Wissenschaftliche Untersuchungen
zum Neuen Testament · 2. Reihe

Herausgeber / Editor
Jörg Frey

Mitherausgeber / Associate Editors
Friedrich Avemarie · Judith Gundry-Volf
Martin Hengel · Otfried Hofius · Hans-Josef Klauck

209

J. de Waal Dryden

Theology and Ethics in 1 Peter

Paraenetic Strategies
for Christian Character Formation

Mohr Siebeck

J. DE WAAL DRYDEN, born 1967; B.E.E., M.Div., Th.M.; 2004 Ph.D. (Cambridge); since then working with L'Abri Fellowship in Greatham, England.

BS
2795.52
.D79
2006

ISBN 3-16-148910-1
ISBN-13 978-3-16-148910-5
ISSN 0340-9570 (Wissenschaftliche Untersuchungen zum Neuen Testament, 2. Reihe)

Die Deutsche Bibliothek lists this publication in the Deutsche Nationalbibliographie; detailed bibliographic data is available in the Internet at *http://dnb.ddb.de*.

The book was printed by Gulde-Druck in Tübingen on non-aging paper and bound by Buchbinderei Held in Rottenburg/N.

Printed in Germany.

Preface

No man is an island, not even the postgraduate research student. No matter how much of a project like this one is the result of personal force of will, the fact remains that it is also the result of a nexus of human connections, each making uniquely different contributions to the whole. But since my name alone accompanies this work, I owe a debt to acknowledge the myriad of support that fostered this thesis on so many fronts.

Firstly, my deep gratitude goes to my Cambridge supervisor Professor Graham Stanton, who always knew how and when to give me a spur and how and when to give me space. I learned much from his scholarship, churchmanship, and above all his graciousness in all circumstances. I am indebted to his care for me and my family during our challenging years in Cambridge.

Our families were a faithful source of encouragement and practical support, and we owe them many thanks for their belief in us and commitment to us. In innumerable practical details they made our life across the Ocean possible. For their understanding, flexibility, and solidarity we are deeply grateful. Special thanks to my dad, Tom Dryden, who proofread this thesis prior to both submission and publication, and to my father-in-law, Woody Harrison, for providing space for me in the library at his law offices to do the final thesis editing prior to submission.

Tyndale House was not only the place where I wrestled for long hours with the matters of this thesis, but was also our home for the three and half years in Cambridge. To the Warden, Bruce Winter, the Librarian, Elizabeth Magba, and the rest of the Staff of Tyndale, I express deep thanks for the way in which they have sustained an environment for sound biblical research. I had many sojourners working along side me at Tyndale, men and women who were trying to scale their own mountains. Each in their own way was a tool of encouragement to me. Of special note were the men of my study group: John Taylor, Bill Salier, Richard Deibert, Daniel Niles, and Dirk Jongkind. I am glad that we got to share in each other's long walk, and am thankful for the ways in which you each contributed to my own understanding of the NT and the ways of the Saviour.

To my college, St. Edmunds, I owe a debt of gratitude for being the face of the university to me. I am thankful for the pleasures of fine formal meals and for financial assistance to aid me in my academic pursuits. Special thanks to my tutor Peter Jackson and his wife for their hospitality.

I also wish to thank the Cambridge Overseas Trust for financial assistance to defray some of the cost of my studies.

I am grateful to Mohr Siebeck for their professionalism and continued commitment to publishing scholarly research. Special thanks to Professor Jörg Frey for accepting my thesis for publication in *Wissenschaftliche Untersuchungen zum Neuen Testament*. Thanks also to theological editor Dr. Henning Ziebritzki, and to production manager Tanja Mix.

We also have a deep sense of gratitude to our friends scattered around the globe who stood by us, each in their own way. Some supported us with regular phone calls, some with financial help, some with a note or a smile or a pint. The hardships of our life in Cambridge made us keenly aware of how important the love and support of friends is to the richness of life, and some days, to survival. Many thanks to you all. To the circle of friends who would later become the Schlupfwinkelbruderschaft I express my deep thanks and affection for how you supported me in this project and especially in the days since.

I also feel indebtedness to all the men and women who have been my conversation partners in the study of 1 Peter, who have dedicated so much work to furthering our understanding of this document so rich with theological depth and human integrity. I am particularly thankful for the commentaries of Bud Achtemeier, Jack Elliott, and Dean Selwyn. (I owe a special thanks to Jack Elliott for giving me access to a draft of his commentary prior to its publication.) Also of special note, the various articles by Willem van Unnik on 1 Peter were of great benefit to me. In addition to these print conversation partners, I wish to thank Dr. Hans Bayer for pushing me in particular in my understanding of the benediction of 1 Peter 1:3-12, and Dr. Robert Yarbrough who introduced me to this epistle in Greek and set alight my passion for it.

Finally, my wife Heather stood by me on the long road of postgraduate research. She always had a keen interest the details of my work as the ideas evolved, sharing in my enthusiasm when the work flowed, and bearing the brunt of my selfishness and myopia when it didn't. She sacrificed much for me and for our son Willem, who was born during the writing of this thesis. I owe the deepest debt to her, for taking hold of me in all my glory and all my shame.

J. Dryden
L'Abri Fellowship
Greatham, England
Christmas 2005

Table of Contents

Preface V
Table of Contents VII
Abbreviations X

Introduction 1
   I. 1 Peter as Paraenesis 5
   II. Plan and Method. 8
   III. Labels and Caveats 9

Chapter One: Paraenesis as an Epistolary Genre 15

   I. The Ethics of Virtue. 15
      A. Habit. 17
      B. Emotions 18
      C. Wisdom 19
   II. Literary Artifacts 20
   III. Ancient Epistolary Types 22
   IV. The Purpose of Paraenesis. 23
   V. Characteristics of Paraenesis: Form and Function 26
      A. Moral Instruction 27
      B. Integration with Worldview 30
      C. Appeals to and Reshaping of Emotional Commitments 32
   VI. Conclusion 35

Chapter Two: The Genre of First Peter 37

   I. Paraenetic Epistle or Baptismal Homily?. 37
   II. The Purpose of 1 Peter 39
   III. The Paraenetic Agenda of 1 Peter 43
      A. A Response to Suffering?. 44
      B. The True Grace of God. 47
      C. A Philosophic Epistle? 49
   IV. Conclusion 52

Chapter Three: Worldview and Story. 55

   I. Worldview and Story in Greco-Roman Paraenetic Literature. 57
      A. Seneca on Paraenesis 58

B. What About the Story? 61
II. Worldview and Story in 1 Peter 64
    A. Mapping the Story 68
    B. The Function of the Story. 81
        1. Contextualizing Ethics 82
        2. Reshaping Values and Priorities. 84
        3. Procuring Allegiance to God 86
III. Conclusion 88

Chapter Four: Conversion and Contrasts 91

I. Conversion in the Greco-Roman World 91
II. Remembrance and Antithesis in Paraenesis 94
III. Remembrance and Antithesis in 1 Peter 98
    A. The Corruptible and the Incorruptible 104
    B. Pure Sincere Love 107
    C. Pure Spiritual Milk. 110
IV. The Function of the Conversion Strategy 113
    A. Clarifying Values. 114
    B. Clarifying Commitments 114
V. Conclusion. 115

Chapter Five: Identity and 'Soft' Difference 117

I. Election, Identity, and Rejection 119
II. Aliens and Strangers. 126
III. Identity and Difference 132
    A. Seneca on Identity and Difference 138
IV. Paraenetic Aims 140

Chapter Six: Moral Instructions. 143

I. Form 143
    A. Exhortation. 144
    B. Exhortation with Motive. 144
    C. Exhortation with Motive and Qualifications. 144
    D. Exhortation with Warrant. 145
    E. Exhortation with Motive and/or Motive with Backing 146
    F. Exhortation w/Qualifications, Warrant and Motive w/Backing. 146
    G.Antithetical Pairs. 147
    H. Combination. 147
II. Function 148
    A. Function in 1 Peter. 151
    B. *Haustafeln* and Wisdom 154

      1. Slaves 156
      2. Wives 158
      3. Husbands 159
      4. Wisdom 160
   III. Conclusion 162

Chapter Seven: Imitatio Christi 163

   I. Example in Greco-Roman Paraenesis 163
      A. Examples and Instructions 164
      B. An Emotional Connection 167
      C. What to Imitate? 169
   II. Christ as Example 172
   III. Imitatio Christi in 1 Peter 174
      A. The Suffering Christ 178
      B. Following in His Steps 185
      C. Following the Shepherd 190
   IV. Conclusion 191

Chapter Eight: Reflections and Prospects 193

   I. Reflections 193
   II. Prospects 197

Bibliography 199

   Ancient Sources 199
   1 Peter Commentaries 201
   1 Peter Studies 203
   Other Works 207

Index of Ancient Sources 215

   Old Testament 215
   New Testament 215
   Greco-Roman 218
   Jewish 220
   Early Church 221

Index of Modern Authors 223

Subject Index 225

Abbreviations

AB	Anchor Bible
AnBib	*Analecta biblica*
ANRW	*Aufstieg und Niedergang der römischen Welt: Geschichte und Kultur Roms im Spiegel der neueren Forschung.* Edited by H. Temporini and W. Hasse (Berlin, 1972–)
ANTC	Abingdon New Testament Commentaries
ASR	*American Sociological Review*
AUSS	*Andrews University Seminary Studies*
BDAG	Bauer, W., F.W. Danker, W.F. Arndt, and F.W. Gingrich. *Greek-English Lexicon of the New Testament and Other Early Christian Literature*, 3rd ed. (Chicago, 1999)
BDF	Blass F., A. Debrunner, and R. Funk. *A Greek Grammar of the New Testament and Other Early Christian Literature* (Chicago, 1961)
Bib	*Biblica*
BNTC	Black's New Testament Commentaries
BTB	*Biblical Theology Bulletin*
CBQ	*Catholic Bible Quarterly*
EKKNT	Evangelsch-katholischer Kommentar zum Neuen Testament
EM	*Moral Epistles*, Seneca
EMSP	European Monographs in Social Psychology
EN	*Nicomachean Ethics*, Aristotle
ExAud	*Ex Auditu*
ExpTim	*Expository Times*
FBL	Foreign Biblical Library
FRLANT	Forschungen zur Religion und Literatur des alten und neuen Testaments
HCRHP	*Handbook of Classical Rhetoric in the Hellenistic Period (330 B.C. – A.D. 400)*. Edited by S.E. Porter. (Leiden, 1997)
HTR	*Harvard Theological Review*
ICC	International Critical Commentary
IDB	*The Interpreter's Dictionary of the Bible*. Edited by G.A. Buttrick (New York, 1962)
Int	*Interpretation*
JBL	*Journal of Biblical Literature*
JETS	*Journal of the Evangelical Theological Society*
JRE	*Journal of Religious Ethics*
JRH	*Journal of Religious History*
JSNTSS	Journal for the Study of the New Testament: Supplement Series
JSOTSS	Journal for the Study of the Old Testament: Supplement Series
KEK	Kritisch-exegetischer Kommentar über das Neue Testament
KTAH	Key Themes in Ancient History
Lange	Lange's Commentary on the Holy Scripture
LEC	Library of Early Christianity

LSJ	Liddel H.G., R. Scott, and H.S. Jones. *A Greek-English Lexicon* (Oxford, 1996)
NABPRSSS	National Association of Baptist Professors of Religion Special Study Series
NewDocs	*New Documents Illustrating Early Christianity*. Edited by G.H. Horsley and S. Llewelyn (North Ryde, NSW, 1981–)
NCB	New Century Bible
NIBCNT	New International Bible Commentary on the New Testament
NICNT	New International Commentary on the New Testament
NovTSup	Novum Testamentum Supplements
NTD	Das Neue Testament Deutsch
NTF	Neutestamentliche Forschungen
NTL	New Testament Library
NTR	New Testament Readings
NTS	*New Testament Studies*
NTTS	New Testament Tools and Studies
RVV	Religionsgeschichtliche Versuche und Vorarbeiten
SBG	Studies in Biblical Greek
SBLDS	Society of Biblical Literature Dissertation Series
SBLMS	Society of Biblical Literature Monograph Series
SBLSBS	Society of Biblical Literature Sources for Biblical Study
SBT	Studies in Biblical Theology
SCHNT	Studia ad corpus hellenisticum Novi Testamenti
SCP	Studies in Classical Philology
SJT	*Scottish Journal of Theology*
SNTSMS	Society for New Testament Studies Monograph Series
SNTW	Studies in the New Testament and its World
SPIB	Scripta Pontificii Instituti Biblici
TDNT	*Theological Dictionary of the New Testament*. Edited by G. Kittel (Grand Rapids, 1964–1976)
TRu	*Theologische Rundschau*
WBC	Word Bible Commentary
WUNT	Wissenschaftliche Untersuchungen zum Neuen Testament
ZNW	*Zeitschrift für die neutestamentliche Wissenschaft und die Kunde der ältern Kirche*

Introduction

It has been many years now since Bernhard Weiß observed that, in 1 Peter 'the way in which the didactic and hortatory elements...are closely interwoven throughout, is characteristically distinct from the Paulines.'[1] Weiß noted two important things: (1) 1 Peter does not follow the Pauline organizing principle of separating 'indicative and imperative',[2] but instead (2) interweaves theology and ethics throughout the epistle. While not an entirely novel insight on the part of Weiß,[3] it is one that has stood the test of time. Throughout subsequent research, this 'unPauline' interweaving of theology and ethics has been a well-rehearsed theme in Petrine studies.[4]

Selwyn, for example, comments that the, 'close interweaving of the two strands [of theology and ethics] makes it difficult to expound the teaching of the Epistle in regard to either without some overlapping.' He warns that, 'we may be most true to its message if we do not try to disentangle them

---

[1] B. WEIß, *A Manual of Introduction to the New Testament*, trans. A.J.K. DAVIDSON, FBL (London: Hodder & Stoughton, 1887), 2:143.

[2] In Pauline studies there are two senses in which the paradigm of 'indicative and imperative' is used. The first can be called the 'organizational' indicative and imperative, where a first major section of theological material is followed by a second major section of ethical implication based upon the first theological section. Thus, imperative follows indicative at both the literary and logical level. The second sense might be called the 'eschatological' indicative and imperative, where Paul places both indicative and imperative immediately together in (eschatological) tension, as in Gal. 5:25: εἰ ζῶμεν πνεύματι, πνεύματι καὶ στοιχῶμεν. It was this second sense of 'indicative and imperative' which was the concern of BULTMANN in his influential essay 'Das Problem der Ethik Bei Paulus,' *ZNW* 23 (1924): 123–40. In referring to the Pauline 'indicative and imperative', I am referring to the first 'organizational' variety. While 1 Peter often places the theological grounds for actions in the immediate context of commands, it does not utilize the second eschatological paradigm either.

[3] FRONMÜLLER, for example, previously noted, 'Dogmatics and Ethics do not occur separately in this Epistle, but are often directly conjoined, and frequently present a quick, even bold transition from the one to the other.' G.F.C. FRONMÜLLER, *The Epistles General of Peter*, trans. J.I. MOMBERT, Lange NT 9.2 (Edinburgh: T&T Clark, 1870), 5.

[4] As a word of clarification, the phrase 'Petrine studies' is used in two distinct senses: the broader sense being the historical study of the person of Simon Peter, the disciple of Jesus, and the writings associated with that name, biblical (Mark, 1 and 2 Peter) and apocryphal (Acts and Apocalypse of Peter), the second more narrow sense being the study of 1 Peter. It is this latter sense that I am using here. The distinction is, of course, general and not airtight, because our knowledge of the person of Peter and his biography informs our understandings of the writings associated with him and vice versa.

too much.'[5] Van Unnik characterizes the epistle as a 'constant dialectical process between dogmatics and ethics,'[6] adding that, 'it is impossible to distinguish as clearly as one can in many of Paul's letters between doctrinal and ethical sections.'[7] More recently Elliott has noted that the 'intricate interrelationship of kerygma and parenesis is one of 1 Peter's most distinguishing features among the epistolary literature of the NT.'[8]

In an attempt to explain this difference between these 'Pauline' and 'Petrine' patterns, Martin has offered a distinction between two different types of Greco-Roman paraenetic texts: 'In the first type, the ontological status and the admonitions are expressed in two distinct sections of the document.'[9] Whereas, 'In the second type of paraenetic structure, the ontology and the admonitions are interwoven. Statements of ontological status are joined directly with their appropriate exhortations.'[10] Thus, the typical Pauline paradigm of 'indicative and imperative' fits with the first type of text, while 1 Peter, where 'statements of ontological status are intercalated with their correlative admonitions,'[11] comports with the second variety. In this way, the difference between Petrine and Pauline styles is understandable in its historical context as choices among available stylistic options.

Martin gives us a place to begin to understand Petrine style, but his distinctions needs nuancing. While it is true that exhortations in 1 Peter are frequently accompanied by immediate justification, it has also been recognized that the theology of the epistle, taken as a *whole*, provides a network of theological grounding for injunctions *throughout* the epistle. Also, while it would be misleading to speak of an 'indicative section' at the beginning of the epistle, it is true that the author has concentrated his theology in 1:3–2:12, and that these verses are recognized to be in some sense foundational to the ethical exhortations of the entire epistle.[12] One

---

[5] E.G. SELWYN, *The First Epistle of St. Peter: The Greek Text with Introduction, Notes and Essays*, 2d ed. (London: MacMillan, 1947), 65.

[6] W.C. VAN UNNIK, 'Christianity According to 1 Peter,' *ExpTim* 68 (1956): 81.

[7] W.C. VAN UNNIK, 'First Letter of Peter,' *IDB*, 3:759. Cf. C.E.B. CRANFIELD, *The First Epistle of Peter* (London: SCM, 1950), 122, 'Whereas others might – more logically and more neatly maybe – put first testimony and then as a separate division the exhortation that follows from it, Peter's way is to weave the two strands together.'

[8] J.H. ELLIOTT, 'The Rehabilitation of an Exegetical Step-Child: 1 Peter in Recent Research,' *JBL* 95.2 (1976): 25.

[9] T.W. MARTIN, *Metaphor and Composition in 1 Peter* (Atlanta, GA: Scholars Press, 1992), 140. He cites the later dialogues of PLATO as indicative of this type.

[10] MARTIN, *Metaphor*, 141.

[11] MARTIN, *Metaphor*, 141. He adds that, 'This compositional structure has always troubled scholars who have approach 1 Peter from a Pauline perspective.'

[12] Cf. D.W. KENDALL, 'The Introductory Character of 1 Peter 1:3–12,' (Ph.D., Union Theological Seminary, 1984), 103–20. Contra E. RICHARD, 'The Functional Christology

example of this is the collocation of corporate identity titles in 2:4–12, which provides normative interpretive images for the whole of the epistle's social ethics. Just as it is now recognized that the old Pauline paradigm of 'indicative and imperative' is not without its difficulties,[13] neither is the alternative paradigm of piecemeal interweaving wholly representative of 1 Peter.

In this brief overview of roughly a hundred years of Petrine scholarship (1886–1992) one is struck by just how little progress has been made in our understanding of the relationship between theology and ethics. The statement of Weiß in the 1880s is comparable to those made today in monographs, commentaries, and NT introductions. Given that, as Elliott said, this is one of 1 Peter's 'most distinguishing features,' it is surprising that our knowledge has progressed little beyond the dictum that the letter does not follow the Pauline pattern but instead interweaves theological and ethical discourse. There is a need for more work that can engender a deeper and more nuanced appreciation of this intertwining of ethics and theology.

At least part of the reason for the meager progress in this area has been the primary concern among Petrine specialists with diachronic form-critical questions. Since Selwyn, form-criticism has been the dominant methodological approach in the study of 1 Peter. This is understandable, since so many questions still survive as to the relation of 1 Peter to the rest of the NT literature (especially the Pauline epistles)[14] and to other early Christian traditions (whether written or oral) incorporated by the author into the epistle. An unfortunate side effect, though, of this approach is the categorical separation of theology and ethics inherent in form-critical methodologies.[15] In distinguishing kerygma

---

of First Peter,' in *Perspectives on First Peter*, ed. C.H. TALBERT, NABPRSSS 9 (Macon, Georgia: Mercer University Press, 1986), 123–4, who recognizes the function of 1:3–12, but argues that, 'From that point on, the letter without fail consists of alternations of imperative and indicative, that is, advice followed by examples or statements of theological justification.'

[13] See V.P. FURNISH, *Theology and Ethics in Paul* (Nashville, TN: Abingdon, 1968), 98–111, where he establishes 'the impossibility of neatly distinguishing between dogmatic and moral themes' (99).

[14] For a recent study, see J. HERZER, *Petrus oder Paulus?: Studien über das Verhältnis des Ersten Petrusbriefes zur paulinischen Tradition*, WUNT 103 (Tübingen: Mohr (Siebeck), 1998).

[15] A seminal expression can be found in M. DIBELIUS, *From Tradition to Gospel*, trans. B.L. WOOLF (London: Ivor, Nicholson and Watson, 1934), 239, 'Thus we see that the hortatory sections of the Pauline epistles have nothing to do with the theoretic foundations of the ethics of the Apostle, and very little with other ideas peculiar to him. Rather they belong to tradition. In this respect Paul is like the other Christian missionaries.'

and paraenesis, form-criticism brings to 1 Peter an agenda of separating the black beads of kerygma from the red beads of paraenesis. While it is certain that the author of 1 Peter has made use of a variety of traditional materials, the author has integrated those traditions to suit his own purposes. This integration of theological and ethical reflections forms an intricate tapestry in 1 Peter that cannot be separated without irreparable damage to the fabric of the epistle. For instance, in a crucial verse like 2:24, *He himself bore our sins in his body on the tree, that we might die to sin and live to righteousness*, how are we to separate theology and ethics without devastating injury to the sense of the verse?[16] If we are to gain an understanding of how theology and ethics function *together* in 1 Peter, then we will need a methodology that does not separate the two *a priori*.

The recent rhetorical analysis of Thurén represents a positive development in this direction. He criticizes form-critical studies of 1 Peter for examining exhortations with an eye only to 'their origin, and not their function in the text.'[17] He argues that a 'diachronic study of different traditions and their origin does not suffice,' and that 'a holistic picture of the letter is required.'[18] He advocates the use of a synchronic functional approach. For Thurén the way in which theology and ethics function *together* is critical. The aim of his work is to uncover how theology works to motivate ethical action. He seeks to produce a distillation of the motivating ideological structure of the letter, while taking into account its paraenetic/rhetorical nature.[19] This differs from my own aims in that, while he is sensitive to how theology and ethics function together, ultimately he still seeks to separate them. I intend to demonstrate how theology and ethics come together to function as paraenesis.

[16] Not that this stopped R. DEICHGRÄBER, *Gotteshymnus und Christushymnus in der frühen Christenheit: Untersuchungen zur Form, Sprache und Stil der frühchristlichen Hymnen* (Göttingen: Vandenhoeck & Ruprecht, 1967), 141, who (albeit cautiously) divides the verse based on his reconstruction of what is confessional and what is an editorial insertion specific to the situation.

[17] L. THURÉN, *Argument and Theology in 1 Peter: The Origins of Christian Paraenesis*, JSNTSS 114 (Sheffield: Sheffield Academic Press, 1995), 20.

[18] THURÉN, *Argument and Theology*, 28.

[19] This is done by using a modified form of the argumentation analysis developed by TOULMIN in *Argument*. THURÉN has applied a similar methodology to Galatians in his recent work *Derhetorizing Paul: A Dynamic Perspective on Pauline Theology and the Law*, WUNT 124 (Tübingen: Mohr (Siebeck), 2000).

I. 1 Peter as Paraenesis

Talking about paraenesis in the context of 1 Peter is nothing new.[20] Dibelius, for example, in opposition to the *religionsgeschichtliche Schule* interpretation of 1 Peter as an early Christian baptismal homily, pointed to the paraenetic nature of 1 Peter revealed in the presence of a *Haustafel*.[21] In a similar vein, many scholars today would loosely characterize 1 Peter as a 'paraenetic epistle.'[22]

Unfortunately, a great deal of confusion surrounds the question of what 'paraenesis' is.[23] For the present study, it is necessary to distinguish between two different senses of the word. The first refers to paraenesis in the sense of a 'form' (*Gattung*), like *Haustafeln*, virtue and vice lists, or collections of ethical maxims. The second sense is a literary genre designation, as in 'paraenetic epistle'.[24] For the sake of clarity, throughout this thesis I will adopt the terminology of 'paraenesis-as-form' to refer to the former and 'paraenesis-as-genre' to refer to the latter.[25] In Petrine studies, the main concern in the past has been with paraenesis-as-form, as a tool for answering diachronic questions. When Lohse, for example, speaks of 'paraenesis' in 1 Peter he is speaking of the paraenetic elements vis-à-vis the kerygmatic, not of 1 Peter as a paraenetic epistle.[26] As we have noted above, this approach is inherently limited in relating theology and ethics because it separates them from the start.

---

[20] To return to our historical starting point, Weiß saw paraenetic characteristics in 1 Peter. See B. WEIß, *Der petrinische Lehrbegriff* (Berlin: Wilhelm Schulze, 1855), 335-53, where he distinguished between paraenesis and paraklesis in 1 Peter.

[21] M. DIBELIUS, 'Zur Formgeschichte des Neuen Testaments (außerhalb der Evangelien),' *TRu* 3 (1931): 232, 'Wir haben hier ein typisches Beispiel ausgeführter Paränese vor uns.'

[22] E.g., J.H. ELLIOTT, *1 Peter: A New Translation with Introduction and Commentary*, AB 37b (New York: Doubleday, 2000), 11, 'The hortatory aim (5:12) and mood of 1 Peter, along with its inclusion of much hortatory and paraenetic material clearly qualify it as a "paraenetic/hortatory letter".'

[23] THURÉN, *Argument and Theology*, 17, complains that, 'The word "paraenesis" often carries a somewhat vague significance.'

[24] Unfortunately, both senses of the word have been used without distinction in form-criticism, and sometimes very closely together; for example, M. DIBELIUS, *James: A Commentary on the Epistle of James*, ed. H. KOESTER, trans. M.A. WILLIAMS, Hermeneia (Philadelphia: Fortress, 1976), 3, 'We may designate the "Letter" of James as paraenesis. By paraenesis we mean a text which strings together admonitions of general ethical content. Paraenetic sayings ordinarily address themselves to a specific (though perhaps fictional) audience, or at least appear in the form of a command or summons.'

[25] These somewhat awkward phrases are necessary, because we will need to retain the use of both senses while clearly distinguishing between them.

[26] E. LOHSE, 'Parenesis and Kerygma in 1 Peter,' in *Perspectives on First Peter*, ed. C.H. TALBERT, NABPRSSS 9 (Macon, GA: Mercer University Press, 1986).

Recently though scholars have begun to pursue the second sense of paraenesis (paraenesis-as-genre), and today there is an 'emerging consensus' that 1 Peter should be read as a paraenetic epistle.[27] While this represents a positive development, it is not without its problems. Unfortunately, the breadth of this consensus is built on a somewhat nebulous use of the phrase 'paraenetic epistle', where this designation means 1 Peter seeks, in some sense, to exhort or encourage. 'Paraenesis' in this sense does not refer to a historical epistolary genre, but instead is a vague description of the authorial aims of the epistle. It is a description of epistolary purpose not epistolary genre. In the end, this description possesses little utility in providing any hermeneutical tools to apply to our text.[28] In contrast to this consensus approach, the present study aims to show how 1 Peter functions as an example of a real epistolary genre from the ancient Greco-Roman world: a paraenetic epistle.[29]

Recent research has advanced our understanding of Greco-Roman paraenetic epistolary traditions considerably and the present study seeks to apply some of these new insights to the study of 1 Peter as an epistle of this type. Wilson's recent study on Colossians, *The Hope of Glory*,[30] represents a promising model for this type of inquiry. Building on Malherbe's work on the Thessalonian correspondence,[31] he interprets the

---

[27] J. PRASAD, *Foundations of the Christian Way of Life According to 1 Peter 1,13–25: An Exegetico-theological Study*, AnBib 146 (Rome: Pontificio Istituto Biblico, 2000), 1: 'After a long period of divergent opinions on the nature of 1 Peter a consensus is emerging among scholars today that it is a paraenetic letter.'

[28] All studies that classify 1 Peter as paraenetic in this general sense draw little if any implications for exegesis from this classification.

[29] MARTIN has done some preliminary work in this area outlining some of the most basic characteristics of paraenesis as a Greco-Roman epistolary genre, and classifying 1 Peter as an example of that genre. But he made little use of this classification in the remainder of his work. He never developed how 1 Peter *functions* as a paraenetic epistle, nor did he seek to draw out implication for the purpose and structure of the epistle from its paraenetic nature. His single chapter on paraenesis is isolated from the rest of his work.

[30] W.T. Wilson, *The Hope of Glory: Education and Exhortation in the Epistle to the Colossians*, NovTSup 88 (Leiden: Brill, 1997).

[31] A.J. MALHERBE, *Paul and the Thessalonians: The Philosophic Tradition of Pastoral Care* (Philadelphia: Fortress Press, 1987), A.J. MALHERBE, 'Hellenistic Moralists and the New Testament,' *ANRW* II.26.1:267–333, and his recent commentary *The Letters to the Thessalonians*, AB 32b (New York: Doubleday, 2000). Although MALHERBE is the real pioneer here, WILSON's work is more suited to my line of inquiry because MALHERBE's focus is on the 'philophronetic' elements in the Thessalonian letters, where Paul emphasizes his personal relationship with his correspondents as a paraenetic rhetorical device. As this emphasis is almost totally absent from 1 Peter, 5:1 being the closest we get to it, his model is of limited value. In contrast, WILSON identifies

author's aims within the categories of paraenetic epistles originating in the Greco-Roman philosophic schools. The purpose of this type of epistle is to exhort the recipients, as relatively new converts to philosophy, to continue on the path they have chosen and to conform their life practice to the teachings they have embraced. The aim of paraenesis is to facilitate growth in moral maturity through various forms of education and exhortation.

In like manner, 1 Peter seeks to confirm young Christian congregations in the new life they have embraced in Christ by facilitating growth in Christian character, chiefly measured in terms of growing moral integrity, and growing practical dependence upon God. This comports with the self-declared confirmatory aim of the epistle to exhort the communities to stand in ἡ ἀληθὴς χάρις τοῦ θεοῦ (5:12). As in Greco-Roman paraenesis, praxis that conforms to beliefs is an essential element in developing Christian maturity. Like Greco-Roman paraenesis, 1 Peter evidences an emphasis on ethical instructions that direct and encourage moral action. As we will see, in addition to this, 1 Peter adopts other modes of instruction common to paraenesis.

The Greco-Roman epistolary genre of paraenesis then represents a workable model to adopt in assessing the nature and aims of 1 Peter. This is not to imply an *exact* correspondence between Christian and philosophic paraenesis,[32] but instead a sufficient overlap in aims and methods to warrant their association. As Wilson has shown with reference to Colossians, paraenetic epistles can provide a useful description in terms of generic style, content, and function.

Wilson's work also forges new ground in the relationship between theology and ethics. He recognizes that Greco-Roman paraenetic epistles were not confined to the use of typically 'paraenetic elements' (paraenesis-as-form), but also incorporated the use of narratives, moral exemplars, and theological/philosophical reflections, all of which were used in conjunction with 'paraenetic elements' to accomplish exhortative goals. His approach opens up new avenues for conceiving of the relationship between theology and ethics because it is unencumbered by a sharp dichotomy between the two. Since all these various literary forms can operate in a paraenetic mode, the hard distinction between paraenesis and kerygma dissolves when theology serves paraenetic ends. As Engberg-Pedersen has recently said with respect to Paul, 'Parenesis consists in reminding and appealing. And

---

several other key literary strategies that are characteristic of paraenesis and applicable to both Colossians and 1 Peter.

[32] A mature Christian character, for example, includes a well-seated active dependence on God, which is absent in the philosophic ideal of maturity.

that is what happens *all through* Paul's letters.'[33] In other words, paraenesis describes not simply some portions of Paul's epistles (paraenesis-as-form), but what his epistles are aiming to accomplish as complete acts of literary communication (paraenesis-as-genre). For Engberg-Pederson, Paul's theology *is* paraenesis,[34] or at the very least, it serves to facilitate paraenetic aims. We will develop this more fully below, but at this point, we can see that the category of Greco-Roman paraenetic epistle not only places 1 Peter within the epistolary writing traditions of its day but also has the potential to unlock new pathways for understanding the relationship between theology and ethics.

II. Plan and Method

The basic agenda for this thesis is to garner evidence of the paraenetic nature of 1 Peter while at the same time highlighting new insights that can be gained by recognizing its paraenetic nature and agenda. The bulk of this thesis, then, will consist in (1) explorations of the nature and function of Greco-Roman paraenetic epistles, and (2) exegetical studies of Petrine texts read against this background.

The first two chapters set out to describe the epistolary genre of paraenesis, and then make a preliminary case for taking 1 Peter as an example of that genre. Chapter one outlines a functional epistolary genre classification for Greco-Roman paraenesis, by rehearsing characteristic literary/rhetorical strategies and how they function within an overall philosophic agenda of eudemonistic life-transformation. Chapter two makes an initial case for recognizing 1 Peter as a paraenetic epistle, by marking the literary features and strategies it shares with Greco-Roman paraenesis. In addition, it demonstrates how these paraenetic strategies are well suited to the epistle's agenda of promoting character growth in the midst of cultural ostracism.

With an initial classification of 1 Peter as a paraenetic epistle as a starting point, the five chapters that follow look in detail at five paraenetic literary strategies utilized in 1 Peter. This is done by first demonstrating how each strategy functions in Greco-Roman paraenesis and then how it

---

[33] T. ENGBERG-PEDERSEN, *Paul and the Stoics* (Edinburgh: T & T Clark, 2000), 302. Italics original.

[34] Cf. ENGBERG-PEDERSEN, *Stoics*, 295, 'Just to state the obvious: on such a reading there will be no valid distinction between "theology" and "ethics" in Paul. All through Paul will be "theologizing" in the sense of spelling out the meaning to human beings of what God has done (to them) through Christ. But all through he will also be concerned with what is the ultimate goal of his "theologizing": practice. Nothing must be torn apart here. It all hangs intrinsically and inextricably together.'

functions in 1 Peter.[35] The first three chapters examine the epistle's main theological discourse in 1 Peter 1:3–2:12, and include chapters dealing with: narrative worldview (chapter three), conversion and the moral antitheses that derive from it (chapter four), and social identity (chapter five). The aim of these chapters is to show how theology functions as paraenesis, i.e., how these literary strategies function to contextualize and motivate considered moral action, and facilitate growth in moral maturity.

The two chapters that follow examine the remainder of the body of the epistle (2:13–5:12) looking at the use of moral instructions/paraenesis-as-form (chapter six) and the use of Jesus as a moral exemplar (chapter seven). Again, the emphasis is on demonstrating the use of these techniques in Greco-Roman paraenesis, their correlate usage in 1 Peter, and how in both settings they function to promote growth in character through practicing moral integrity.

Finally, chapter eight summarizes the findings of the thesis and its implications for Petrine studies as well as the study of other examples of early Christian epistolary literature.

III. Labels and Caveats

While the method of the above plan is quite straightforward, in the sense that it involves the reading of 1 Peter in the light of an ancient epistolary genre, providing a label to accompany this methodology proves quite difficult. The emphasis on the character forming agenda of the epistle means that it has great affinities with what is now being called 'character ethics interpretation'.[36] But as this is a very young interdisciplinary subdiscipline in biblical research, it has yet to develop anything like a coherent methodology or set of methodologies.

My goals and methods probably have the greatest resonance with what is often called 'socio-rhetorical analysis', which combines elements of both social-scientific and rhetorical analysis. With rhetorical analysis, I share a fundamental concern for how the author uses rhetorical devices to shape the lives of Christian communities and the individuals that constitute those communities. However, while my study is *functional*, it is not strictly

---

[35] One of these paraenetic strategies, social identity, is in fact a Christian paraenetic strategy (derived from analogous Jewish traditions) and so is not characteristic of Greco-Roman paraenesis, for reasons we will see later. Even so, social identity does operate in 1 Peter as a paraenetic strategy. This is one example of the flexibility of the methodology adopted here, which does not confine itself to strict 'parallels'.

[36] See, e.g., W.P. BROWN, ed., *Character and Scripture: Moral Formation, Community, and Biblical Interpretation* (Grand Rapids: Eerdmans, 2002).

speaking rhetorical analysis, since I do not use the categories of either
ancient or 'universal' rhetoric. Also, while I am concerned to map the
function of certain literary/rhetorical strategies from the Greco-Roman
world onto 1 Peter, I follow the growing consensus as to the limited
usefulness of 'classical rhetorical handbooks' in studying NT epistolary
literature.[37] In addition, my concern for the functionality of 1 Peter goes
beyond the question of how the text seeks to affect its readers via
persuasion, which is, strictly speaking, the focus of rhetorical study.

With social-scientific criticism, I share a concern for realities that
extend beyond the individual and which penetrate into the social world and
makeup of both the addressees and the author. Because of this I do adopt,
to a limited degree, some basic terminology common to social-scientific
criticism (e.g., identity, difference, and the other). That said, one will not
find in what follows anything like a full-fledged social-scientific study of
1 Peter.

My practice has been to adopt a methodological eclecticism, which is
governed by a set of exegetical convictions informed by discourse analysis
(sometimes also called 'textlinguistics').[38] Now, just as this is not an
experiment in social-scientific criticism, neither is it a linguistic study; one
will only rarely find in what follows the highly specialized terminology
familiar only to discourse analysts. But the principles that have guided my
eclecticism are deeply influenced by the basic tenets of discourse analysis.

Discourse analysis is centrally concerned with what linguists call
'pragmatics',[39] what people *do* through acts of communication. As Brown
and Yule say, 'In discourse analysis...we are concerned with [1] what
people using language are doing, and [2] accounting for the linguistic
features in the discourse as the means employed in what they are doing.'[40]
Likewise, my concern here is with what the author is trying to accomplish
in writing his epistle to these beleaguered churches in Asia Minor and how
he does it. This goes beyond an analysis of what the text 'means', to the
intentional pragmatics of the author revealed in the linguistic data and

---

[37] See, e.g., P.H. KERN, *Rhetoric and Galatians: Assessing an Approach to Paul's
Epistle*, SNTSMS 101 (Cambridge: Cambridge University Press, 1998).

[38] For an excellent introduction see J.T. REED, *A Discourse Analysis of Philippians:
Method and Rhetoric in the Debate Over Literary Integrity*, JSNTSS 136 (Sheffield:
Sheffield Academic Press, 1997), 16–33.

[39] Cf. G. BROWN and G. YULE, *Discourse Analysis*, Cambridge Textbooks in
Linguistics (Cambridge: Cambridge University Press, 1983), 26, '"Doing discourse
analysis" certainly involves "doing syntax and semantics", but it primarily consists in
"doing pragmatics".' They also note that, 'Any analytical approach in linguistics which
involves contextual considerations [i.e., paralinguistic considerations], necessarily
belongs to that area of language study called pragmatics.'

[40] BROWN and YULE, *Discourse Analysis*, 26.

form of the text. So, in looking at how the author of 1 Peter utilizes certain paraenetic literary strategies, the concern here is with the *functionality* of those strategies – what they are suited to do and what our author seeks to accomplish by using them.[41]

So, while not appropriating many of the specialized tools of discourse analysis, this thesis is shaped by its fundamental tenets. One example of the practical outworking of these tenets might prove illustrative. Discourse analysis owes its origins in part to 'speech-act theory' developed by Austin and Searle.[42] Vanhoozer helpfully summarizes its core concept:

> The main point is that in speaking we also do certain things. Words do not simply label; sentences do not merely state. Rather, in using language we do any number of things: question, command, warn, request, curse, bless and so forth. A speech act has two aspects: propositional content and illocutionary force, the "matter" and "energy" of communicative action. The key notion is that of illocution, which has to do not simply with locuting or uttering words but with what we do *in* uttering words.[43]

Speech act theory, like discourse analysis, places the emphasis on the 'energy' of communication (i.e., what it seeks to accomplish). One of the important implications of this focus on action is that the illocutionary force of a 'locution' is not necessarily tied to its grammatical form, but is dependent upon its context (linguistic and/or paralinguistic). For example, the declaration, 'There is no salt on the table,' can carry the illocutionary force of, 'Please bring the salt when you come back to the table.'[44]

Perhaps surprisingly, this has implications for our interpretation of 1 Peter, and the relationship between theology and ethics. As we have said, our concern is with textual pragmatics. When we are approaching the theology of the epistle we will want to be sensitive to what the author is trying to accomplish by means of his theological discourse, paying close attention to the particular literary strategies he is adopting to help us determine his illocutionary objectives. In practice, this means that discourse function is not *necessarily* tied to grammatical mood. The

---

[41] This is the sense in which discourse analysis has affinities with socio-rhetorical analysis, since both attempt to analyze texts in terms of social function. As REED, *Discourse*, 29, says, '[One] tenet of discourse analysis is that discourse should be analysed for its social functions and, thus, in its social context.'

[42] J.L. AUSTIN, *How to Do Things with Words* (Cambridge, MA: Harvard University Press, 1962), and J.R. SEARLE, *Speech Acts: An Essay in the Philosophy of Language* (Cambridge: Cambridge University Press, 1969).

[43] K.J. VANHOOZER, *First Theology: God, Scripture & Hermeneutics* (Downers Grove, IL: IVP, 2002), 118.

[44] This also means that the same utterance 'It's quarter to eight,' can have different illocutions, 'Hurry up we're late,' or 'Don't worry, the performance isn't until nine,' depending on the context.

functionality of statements in the indicative cannot be confined to 'informing'. Thus, the traditional distinction between 'indicative' and 'imperative', while useful in many regards, is problematic when it implies that the function of indicatives is to 'inform' or 'instruct', while imperatives 'exhort'. As we have just seen in our domestic example above, indicatives can function, at the illocutionary level, as imperatives.

This understanding is foundational to my speaking of 'paraenetic theology' in analyzing the pragmatics of theological discourse in 1 Peter. My concern is to demonstrate how theology functions in a paraenetic mode to facilitate the paraenetic agenda of the author, where theology is shaped *pragmatically* to aid in the author's program of promoting growth in Christian character. The organization of theological materials in 1 Peter is chiefly determined by these pragmatic goals, not by systematic or logical concerns. This explains why, in the history of Petrine research, outlining the epistle has proved to be an activity with few, if any, exegetical rewards.

This leads to the first of two caveats. Since we are concerned here with the functionality of the epistolary genre of paraenesis, the correlation between 1 Peter and literature of the Greco-Roman philosophic schools that we will attempt to demonstrate and utilize is a *functional* one. Our concern here is not with demonstrating 'micro-parallels' of phraseology or keywords, but instead with 'macro-parallels' of generic function. Thus, the aim is to demonstrate correlations in terms of the overall agendas pursued in both Greco-Roman paraenetic epistles and 1 Peter, and also correlations in the ways in which they both go about actualizing those agendas.

This also means that this study relates 1 Peter and Greco-Roman paraenetic epistles by analogy not genealogy. To a certain extent this is unusual, since the normal approach is to first establish a genealogical link between historical texts and then to talk about one text in relation to another (e.g., this text is dependent on that one) and then to make exegetical judgments based on this (e.g., therefore this author is agreeing with or disagreeing with the previous author). My approach here has been to bypass the question of genealogy and to compare texts analogically. In practice this is simply placing two texts from the ancient world next to each other and noting the similarities in functionality and drawing exegetical implications from those functional parallels. Obviously it assumes *some* genealogical relationship must exist, but seeks neither to chart that relationship nor to draw any conclusions from that relationship.

The second caveat is somewhat mundane but necessary. I do not adopt the traditional distinction between 'letter' and 'epistle'. While at one time the distinction championed by Deissmann[45] was useful for rescuing the 'letters' of Paul from dogmaticians and emphasizing their essential historical character, subsequent research has shown that a hard distinction between 'letter' and 'epistle' is difficult to maintain, and at best these terms represent poles on a continuum.[46] The epistolary writings of the NT reside at varying places along the continuum between 'letter' and 'epistle'. They are examples of genuine correspondence, but they also show signs of careful composition and being intended for varying degrees of public consumption. On these grounds, I will use the two terms interchangeably and without any connotation of relative place on the continuum.

With these caveats in place, we are prepared to begin our study with an examination of the nature of paraenetic correspondence in the Greco-Roman philosophic schools.

---

[45] See G.A. DEISSMANN, *Light From the Ancient East: The New Testament Illustrated by Recently Discovered Texts of the Graeco-Roman World*, trans. L.R.M. STRACHAN (London: Hodder and Stoughton, 1927), 227–51.

[46] From an examination of ancient letter writing traditions W.G. DOTY, 'Epistolary Literature,' *CBQ* 31 (1969): 198, concludes that, 'The absolute distinction between Letter and Epistle should be dropped.' Cf. K. BERGER, 'Hellenistische Gattungen im Neuen Testament,' *ANRW* II.25.2: 1133, 'Die Einteilung Deissmanns...ist nicht mehr haltbar.'

Chapter One

Paraenesis as an Epistolary Genre

The purpose of this chapter is to outline the basic features of paraenesis as an epistolary genre within its setting in the Greco-Roman philosophic schools. As we said in the introductory chapter, the aim of this study is to foster new ways for relating theology and ethics in 1 Peter. Our hope is that an understanding of how 1 Peter functions as a paraenetic epistle will serve to facilitate that aim. We begin this study with an exploration of the form and function of paraenetic epistles in the Hellenistic environment, in light of recent research in this area.

As a literary genre paraenesis was a widespread phenomenon in the ancient Mediterranean world. In addition to well-known Greco-Roman examples like Isocrates and Seneca, one can also find examples of paraenesis in, among other places, Egypt and Israel.[1] In all these settings, paraenesis concerned itself with giving practical advice as an act of confirming the reader in a recently undertaken pursuit. Gammie rightly classifies it as a form of wisdom literature.[2] While all forms of paraenesis share some common literary characteristics, each unique cultural setting produced specific forms to suit its own environment. Our interest in this study is the form of paraenesis that arose in the Greco-Roman world, where it developed as a tool of the philosophic schools to promote growth in moral character. So, to understand the function of paraenesis, we first must review a few of the basic contours of Greco-Roman philosophy, with special emphasis on its understanding of moral development and moral virtue.

I. The Ethics of Virtue

In the last quarter century the scholarly study of ethics has seen a resurgence of interest in Greco-Roman (and especially Aristotelian) ethical

---

[1] Among the Egyptian examples given by J.G. GAMMIE, 'Paraenetic Literature: Toward the Morphology of a Secondary Genre,' *Semeia* 50 (1990): 49–50, see 'The Instruction for King Meri-ka-Re' or the 'Instructions of Amen-em-Opet'. For Israel, Deuteronomy is the quintessential example of paraenesis in the Hebrew Bible.

[2] See GAMMIE, 'Paraenetic Literature,' 45.

theories. Of particular interest to contemporary ethicists is the ancient teaching on moral virtue. This aspect has become so central to the research of some that these ethicists have come to refer to their work simply as 'virtue ethics'.[3] Virtue based theories emphasize the character of the moral agent and how that character is developed over time through moral choices. Virtue ethics places itself in contrast to modern (deontological and consequentialist) theories that examine moral questions with little regard for the history of the agent.[4]

Because virtue ethics is a contemporary ethical theory, formed in relation to other contemporary theories and to some degree dependent upon them, it is of limited value in informing us directly about Greco-Roman ethics. It is, however, a helpful reminder of the distance between ancient virtue-based theories and their modern counterparts, and consequently that the context within which the ancients conceived of and practiced ethics was considerably different from our own.

In what follows, I aim to give a brief outline of Greco-Roman ethics and the place of virtue within it. Immediately, of course, there are major liabilities in any such endeavor. The ancient world was no less diverse than our own, and it is questionable whether or not the idea of 'Greco-Roman ethics' is simply an imposition of uniformity on an irreducibly diverse collection of schools and theories. Mindful of this diversity, I hope to outline those basic contours of thought, finding their root in Aristotle, which the later Hellenistic schools and their Roman counterparts held in common and which formed the backdrop for their differences.

Aristotle begins his *Nicomachean Ethics* with the observation that, 'Every craft and every line of inquiry, and likewise every action and decision, seems to seek some good.'[5] He goes on to apply this principle to the whole of life, and concludes that the good to which human life aims is 'happiness' (εὐδαιμονία). How then does one achieve this state of 'happiness'? Aristotle argues that, 'the human good proves to be activity of the soul in accord with virtue (ἀρετήν),' and adds that this activity must

---

[3] For introductions, see the collections by R. CRISP and M.A. SLOTE, eds., *Virtue Ethics, Oxford Readings in Philosophy* (Oxford: Oxford University Press, 1997), and also D. STATMAN, ed., *Virtue Ethics: A Critical Reader* (Edinburgh: Edinburgh University Press, 1997). For examples, see the influential A.C. MACINTYRE, *After Virtue: A Study in Moral Theory*, 2nd ed. (London: Duckworth, 1985), or the more recent R. HURSTHOUSE, *On Virtue Ethics* (Oxford: Oxford University Press, 1999). For an application to theology see S. HAUERWAS and L.G. JONES, eds., *Why Narrative?: Readings in Narrative Theology* (Grand Rapids: Eerdmans, 1989)

[4] This emphasis on the moral agent means that virtue ethics is sometimes alternatively referred to as 'agent-based ethics'.

[5] ARISTOTLE, *EN*, 1094a.

occupy 'a complete lifetime (ἐν βίῳ τελείῳ).'[6] Thus, the goal (τέλος) of life is happiness, and the means to that end is virtue.

As mentioned before, the appeal of Aristotelianism for virtue ethicists is its concern with the life of the moral agent as the context for moral deliberation, in contrast to other approaches that treat moral choices as isolated events. These latter approaches are *centrally* concerned with the question, what shall I do? Whereas Aristotelian approaches are *centrally* concerned with, what kind of person should I be(come)? So, for Aristotle the central question is that of moral character, with choice being the means of shaping character over the course of a lifetime. This basic notion of the centrality of character was simply *assumed* by the later Hellenistic schools. As Annas notes, 'Ancient ethical theories are concerned with the agent's life as a whole, and with his character. Concern with character and choice, with practical reasoning and the role of the emotions, is central rather than marginal.'[7] So, for Aristotle and the schools the chief concern was with character development (ἠθοποιία), which practically speaking meant the inculcation of the virtues.

To understand why the virtues were so central, we first must understand what they are. What do virtues like courage, temperance, fidelity, and truthfulness hold in common and how do they function within the project of character formation? Annas lists three attributes that were at the heart of the ancient understanding of the virtues:

1. Virtues are *dispositional*.
2. Virtues have an *affective* aspect: they involve our feelings, especially our feelings of pleasure and pain, and developing a virtue involves habituating our feelings in certain ways.
3. Virtues have an *intellectual* aspect: they involve reasoning about, and grasp of, the right thing to do, and developed virtue implies good practical reasoning or practical intelligence.[8]

A. Habit

To say that the virtues are *dispositional* means they are more than simply noble ideals; they are states of the soul. A virtue is a learned disposition or inclination of the soul to do the right thing in a particular circumstance. For example, if someone has developed the virtue of courage, then, when challenged by the temptation to either cowardice or recklessness, that person will have the inclination and desire to do what is courageous. Virtues are not simply dispositions of temperament given at birth, but rather they are *learned* dispositions developed over years by habit. Thus, in

---

[6] ARISTOTLE, *EN*, 1098a.
[7] J. ANNAS, *The Morality of Happiness* (Oxford: Oxford University Press, 1993), 4.
[8] ANNAS, *Happiness*, 48–9.

Greco-Roman ethics choices have a cumulative effect on one's character and dispositions toward virtue or vice.

To say that virtues are dispositions formed by habit is not to say that they become 'mindless habits'. We might describe the virtues as dispositions that are stable, but not static. To have a certain virtue one must have a well-seated disposition toward that virtue, but it always can be (and needs to be) strengthened by continuing to choose what that virtue calls for.

Immediately, we can see why thinking of one's life *as a whole* is so central to ancient ethics. No choice stands in isolation. Each choice is affected by the weight of past choices and the dispositions they have created. Likewise, each choice contributes to the state of the agent's soul and abilities in choosing well in the future. Thus, each choice is immediately placed within the context of one's life as a whole, and the direction of that life. Every choice in line with virtue is one that enables virtuous living in the future, and thereby enables movement toward the goal of εὐδαιμονία. The virtues then become an aid for procuring happiness through dispositions that enable virtuous living.

B. Emotions

To say that the virtues have an *affective* aspect means, first, that they are not to be thought of as solely intellectual dispositions, and secondly, that they are not accurately portrayed as commitments to be held in *opposition* to emotions. Having virtue is not simply having self-control in the face of desire for some corrupt gain. The fostering of a virtuous disposition also fosters one's desire *for* virtue. The virtuous agent is one who not only has the inclination to do the right thing and performs the right action, but also one who desires that action and takes pleasure in the performance of it.[9] An agent who performs the right action, but does so in labored opposition to his emotions and desires may be on the road to virtue, but he has not yet attained it.

Two things follow from this: first, the emotions are an essential part of right action and virtuous living, and second the emotions can be *shaped* through habitual virtuous choices, in the same way that one develops the virtues themselves. Virtuous choices instill a growing desire for virtue in the moral agent. If one is to become virtuous, then one must learn to love the right and hate the wrong, and one does this by means of making

---

[9] Cf. MACINTYRE, *After Virtue*, 149, 'Virtues are dispositions not only to act in particular ways, but also to feel in particular ways. To act virtuously is not, as Kant was later to think, to act against inclination; it is to act from inclination formed by the cultivation of the virtues. Moral education is an "éducation sentimentale".'

virtuous choices. So, as before, habit in line with virtue becomes the essential means of becoming virtuous.

It should be noted that on this particular point of the affective aspect of virtue there is some diversity among the Hellenistic schools. The Stoics developed a theory of virtue with a decidedly more intellectual bent than the Aristotelian model. They saw emotions as ultimately having nothing to contribute to right actions, since the only reason for choosing a right action is its accordance with Nature/reason. They conceived of emotions primarily as contenders with virtue, and thus ἀπάθεια became *the* Stoic virtue.[10]

C. Wisdom

Finally, to say that the virtues possess an *intellectual* aspect means that, while they are developed by habit, the virtues never become mindless automatic responses to circumstance. The virtuous person is not 'programmed' by habit to do the right thing. He must understand what it is he is doing and why. For an agent to perform a virtuous act he must not only have the inclination and desire for that act, but must also understand *why* that act is virtuous. He should understand how a particular act in a particular circumstance could, for example, be brave or temperate. Thus, he must understand how to relate the *general* principles of virtue to *particular* situations.

This skill of recognizing the virtuous act in a particular situation Aristotle called φρόνησις, which can be loosely translated as 'discernment' or 'wisdom'. Once again, this aspect of virtuous living is developed over time. Through the repeated act of making decisions in line with virtue, one develops the skill of discernment. Wisdom is a learned skill that needs to be fostered over time for the flourishing of virtue. Wisdom is not merely knowledge of general principles, but rather the skill of applying them to life; it requires a great sensitivity to the complex circumstances of individual situations in weighing the right course of action. No two situations are exactly alike, and therefore general dictums (though necessary) are not enough; the skill of φρόνησις is required to discern the virtuous act in a particular situation. Once again, we see how this places virtue within the course of one's life as a whole. This intellectual aspect of

---

[10] This difference in thought is indicative of the entire Stoic project, not simply a small critique of Aristotle. The Stoics critiqued the other schools on the grounds that their theories could not secure happiness, because they left individuals vulnerable to the vicissitudes of life. Their solution was a life of 'detachment', free from the devastating force of calamity on one's life. On this theme, see the two monographs of M.C. NUSSBAUM, *The Fragility of Goodness: Luck and Ethics in Greek Tragedy and Philosophy* (Cambridge: Cambridge University Press, 1986) and *The Therapy of Desire: Theory and Practice in Hellenistic Ethics* (Princeton: Princeton University Press, 1994).

virtue – wisdom – is one that draws on life experience and whose future development is dependent on wise choices in the present.

From these points, we can summarize a few key strands. Greco-Roman ethics places at its center a concern for the character of the moral agent. (Like all ethical programs, it has a concern for the right thing to do in a given situation, but it does this within the wider context of virtue.) Because of this concern for character development, it devotes a great deal of energy to exploring the nature of character and the various means of influencing it. This can be seen in its keen interest in the emotional and psychological sides of character as well as its emphasis on habit as a tool for enabling moral progress.

In Greco-Roman ethics, the life of the virtuous agent becomes a life with a vector pointed at an ideal, where each moral choice is made with the course of one's life in mind. If I want to be this kind of person, which choice shall I make? Or, if I make this choice, what kind of person will it make me? Thus, choices are placed in the context of seeing one's life as a whole – as a kind of linear narrative directed toward a τέλος.

II. Literary Artifacts

Inevitably, these basic concepts found expression in the arts. After Aristotle, Greek tragedies became expositions of moral character, using calamity to reveal virtues and vices.[11] Likewise, biographies were written to not only to give an account of lives of great men but also to extol the virtues that made their lives great.[12] If we turn to philosophic literature, then we are inclined to think of formal treatises or, in the case of Plato, the dialogues. But the philosophic schools also possessed a rich letter writing tradition. As Stowers notes, 'Going back to Aristotle's famous *Protrepticus* there was a long tradition of putting exhortations to the philosophical life into the form of letters.'[13] This use of letter writing became increasingly important in the Hellenistic period when Greek philosophic ideas, as well as philosophers, spread throughout the Mediterranean world and philosophic pursuits were no longer confined to

---

[11] Cf. EPICTETUS, *Discources*, 1.4.26, 'For what are tragedies then but the portrayal in tragic verse of the sufferings of men who have admired things external?'

[12] See PLUTARCH, *Pericles*, 1.3–4; 2.2–4.

[13] S.K. STOWERS, *Letter Writing in Greco-Roman Antiquity*, LEC 5 (Philadelphia: Westminster, 1986), 37.

Athens. Letter writing became an essential tool for philosophers to continue the tutelage of their students over large distances.[14]

Another important consequence of the process of Hellenization for the philosophic schools is a change in the typical audience for philosophic teaching and literature. In the time of Plato and Aristotle, the ideal moral agent was an adult male Athenian, with a good upbringing in a respectable family. All philosophy was conceived of within the context of the Athenian city-state; thus, Aristotle's *Nicomachean Ethics* is a complement to his *Politics*. This was not so for the Hellenistic schools. The audience for their philosophy was more likely to be an adult 'convert'[15] from paganism.

Within this context, the Hellenistic schools developed two main types of epistolary literature: *protreptic* and *paraenesis*. Both protreptic and paraenesis are types of exhortation, but over time the schools developed a loose distinction between protreptic as an exhortation to *enter into* the philosophic life and paraenesis as exhortation to *continue on* in the philosophic life.[16] Both extol virtue as the means of reaching the goal of

---

[14] Cf. D.E. AUNE, *The New Testament in its Literary Environment*, LEC 8 (Philadelphia: Westminster, 1987), 167, 'The first century A.D. was a period when moral philosophers increasingly made use of the letter form as a vehicle for instruction. The letters of Plato and Aristotle were important models in this development.'

[15] This is not to say that *all* members of the schools should be classified as 'converts'. There were still those who were educated in a system analogous to the Classical model, where philosophy was the final step in the molding of a Roman gentleman. At this point we can loosely classify two types of philosophic neophytes: adherents and converts. Both have made a strong commitment to the philosophic life, but the latter has a stronger sense of *discontinuity* with his previous life. This distinction is pursued in more detail below in Chapter 4, which deals in depth with conversion.

[16] A long-standing debate persists on the distinction between paraenesis and protreptic. STOWERS, *Letter Writing*, 92, states that he 'will use *protreptic* in reference to hortatory literature that calls the audience to a new and different way of life, and *paraenesis* for advice and exhortation to continue in a certain way of life,' even though he freely admits that, '[t]he terms, however, were used this way only sometimes and not consistently in antiquity.' In fact T.C. BURGESS, *Epideictic Literature*, SCP (Chicago: University of Chicago Press, 1902), 230n2, notes that, 'in many cases the words seem to be used even by technical writers as fully interchangeable,' although he agrees to, 'a more or less noticeable predominance of the precept character in the word παραινῶ and its derivatives.' GAMMIE, 'Paraenetic Literature,' 52, builds on this and shows that while a possibility in protreptic, 'the presence of precepts and a commending of them as a way of life...is not an optional feature for paraenesis.' In addition he notes that, 'protreptic seeks to persuade frequently through a sustained demonstration. The demonstration in protreptic is more systematic, organized and regular than it is in paraenesis' (53). Thus, paraenesis is *typically* addressed to neophytes and contains precepts pertaining to various spheres of life. Protreptic is *typically* addressed to potential members using a sustained argument to extol the life of virtue.

happiness, but paraenesis is concerned with the practical facilitation of that goal through moral education and transformation.

III. Ancient Epistolary Types

It might prove helpful at this point to place these two philosophic epistolary genres within the context of ancient letter writing practices. The professional letter writing 'handbooks' that we possess from the Greco-Roman world differentiate epistolary types/genres primarily based on *social function*.[17] For example, the *Epistolary Types* of Demetrius describes twenty-one types of letter (e.g., friendly, commendatory, blaming, reproachful, consoling, censorious, admonishing or threatening). Demetrius stresses that each letter must be written to 'fit the particular circumstance.'[18] For each type, he includes a short sample letter, which contains typical literary elements that are appropriate to the social function that type aims to accomplish. Likewise, Libanius also articulates an epistolary genre classification focused on social function, listing forty-one types in his *Epistolary Styles*. Stowers summarizes the function served by these handbooks:

> The concept of epistolary types provided the ancient writer with a taxonomy of letters according to typical actions performed in corresponding social contexts and occasions. The types in the handbooks give a sample, in barest outline, of form and language that is appropriate to the logic of the social code in a particular instance. The author, then, could elaborate, combine, and adapt this ideal according to the occasion in view, his purpose and his literary abilities. Rhetorical training provided the letter writer with techniques for the endless elaboration and development of the basic ideal captured in the handbook descriptions.[19]

Thus, the handbooks are evidence of recognized epistolary genres of the day, which were primarily understood in terms of social function. While certain literary characteristics are given, these sample letters are deliberately brief, affording the greatest flexibility within the form. So, how do these types relate to our two philosophic epistolary genres of paraenesis and protreptic? Aune argues that 'most' of these epistolary types 'are subtle variations of the Greek letter of advice (*logos protreptikos*

---

[17] These handbooks have no formal connection to ancient 'rhetorical handbooks'. On the relationship between classical rhetoric and epistolary writing, see J.T. REED, 'Epistle,' *HCRHP*, 171–93.

[18] (PSEUDO-) DEMETRIUS, *Epistolary Types*, 1.

[19] STOWERS, *Letter Writing*, 56. He adds that, 'The modern student of ancient letters should understand both the limitations and the logic which the various types represent and the enormous flexibility in composition which they allow.'

or *logos parainetikos*).' While there is some merit to this suggestion, in connection with paraenesis and protreptic, it is probably more helpful to think of most of these various epistolary types as sub-genres or 'forms' (*Gattungen*) utilized in paraenetic and protreptic letters.[20] While these various epistolary types can describe the sole purpose of a letter, a letter of commendation, for example, they can also be combined to form more complex letters performing several complementary social functions. Recognizing this, Libanius simply calls his final epistolary type 'mixed'.[21] Paraenesis and protreptic then are 'mixed' epistolary genres utilizing various other sub-genres as needed to accomplish their aims.[22]

What is most important for our study is to see that Demetrius and Libanius classified epistolary genres, like paraenesis and protreptic, primarily in terms of their *social function*. Genres were not *primarily* differentiated by literary characteristics. The utility of such functional epistolary genre classifications lies in their flexibility of form, which enabled them to, as Demetrius said, 'fit the particular circumstance.' Likewise, our epistolary genre category of paraenesis will emphasize functionality and will examine literary strategies in terms of how they further the author's paraenetic aims. Our next concern, then, is to map out the function of paraenesis.

IV. The Purpose of Paraenesis

Paraenesis seeks to facilitate progress (προκοπή) in moral virtue. Ancient philosophy saw happiness in the *conformity* of one's life with virtue, not simply a belief in virtue.[23] Not surprisingly then, paraenesis is concerned with the transformation of life to conform to beliefs. It is only in living out his beliefs that a neophyte can enjoy the freedom that was promised him as a fruit of adopting the philosophic path. As we saw above in our discussion

---

[20] AUNE, *Literary Environment*, 161. Since paraenesis and protreptic are epistolary categories describing moral exhortation it is probably an overstatement of AUNE to subsume 'most' of these types under these headings. The types laid out in the handbooks have a much broader scope, and are not primarily focused on moral education or exhortation. It is hard to interpret, for example, a letter to a Roman State official from a lesser being thought in terms of protreptic or paraenetic.

[21] (PSEUDO-) LIBANIUS, *Epistolary Styles*, 45.

[22] The epistolary types of Demetrius and Libanius do not represent an exhaustive list of 'forms' for use in paraenesis, as will be seen shortly.

[23] Cf. the advice of M. RUFUS, in *Fragmenta* 1.5.15–1.6.3, 'whatever exhortations (οἱ παραινούμενοι) he is persuaded are true, there he must follow out in life (βίος); for only in this way will anyone profit from philosophy, if to sound teachings one adds works (τὰ ἔργα) in harmony with them.' Translation and text: WILSON, *Hope*, 94.

of virtue, the means of appropriating this new life is acquiring the virtues in greater and greater measure. This explains why paraenesis emphasizes the moral sphere of life and is so replete with moral maxims and precepts. Paraenesis is concerned with developing virtue – with the transformation of character – through practical instruction.

Libanius, in his handbook, states that, 'Paraenesis is divided into two parts, encouragement and dissuasion (προτροπὴν καὶ ἀποτροπήν).'[24] Paraenesis operates simultaneously on two fronts: the promotion of virtue and the denigration of vice. As Isocrates says to Demonicus, 'I am going to counsel you on the objects to which young men should aspire and from what actions they should abstain.'[25] The most succinct expression of this in paraenesis is found in lists of contrasting virtues and vices. But this consciousness of what wisdom literature calls the 'Two Ways' is characteristic of paraenesis.[26] The goal of this form of teaching is to inculcate virtues while at the same time weakening the hold of vices.

In the context of conversion to philosophy, one of the greatest obstacles to growth is the convert's own past. Just as one develops good dispositions by living in accordance with virtue, so also one develops bad dispositions by living in accordance with vice. So, for the convert the path of life is not only trying to instill new virtues, but also trying to extirpate well-rehearsed vices. Thus, the literary strategy of antithesis has a special potency for the convert.

In the ancient world the experience of conversion often entailed a radical reorientation, involving a degree of estrangement, not only from one's old beliefs, but also from a society that endorsed them. Thus, entrance into a philosophy often involved a process of re-socialization into a new society of the philosophic 'community'. Paraenesis is especially suited to converts at this crossroads, which sociologists refer to as the 'liminal' phase of socialization. During this phase a convert is still struggling with breaking old ties, incorporated in countless attitudes, habits, ritual practices and relationships, and establishing new ties through adopting new practices and attitudes, which center the convert's identity within the circle of the new community.

Paraenesis is directed at reinforcing one's social and emotional commitments to the new path and disparaging one's emotional and social ties to the past. Paraenesis is concerned with more than simply supplying moral instruction. It aims at the transformation of a life in all its

---

[24] (PSEUDO-) LIBANIUS, *Epistolary Styles*, 5.

[25] ISOCRATES, *Demonicus*, 5.

[26] Cf. GAMMIE, 'Paraenetic Literature,' 56, 'Comparison or contrast between alternative entities, ways or styles is an exceedingly old and yet persistent device in Paraenetic Literature.'

complexity. The goal of this transformation is happiness, which only comes about through attaining virtue, but paraenesis recognizes the intricacy of the human soul, and the multiple levels on which it must operate to bring about moral transformation.[27] Thus, it seeks to persuade the neophyte in diverse ways to confirm him in the course he has chosen. Wilson describes paraenesis as:

> [A] teacher's commendation, through moral exhortation, instruction, and correction, of a prescribed way of life to individuals who are at a novice or liminal stage of development within their philosophical group. This manner of address is delivered within the framework of a previously-shaped and comprehensive understanding of reality that derives from the movement's particular teachings. ...Because the recipients of paraenesis find themselves at a cross-roads, both in life and in terms of their training within the school, the formulation of paraenesis will take into account facets of prior competing worldviews, which possess their own agendas for human thriving. Since it is oriented towards the personal formation and palpable moral progress of students, paraenesis exhibits a clear persuasive interest, as it seeks to shape the concrete behavior and decision-making process of neophytes so that every aspect of their lives corresponds with and verifies the teachings to which they subscribe.[28]

Wilson exhibits an appreciation for the complexity of the situation typically addressed in paraenesis, as well as for the diversity of literary strategies that an author can bring to bear in response to that complexity.

Among these, Wilson mentions the integration of moral instruction with the basic 'worldview' of the philosophy. As a form of exhortation aimed at the transformation of an individual's character in all its complexity, paraenesis does not confine itself to lists of moral maxims.[29] It is not surprising then that the basic teachings of the philosophy have a role to play in contextualizing ethical instruction and providing ideational grounding for considered moral actions.

---

[27] At first this may sound like we are attributing too much to the ancient philosophers but H.D. BETZ, 'Introduction,' in *Plutarch's Ethical Writings and Early Christian Literature*, ed. H.D. BETZ, SCHNT 4 (Leiden: Brill, 1978), 2, notes that, 'In the Hellenistic and Roman periods especially, philosophers were engaged in the practice of what we would call today, "psychological counseling" or "psychotherapy," that is, using ethical theory in a simplified and practical form in order to educate themselves and others to accept and carry through a reasonable way of life.'

[28] WILSON, *Hope*, 12.

[29] Cf. MALHERBE, 'Hellenistic Moralists,' 279. 'The insights gained by DIBELIUS and his successors are valuable, but their interest in form and origin has led to too narrow understanding of paraenesis. If the investigation is to proceed significantly a broader approach must be adopted. In particular, a fresh look should be taken at the characteristics of paraenesis, especially those features that may take us beyond a concern with the form and origin of *topoi*, virtue and vice lists, diatribe, lists of duties of members of a household, and the like.'

Because it addresses those who already possess a basic knowledge of the school, paraenesis does not typically lay out the tenets of the philosophy in a systematic or comprehensive way, but only in a summary fashion. (Hence the familiar observation that paraenesis does not introduce new doctrines.) The reasons governing choices of content and arrangement in such summaries are *pragmatic*. The reiterations of doctrine are chosen for their usefulness in promoting the paraenetic aims of the author (e.g., contextualizing ethical instruction or reinforcing affective commitments to virtue).

Summarizing, the purpose of paraenesis is life transformation. Taking into account the complexities of life, it utilizes a host of literary strategies to redirect the neophyte's commitments from his old way of life to his new path of virtue. We have seen that paraenesis operates in three primary modes: ethical instruction, integration with worldview, and reformation of affective commitments. These three spheres or modes of operation afford a helpful heuristic grouping for looking at some of the distinctive features of paraenetic literary strategies.

V. Characteristics of Paraenesis: Form and Function

The descriptions of the form of paraenesis that follow draw heavily on Isocrates' letter to Demonicus and Seneca's *Moral Epistles* ninety-four and ninety-five. The epistles of Isocrates have long been recognized as a quintessential example of Greco-Roman paraenesis.[30] Its main use here is in providing examples of characteristically paraenetic expressions. The two epistles of Seneca are invaluable because they represent a self-conscious reflection from an ancient philosopher on the *role* of paraenesis in forming character. Seneca is also important because, not only was he a contemporary of the first Christians,[31] but his particular eclectic brand of Stoicism was, in the opinion of many early church fathers, both admirable for its persuasive moral teaching and amenable to Christianity.[32] Thus, his thoughts on the nature of paraenesis and its role in moral

---

[30] See e.g., DIBELIUS, *James*, 5. ISOCRATES lived from 436–338 BC.

[31] SENECA died by his own hand in AD 65, at roughly 70 years of age. His *Epistles* were written in his later years.

[32] Cf. MALHERBE, 'Hellenistic Moralists,' 269–70, 'The respect with which the moral philosophers were viewed is well illustrated the growing Christianization of Seneca in the early church. Whereas Tertullian referred to him as *Seneca saepe noster*, two hundred years later Jerome dropped the qualifying adverb and called him *noster Seneca*. In the intervening period a collection of fourteen letters purporting to have passed between Paul and Seneca had come into existence. These spurious writings reflect the tacit assumption that Paul and Seneca have much in common.'

formation offer an invaluable insight into the nature of paraenetic literature. Where illustrative, other ancient authors are utilized to supplement these two primary sources.

A. Moral Instruction

Moral instructions (paraenesis-as-form) are the most obvious characteristic literary strategy adopted in paraenesis. As Gammie says, 'Paraenesis is a form of address which not only commends, but actually enumerates precepts or maxims which pertain to moral aspiration and the regulation of human conduct.'[33] There are four main types of moral instruction: (1) maxims, (2) exhortations and admonitions, (3) virtue and vice lists, and (4) moral exemplars.

Before we look at each of these types, it is important to note that the content of all these types of moral instruction is *traditional* and *uncontestable*. Paraenetic writers do not aim at originality; they freely admit to borrowing from traditional sources and even other philosophic schools for their instructions.[34] Instructions require no polemic to convince the audience of their validity. As Seneca says, 'Such maxims need no special pleader (*advocatum ista non quaerunt*); they go straight to our emotions, and help us simply because Nature is exercising her proper function.'[35] Therefore, the aim of moral instruction is not inventing new precepts, but to instruct and exhort.

A *maxim* is a statement (sentence or phrase) given in the indicative with transparent moral implicatures. For example, 'If you admit to your friendship men who seek your favor for the lowest ends, your life will be lacking in friends who will risk your displeasure for the highest good.'[36]

An *exhortation* is moral advice given in the imperative calling the hearer to adopt a certain attitude or to perform a specific action. For example, 'Be courteous in your manner, and cordial in your address (τῷ μὲν τρόπῳ γίγνου φιλοπροσήγοριας, τῷ δὲ λόγῳ εὐπροσήγορας).'[37]

---

[33] GAMMIE, 'Paraenetic Literature,' 51.

[34] ISOCRATES, for example writes, 'With these examples (παραδείγμασι) before you, you should aspire to nobility of character, and not only abide by what I have said, but acquaint yourself with the best things in the poets as well, and learn from the other wise men also any useful lessons they have taught. For just as we see the bee settling on all the flowers, and sipping the best from each, so also those who aspire to culture ought not to leave anything untasted, but should gather useful knowledge from every source' *Demonicus*, 51–2.

[35] SENECA, *EM*, 94.28. Cf. (PSEUDO-) LIBANIUS, *Epistolary Styles*, 5, 'Paraenesis is hortatory speech that does not admit of a counter-statement.'

[36] ISOCRATES, *Demonicus*, 30.

[37] ISOCRATES, *Demonicus*, 20.

An *admonition* is moral advice given in the imperative warning the hearer to abstain from a particular attitude or action. Such as, 'Never allow yourself to be put under oath save for one of two reasons – in order to clear yourself of disgraceful charges or to save your friends from great dangers.'[38] Exhortations and admonitions are frequently accompanied by *motive clauses*. For example, 'Be not fond of violent mirth, nor harbor presumption of speech; for the one is folly, the other madness.'[39]

Finally exhortation and admonition can be used together to form an *antithetical pair*, for example: 'Never emulate those who seek to gain by injustice (μηδένα ζήλου τῶν ἐξ ἀδικίας κερδαινόντων), but cleave rather to those who have suffered loss in the cause of justice (ἀλλὰ μᾶλλον ἀποδέχου τοὺς μετὰ δικαιοσύνης ζημιωθέντας).'[40]

Exhortations and admonitions are both general and specific at the same time. They give advice for *specific* spheres of life (e.g., family, friends, possessions) but the advice is *general* and often merely specifies the *attitude* one should adopt toward that sphere of life. The benefits of this are specificity and flexibility. Instructions apply the virtues to specific life situations and are therefore useful in helping someone find his way on the path to virtue. At the same time, they are general enough to apply to virtually anyone at almost any time and place.

Maxims, exhortations and admonitions function at several different levels. First, they simply tell the neophyte what to do, providing directives to young philosophers on how to live out their philosophy practically. Seneca argues that, 'If you rid a man of insanity, he becomes sane again, but if we have removed false opinions, insight into practical conduct does not at once follow. Even though it follows, counsel will none the less confirm (*tamen admonitio conroborabit*) one's right opinion concerning Good and Evil.'[41] Moral instructions give practical advice to young students who are just learning what it means to live out their beliefs; they need practical instruction on what to do. In addition, instructions also provide landmarks on the neophyte's moral landscape, confirming him in his choices.

Secondly, moral instructions also aid in the development of practical wisdom: φρόνησις. By giving situationally specific instructions, the convert gains experience in applying the virtues to life and thereby shaping his moral imagination. Seneca argues that, 'We are hindered from accomplishing praiseworthy deeds...by want of practice in discovering the demands of a particular situation. Our minds are often under good control,

---

[38] ISOCRATES, *Demonicus*, 23.
[39] ISOCRATES, *Demonicus*, 15.
[40] ISOCRATES, *Demonicus*, 39.
[41] SENECA, *EM*, 94.36.

and yet at the same time are inactive and untrained in finding the path of duty – and advice makes this clear (*admonitio demonstrat*).'[42] Instructions then facilitate the development of the skill of applying principles to specific situations.

Finally, the most obvious function served by instruction is simply provoking someone to action, by concentrating the mind on duty and exhorting him to action. As Seneca says, 'Advice is not teaching; it merely engages the attention and rouses us, and concentrates the memory, and keeps it from losing grip. We miss much that is set before our very eyes. Advice is, in fact, a sort of exhortation (*admonere genus adhortandi est*).'[43] Here Seneca is making two points. The first is that instruction gives commands and rouses the soul of the listener from complacency or mere contemplation. Secondly, he says that it serves as a reminder of one's duties; as such things can (conveniently) be easily forgotten.

It is important to remember that there is value within the philosophic schools to simply doing the right thing. It is important to understand why one does it, and to want to do it, but if those things are not present in their fullness, as happens often, there is still a value to right action. First, it is a good in and of itself to do the right thing. Secondly, it shapes the soul in the direction of virtue. Because one develops the virtues by habit, action is a necessary component of learning to live virtuously. So, exhortation and admonition prove to be essential tools in moral education.

Virtue and vice lists give lists of virtues and virtuous attitudes to be honored and practiced, in contrast to vices to be avoided and eradicated. For example, 'Shun not only the worst evils, injustice and self-indulgence, but also their causes, pleasures. ...And pursue not only the best goods, self-control and perseverance, but also their causes, toils.'[44] Lists of virtue or vices can also appear on their own: 'Practice self-control in all the things by which it is shameful for the soul to be controlled, namely, gain, temper, pleasure, and pain.'[45]

With regard to function, virtually everything that has been said for exhortations and admonitions applies to the lists as well.[46] In addition, the lists add a clarifying element of contrast. Paraenesis is written to *per*suade and to *dis*suade, and often adopts antithetical language to contrast 'Two Ways' of life, as another system of landmarks on the moral landscape, providing reference points for moral action.

---

[42] SENECA, *EM*, 94.32.
[43] SENECA, *EM*, 94.25.
[44] (PSEUDO-) CRATES, *Epistle* 15. Cf. DIO CHRYSOSTOM, *Orations*, 44.10.
[45] ISOCRATES, *Demonicus*, 21.
[46] Cf. SENECA, *EM*, 95.65–7.

Finally, *moral exemplars* are used as models to be admired and imitated for their virtuous lives. For example, as Isocrates tells Demonicus:

If you will but recall also your father's principles, you will have from your own house a noble illustration of what I am telling you. For he did not belittle virtue nor pass his life in indolence; on the contrary, he trained his body by toil, and by his spirit he withstood dangers. Nor did he love wealth inordinately; but, although he enjoyed the good things at his hand as became a mortal, yet he cared for his possessions as if he had been immortal.[47]

Moral exemplars function in similar ways to maxims, exhortations, and admonitions, but they add a personal element to instruction; they are *embodied* exhortations. Through them, the neophyte is not simply asked to follow a precept, but to emulate and copy the life of an individual. The force of this is to personalize instructions and to bring them into the realm of actuality. The exemplar is a real person with whom the young philosopher can identify. (Precepts do not have struggles, and they do not make courageous choices.) In this way, instructions take on a human dimension, which also brings a sense of realizability to instruction. The exemplar, with whom the convert is asked to identify, has lived a life of realized virtue; he has struggled to conform his life to virtue and has reaped the rewards of honor and happiness. Thus, exemplars personify the goal of paraenesis – the soul transformed in the image of virtue.

B. Integration with Worldview

In Seneca's ninety-fourth epistle, he argues that moral instructions (what he calls 'precepts') are necessary for effective paraenesis. In epistle ninety-five, he makes the complementary point that precepts must be combined with a comprehensive understanding of reality (in present-day terminology, a worldview) if they are to be effective. He says that, 'It is not enough, when a man is arranging his existence as a whole, to give him [only] advice about details.'[48] Rather, if precepts are to be effective, then they need to be placed in context, given grounding, and integrated with all of life. Seneca argues that, 'Precepts by themselves are weak and, so to speak, rootless if they be assigned to the parts and not to the whole. It is the doctrines which will strengthen and support us in peace and calm, which will include simultaneously the whole of life and the universe in its completeness (*quae totam vitam totamque rerum naturum simul contineant*).'[49]

---

[47] ISOCRATES, *Demonicus*, 9.
[48] SENECA, *EM*, 95.44.
[49] SENECA, *EM*, 95.12. Cf. *EM*, 95.59.

Paraenesis then promotes virtues by 'picturing a world in which such conduct is only common sense.'[50] To be effective, paraenesis must integrate moral instructions with worldview; instructions then are not simply conceived on their own, but integrated within an all-encompassing picture of reality. Because it seeks to transform the life of the convert, in its entirety, to live out his beliefs, it is not surprising that paraenesis takes such a 'holistic' approach.

Wilson describes a worldview as, 'a particular way of looking at the world, of integrating different provinces of knowledge and experience into a symbolic totality, a symbolic universe.'[51] Worldviews possess huge integrative power by giving an interpretive framework of philosophic reflection about the nature of the world, and human flourishing within it, with which to interpret human existence. They provide universal context and grounding for action, and place human life within a larger framework. As Wilson says:

Functionally, this [symbolic] universe serves as a map of fact and value for a person, legitimating all roles, priorities, and institutions by situating them in the context of the broadest horizon of reference conceivable, bestowing meaning on all domains of life. In adopting the elements of a worldview cognitively and normatively, individuals are able to "locate" themselves; all of history and the entire biography of the individual are seen as events occurring in this world.[52]

Worldview then provides a context for conceiving of one's life as a whole, as a kind of linear narrative within a larger (cosmic narrative) world. The τέλος of that world subsequently becomes a reference point for all action. As Seneca teaches, 'No one will do his duty as he ought unless he has some principle to which he may refer his conduct. We must set before our eyes the goal of the Supreme Good, towards which we may strive, and to which all our acts and words may have reference (*ad quem omne factum nostrum dictumque respicitat*) – just as sailors must guide their course according to a certain star.'[53] Therefore, philosophic doctrine in paraenesis serves to contextualize moral instructions and provide a reference framework for deliberate moral action.

As mentioned above, because paraenesis is directed to those already within the school, it does not incorporate its doctrinal teaching in a systematically argued way, as in protreptic. Rather it utilizes short summary statements and slogans of the philosophic school to remind the

---

[50] C. GEERTZ, 'Ethos, World View, and the Analysis of Sacred Symbols,' in *The Interpretation of Cultures* (New York: Basic Books, 1973), 129.
[51] WILSON, *Hope*, 100.
[52] WILSON, *Hope*, 100.
[53] SENECA, *EM*, 95.45.

reader of basic beliefs and to point to the larger framework already known
to them. There is no need for new instruction, only reminders of a few key
points. The content of this instruction is chosen for its pragmatic value for
reinforcing beliefs and contextualizing moral instruction. It emphasizes
those elements of the school's worldview that the author believes will most
benefit his reader and suits his purpose. Thus, the philosophic constructs
given in paraenesis are pragmatic.[54] This 'pragmatic philosophy'[55] is
another literary strategy at the author's disposal to transform the life of his
reader.

C. Appeals to and Reshaping of Emotional Commitments

As we have noted before, Greco-Roman philosophers were quite
sophisticated in their approaches to moral transformation. They possessed
a deep appreciation for the emotional life of the convert, and how emotions
can be both an aid and a hindrance to virtue. Seneca, for example, bemoans
that, 'We are hindered from accomplishing praiseworthy deeds...by our
emotions.'[56] Paraenesis involves not only moral instruction, but also a kind
of emotional therapy.[57] It seeks to break not only bad habits, but also
unhealthy devotions, and in place of these, to foster desire for virtue. Once
again, we see the typical double-barreled approach of paraenesis: checking
bad emotional commitments and instilling good ones.

Seneca argues that, 'Certain things sink into us, rendering us sluggish in
some ways, and hasty in other. These two qualities, the one of recklessness
and the other of sloth, cannot be respectively checked or roused unless we
remove their causes, which are mistaken admiration and mistaken fear
(*falsa admiration et falsa formido*).'[58] Seneca recognizes the negative
power of emotional ties. Recklessness and sloth are both powerful vices,
but their effective elimination is dependent upon the removal on their
emotional causes – mistaken admiration and mistaken fear.[59] It is only

---

[54] Cf. WILSON, *Hope*, 92–3.

[55] The technical term for this is 'ideology', but I will use the (admittedly more
cumbersome) expressions 'pragmatic philosophy' and 'pragmatic theology', because they
are free from both the pejorative and pseudo-objective connotations of 'ideology'.

[56] SENECA, *EM*, 94.32.

[57] Cf. A.J. MALHERBE, *Moral Exhortation: A Greco-Roman Sourcebook*, LEC 4
(Philadelphia: Westminster, 1986), 48, 'The moral philosophers gave considerable
attention to developing methods by which to cultivate moral growth. These methods,
which were perpetuated and further developed in later Christian monastic orders,
included what we would call psychotherapy, psychological and pastoral counseling,
spiritual direction or soul care, and the most general exhortation. The term used to
describe this entire range of activity is "psychagogy."'

[58] SENECA, *EM*, 95.37.

[59] For example, 'A man may know that he should fight for his country, but fear will
dissuade him.' SENECA, *EM*, 95.37.

when *these* are removed that one is freed to follow moral instructions. He concludes that, 'It will therefore be of no avail to give precepts unless you first remove the conditions that are likely to stand in the way of precepts.'[60] The answer, in the end, is a re-education of the emotions. Paraenesis seeks to give the convert a disdain for vices like cowardice, sloth, and greed and a love for virtues like courage, amiability, and truthfulness. Seneca depicts this devotion to virtue in the strongest possible terms:

Just as a soldier's primary bond of union is his oath of allegiance and his love for the flag, and a horror of desertion, and just as after this stage, other duties can easily be demanded of him, the trusts given to him when once the oath has been administered; so it is with those whom you would bring to the happy life: The first foundation must be laid, and virtue worked into these men. Let them be held by a sort of superstitious worship of virtue; let them love her; let them desire to live with her, and refuse to live without her.[61]

Paraenesis then seeks to instill in the convert an array of emotional attachments to virtue. This, in turn, will free the convert to act out his beliefs, and to do so in a virtuous way, where right desires accompany right actions.

In accomplishing these twin goals of deflating the power of mistaken devotions and instilling true ones, paraenesis is at its most rhetorical. Because it is designed to reshape emotional attachments, paraenesis is aimed directly at the heart with rhetorical language of disparagement for vice and praise for virtue. In fact, this is another function of the virtue and vice lists. They not only enumerate the vices and virtues, but are also designed to affect one's attachment to them. Virtue and vice lists provide a moral and emotional 'either/or' for the convert. They call for an allegiance to virtue and a break with vice.

As we saw above, the use of *antithesis* is another typical literary strategy in paraenesis. By placing objects of devotion on either side of a fence, it clarifies emotional attachments and calls for a realignment of them. In this strategy, one important tool is the language of conversion. As we have said, the experience of conversion often involved a break with family, friends, and the society as a whole. The paraenetic writer often utilizes the convert's own experience of conversion to remind him that he has passed from ignorance and vice to knowledge and virtue. In this way, the author draws the sharpest possible distinction between the convert's past life and his new one. This serves to sever emotional commitments to the past while fostering emotional attachment to his new philosophic life. Friends, family, and society in general are depicted as unenlightened and

---

[60] SENECA, *EM*, 95.38.
[61] SENECA, *EM*, 95.35.

base to facilitate breaking ties to them and their way of life. Meanwhile the ties of friendship with others in the school are depicted as surpassing previous relationships, because real friends care about the soul of the other and are thus willing to rebuke and admonish one another.

In addition, the paraenetic author often depicts the act of conversion itself as irreversible. This serves to strengthen the antithesis, thereby cutting off the possibility of the convert returning to his old life, which he is tempted to do each time he entertains a tie to his old life. Antithesis in this form leaves no room for indecision, and helps the convert to evaluate his emotions in the context of his experience of conversion and his desire to carry through on his initial commitment. It instills in him a distaste for the vices of his old life as well as a desire for the virtues of the new. In this way, it is a therapy for the emotional ambivalence he feels in this transitional phase within his philosophic journey.

Moral exemplars are another useful tool for emotional education. While negative examples are sometimes given for contrast, in most cases the examples given are positive ones to be followed. These depictions are usually heavily rhetoricized encomia. The goal in this is the veneration of great men and their lives of virtue. Here the reader not only learns what virtue is, but develops admiration for embodied virtue. Through examples the neophyte learns to venerate virtuous character traits, and to seek them for himself. In using moral exemplars, paraenesis seeks to transform the reader's life in all its complexity – intellectual and emotional – in the image of virtue, or here, virtuous men.

Finally, paraenetic authors attempt to cultivate desire for virtue by reminding their hearers of the fruit of virtue: the pleasure of εὐδαιμονία. As Isocrates says, 'But most of all would you be spurred on to strive for noble deeds if you should realize that it is from them most of all that we also derive pleasure in the true sense (τὰς ἡδονὰς ἐκ τούτων μάλιστα γνησίως ἔχομεν).'[62] The virtuous life is one that gives pleasure, peace, and fulfillment. These reminders of the fruits of virtue are another rhetorical means available to the author to entice his pupil to seek virtue. As Seneca says, 'The counsel which assists suggestion by reason – which adds the motive for doing a given thing and the reward which awaits one who carries out and obeys such precepts – is more effective and settles deeper in the heart.'[63] He argues that, in the work of life transformation, a combination of instruction, motive, and benefits is more effective than any one by itself.

---

[62] ISOCRATES, *Demonicus*, 46.
[63] SENECA, *EM*, 94.44.

VI. Conclusion

Our aim in this chapter has been to sketch some of the basic features of the epistolary genre of paraenesis, which developed as a tool of the philosophers of the Hellenistic schools. We began by rehearsing some of the fundamental contours of Greco-Roman philosophy, with a special emphasis on ideas of moral character and virtue. We saw that paraenesis grew out of the fundamental needs and concerns of the philosophic schools in the Hellenistic period, as a way of promoting growth in moral maturity.

We observed that paraenesis works in three primary modes: by providing moral advice, contextualizing moral instruction within worldview constructs, and reorienting affective commitments. In paraenesis, these three basic modes of operation find expression in a host of literary strategies aimed at aiding the paraenetic enterprise of character formation (ἠθοποιία). Paraenesis seeks, through a diverse collection of literary-rhetorical devices, to aid the student in his attempt to transform his life and obtain the happiness that comes from virtue. As we saw, paraenesis is not limited to simply supplying moral instructions, but is a multifaceted approach to character transformation, which takes into account the history of the agent and the complexities of emotional and social ties that can impede progress in conforming one's life to one's convictions.

We have sketched out a functional genre classification for paraenesis as an epistolary genre, which combines the function of paraenesis (promoting growth in moral maturity) with a collection of typical literary strategies. Our next task is to see how 1 Peter might fit this model.

Chapter Two

The Genre of 1 Peter

Having established in the previous chapter the basic features of paraenesis as an ancient epistolary genre, the task at hand is to tender evidence for taking 1 Peter as an example of that genre. Our functional classification described paraenesis in terms of (1) function (i.e., seeking to promote growth in moral character) and (2) typical paraenetic literary strategies. So, if 1 Peter is a paraenetic epistle, then it will exhibit both paraenetic literary devices and a concern for growth in moral maturity. The aim of this chapter is to make the initial case that 1 Peter is a paraenetic epistle, and to offer answers to some possible objections to this classification. The remainder of the thesis will supply further confirmation of the paraenetic nature of 1 Peter while exploring various exegetical implications that arise from recognition of the epistle's paraenetic nature.

I. Paraenetic Epistle or Baptismal Homily?

Genre has proved a surprisingly contentious topic in the history of Petrine research. Beginning with Harnack, an entire generation of scholars argued that 1 Peter was not a genuine epistle at all, but actually a 'baptismal homily' dressed in the trappings of an epistle.[1] Beare, for example, argues

---

[1] A. HARNACK, *Die Chronologie der altchristlichen Literatur bis Eusebius*, 2 vols., *Geschichte der altchristlichen Literatur bis Eusebius* (Leipzig: J. C. Hinrich, 1897), 1:451 argued that, 'Sieht man von 1, 1.2 u. 5, 12–14 zunächst ab, so stellt sich das Schriftstück, ähnlich wie der Epheserbrief, nicht als ein eigentlicher Brief, sondern als ein homiletischer Aufsatz dar.' The reason for HARNACK's speculation here was not the literary characteristics of the letter, but a long-standing difficulty in identifying the recipients of the letter who are addressed as converts from paganism in the body of the letter and as διασπορά (a seemingly obvious reference to the Jewish makeup of the audience) in the salutation of the letter. He solved the difficulty by positing that the greeting and closing were added to an already existing 'homiletic discourse'. HARNACK's comment was more fully developed in the influential work of E.R. PERDELWITZ, *Die Mysterienreligion und das Problem des 1. Petrusbriefes: Ein literarischer und religionsgeschichtlicher Versuch*, RVV 11.2 (Giessen: Töpelmann, 1911). Others who refined this line of thinking are PREISKER in his appendix to WINDISCH's commentary (157), F.L. CROSS, *1. Peter: A Paschal Liturgy* (Oxford: A.R. Mowbray, 1954), B.I.

that 'The long section from 1:3 to 4:11 is not epistolary in form or in content,' and concludes that, 'it is not a letter but a sermon.'[2] He describes this sermon as 'a baptismal discourse, addressed to a group of recent converts.'[3] While this view 'had become all but axiomatic'[4] in its day, the consensus among scholars today is that there is a scarcity of evidence to support the theory of a cloaked baptismal homily, and that 1 Peter is a genuine epistle.[5]

Dibelius was one of the early critics of the sermonic hypothesis. Pointing specifically to the *Haustafel* in 2:18–3:7, he argued that 1 Peter was a 'typical example of paraenesis,'[6] and therefore a genuine epistle. By observing forms, he was able to determine genre. In a similar vein, our first step in demonstrating the paraenetic nature of 1 Peter is to document the presence of the various paraenetic literary strategies cataloged in the previous chapter; later we will examine the question of epistolary function.

We start by noting that more than half of the epistle (2:13–5:12) is devoted to moral instructions. The bulk of this ethical material is taken up with exhortations and admonitions on various topics. The *Haustafel*, mentioned by Dibelius, is, as we will see later, just a specialized form of traditional moral instruction concerned with οἰκονομία.[7] In addition, we can note the presence of lists of virtues (3:8) and vices (4:3; also see 2:1), and the use of moral exemplars: both Sarah (3:5–6) and Jesus (2:21–25;

REICKE, *The Epistles of James, Peter, and Jude*, AB 37 (Garden City, N.Y.: Doubleday, 1964), and F.W. BEARE, *The First Epistle of Peter: The Greek Text with Introduction and Notes*, 3rd ed. (Oxford: Blackwell, 1970).

[2] BEARE, *1 Peter*, 25.

[3] BEARE, *1 Peter*, 26. He adds that the 'later part of the book [4:12ff] is truly epistolary in form and in content and to this the address (1:1–2) and the closing greetings (5:12–14) properly belong. Into this framework, the baptismal discourse has been intruded, possibly by a later editor, but more probably by the writer himself.'

[4] P.J. ACHTEMEIER, 'Newborn Babes and Living Stones: Literal and Figurative in 1 Peter,' in *To Touch the Text: Biblical and Related Studies in Honor of Joseph A. Fitzmyer, S.J.*, ed. M.P. HORGAN and P.J. KOBELSKI (New York: Crossroad, 1989), 208.

[5] E.g., P.J. ACHTEMEIER, *1 Peter: A Commentary on First Peter*, Hermeneia (Minneapolis: Fortress, 1996), 61–2, 'As a result of continuing work on the content and style of 1 Peter, the emerging scholarly consensus is that far from being a composite work, the letter must rather be seen as a literary unity. That is due on the one hand to the fact that advocates of the embodiment of some sort of baptismal homily or liturgy have been unable to find agreement among themselves about either its nature or its extent, and on the other hand to the fact that there is no compelling internal evidence against its literary integrity. As a result, the letter is probably best understood as a piece of genuine correspondence that, whatever elements may have gone into its composition, has received in its present form from its final author its point, direction, and meaning, thus forming it into a unified whole.'

[6] DIBELIUS, 'Formgeschichte,' 232.

[7] Cf. SENECA, *EM*, 94.1.

3:18; 4:1). These various forms of moral instruction, which constitute the majority of the letter, are compelling evidence of its paraenetic nature.

In addition to this, as in Greco-Roman paraenesis, the letter emphasizes conversion as a life-defining choice. The baptismal homily hypothesis does contain a grain of truth. While baptism is only explicitly mentioned once in 3:21, conversion (of which baptism is the sign) *is* a major theme in the epistle. The readers are told that they have been given new birth (1:3, 23), and have been redeemed (1:18) and purified (1:22). They are 'like newborn babes,' having 'tasted that the Lord is good' (2:2–3). Once they were not a people, but now they are the chosen people of God (2:9–10). Again and again, the author reminds them of their conversion and draws out moral implications, calling for a break with their past way of life, and a renewed dedication to pursuing of their new life in Christ. This stock paraenetic strategy is further evidence of the paraenetic nature of the letter.

As we will see in the next chapter, the letter also uses theology to provide an ideational context for moral action. By constructing a narrative worldview of God's action in the world in 1:3–12, the author places the lives of the readers within a framework that provides a means of both interpreting adverse circumstances and contemplating concrete moral actions. In this way, our author engages in the typically paraenetic enterprise of integrating moral instruction with worldview, which Seneca argued is necessary for paraenesis to be effective.

So, in terms of form, 1 Peter possesses the hallmarks of a paraenetic epistle: exhortations, virtue and vice lists, moral exemplars, an emphasis on the moral implications of conversion, and theological constructs pragmatically shaped to contextualize moral deliberation. Our first criterion is satisfied; the form is paraenetic. We now turn to the question of function in order to confirm our designation of paraenetic epistle. What was the author's *aim* in writing his epistle? Does it show evidence of the typically paraenetic project of promoting growth in moral character?

II. The Purpose of 1 Peter

To uncover the purpose of 1 Peter we must first grasp the situation of the readers to which the author felt compelled to respond, and then look at his strategy in responding. Most students of the epistle point to persecutions among these Anatolian congregations as the key to understanding the situation and therefore the purpose of 1 Peter.[8] Suffering is certainly one of

---

[8] E.g., P.H. DAVIDS, *The First Epistle of Peter*, NICNT (Grand Rapids: Eerdmans, 1990), 23, 'The central concern of 1 Peter is clearly the issue of the suffering of the Christians in Asia Minor.' Compare the comment by A. SCHLATTER, *Petrus und Paulus*

the key themes of the epistle. While a previous generation of scholars saw these sufferings as a result of Roman state persecution,[9] over the last few decades the consensus has grown that the persecutions and sufferings faced by these churches were, as Kelly describes them, 'private and local, originating in the hostility of the surrounding population.' He explains that, 'The picture we obtain [in 1 Peter] is of minority groups living in an environment charged with dislike, misrepresentation and positive hostility, probably with sporadic explosions of violence.'[10] Their persecutions were characterized by slander and ostracism from their pagan neighbors, on account of their distinctive lifestyle (see 3:16; 4:4), and probably their abstention from public and domestic cultic practices.[11]

What then is the author's response to these persecutions? Many have understood the epistle as a consolation and encouragement amidst circumstances where the readers are apt to despair. Lohse, for example, states that, 'The epistle is addressed to Christians who are suffering and afflicted. It is the author's aim to strengthen and comfort them in this time of trial.'[12] He sees consolation as the purpose of the epistle. Like others, Lohse roots this consolation in the eschatological hope mentioned in 1:3–5. He summarizes the message of the epistle as: 'for a short time, if it is God's will, the Christians undergo suffering in various kinds of πειρασμοί (1:6–8), but the suffering is superseded by the eschatological rejoicing that is already being sounded in the church.'[13] It is along such lines that others have characterized 1 Peter as an epistle of hope,[14] with a message akin to Paul's in Rom. 8:18.

While this theme of consolation has its place in 1 Peter, it can hardly be called *the* 'theme' or 'purpose' of the epistle as it receives surprisingly little attention in the letter. Apart from possible allusions via the ὀλίγος in 1:6 and 5:10, the only explicit endorsements of this type of consolation comes in 4:13 and (maybe) 5:1. This is not to downplay the strong eschatological bent of the epistle, but to clarify that eschatology does not

---

nach dem Ersten Petrusbrief (Stuttgart: Calwer, 1937), 13, that the purpose of the epistle was 'daß die Kirche zum Leiden angeleitet werden muß.'

[9] E.g., BEARE, *1 Peter*, 33.

[10] J.N.D. KELLY, *A Commentary on the Epistles of Peter and Jude*, BNTC (London: Black, 1969), 10.

[11] Cf. ACHTEMEIER, *1 Peter*, 34–5.

[12] LOHSE, 'Parenesis and Kerygma,' 42.

[13] LOHSE, 'Parenesis and Kerygma,' 50. See also his conclusion, 'As strangers and sojourners in this world, however, they are on the way to their heavenly home with joyous hope' p. 59.

[14] E.g., D. GUTHRIE, *New Testament Introduction*, 4th ed. (Downers Grove, IL: IVP, 1990), 781, 'The keynote of the letter is hope.' Cf. N. BROX, *Der erste Petrusbrief*, EKKNT 21 (Zürich: Benziger Verlag, 1993), 17, 'Das Thema ist die Hoffnung (3,15).'

function in this way; rather eschatological hope most often serves as a motivation for ethical action,[15] as in 4:7: *The end of all things is at hand* (πάντων δὲ τὸ τέλος ἤγγικεν); *therefore keep sane and sober for your prayers* (σωφρονήσατε οὖν καὶ νήψατε εἰς προσευχάς). Further, as we have seen above, the majority of the epistle is taken up with moral instructions applying to both general and specific life situations. The advice in 2:1 to *put away all malice and all guile and insincerity and envy and all slander* (πᾶσαν κακίαν καὶ πάντα δόλον καὶ ὑποκρίσεις καὶ φθόνους καὶ πάσας καταλαλιάς), which is typical of the ethical discourse in the letter, does not function well as consolation.

More recently, some scholars have been able to integrate such ethical instructions into the purpose of the epistle by focusing on the social pressures placed on the addressees by persecution, and seeing the moral instructions as counteracting these social tensions. In his work on the *Haustafel* in 1 Peter, Balch argues that, 'one primary purpose of proper household behavior was to reduce the social-political tension between society and the churches.'[16] Thus, the purpose of the *Haustafel* in 1 Peter is to curb the cultural distinctiveness of the churches, which is the cause of their persecution. By acting in a way that conforms to the social mores of Greco-Roman society, the churches will win over their neighbors and curtail their social ostracism (2:12, 15). As Balch argues, 'The author of 1 Peter exhorted the recipients of his letter to the behavior outlined in the code with the intention of encouraging conduct which would contradict the Roman slanders.'[17] Thus, according to him, the purpose of the ethical formation of the community was to promote their assimilation into the culture and thereby allay their suffering and persecution. His approach has much to recommend it, especially its ability to integrate the ethical teaching of the epistle, or at least a major portion of it, with the situation of persecution and the purpose of the epistle. The trouble with his thesis is that this agenda of assimilation does not comport well with the overall thrust of the epistle. As Achtemeier remarks, 'if one gains any impression from the whole of 1 Peter, it would have to be that the farthest thing from the author's mind is accommodation to Hellenistic culture; 4:1–4 ought to make that clear enough.'[18] In fact, as Elliott insists, 'It was precisely a

---

[15] Cf. J. PIPER, 'Hope as the Motivation of Love: 1 Peter 3:9–12.' *NTS* 26 (1979–80): 212–31.

[16] D.L. BALCH, *Let Wives be Submissive: The Domestic Code in 1 Peter*, SBLMS 26 (Chico, CA: Scholars Press, 1981), 81.

[17] BALCH, *Wives*, 65–80, documents how this type of slander was typical of Greco-Roman criticism of 'Eastern religions'.

[18] ACHTEMEIER, 'Newborn Babes,' 219.

temptation to assimilate so as to avoid further suffering that the letter intended to counteract.'[19]

Elliott sees the purpose of the letter as reinforcing the identity of the community against this threat of assimilation. He argues that, unless checked, 'social tensions with outsiders would eventually undermine the confidence, cohesion, and commitment within the community.'[20] 'In general,' he says, 'the injunctions, contrasts, imagery, and traditions in 1 Peter all served the common aim of reinforcing a sense of identity, promoting the internal cohesion of the community, and providing it with a persuasive sustaining rationale for continued faith, commitment, and hope.'[21] Thus, according to Elliott the purpose of the epistle is to bolster community identity by emphasizing the lines of distinction between the churches and the pagan world around them, and by building interpersonal cohesion within the community. It should be noted, since it is often overlooked, that Elliott's interpretation is concerned with more than simply 'boundary maintenance'; he also stresses elements of the epistle that foster the internal life of the community.

Elliott's program, like that of Balch, is commendable for its ability to integrate the ethical portions of the epistle into an overall agenda that responds to the problem of social ostracism. The difficulty with his approach is that it confines itself to the social sphere. Only those aspects that pertain to community life are visible through his methodological prism. While I would not question the bulk of his conclusions, the approach is too narrowly focused. For him the ideology of the epistle is designed to produce results in the social sphere alone. Since there is such a strong emphasis in 1 Peter on integrity in social relationships, both with insiders and outsiders, Elliott's method is particularly enlightening in reading some of the letter (e.g., 2:4–12). However, there are other points where the method is less helpful. For example, in 1:3–12 one agenda of the author is to win the allegiance of the readers to God in the midst of practicalities that seem to speak against his faithfulness. Since this has little immediate social relevance, within Elliott's model it fades from view. In addition, Elliott's focus on the sociological aspects of the letter's agenda necessarily downplays how the letter seeks to transform *individual* lives

---

[19] J.H. ELLIOTT, '1 Peter, Its Situation and Strategy: A Discussion with David Balch,' in *Perspectives on First Peter*, ed. C.H. TALBERT, NABPRSSS (Macon, GA: Mercer University Press, 1986), 72–3. Cf. ACHTEMEIER, 'Newborn Babes,' 219, 'Indeed, it is not the danger of avoiding acculturation, but the temptation to lapse into acculturation that seems uppermost in our author's mind.'

[20] ELLIOTT, 'Situation and Strategy,' 68.

[21] ELLIOTT, 'Situation and Strategy,' 66.

within the community.[22] As is often the case with social-scientific approaches, individual and transcendental elements tend to become eclipsed by or subsumed under social realities.

None of the proposals we have outlined here has produced an explanation of the purpose of 1 Peter that is sufficient to explain the epistle as a whole. Each highlights certain aspects, but none gives a cohesive vision. Producing such a cohesive vision has proven to be one of the perennial difficulties in Petrine studies.[23] In what follows, we will attempt to address this difficulty by showing how 1 Peter functions as a paraenetic epistle by confronting the moral challenge of suffering and promoting growth in Christian character.

III. The Paraenetic Agenda of 1 Peter

We have already noted the formal paraenetic elements of (1) moral instructions, (2) an emphasis on conversion, and (3) pragmatically shaped worldview constructs as evidence of the paraenetic *form* of 1 Peter. Not surprisingly, these elements are also evidence of the paraenetic *agenda* of the epistle. Form follows function and vice versa.

The epistle's moral instructions function at multiple levels to accomplish the paraenetic aims of the author. First, they focus attention on the moral sphere of life as the primary arena in which their salvation is to bear fruit. Secondly, they facilitate moral action simply because they command good deeds. Thirdly, they promote the acquisition of discernment by giving advice that is both situationally specific (i.e., addressing a particular social sphere or relationship) and general (i.e., prescribing governing attitudes). In this way, the readers acquire experience in seeing foundational principles applied to real life circumstances. This in turn gives these converts a model for applying their beliefs to analogous situations, which involves practice in the art of discernment.

Likewise, the strong emphasis on images of conversion, especially in 1:13–2:3, is tailored to the author's paraenetic agenda. By placing an

---

[22] When I am speaking of ELLIOTT's 'program' or 'method', I am referring to his work laid out in *Home*. In his commentary, ELLIOTT would likely endorse the alternate agendas I have pointed out. But he does not intend to write a social-scientific commentary on 1 Peter. While he incorporates many of his previous insights into the social agenda of 1 Peter, he does not limit himself to this sphere, nor attempt work out a socio-scientific reading of each passage in 1 Peter. Thus, my criticisms of the narrowness of method are directed at his model developed in *Home*, which is incorporated to some extent, but by no means consistently, in his commentary.

[23] See the *Forschungsbericht* in MARTIN, *Metaphor*, 3–39.

absolute antithesis between life before and after conversion, and by deprecating the former while extolling the latter, our author facilitates a break with past practices and fosters the adoption of new ones. The image of new birth in 1:3, echoed in images like ἀρτιγέννητα βρέφη (2:2), creates an absolute antithesis between life before and after conversion. There is no possibility of going back, of being unborn. This translates into an absolute renunciation of the patterns of life that characterized life prior to conversion. The author's aim is to aid these Christians in the process of breaking the ties of their previous ἀναστροφή, powerful though they may be, and embracing their new found path. The (typically paraenetic) agenda here is to promote praxis that conforms to core beliefs.

Also typical of paraenetic practice is an integration of ethical instruction with worldview constructs. This is chiefly seen in the way that the epistle's theology is pragmatically shaped to aid in the author's paraenetic agenda. As Beare contends,

> The Epistle is in no sense a theological treatise. The central doctrines of Christianity are presupposed, but they are not expounded or discussed... The writer is concerned to set forth the manner of life to be followed by the Christian in the Church and in the world, and he refers to the doctrines of the faith only as to principles held in common by him and his readers, to which he may therefore appeal with confidence in *seeking to direct their conduct*.[24]

As we will see in the following chapter, the author of 1 Peter uses theological discourse to construct the boundaries of a theological narrative worldview that serves as a contextualizing moral vision, which informs moral deliberation and facilitates the appropriation of moral instructions. In 1 Peter theology operates in a paraenetic mode.

A. A Response to Suffering?

How then do the author's paraenetic aims address the problem of persecution? As we have already noted, calls to renounce vice and to 'do good' hardly seem appropriate responses to suffering. But they are appropriate, if the author's concern is with the *moral* challenge of suffering. If the author sees the greatest challenge produced by suffering as an invitation to hatred or vengeance and not simply despair, then his response would entail a call to maintaining moral integrity in the face of insults and abuse. Encountering persecution for their faith and distinctive lifestyle, these Christians are faced with two opposite but equally compelling temptations: to retaliate in kind or to disengage. The author's aim is to deny them both of these sinful responses. Instead, he enjoins his

---

[24] BEARE, *1 Peter*, 50. Italics added.

readers to remain steadfast in their good conduct and to show integrity in relationships with their persecutors.

We noted above that paraenesis addressed to converts is especially sensitive to the 'liminal' phase of socialization, when neophytes are struggling to cut attachments to old familiar habits and associations, while establishing new connections and commitments. 1 Peter is addressed to young converts in this liminal phase, as evidenced in the emphasis on conversion we have already noted.[25] Paraenesis is aimed at aiding neophytes over this obstacle by facilitating progress in moral maturity. For the converts addressed in 1 Peter this liminal struggle is *exacerbated* by suffering. Their difficulties are not only a product of their persecutions, but are also generic to their status as converts. Thus, the issues addressed by the author go beyond a response to suffering to address underlying struggles, which are *intensified and exposed* by suffering. The occasion of the epistle is the painful persecutions that these Anatolian churches are called to endure, but the challenges addressed do not arise solely out of suffering. Suffering has exposed the soft underbelly of Christians already engaged in trying to transform their lives to conform to their new beliefs. Persecutions have merely intensified temptations to assimilation and isolation, and intensified the need for safeguards against them.

The author's aim is not limited to helping these communities merely *survive* persecution, but is actually focused on *growth* in maturity in the midst of persecutions. This agenda of character growth, which is typical of paraenesis, is not tempered by suffering. In fact, the author interprets their situation of suffering as a means for bringing about growth. Persecution is

---

[25] 'Young converts' is an ideal audience category. It does not mean that *all* the addressees were in fact young converts from paganism. 5:1–5 tells us there were elders in the church who, in all likelihood, were older in the faith as well as in years. Also, it is not unlikely that there were Jewish Christians amongst the congregations. The ideal audience category of 'young converts' is how the author has chosen to envision the status of his audience (e.g., 2:2) for the purpose of addressing them and their situation. Presumably, since the author is aiming for some degree of relevance, there is a correlation between this category and the general makeup of the churches. 'Young' is also an ideal and relative term. The Hellenistic schools were very conscious of progress and the different stages one went through in becoming 'mature'. The Epicureans, for example, made a distinction between advanced students and novices as well as different levels of maturity and authority (see R.S. ASCOUGH, 'Greco-Roman Philosophic, Religious, and Voluntary Associations,' in *Community Formation: In the Early Church and in the Church Today*, ed. R.N. LONGENECKER (Peabody, MA: Hendrickson, 2002), 8). 'Young converts' refers to those in the liminal 'hump' of progress, from novice to advanced student. At the same time, the category of maturity is relative. No philosopher ever reached perfection, so there was always room for more growth in virtue and hence a continuing need for exhortation. Thus, paraenesis was fruitful for all philosophers, whether nascent or mature; but at the same time, it had a special potency for the recent convert.

not simply something to be endured but an *opportunity for growth*. In 1:6–7 the author interprets suffering as a 'refining fire', which produces a refined faith, a matured character – mature in its convictions and its moral integrity.

This refined faith is not, however, an automatic byproduct of suffering. Suffering is more likely to produce bitterness and selfishness than it is growth in moral character, as every piece of tragic theater from the ancient world attests. It is only when suffering is met with moral fortitude that it produces a refined character. Our author's agenda is to promote such a response to persecutions. This explains how it is that our author can respond to suffering with calls to renounce vice and to persevere in well-doing. The author's paraenetic aim is growth in Christian maturity, which is seen primarily in terms of growth in moral character, as both an expression of maturity and a means of growth.

But the author's aims are not limited to the moral sphere alone. For our author, growth in Christian maturity, while primarily seen in terms of moral transformation, also entails growth in active dependence upon God – what 1 Peter calls 'faith/hope'. Along with addressing the *moral* challenge of suffering, 1 Peter also addresses the *theological* challenge of suffering. In the face of persecutions, these young churches are bound to question God's care for them. The author of 1 Peter is sensitive to this struggle as well, and peppers his epistle with reminders of the grace that God has shown, is showing, and will show to his chosen people. The opening section (1:3–12) is an intricately constructed collection of such reminders of God's grace and goodness. The image of the refining fire just mentioned is just one facet of this exordium, but is especially important as it reinterprets present trials as a means of furthering the process of salvation, of growth in maturity. Suffering is no longer a proof of God's neglect, but instead becomes a sign of his fatherly hand at work to bring about salvation among his people. In this way, trials are a cause to rejoice, even though they are painful.[26]

It is important to realize that in 1 Peter these two agendas, moral and theological, are two sides of the same coin. They are inseparable, primarily because faith/hope in 1 Peter is always an active concern and never an enterprise that can be confined to cognition alone. Growth in faith entails

---

[26] As CALVIN said so well, 'the faithful are not logs of wood, nor have they so divested themselves of human feelings as to be unaffected by sorrow, unafraid of danger, unhurt by poverty, and untouched by hard and unbearable persecutions. Hence, they experience sorrow because of evils, but it is so mitigated by faith that they never cease at the same time to rejoice. Thus sorrow does not prevent their joy, but rather gives place to it.' J. CALVIN, *The Epistles of Paul the Apostle to the Hebrews and the First and Second Epistles of St. Peter*, trans. W.B. JOHNSTON, Calvin's NT Commentaries 12 (Grand Rapids: Eerdmans, 1994), 234.

growth in active obedience and vice versa. Good works are an outcome of faith, but at the same time, good works are a means of growth in faith. Balancing these twin elements correctly is no easy task, but a proper understanding of their relationship is vital for understanding the author's agenda in addressing his readers. Logically (and theologically) speaking, faith has a priority as the more primary element. Good works are a product of faith, and the epistle repeatedly gives reverence for God as the fundamental motivation for moral deliberation and action (e.g., 2:17–19; 3:2). At the same time, 1 Peter shares with Greco-Roman philosophy the conviction that virtuous deeds are the engine of character formation. So, in practice there is a priority given to praxis and the exhibition of one's faith in the social/moral sphere. In 1 Peter, the means for bringing about growth in Christian character, seen as a well-formed dependence upon God and moral integrity, is good works. Thus, the overall emphasis of the epistle is on sustaining good conduct, but this emphasis in always grounded in the final motivation of reverence for God. A prime example of this balance is found in the letter's final summary statement of how these churches are meant to respond to suffering in 4:19.[27] *Therefore let those who suffer according to God's will* (ὥστε καὶ οἱ πάσχοντες κατὰ τὸ θέλημα τοῦ θεοῦ) *do right and entrust their souls to a faithful Creator* (πιστῷ κτίστῃ παρατιθέσθωσαν τὰς ψυχὰς αὐτῶν ἐν ἀγαθοποιΐᾳ). Here the author's rejoinder to those that are suffering is to entrust themselves to their faithful creator. [28] What is interesting is that they are to do this by means of 'doing good' (ἐν ἀγαθοποιΐᾳ). Through this activity they express their trust in God's faithfulness to them. Thus, the two elements are distinguishable but inseparable.

B. *The True Grace of God*

One final element that again points to the paraenetic nature of 1 Peter is the author's concluding exhortation in 5:12b, where the author supplies us

---

[27] Cf. L. GOPPELT, *A Commentary on 1 Peter*, ed. F. HAHN, trans. J.E. ALSUP (Grand Rapids: Eerdmans, 1993), 334, 'Here the parenetic conclusion is drawn from vv. 17f. as well as from the entire section.'

[28] It is interesting that the author focuses on God as creator here. Especially considering this is the only instance in the NT writings where God is called κτίστης. The emphasis is most likely not on God's role as one-time creator, but on the activity of providential oversight that is the prerogative and responsibility of a faithful creator. As C. BIGG, *A Critical and Exegetical Commentary on the Epistles of St. Peter and St. Jude*, ICC (Edinburgh: T&T Clark, 1902), 182, says, 'the title Creator…involves power which is able, and love which is willing to guard His creatures.'

with his own summary of his agenda in writing the epistle.[29] *I have written briefly to you, exhorting and declaring that this is the true grace of God; stand fast in it* (δι᾽ ὀλίγων ἔγραψα παρακαλῶν καὶ ἐπιμαρτυρῶν ταύτην εἶναι ἀληθῆ χάριν τοῦ θεοῦ εἰς ἣν στῆτε).

He has written testifying to the grace of God that his readers have received, exhorting them not to falter in their faith but to stand firm in that grace. As we have seen before, Greco-Roman paraenetic epistles are written for the purpose of confirming neophytes in the philosophic path they have undertaken. In the same way, the author of 1 Peter characterizes his aim in writing as a confirming one.

This can be seen in his summary of the contents of the epistle as a witness to ἡ ἀληθής χάρις τοῦ θεοῦ.[30] Three simple observations flow from this description. First, what is being advocated here to the churches is χάρις, which is a gift of favored status. 1 Peter 4:1 speaks of grace as a multi-faceted reality (ποικίλης χάριτος), which, while only fully realized in the future (1:13), is being revealed and multiplied in the present realities of Christian existence (1:2; 2:19–20; 4:10; 5:5). Secondly, this grace is 'true', not primarily in the sense of true as opposed to a 'false grace', as though the epistle were written to oppose heretical teaching, but rather true in the sense of 'authentic and to be relied upon.'[31] This grace is trustworthy and therefore it is not folly to put one's faith in it; it is a wall that will not collapse when leaned upon. This surety and trustworthiness ultimately rests in, and this is the third point, the fact that this grace is *from God*. It is not simply the grace of God that the author is calling his readers to believe in, but in God *himself*, ὁ θεὸς πάσης χάριτος, as he is called two verses earlier. It is the dependability, trustworthiness, and goodness of God that makes this grace worthy of faith, commitment, and action. And so, it makes sense that the author has not simply testified to this grace but also exhorted his readers to stand firm in it. All other securities are fading and temporary; only God himself is eternal and good (cf. 1:23–25).

---

[29] Cf. BEARE, *1 Peter*, 25, and W. SCHRAGE and H.R. BALZ, *Die katholischen Briefe: die Briefe des Jakobus, Petrus, Johannes und Judas*, NTD 10 (Göttingen: Vandenhoeck & Ruprecht, 1973), 64.

[30] The αὕτη in 5:12b could refer to one of three things. First, the χάρις that follows closely after and is the only object in the sentence with which it agrees. If this is true, then the sense of the clause could be rendered as 'this grace is the true grace of God'. Second, the persecutions that the churches are having to endure which in 2:19–20 are referred to as χάρις (so BROX, *1. Petrusbrief*, 245). Third, the contents of the entire epistle. This last solution seems the most plausible, since in the immediate context 'this' refers to what 'I have briefly written to you.' So, ACHTEMEIER concludes that the referent here is 'the epistle itself in the sense of its content' (352). Cf. BIGG, *1 Peter*, 196, '"This" refers to the whole contents of the Epistle, whether doctrine or exhortation.'

[31] KELLY, *Peter & Jude*, 216.

Two things need to be stressed about 'standing firm' in the grace of God. First, it is an *activity*, not simply an internal commitment, but a commitment to God that is lived out in the everyday practical challenges of retaining a distinctive Christian ἀναστροφή in the midst of a hostile culture. Second, the scope of this activity is as broad as the multi-faceted grace it is committed to. It involves the practical belief in what God has done, will do, and is doing for his chosen people. It is a practical commitment to God's comprehensive work of salvation. At the center of this is a commitment to God's sanctifying work of character development. As we have already noted, trials become a refining fire when persecutions are met with moral integrity. Likewise, a commitment to put the reality of new birth into practice by shedding sinful practices is also an example of standing firm in the grace of God.

Here in 5:12, the author once again shows his practical bent by not simply exhorting intellectual belief in the grace of God, but rather calling for action flowing from the firm foundation of God's grace. In calling his readers to reaffirm their commitment to their God and his program of salvation, the author is engaged in a typically paraenetic confirming exercise.

C. A Philosophic Epistle?

One possible objection to the line of interpretation outlined here is that paraenesis as an epistolary genre was native to the philosophic schools, and thus was a phenomenon limited to a highly educated and (for the most part) elitist class. What do the practices within philosophic circles have to do with those within first-century Christianity, which had few conscious or explicit links with either the philosophic schools or the cultural and political Roman elite?

Such an objection, while *prima facie* compelling, fails to reckon with the pervasive nature of Hellenization in the ancient world. This is not to say that every slave read Plato, but that Hellenistic culture and modes of thought and expression substantially infiltrated the assumptions and practices of all the peoples of the ancient Mediterranean world. This was even more so in those contexts, like Judaism, where there was a resonance of beliefs and convictions. Greco-Roman philosophy had a long, if sometimes weak, tradition of monotheism, but even more importantly a strong emphasis on the central importance of moral reform. In these areas, Judaism found deeper resonances with Greco-Roman philosophy than with its contemporary religions.[32] It is probably for these reasons that Judaism

---

[32] It is for this reason that many scholars have argued, with L. ALEXANDER, 'Paul and the Hellenistic Schools: The Evidence of Galen,' in *Paul in His Hellenistic Context*, ed. T. ENGBERG-PEDERSEN, SNTW (Minneapolis: Fortress, 1995), 60, that, 'to the casual

(and later Christianity) found Hellenistic modes of expression congenial to
its goals and convictions. The typical example of this is Philo, but
Josephus is just as illustrative. Likewise, 'Hellenistic' Jewish writings like
1–4 Maccabees are examples of Jewish ideology dressed in Hellenistic
modes of expression. Most likely, it was through this Jewish heritage that
Christianity acquired Hellenistic forms like the *Haustafeln* and virtue and
vice lists. If we assume that philosophy was in some sense confined to an
elite circle then such phenomena in early Christian literature are simply
inexplicable. And it is this place that we have to begin, with the hard
evidence of the various Hellenistic literary forms (*Gattungen*) that we find
in early Christian literature. The place we begin is analogy not genealogy.
Genealogy is a secondary step to attempt to explain the reality of analogy.

We begin with the evidence of forms like the *Haustafeln* that we find in
both Christian literature and Hellenistic philosophy. From there we can ask
the questions of genealogy. The idea that we begin with genealogy, and
then this gives us the justification to compare things analogically is
mistaken. If the analogical evidence did not exist, then the genealogical
speculation would not begin; we would not begin to seek a historical
connection unless we had evidence of a connection in the first place. The
genealogist is like the homicide detective; he begins with a cold body and
tries to unravel the details of the murder. The genealogist begins with the
evidence of analogy, and then by supposition tries to reconstruct a history.

As mentioned above, the methodology of the present study will be to
begin with analogy and to stay there. The genealogical history has been,
and continues to be, the work of others. This does not mean that the
genealogical task is not important, but that it is not always a necessary
prerequisite to comparing ancient sources. Again, often it is assumed that
unless the genealogical link can be *firmly* established between two texts,
then it is illegitimate to compare them. So then it is only after a genealogy
is proved that analogical analysis begins. My practice here will be to
demonstrate the reality of analogy between philosophic paraenesis and
1 Peter, and then draw exegetical inferences from the reality of analogy,
without speculating as to the genealogical relationship.

This means that I assume that *some* genealogical relationship exists, but
that it is not necessary to map it out precisely before proceeding with
analogical analysis. Nevertheless, I would agree that some genealogical

---

pagan observer the activities of the average synagogue or church would look more like
the activities of a [philosophic] school than anything else. Teaching or preaching, moral
exhortation, and the exegesis of canonical texts are activities associated in the ancient
world with philosophy, not religion.' Along similar lines, see the influential essay by
E.A. JUDGE, 'The Early Christians as a Scholastic Community,' *JRH* 1 (1960-61), 4–15;
125–37

relationship must exist, and must be plausible, if the analogy is claiming to be historical. We could compare Jesus and Confucius analogically quite fruitfully, but it would be wrong to make conclusions about any historical connection between the two. Analogy does not prove genealogy.

Because the present study is attempting to place 1 Peter in its historical context, as a piece of literature from the ancient world, a case for the possibility of a plausible genealogy is necessary, even if an exact map isn't. So, we have to make it possible to get from point A to point B, but it is not necessary to know the exact route to say there is a road between them. The traveler who leaves A and arrives at B is proof enough, as long as point A and B are on the same continent. So, in our case, the evidence of analogy is sufficient to say that a connection exists, as long as it is within the realm of historically plausibility.

So is it plausible that the author of 1 Peter adopted the literary strategies of the Greco-Roman philosophic schools? First, we have already noted that paraenesis as a form of wisdom literature was present in various ancient cultures, including Judaism. Secondly, the specific Greco-Roman variety of paraenesis had a long tradition going back to the Classical period, which only grew stronger in the Hellenistic period. So Malherbe can report with confidence that, 'By the first century A.D. the paraenetic letter was established as a form of hortatory address.'[33] Thirdly, paraenetic letter writing was not confined to the elitist circles of influential philosophers like Seneca, as the example of papyrus 3069 from Oxyrhynchus demonstrates.[34] Fourthly, by the time of 1 Peter's composition,[35] such paraenetic strategies were already common in the letter writing traditions of early Christianity. Finally, the literary skill with which 1 Peter is composed suggests that its author/amanuensis[36] was schooled in the art of letter writing, and thus would have been familiar with the basic ingredients of paraenetic epistolary composition.[37]

---

[33] MALHERBE, 'Hellenistic Moralists,' 284.

[34] I owe the reference to STOWERS, *Letter Writing*, 99. Cf. *NewDocs* 4 (North Ryde, NSW: Macquarie University, 1987), 67–70.

[35] In terms of dating, I adopt the consensus that places the date of composition in the latter third of the first century.

[36] For the present study, the question of authorship is not an integral one. Because the author does little to utilize the position and authority associated with the name of the apostle Peter, and because this study is, at heart, a synchronic functional one, the identity of the author is of little practical importance. Consequently, I will refer to the writer simply as 'the author,' and leave the issue undecided.

[37] In addition it must be stated that genres rarely operate at a conscious level; most often they are learned by a kind of cultural osmosis and adopted automatically to suit a particular situation. To give a contemporary example, one writes a letter to the editor differently than a letter to a friend, but very rarely are these generic differences conscious choices. (It is when we are examining human communication from a culture *different*

So we can say that we have grounds to reckon on the historical probability of a genealogical connection between Greco-Roman philosophic paraenesis and 1 Peter, whatever it may be. Therefore if a strong analogy can be demonstrated, in terms of generic form and function, it would be valid to compare the documents in analogical analysis, letting the genre of paraenesis inform our exegesis of 1 Peter.

IV. Conclusion

The goal of this chapter has been to make an initial case for the claim that 1 Peter is a paraenetic epistle. We have seen that in form and function it evidences characteristics that are consistent with paraenetic epistolary practices. As to form, we noted the prevalence and diversity of moral instructions. This combined with a stress on conversion as a life-defining reality and pragmatically shaped theology points to the paraenetic nature of 1 Peter. With respect to function, we also saw that 1 Peter shares with Greco-Roman paraenetic epistles a central concern for promoting growth in character through moral transformation. In addition, they also share a core conviction that virtuous living is the primary means of facilitating positive character formation.

We also saw how this agenda is a response to the moral and theological challenges both produced by and exacerbated by suffering. The author's repeated exhortation to do good not only facilitates growth in moral character, but also counters temptations to assimilation, isolation, and retaliation that arise in the context of persecution. In fact, the author sees persecution as the context for growth, not only as something to be endured but also as something to rejoice in, because through it God refines the hearts of his people. Thus, even in the midst of persecution these struggling Christian communities are reminded of God's fatherly care for them.

The author's purpose in writing is a multifaceted one, but, as we have seen, his agenda has deep resonances with the typically paraenetic agenda of confirmation through facilitating moral growth. Thus, the function of the letter points to its nature as a paraenetic epistle. In the chapters that

---

from our own that questions of genre become more difficult and more explicit.) So, the author of 1 Peter need not have *consciously* adopted certain paraenetic literary strategies for them to be present in his epistle. Equally, it is not necessary that the audiences of the epistle *consciously* recognized it as an example of paraenesis for them to have understood it. For more on the practical functionality of genres see A. FOWLER, *Kinds of Literature: An Introduction to the Theory of Genres and Modes* (Cambridge, MA: Harvard University Press, 1982).

follow, we will continue to accumulate confirming evidence of the paraenetic nature of 1 Peter. In addition, we will begin to work out implications for the functionality of particular texts within the epistle's overall paraenetic agenda.

Chapter Three

Worldview and Story

The concept of worldview is a powerful sociological tool for describing the cultural density of belief systems, providing a window into how beliefs shape culture, and how they are, in turn, themselves shaped by culture.[1] At the most basic level worldviews are, in the words of Wright, a 'grid through which humans perceive reality.'[2] A worldview is an all-encompassing picture of reality touching all spheres of human knowledge and activity that serves to integrate human existence into a comprehensible unity. While possessing intellectual elements, a worldview finds embodiment in a particular cultural ethos, giving expression to various cultural artifacts: pottery, architecture, literature, clothing, philosophy, and sports, to name just a few. Functionally, a worldview is a means of ascribing meaning and value to the particularities of life. Wilson describes it as, 'a map of fact and value...legitimating all roles, priorities, and institutions by situating them in the context of the broadest horizon of reference conceivable, bestowing meaning on all domains of life.'[3] Worldviews provide not only an interpretive lens to understand reality, but also a place for individuals within that reality. 'In adopting the elements of a worldview,' Wilson argues, 'individuals are able to "locate" themselves; all of history and the entire biography of the individual are seen as events occurring in this world.'[4] Thus, a worldview provides an interpretation of an individual's life story within an all-encompassing picture of reality that brings significance and meaning to their actions.

Practically, worldviews can be communicated in many different ways. The most obvious form involves a systematic formulation and presentation

---

[1] Historically, worldview has proved difficult to define precisely because different philosophical/sociological traditions define it in their own particular way. For a survey, see A.M. WOLTERS, 'On the Idea of Worldview and its Relation to Philosophy,' in *Stained Glass: Worldviews and Social Science*, ed. P.A. MARSHALL, S. GRIFFIOEN, and R.J. MOUW, *Christian Studies Today* (Lanham, MD: University Press of America, 1989). Within the scope of this study, I shall use the basic concepts of worldview that are foundational and common to all these fine-tuned variations.

[2] N.T. WRIGHT, *The New Testament and the People of God* (London: SPCK, 1992), 38.

[3] WILSON, *Hope*, 100.

[4] WILSON, *Hope*, 100.

of the fundamental doctrines of a particular worldview. Less obvious perhaps, but often more effective, is the use of story to communicate worldview.[5] All cultures possess a cluster of defining stories that illustrate and reinforce those values that are most prized within that culture's worldview.[6] Narratives communicate beliefs through the actions of their characters. The deliberate actions of gods, heroes, and villains demonstrate core beliefs in a realized form. Their decisions, desires, hopes and fears embody and enforce a particular worldview's ethos. Thus, narrative is a powerful way to communicate worldview in a concrete form that embodies both beliefs and ethos.

In addition to using a *set* of stories that communicate worldview, narrative can also be used to construct worldview by depicting all of reality as a single unfolding meta-narrative – a universal history with a beginning, middle, and end. This 'narrative worldview' communicates a worldview in a concrete form as a realized picture of reality, not simply a set of ideas. Additionally it *shows* the relationships of different persons and realities within the worldview, instead of having to define them abstractly. Creating a narrative worldview also gives a teleological structure to reality, since it points towards a specific fulfillment/conclusion that embodies the worldview's fundamental values. Narrative worldviews are able to communicate beliefs and ethos together, and for this reason are often more effective than doctrinal abstractions.

Human beings, whether consciously or not, experience life as a story: a series of events encountered chronologically and contingent upon their choices as active agents, much like characters in a narrative.[7] Human beings do not meet ideas in the street, but they understand stories because they experience them directly (in their own lives) and indirectly (in the lives of those known to them) every day. Wilson argues that stories 'constitute one of the rudiments of human life and consciousness. Stories are the mechanisms with which people comprehend reality, articulate belief systems, and establish standards of behavior.' He contends that, 'An essential function of worldviews, then, is to provide such stories, to

---

[5] I am not adhering to the distinction between 'narrative' and 'story', because within the scope of this thesis it is neither necessary nor advantageous to do so. Consequently, I will use the terms interchangeably. For an overview of the distinction see G. LOUGHLIN, *Telling God's Story: Bible, Church and Narrative Theology* (Cambridge: Cambridge University Press, 1996), 52–63.

[6] The most obvious example from the Classical world would be the epic works of HOMER.

[7] Cf. S. CRITES, 'The Narrative Quality of Experience,' in *Why Narrative?: Readings in Narrative Theology*, ed. S. HAUERWAS and L.G. JONES (Grand Rapids: Eerdmans, 1989), 65-88, and C. TAYLOR, *Sources of the Self: The Making of the Modern Identity* (Cambridge: Cambridge University Press, 1989), 47.

create…a narrative universe that bestows meaning, defines necessary criteria for evaluation, and explains the motivations of the actors that the stories contain.'[8] A narrative worldview presents a story that provides meaning and moral direction to the individual's story. The τέλος of the meta-narrative defines the τέλος for the individual. As MacIntyre says, 'I can only answer the question "What am I to do?" if I can answer the prior question "Of what story or stories do I find myself a part?"'[9]

I. Worldview and Story in Greco-Roman Paraenetic Literature

Since worldview is as much a cultural ethos as it is a system of beliefs, it is no surprise, then, that worldviews are transmitted and learned through a process of 'socialization'. This process may be conscious and deliberate on the part of an 'instructor' and 'pupil', but it is just as likely to be simply an imbibing of cultural norms through lived experience. Worldviews then can often be held without any self-reflection on the part of the individual. But sometimes such self-reflection becomes a necessity (e.g., in conversion to a new belief system), and then the doctrines of one's worldview come under scrutiny. At such a time, the philosophical underpinnings of a worldview become exposed and are judged according to some theory of truth (e.g., correspondence or coherence). The worldview's philosophic doctrines then serve either to legitimate or to discredit that worldview.

In the context of conversion, this may lead to a radical reshaping of worldview. Converts often need to adopt a new picture of reality and with it a new system of moral and aesthetic values. The degree of reshaping will be dependent on the *distance* between the convert's previous worldview and their target worldview. This process will involve new social customs and roles, but it will especially involve philosophic reflection to legitimate the new worldview and to discredit the old. So acquiring a new worldview is a process often focused on the new beliefs of the worldview, but at the same time involving new praxis. This process is deliberate and concentrated, as the convert undergoes a process of re-socialization, whereby he consciously directs his life to conform with his new beliefs as well as consciously breaking the well-formed beliefs and practices of his previous worldview. This *intentionality* of worldview acquisition for the convert is in contrast to the way that a native worldview is often simply imbibed.

Paraenesis is aimed at aiding the convert in this process of re-socialization. Worldview 'maintenance' is therefore an essential part of

---

[8] WILSON, *Hope*, 189.
[9] MACINTYRE, *After Virtue*, 216.

paraenesis. Paraenesis works to promote and crystallize the neophyte's acquisition of his new worldview, while at the same time disparaging and destabilizing his old worldview. So, it is common in paraenesis to have bi-polar language discussing the benefits of life in the new worldview as well as the liabilities of life in the old. This re-socialization is a process of re-education, and so paraenesis involves a great deal of instruction about the beliefs of the worldview and their integration into life practice. As Wilson says:

> The presentation of worldview in this literary context [i.e., paraenesis] is conducted so as to aid the readers (neophytes in the movement who are still developing their new self-identity) in assimilating this worldview in such a manner and to such a degree that it informs every aspect of life, particularly as regards their progress of moral reasoning and conduct. This objective is foundational for the character of paraenesis as an instrument of guidance that directs the personal transformation of its recipients as they overcome specific challenges.[10]

In Greco-Roman paraenesis, this is often reflected in the integration of philosophical and ethical instruction. While it is true that moral instructions can appear on their own, just as often they appear in conjunction with some basic philosophic beliefs. As we saw before, Seneca argues that in order for precepts (moral instructions/paraenesis-as-form) to be effective it is necessary that they be wed to a system of beliefs.[11] As he says, 'As leaves cannot flourish by their own efforts, but need a branch to which they may cling and from which they may draw sap, so your precepts (*praecepta*), when taken alone, wither away; they must be grafted upon a school of philosophy (*sectae*).'[12]

A. Seneca on Paraenesis

Seneca's basic argument is that moral instructions alone are ineffective and need grounding in beliefs. Precepts alone will not bring about moral transformation. First, precepts cannot be given for every situation in life and therefore reason is needed to deduce the right action in particular situations (as in the Aristotelian concept of φρόνησις). Seneca argues that, 'No man can duly perform right actions except one who has been entrusted with reason (*ratio*), which will enable him, in all cases, to fulfill all the categories of duty.'[13] Secondly, as Seneca says, 'Philosophy is both theoretic and practical (*philosophia autem et contemplativa est et activa*);

---

[10] WILSON, *Hope*, 209.

[11] In the 'previous' epistle, *EM* 94, he argues that *doctrines* alone are insufficient and that precepts are necessary as well.

[12] SENECA, *EM*, 95.59.

[13] SENECA, *EM*, 95.12.

it contemplates and at the same time acts (*spectat simul agitque*).'[14] Philosophy cannot be confined to giving moral advice alone; it is a holistic system aimed at the reorientation of the whole person. As he says, 'It is not enough, when a man is arranging his existence as a whole, to give him [only] advice about details (*in particulas suasisse totum ordinanti parum est*).'[15] Philosophy aims at an alignment of both thought and action in accord with Nature.

Thirdly, this is important because false beliefs *obstruct* the power of precepts to educate, motivate, and transform. When the beliefs and desires of the individual are not molded by virtue, then precepts become impotent. Seneca declares that, 'It will therefore be of no avail to give precepts unless you first remove the conditions that are likely to stand in the way of precepts (*nisi prius amoveris obstatura praeceptis*).' Therefore, '[t]he soul, in order to deal with the precepts which we offer, must first be set free.'[16] And how is the soul to be set free? False beliefs must be checked by sound doctrine. 'In order to root out a deep-seated belief in wrong ideas (*ut revellatur penitus falsorum recepta persuasio*), conduct must be regulated by doctrines (*decretis agendum est*). It is only when we add precepts, consolation, and encouragement to these, that they can prevail; by themselves they are ineffective (*per se inefficases sunt*).'[17]

The problem, as Seneca sees it, is one of valuing things properly. He says that, 'Certain things sink into us, rendering us sluggish in some ways, and hasty in others. These two qualities, the one of recklessness and the other of sloth, cannot be respectively checked or roused unless we remove their causes, which are mistaken admiration and mistaken fear (*falsa admiratio et falsa formido*).'[18] For Seneca, people are controlled by the things they value or fear the most. He gives the example of a man who knows that he ought to provide for his family and friends, but is controlled by greed or fear of financial risk. Seneca sees these two psychological defects (mistaken admiration and mistaken fear) as rooted in mistaken *values*, or more properly, an inability to value things properly. What is needed then is a system of values that touches all possible objects of admiration, whether people, ideas, or possessions. As he says, 'It is useless for us to have mouthed out precepts, unless we begin by reflecting what opinion we ought to hold concerning everything (*qualem de quacumque re*

---

[14] SENECA, *EM*, 95.10.
[15] SENECA, *EM*, 95.44.
[16] SENECA, *EM*, 95.38.
[17] SENECA, *EM*, 95.34.
[18] SENECA, *EM*, 95.37.

habere debeamus opinionem) – concerning poverty, riches, renown, disgrace, citizenship, exile.'[19]

According to Seneca, for precepts to be effective they must be married to a universal map of fact and value – a worldview. As he says, 'Precepts by themselves are weak and, so to speak, rootless if they be assigned to the parts and not to the whole. It is the doctrines which will strengthen and support us...which will include simultaneously *the whole of life and the universe in its completeness* (*totam vitam totamque rerum naturam simul contineant*).'[20] Thus, what is needed is an all-encompassing picture of reality that is able to relate the teleological place and ontological value of all things. Granted, ancients like Seneca did not grasp the sociological aspects of knowledge embodied in the modern concept of worldview, but we could rightly call what he is referring to here a philosophic worldview.[21]

So, for Seneca, if paraenesis-as-form is to be effective it must be set in the context of a worldview, which provides a map of fact and value for all of reality. Only thus can someone be set free from mistaken and erratic desires. He says:

> If you would always desire the same things, you must desire the truth. But one cannot attain the truth without doctrines; *for doctrines embrace the whole of life* (*continent vitam*). Things good and evil, honourable and disgraceful, just and unjust, dutiful and undutiful, the virtues and their practice, the possession of comforts, worth and respect, health, strength, beauty, keenness of the senses – all these qualities call for one who is able to appraise them (*haec omnia aestimatorem desiderant*). One should be allowed to know at what values every object is to be rated on the list; for sometimes you are deceived and believe that certain things are worth more that their real value; in fact, so badly are you deceived that you will find you value at a mere penny-worth those things which we men regard as worth most of all – for example, riches, influence, and power.[22]

Thus, for paraenesis-as-genre to be effective it must include not just precepts but also a complementary picture of reality that is able to properly value all things. Precepts, then, are only effective if they are married to a worldview that compliments, informs, reinforces and contextualizes them; *effective* paraenesis weds beliefs and instructions.

---

[19] SENECA, *EM*, 95.54.

[20] SENECA, *EM*, 95.12. Italics added.

[21] As we said before, in the context of conversion the *philosophic* side of worldview has a prominent place in the process of re-socialization. It is not surprising then that SENECA here is concentrating on the philosophic side of worldview. The responsibility to 'teach' the other aspects of the worldview of the Stoics resides in shared rituals, dramas, clothing, food, etc. Here, in this didactic setting, he can most effectively communicate the philosophic beliefs of Stoicism.

[22] SENECA, *EM*, 95.58–9. Italics added.

In his 95th epistle, Seneca provides exemplary passages of integrated paraenesis. He discusses proper belief and behavior under three 'subject headings': God, man, and possessions. In his first section on God he argues that, 'Although a man hear what limit he should observe in sacrifice, and how far he should recoil from burdensome superstitions, he will never make sufficient progress until he has conceived the right idea of God (*nisi qualem debet deum mente conceperit*) – regarding Him as one who possesses all things, and allots all things, and bestows them without price.'[23] He shows how a proper conception of God is necessary for progress. His second subject, on the question of relating to others, is a brilliant example of this marriage of ethics and beliefs.

> Then comes the second problem – how to deal with men. ...Shall we advise stretching forth the hand to the shipwrecked sailor, or pointing out the way to the wanderer, or sharing a crust with the starving? Yes, if I can only tell you first everything which ought to be afforded or withheld; meantime, I can lay down for mankind a rule, in short compass, for our duties in human relationships: all that you behold, that which comprises god and man, is one – we are the parts of one great body (*membra sumus corporis magni*). Nature produced us related to one another (*natura nos cognatos edidit*), since she created us from the same source and to the same end. She engendered in us mutual affection (*haec nobis amorem indidit mutuum*), and made us prone to friendships (*sociabiles fecit*). She established fairness and justice; according to her ruling, it is more wretched to commit than to suffer injury. Through her orders, let our hands be ready for all that needs to be helped. Let this verse be in your heart and on your lips: *I am a man; and nothing in man's lot do I deem foreign to me.*[24] Let us possess things in common; for birth is ours in common (*habeamus in commune; natisumus*).[25]

Here Seneca roots the ethics of human relationships in the decrees and purposes of Nature. Given this belief, attitudes of kindness and brotherly affection are literally quite 'natural', and to act in such a way is simply to do what is in accord with one's reasonable nature. Thus, right doctrine contextualizes and reinforces right behavior. Worldview and moral instruction operate together for the purpose of moral transformation.

B. What About the Story?

In all of this the element of story mentioned above seems to be missing. Seneca's worldview is expressed as a system of beliefs, not an all-encompassing meta-narrative. But is there perhaps a hidden narrative structure to the worldview Seneca puts forth? The short answer is: No. There *is* a strong narrative element in Greco-Roman ethics, which conceives of the life of the *individual* as a journey of enlightenment and

---

[23] SENECA, *EM*, 95.48.
[24] TERENCE, *Self-Tormentor*, 77. Homo sum, humani nihil a me alienum puto.
[25] SENECA, *EM*, 95.51–3.

maturation, directed toward the goal of contentment/fulfillment/happiness. Thus, at the level of the individual there is a strong narrative element, where lives are taken as a whole, as a kind of narrative directed towards a goal. But, generally speaking, in Greco-Roman philosophy Nature and the κόσμος have no teleology.[26] They are not moving toward a goal of maturation, they simply are. God may act, but there is no grand narrative to speak of; he is not directing the universe toward a goal. So, Greco-Roman philosophy, on the whole, lacks meta-narrative in this strict sense of the word.[27] Persons can have a τέλος, and therefore narrative does have a strong role to play in the conception and development of the life of the individual,[28] but the narrative element does not go beyond this to the level of meta-physical meta-narrative or narrative worldview.[29]

Here Philo's Judaism-cum-Platonism presents us with an opportune and intriguing bridge. In his project to present Judaism as a Hellenistic philosophy, he provides an example of how a narrative worldview (here Judaism) functions in the context of Greco-Roman ethics. At the center of Philo's apologetic enterprise is Moses, whom he portrays as a great Hellenistic philosopher. At the beginning of his *On the Creation* he explains that Moses is a superior philosopher because he does not move immediately to expound laws, but first tells the story of creation, thereby providing a framework in which to comprehend and appropriate his laws. He writes:

While among other lawgivers (νομοθετῶν) some have nakedly and without embellishment drawn up a code of the things held to be right among the people, and others, dressing up their ideas in much irrelevant and cumbersome matter, have befogged the masses and hidden the truth under fictions, Moses, disdaining either course, ...introduced his laws with an admirable and most impressive exordium (ἀρχήν). He refrained, on the one hand, from stating abruptly what should be practiced or avoided, and on the other hand, in face

---

[26] Cf. the fascinating (if misguided) study by ENGBERG-PEDERSEN, *Stoics.* In his project to remold Paul as a Stoic, he first removes Paul's 'theology cum cosmology' on the grounds that it 'does *not* constitute a real option for us,' (19) and then goes on to highlight the similarities in the ethical structures of Paul and the Stoics, both seeing life as a journey of moral transformation and maturation. Thus, he recognizes that Stoicism has no place for meta-narrative, but does rely on personal biography as important element in moral education.

[27] In contemporary post-modern discourse the term 'meta-narrative' can be used to refer to *any* philosophic or religious explanation of reality, whether or not it contains 'narrative' elements. I am using the term in a more precise sense to refer to all-encompassing pictures of reality that have a fundamentally narrative structure (i.e., they explain reality in terms of a story). Non-teleological pictures of reality are not meta-narratives in this limited sense.

[28] We will see this later on in our study of moral exemplars and the *imitatio Christi* motif.

[29] Contra WILSON, *Hope*, 208–9.

of the necessity of preparing the minds of those who were to live under the laws for their reception, he refrained from inventing myths himself or acquiescing in those composed by others. His exordium...consists of an account of the creation of the world, implying that the world is in harmony with the Law, and the Law with the world (ὡς καὶ τοῦ κόσμου τῷ νόμῳ καὶ τοῦ νόμου τῷ κόσμῳ συνᾴδοντος), and that the man who observes the law is constituted thereby a loyal citizen of the world (καὶ τοῦ νομίμου ἀδρὸς εὐθὺς ὄντος κοσμοπολίτου), regulating his doings by the purpose and will of Nature, in accordance with which the entire world itself also is administered (ὁ σύμπας κόσμος διοικεῖται).[30]

Thus, the account of creation in Genesis provides a metaphysical framework for the laws that will come later in the Pentateuch. Philo says that Moses recognized the need for adequately preparing the minds of his readers to appropriate his moral precepts. Just as Seneca argues that worldview is necessary for moral instruction, Philo argues that the creation story provides an essential framework for the subsequent laws. As he says elsewhere, 'In relating the history of early times, and going for its beginning right to the creation of the universe, he wished to show two most essential things: first that the Father and Maker of the world was in the truest sense also its lawgiver (πατέρα καὶ ποιητὴν τοῦ κόσμου καὶ ἀληθείᾳ νομοθέτην), and secondly that he who would observe the laws will accept gladly the duty of following nature (ἀκολουθίαν φύσεως) and live in accordance with the ordering of the universe, so that his deeds are attuned to harmony with his words and his words with his deeds.'[31] So, the creation account serves not only to give instruction about the creator and his creation, but also to provide a reasonable context for living rightly (i.e., in accord with Nature). The creation narrative provides a story that brings an integration of fact and value, belief and action, or as Philo says, 'words and deeds.' It relates the nature of the universe to moral actions and thus provides a unifying picture of reality that carries with it moral structure.

For Philo this is sufficient evidence that Moses is a superior philosopher (and *eo ipso* that Judaism is a superior philosophy). Moses not only gives sound moral advice and precepts, but he gives it within the context of an overarching understanding of reality that contextualizes his moral instructions. The creation narrative serves as a narrative framework providing a picture of reality that serves as a map of fact and value. Philo praises Moses for this integration of narrative worldview with moral instruction, and intriguingly calls this practice 'exhortation'. He says concerning Moses, 'In his commands and prohibitions he suggests and admonishes (ὑποτίθεται καὶ παρηγορεῖ) rather than commands (κελεύει) and the very numerous and necessary instructions which he essays to give

---

[30] PHILO, *On Creation*, 1.1–3.
[31] PHILO, *Moses*, 2.48.

are accompanied by forewords and after-words (μετὰ προοιμίων καὶ ἐπιλόγων), in order to exhort (προτρέψασθαι) rather than to enforce.'[32] Thus, the thing that separates exhortation and admonition from mere commands is the inclusion of a narrative worldview to ground and reinforce moral advice. Philo only gives us a taste of the implications of this idea, but it is enough to move on to see how the author of 1 Peter uses narrative worldview to contextualize and reinforce his ethical instructions in the process of his 'exhortation'.

II. Worldview and Story in 1 Peter

The author's aim in 1 Peter is to encourage young Anatolian churches to live out their beliefs in the midst of social hostility. He uses theology foremost as a tool to shape their way of looking at the world, and through this, their way of living in the world. He describes a universe that contextualizes and reinforces his agenda of moral transformation. Before giving them moral instructions, he gives them a moral vision that places them within a moral universe. He does this by depicting not simply a theological worldview, but a *narrative* theological worldview. He is not giving simply ontological statements about how the world is, but weaving together a *story* of how the world is; and this story becomes the context for their own stories as individuals and as a community.[33] This is the sense in which the narrative world of 1 Peter contextualizes the lives of the readers and their moral choices. It places their lives within a story of the world conceived on the largest possible canvas – a story of creation, fall, redemption, and consummation.[34] What God is doing in their midst is part of the grand narrative of his plan to redeem his creation and a people for himself. Thus, the world is not spinning aimlessly, but headed toward a goal. In this context, daily choices, as the means by which they appropriate their salvation in the present, take on truly cosmic significance.[35]

---

[32] PHILO, *Moses*, 2.51.

[33] In modern sociological terms, the author portrays a symbolic universe into which their personal biographies might fit. Cf. P.L. BERGER and T. LUCKMANN, *The Social Construction of Reality: A Treatise in the Sociology of Knowledge* (Garden City, NY: Anchor Books, 1967), 110–22.

[34] Creation is mentioned in 1:20 and 4:19. References to redemption (e.g., 1:18–19) and consummation (e.g., 1:5) are ubiquitous. Some type of 'Fall' is implied in the need for redemption, and can be assumed here as a stock element common to both Jewish and Christian thought.

[35] In this way, 1 Peter shares more with Judaism and especially Jewish apocalyptic than it does with Greco-Roman philosophy, which as we saw has little room for meta-narrative. 1 Peter cannot be characterized as an apocalypse, since it lacks many of

This understanding of 1 Peter is not as altogether idiosyncratic as it may sound. Selwyn argued that, 'the general ethical teachings [of the epistle] are intimately associated with ideas, events, images, and religious ordinances which constitute the *Weltanschauung* of Christianity.'[36] He also noted how theology and ethics are 'organically united...to supply the moral life with a basic vision, and to require of faith a practical fruit, which give to the Christian ethic a peculiar strength and vitality.'[37] Elsewhere, he maintains that, 'St. Peter is bidding his readers...to chart their lives...on a large map.'[38]

These ideas of narrative worldview, which were nascent in Selwyn,[39] become explicit in Boring, who states that 'the author is not attempting to teach or explain theology as such, but addresses the experienced concerns of the readers from within the *narrative world* presupposed by the letter.'[40] He argues that:

The author places their experience within the framework of the real world constituted by God the creator who has acted in Christ, who is presently at work within them, and who takes responsibility to bring the world to a worthy conclusion. The author does this not by explaining metaphysics, history, or cosmology, to them, but by addressing them from

---

the crucial elements of the genre (e.g., a heavenly vision communicated by a patriarch), but Achtemeier, *1 Peter*, 105, rightly says it is 'appropriate to speak of elements of an apocalyptic eschatology' in 1 Peter. The letter shares with apocalyptic literature a belief in the present as a time of fulfillment of the OT prophecies of God's cosmic eschatological salvation. It is also keen to portray this in the context of a sweeping historical narrative beginning with creation and fall, and ending with vindication and salvation. Achtemeier, *1 Peter*, 107, also notes that, 'Perhaps most characteristic of 1 Peter are those elements that interpret present, earthly circumstances in light of the supernatural world and the future (e.g., 1:6–7; 4:12–13, 15–18; 5:1–4, 9–10) and seek in that way to influence both the understanding and behavior of the readers (e.g., 1:10–17; 4:4–5; perhaps also 2:18–24 and 3:17–18).' Along with this, he notes how the eschatological tension between present and future undergirds the paraenesis of the letter, as is also common in apocalyptic.

[36] Selwyn, *1 Peter*, 108. While the concept of worldview has gone through significant development and refinement since Selwyn's day, the '*Weltanschauung*' he speaks of here is not too far different from what today would be called worldview.

[37] Selwyn, *1 Peter*, 109. To be precise, he saw here the union of three different types of sources: (1) basic principles of conduct finding their root in Jewish and Gentile moralities and 'expressed in rules or maxims,' (2) a proper Christian ethic 'based upon the Old Testament and the teaching of Christ,' and (3) Christian theology. The simple point I am drawing from his work is unaffected by my abridgement of detail here.

[38] Selwyn, *1 Peter*, 79.

[39] Selwyn was discussing essentially the same ideas, but without the terminology (then unavailable) of 'narrative world' or 'symbolic universe'.

[40] M.E. Boring, *1 Peter*, ANTC (Nashville: Abingdon Press, 1999), 183. Italics added.

within this world, confirming the new world they received at their new birth, and by deepening and widening their perception of the new reality in which they live.[41]

Thus, the author's strategy in shaping their lives as Christians is to confirm and deepen their understanding of how their lives fit within the greater story of God's 'plan of salvation'.

In 1 Peter this narrative world is presupposed in two senses. First, the author only refers to key elements of the story of salvation to evoke an entire narrative worldview that is familiar to both author and readers. This sort of shorthand description of key elements is, as we have noted before, typical of paraenesis, where only a few key points need to be reviewed and emphasized. Thus, what we have access to in the epistle is that portion of the entire presupposed narrative theological worldview that the author found it useful to highlight. The author's goal is to be relevant not comprehensive.

Secondly, the narrative world is presupposed in that, while 1 Peter is an epistle and not a narrative, it is governed by what Hays has termed a 'narrative substructure.'[42] That is, it refers not only to *realities* within and beyond the experience of its readers, but more importantly, it refers to a series of *events* that adhere together in an intuited sequence. It is these chronologically related events (with a beginning, middle and end) that make up a story. Thus, while non-narrative in genre, 1 Peter utilizes an *implied* narrative that unifies all the 'salvation-historical' events it references. It describes a world that is governed by a story – the story of God's salvation.[43]

The author introduces this story in his epistolary prescript (1:1–2). *To the elect exiles of the Dispersion* (ἐκλεκτοῖς παρεπιδήμοις διασπορᾶς) *in Pontus, Galatia, Cappadocia, Asia, and Bithynia, according to the foreknowledge of God the Father* (πρόγνωσιν θεοῦ πατρὸς) *in the*

---

[41] BORING, *1 Peter*, 184. See his 'Appendix 1: The Narrative World of 1 Peter,' in which he tabulates 157 distinct 'events' in the narrative world depicted in 1 Peter.

[42] R.B. HAYS, *The Faith of Jesus Christ: An Investigation of the Narrative Substructure of Galatians 3:1–4:11*, SBLDS 56 (Chico, CA: Scholars Press, 1983), 1–30. Cf. N.R. PETERSEN, *Rediscovering Paul: Philemon and the Sociology of Paul's Narrative World* (Philadelphia: Fortress Press, 1985), 1–42, and E. ADAMS, *Constructing the World: A Study in Paul's Cosmological Language*, SNTW (Edinburgh: T&T Clark, 2000), 3–7, 23–8.

[43] Cf. B.W. LONGENECKER, 'Narrative Interest in the Study of Paul,' in *Narrative Dynamics in Paul: A Critical Assessment*, ed. B.W. LONGENECKER (Louisville, KY: Westminster John Knox, 2002), 4, '[Paul's] letters do not simply offer independent snippets of "truth" or isolated gems of logic, but are discursive exercises that explicate a narrative about God's saving involvement in the world.' He argues that, 'Paul's epistolary discourse is like a membrane that is tightly stretched over a narrative framework, revealing many narrative contours from beneath' (3–4).

sanctification of the Spirit (ἐν ἁγιασμῷ πνεύματος) *for obedience and sprinkling with the blood of Jesus Christ.* The 'titles' by which the author addresses the churches (ἐκλεκτοῖς παρεπιδήμοις διασπορᾶς) point to their place and identity in the story of salvation. Within God's plan, they are 'elect strangers'[44] scattered throughout Northern Asia Minor. It is their new status as a distinct people of God that makes them strangers within their own culture.[45] They are strangers because they are called to live differently from those around them and are thus to expect some animosity on the part of their neighbors. This is their story as suffering Christian communities, which is related to the larger story of God's salvation.

Their new status originates in the πρόγνωσις θεοῦ πατρός. The source of their election and their current status as strangers is the choice of their father God. A choice finding its fruition in their present, but predating creation itself (cf. 1:20). Thus, their personal and corporate stories are caught up into the larger story of God's work of salvation. As Boring says, 'Their life is lived on the historical sojourn between creation and eschaton...with their new identity as the people of God who are always in tension with the structures and values of this world and its powers.'[46] They are a people set apart by the Spirit (ἁγιασμῷ πνεύματος) to live lives characterized by obedience to God as an expression of their covenantal relationship with him, sealed in the blood of Jesus Christ.[47]

---

[44] Where ἐκλεκτοῖς is best taken as an adjective modifying the substantive παρεπιδήμοις, so ELLIOTT, *1 Peter*, 315, and BIGG, *1 Peter*, 90.

[45] So GOPPELT, *1 Peter*, 67, 'Christians are foreigners among their fellow human beings, even among relatives and acquaintances, because their existence has been established on a totally new basis.' In contrast ELLIOTT argues that παρεπίδημοι along with παροικία (1:17) and πάροικοι (2:11) are to be taken in a *literal* sense referring to socio-political status as strangers and resident aliens in society. While ELLIOTT is correct to discount the metaphorical sense of παρεπίδημος as, 'an exile from heaven, his true home,' (BIGG, *1 Peter*, 90) he has overcorrected by insisting that the status of these 'strangers' is not brought about by their new status as elect, but is what they already were. The most natural sense is to take παρεπίδημοι in the metaphorical sense of 'a group that is estranged from the larger society', and that the root of that estrangement is in fact their conversion to Christianity, 'rather than in the political situations of the first century,' ACHTEMEIER, *1 Peter*, 82. Cf. ACHTEMEIER, 'Newborn Babes'. We will examine the benefits and liabilities of ELLIOTT's approach more fully below in chapter 5.

[46] BORING, *1 Peter*, 58.

[47] This is the general thrust of the difficult phrase: ἐν ἁγιασμῷ πνεύματος εἰς ὑπακοὴν καὶ ῥαντισμὸν αἵματος Ἰησοῦ Χριστοῦ. Efforts have been made to relate Ἰησοῦ Χριστοῦ to ὑπακοήν, but this would mean that it would have to be in a similar relationship to ῥαντισμόν, which is most unlikely. So Ἰησοῦ Χριστοῦ only specifies the αἵματος which is to be 'sprinkled', and 'obedience and sprinkling' are to be seen as the purposes (the most natural sense of εἰς) of the Spirit's sanctifying work. ACHTEMEIER points to the establishment of the covenant in Exod. 24:3–8 as the most likely parallel to 'obedience and sprinkling'. There Israel pledged its obedience and then sacrificial blood was

We can see here how the author has already introduced us to several events in a storyline. God has chosen a people according to his foreknowledge and set them apart by the Spirit to live out the covenant he has established with them through the blood of Christ. In this way, the readers' lives are placed within an unfolding drama to which their present status as 'elect strangers' is directly related because, it too, derives from the intention of God.[48]

Thus, already in the epistolary prescript the author has given us a brief introduction to the narrative he wishes to develop. One important feature to note here is the author's intertwining of *two stories*: the grand 'meta-narrative' of God's plan of redemption and the story of the readers, i.e., their election and resulting estrangement from society.[49] This intertwining of stories is essential, because the purpose of utilizing a narrative worldview is to root the lives of the readers within a larger story. As Wilson says, 'The narrative dimension lends to the worldview shape and direction, demonstrating how it relates concretely to the experiences, history, and expectations of people who are themselves living out a kind of "story."'[50] This is why the author highlights their current 'story' as strangers, and interprets it by relating it to their election and God's plan of salvation for them. He is mapping their life experiences directly onto the grand narrative of salvation, from creation to eschaton, and thus placing their lives (personal and corporate) within the context of an overarching narrative worldview.

A. Mapping the Story

Whether we are thinking of ethical instructions or theological discourse, this meta-narrative of God's work of salvation undergirds the entire epistle. The explicit references to this narrative are heavily concentrated in

---

sprinkled on the altar. Then after they again pledged their obedience the remaining blood was sprinkled on them. 'Thus,' ACHTEMEIER argues, 'the two elements in the ceremony, obedience and sprinkling of blood, reflect the order and content of 1 Pet 1:2' (*1 Peter*, 88). This interpretation is the only one that makes sense of the phrase in its context while doing justice to the syntax. Cf. BROX, *1. Petrusbrief*, 57, and SCHRAGE and BALZ, *Die katholischen Briefe*, 67.

[48] Cf. SCHLATTER, *Petrus und Paulus*, 17. 'Der Ursprung der Kirche ist Gottes gnädiger Wille.'

[49] Strictly speaking, there are three stories since there is also the story of the 'Apostle Peter', the implied author of the text, which includes his relationship with Christ and with the churches addressed. Unlike many of the Paulines, this story receives short shrift in this epistle (1:1a; 5:1, 12–14); and since it plays no crucial part in the other stories, it can be ignored with little detriment.

[50] WILSON, *Hope*, 189.

the first major section of the body of the epistle (1:3–2:10).[51] As noted before, it is impossible to draw hard lines of demarcation between 1 Peter's theological and ethical discourses; but we can draw rough (if permeable) boundaries. Especially if we momentarily set aside the *imitatio Christi* passages, which will be dealt with on their own in chapter seven, then nearly all of the 'theology' of the epistle falls in this first major section of the body.

Within this major section we can also delineate three subsections (1:3–12; 1:13–2:3; and 2:4–10). The first subsection is of particular interest here, as its chief concern is with laying the foundation of the narrative worldview of the letter. We will begin with a study of the first subsection (1:3–12) on its own, and in subsequent chapters examine the two subsections that follow. (These later subsections will build on the foundation laid here and extend this narrative in particular directions.)

Beginning with εὐλογητὸς ὁ θεός, the first subsection can properly be called a 'benediction'. In Greek, this benediction is a single intricate sentence crafted as a string of relative coordinating and subordinating clauses. Its purpose is to paint a portrait of reality governed by God's saving work, commencing in the past, continuing in the present, and culminating in the future. With this salvation-historical narrative it intertwines the history of the readers, showing how they fit into this larger narrative and showing that their conversion, present trials, and future glorification are a piece of this greater story. Just as in the prescript, the author is telling a single story that is made up of two interconnected stories, one is the grand narrative of God's saving work (with a particular emphasis on the death and resurrection of Jesus) and the other is the story of the readers (with a particular emphasis on their conversion and present sufferings). The benediction can also be divided into three smaller subunits (3–5; 6–9; 10–12).[52]

The first subunit begins in verse 3 by praising God, *Blessed be the God and Father of our Lord Jesus Christ,* using the common Jewish formula εὐλογητὸς ὁ θεός[53] augmented with an appropriate Christian title of God as

---

[51] This section is clearly marked at the front end by the transition from the end of the epistolary prescript in 1:2 and the beginning of the body in 1:3 with εὐλογητὸς ὁ θεός, and at the back end by the beginning of a new section in 2:11 with the vocative ἀγαπητοί. Also the ἔλεος of 1:3 and the ἐλεέω of 2:10 form an inclusio.

[52] The transitions are marked by anaphoric relative pronouns that begin a new thought unit, yet refer back to the immediate context. Cf. ACHTEMEIER, *1 Peter,* 90.

[53] E.g., in the LXX: Gen. 14:20; 1 Kgs. 5:21; 1 Esd. 4:40; Tob. 11:17; 13:2, 18; Ps. 17:47; 65:20; 67:36. This blessing also became a 'stock phrase' in synagogue liturgy. See DEICHGRÄBER, *Christushymnus,* 40-3. The verb of being, either ἐστίν or more probably εἴη, is assumed.

πατὴρ τοῦ κυρίου ἡμῶν Ἰησοῦ Χριστοῦ.[54] The next clause gives the warrant for this blessing, *by his great mercy* (κατὰ τὸ πολὺ αὐτοῦ ἔλεος) *we have been born anew* (ἀναγεννήσας ἡμᾶς). Already we have the strong intertwining of the two stories. In his mercy, God has acted to give these Christians new birth in their conversion.[55]

The meaning and purpose of this new birth is expounded in three εἰς clauses: εἰς ἐλπίδα..., εἰς κληρονομίαν..., εἰς σωτηρίαν...,[56] which constitute the remainder of the first subunit of the benediction (3c–5). These clauses describe three eschatological realities that are gifts of the (eschatological) new birth. It is important to note here that eschatology in 1 Peter (as with many other NT writings) is not viewed as a future reality only, but rather as something that has already begun and that will reach its culmination in the future. The eschaton is the messianic age, which was inaugurated with the coming of the Messiah Jesus and in his resurrection from the dead (see 1:20). As Selwyn says, 'Our author...conceives of the end as organically linked with what has already occurred, in the case both of Christ and of the Church: it is not a matter of something wholly novel but of the culmination of something already experienced and known.'[57] This is especially important as we observe how the author relates God's eschatological plans and glories with the current life situations of those addressed; they are already living in the eschatological age, directed towards their final salvation.[58] As Elliott says, 'In temporal perspective vv 3–5 thus describes the totality of reborn Christian existence from its inception to its final outcome.'[59]

---

[54] The exact same Christian benediction is found in 2 Cor. 1:3 and Eph. 1:3, in place of the more common Pauline thanksgiving. See DEICHGRÄBER, *Christushymnus*, 63–87.

[55] Actually the author includes himself (and possibly other Christians and churches) in this statement, since he says ἀναγεννήσας ἡμᾶς. So to be precise there is at least one other 'story' involved here as well. But its involvement is inconsequential to what is being said; the author's story will drop out in the next verse, where he shifts the focus to his readers speaking of the inheritance τετηρημένην ἐν οὐρανοῖς εἰς ὑμᾶς (4b).

[56] Cf. ELLIOTT, *1 Peter*, 333, where he designates εἰς ἐλπίδα ζῶσαν as 'the first of three successive *eis* ("for") phrases (vv 3a, 4a, 5b) identifying three related results or benefits of God's regenerating action (see BDF §21 for this syntactical use of the preposition *eis*).' Cf. BEARE, *1 Peter*, 82.

[57] E.G. SELWYN, 'Eschatology in 1 Peter,' in *The Background of the New Testament and Its Eschatology: Studies in Honour of C.H. Dodd*, ed. W.D. DAVIES and D. DAUBE (Cambridge: Cambridge University Press, 1956), 397.

[58] Cf. SELWYN, 'Eschatology,' 395–6, 'The end, then, has supervened; the eschatological Messiah has entered history; the eschatological community has been called out of the Jewish and Gentile world and brought into being through conversion and baptism.'

[59] ELLIOTT, *1 Peter*, 338.

The first εἰς clause illustrates this nicely. They have been born *into a living hope through the resurrection of Jesus Christ from the dead* (εἰς ἐλπίδα ζῶσαν δι' ἀναστάσεως Ἰησοῦ Χριστοῦ ἐκ νεκρῶν). Hope (ἐλπίς) is quite obviously eschatological, signifying the believers' sure confidence in the things God has promised. But what can be meant by an ἐλπίς ζῶσα?[60] The answer is quite simple if we keep in mind 1 Peter's eschatology. It is a living hope because it is an *active* hope, not *only* looking to the future, but being realized now and rooted in the past. It derives its confidence from being rooted in what God has already done in the resurrection of Christ.[61] In addition, it is a living hope because it is *already active*; the audience of this letter lives between the time of the resurrection and the final consummation. This living hope is something that is partially realized in the past (in the resurrection), in the present (in its transforming power in the churches) and which will be fully realized in the future.[62] Thus, we have here another clear example of the intertwining of the two stories. The framework for living in the present is the living hope given by God as a sure hope of future salvation and rooted in his action in the past (i.e., the resurrection). Petrine eschatology then emphasizes how present existence is lived *within* the eschatological age, not simply in expectation of it. Therefore, eschatology, as the unfolding of God's plan of salvation becomes the context for all of life.

The next εἰς clause in verse 4 also expresses this eschatological perspective. It speaks of new birth *into an inheritance which is imperishable, undefiled, and unfading, kept in heaven for you* (εἰς κληρονομίαν ἄφθαρτον καὶ ἀμίαντον καὶ ἀμάραντον, τετηρημένην ἐν οὐρανοῖς εἰς ὑμᾶς). Again, the referent here (κληρονομία)[63] is unmistakably

---

[60] This is a question that continues to puzzle commentators. BEARE, *1 Peter*, 82, suggests that, 'The words undoubtedly suggest a vigorous, firm, vivid hope, in contrast with any lifeless philosophical doctrine of immortality or any wavering anticipation of blessedness.' Cf. J.R. MICHAELS, *1 Peter*, WBC 49 (Waco, TX: Word, 1988), 19, 'If any contrast is intended, it is with the hopelessness of pagan religion.' ACHTEMEIER, *1 Peter*, 95, argues that living hope is 'to be understood in contrast to a dead or vain hope, one that is based on no reality and hence has neither present nor future validity.' SELWYN, *1 Peter*, 124, calls it 'a hope that is never extinguished by untoward circumstances, just as "living waters" are waters flowing fresh from a perennial spring.'

[61] Cf. ACHTEMEIER, *1 Peter*, 95, 'Christian hope is a living hope rather than a futile hope because it is linked to, and grounded in, the resurrection of Jesus Christ.'

[62] Cf. J.E. HUTHER, *Critical and Exegetical Handbook to the General Epistles of Peter and Jude*, trans. D.B. CROOM, KEK 12 (Edinburgh: T&T Clark, 1881), 55, 'ἐλπίς need not be conceived as representing *one single* side of the Christian life, but under it may be understood the whole Christian life in its relation to the future σωτηρία.'

[63] In the OT 'inheritance' (MT: נַחֲלָה; LXX: κληρονομία) most often refers to the land promised to the people of Israel, and was a sign of their covenant relationship with God going back to Abraham (Gen. 12:7). Not surprisingly, it is a keyword in Numbers,

eschatological. This is emphasized by the three α-privative adjectives that place this inheritance beyond the touch of human corruption,[64] and hence ἐν οὐρανοῖς. Along with this future element, the *present* activity of God is intimated in the perfect participle τετηρημένη, emphasizing the present state of the inheritance and God's work (divine passive) of watching over it. Thus, God is guaranteeing their inheritance in the future. The present work of God becomes explicit in verse 5 in the subordinate clause modifying ὑμᾶς: τοὺς ἐν δυνάμει θεοῦ φρουρουμένους διὰ πίστεως. Thus, God is working at both ends: guarding their inheritance in heaven, and also guarding them in the present. They are protected[65] by the power of God, most intriguingly, διὰ πίστεως. Their faith is the instrument by which God is saving and guarding them.[66] Once again, we see the juxtaposition of future and present realities and the interconnecting of the meta-narrative of salvation with the story of the readers. God guarantees an incorruptible inheritance now as their possession in the future. At the same time, he is at work in them via their faith to guard their life for their future salvation.

The eschatological storyline is carried through in the final εἰς clause in 5b, which speaks of their new birth into *a salvation ready to be revealed in the last time.* In 1 Peter, σωτηρία can refer to the *entirety* of salvation from inception to consummation (1:10),[67] or to a *part* or a *period* of the whole: as in 'growing up' in salvation (2:2). Here it is called the salvation 'ready (or waiting) to be revealed' and thus refers to the future consummation of salvation. So, the entire phrase εἰς σωτηρίαν ἑτοίμην ἀποκαλυφθῆναι ἐν καιρῷ ἐσχάτῳ is looking forward to the final form of salvation to be revealed by God in the future.

But here it seems that our 'eschatological paradigm' has broken down; this clause speaks of the future of salvation *only* without reference to its present complementary reality. The next phrase, *in this you rejoice* (ἐν ᾧ

Deuteronomy, and especially Joshua. In post-exilic Judaism, however inheritance was often taken in a metaphorical sense of salvation or eternal life (Dan. 12:13; Ps. Sol. 14:10; 15:5; 1QS 11:7). Thus, at the time of the NT, this metaphorical sense of κληρονομία was already in the air.

[64] Cf. ACHTEMEIER, *1 Peter*, 95, and KELLY, *Peter & Jude*, 51.

[65] φρουρέω has a strong sense of guarding. Its related noun φρουρά can have the sense of 'prison', or 'garrison', and the literal sense of the verb can mean 'guard' in this military/police sense, as in 2 Cor. 11:32. It can also be taken, as it is here, in a transferred sense of 'guard', 'watch over', cf. Gal. 3:23, Phil. 4:7.

[66] Cf. ACHTEMEIER, *1 Peter*, 97, 'That divine guarding is now visibly appropriated by the Christians' trust (διὰ πίστεως), which becomes the instrument whereby the divine protection becomes reality.' Also cf. F.J. HORT, *The First Epistle of St. Peter I.1–II.17: The Greek Text with Introductory Lecture, Commentary, and Additional Notes* (London: Macmillan, 1898), 38.

[67] Cf. ELLIOTT, *1 Peter*, 335–6. Contra MICHAELS, *1 Peter*, 23, '"Salvation," as elsewhere in 1 Peter (i.e., vv 9–10; 2:2) is essentially future.'

ἀγαλλιᾶσθε), which is a relative clause that marks the transition from this first subunit (3–5) to the second subunit (6–9), speaks of rejoicing in the present. Could this be the link between future and present salvation we would expect? We will have to suspend judgment on this question momentarily as we sort out this phrase: ἐν ᾧ ἀγαλλιᾶσθε.

This short phrase is notoriously difficult to unpack. The main problem is locating the antecedent of ᾧ.[68] If taken as masculine it most likely refers back to the καιρός of ἐν καιρῷ ἐσχάτῳ.[69] If taken as a neuter, then it refers back to all that has been said in verses 3–5 (i.e., the eschatological gifts of salvation that come with the new birth). The proximity of ἐν καιρῷ ἐσχάτῳ argues in favor of the first (masculine) alternative, but the difficulty with this reading is the present aspect of ἀγαλλιᾶσθε. What sense does it make to say *in the last time* (future) *you rejoice* (present)? This difficulty has led many commentators to take the ᾧ as neuter and refer it back to all that has been said before.[70] By contrast, those who still believe that ᾧ refers to καιρός take ἀγαλλιᾶσθε as a present aspect verb with *future* sense, *in this you will rejoice*.[71] These are the two options given by the commentators, but a third possibility springs naturally from what we have said about Petrine eschatology. The καιρός ἔσχατος does not refer to the *future only*, but to the *entirety* of the messianic age, including the present, and the future consummation. If we take this approach then it makes perfect sense to say ἐν καιρῷ ἐσχάτῳ ἀγαλλιᾶσθε. In this way we are not forced to take a present as a future[72] or to take ᾧ as referring to all that comes before it.[73]

---

[68] It is possible, as noted by T. MARTIN, 'The Present Indicative in the Eschatological Statements of 1 Peter 1:6, 8,' *JBL* 111.2 (1992): 309, that the ἐν ᾧ can be used absolutely, i.e., without an antecedent with the sense of 'therefore' (see H.W. SMYTH, *Greek Grammar* (Cambridge, MA: Harvard University Press, 1980), §2511). This actually occurs in 2:12; 3:16, but both times immediately following ἵνα, and plainly without an antecedent. The use of ἐν ᾧ in 3:19 with an immediate antecedent πνεύματι, is a much more convincing parallel to 1:6. As MARTIN himself concludes, '[the] argument for the absolute use of ἐν ᾧ is not convincing.'

[69] It could possibly refer to θεός, or πατήρ, or even ἀναγεννήσας (in 1:3), but καιρός is more compelling on account of its proximity. It cannot possibly refer to ἐλπίς (fem.) as suggested by DAVIDS, *First Peter*, 54–5.

[70] So ACHTEMEIER, *1 Peter*, 100–1, ELLIOTT, *1 Peter*, 338–9, BROX, *1. Petrusbrief*, 63, and SELWYN, *1 Peter*, 125–6.

[71] So MICHAELS, *1 Peter*, 27–28, GOPPELT, *1 Peter*, 88–9, MARTIN, 'Present Indicative,' 307–14, and SCHLATTER, *Petrus und Paulus*, 47, 57.

[72] This seems unlikely here. While it is true that 'the tenses of ancient Greek do not signal time except by implication from their relationship to their context,' (K.L. McKAY, *A New Syntax of the Verb in New Testament Greek*, SBG (New York: Peter Lang, 1994), 39) the use of present with reference to an action in the future is rare. In the NT it is almost completely dominated by verbs of motion (e.g., ἔρχομαι), and is more normally used with a durative sense. It can, usually in narrative, be used to refer to an action completely in the future when it is used in a prophetic context. In this case, it is used as a

The difficulty with this is that we have already said that καιρός ἔσχατος in verse 5b refers not to the whole messianic age but to the *future* time when salvation will be revealed in all its glory. Καιρός ἔσχατος cannot mean the end of time (5b) and then the whole of the messianic age (6a). Or could it? Similar to what we saw with σωτηρία, καιρός ἔσχατος can refer to either *part* of the last times or to the *whole* of it. In verse 5b it refers to part (i.e., the time of final consummation), and in verse 6a it refers to the whole last time. It all sounds like special pleading, until we look at verse 10.

There we have the benediction's other major transition (from 6–9 to 10–12). As in verse 6, the transition is accomplished using a relative pronoun referring back to a *Stichwort* in the previous verse: σωτηρία. Verse 9b speaks of the salvation of your souls ([ὑμῶν] σωτηρία ψυχῶν), and this is picked up in verse 10a with περὶ ἧς σωτηρίας. The σωτηρία of verse 9 refers to the appropriation of salvation in the present,[74] whereas in verse 10 it refers to the entire plan of salvation. So, in verse 9b σωτηρία

---

vivid expression of a future event as though it were happening in the present (i.e., as 'a counterpart to the historical present', BDF §323). See B.M. FANNING, *Verbal Aspect in New Testament Greek* (Oxford: Clarendon, 1990), 221–6, where he specifies four types of 'futuristic present'. Our verb might possibly fit into his final category, but it has little in common with his examples.

[73] As a general rule, one should attempt to find a definite referent for a relative pronoun in its immediate context. While this is not always the case, it does make a good *prima facie* case against ᾧ referring to all that precedes it. This general rule is especially important in this benediction, where the structure of the period is defined by a series of relative clauses linked together by relative pronouns and catchwords. To take ᾧ as referring to the content of vv. 3–5 would break this chain. ACHTEMEIER, *1 Peter*, 100, argues that on the basis of 4:4, where 'the ἐν ᾧ is used proleptically, anticipating the ensuing genitive absolute (μὴ συντρεχόντων ὑμῶν), ...and bears the meaning "therefore," or "for that reason,"' that 'it is preferable to find here as well the meaning "for that reason."' First of all, he misses the importance of the literary structure of the benediction as compared with the remainder of the book. Second, his implication from the fact that the relative is used proleptically is that the relative is used *loosely*. He is not arguing that the ἐν ᾧ of 1:6 is used proleptically, neither interpretation would be favored by such an approach. In fact, the example proves that relatives are not used loosely, since it has an immediate kataphoric referent in the genitive absolute. It is not used proleptically to refer to all that follows, but has a *definite* referent.

[74] This will be shown below. There is an interpretive issue here as to whether this is referring to salvation in the present or salvation in the future. The issue turns on whether the ἀγαλλιᾶσθε of v. 6 is taken with present or future sense, because there is another ἀγαλλιᾶσθε at the beginning of v. 9, which will necessarily have the same sense (present/future) due to proximity and context. So the present or future sense of ἀγαλλιᾶσθε will determine the present or future sense of σωτηρία in v. 9. Since we have shown that ἀγαλλιᾶσθε should be taken with present sense in v. 6, then σωτηρία refers to the present appropriation of salvation in v. 9. Even if σωτηρία referred to future salvation, the point being made above still holds, since this is also a specific *period* or *part* of salvation.

means a part of salvation and in verse 10a it means the whole of salvation. A similar semantic shift is happening with καιρός ἔσχατος in the transition from verse 5b to verse 6, where the move is also from a *portion* (the end) to the *whole* messianic age. In both cases, a relative pronoun is used to begin a new thought unit, loosely connecting it to the previous subunit via a *Stichwort*.

Thus, the ἐν ᾧ ἀγαλλιᾶσθε, which marks the transition from subunit one (3–5) to subunit two (6–9), completes the thought of verse 5 and begins the thought of verses 6 and following. Through its semantic shift, it relates *future* salvation with rejoicing in the *present* 'last time'. At the same time, it begins the thought of the next subunit, which talks about rejoicing in the salvation that is being realized through trials. Although awkward, this complex transition fits well into its context. These two subunits are approaching the story of salvation from complementary temporal perspectives. The first subunit describes how *future* salvation relates to the *present*, while the second subunit describes how the *present* trials and salvation relate to the *future*. In a sense, the whole of subunit two (6–9) is the present counterpoint to verse 5b, where salvation as an eschatological reality is appropriated in the present, as in verse 9, which speaks of rejoicing in receiving salvation as a present sanctifying reality.

The second subunit of the benediction, then, continues the pattern of the intertwining of the meta-narrative with the story of the readers, this time focusing on the readers. Immediately following the ἐν ᾧ ἀγαλλιᾶσθε, we are introduced for the first time to the situation of the churches: *though now for a little while you may have to suffer various trials* (ὀλίγον ἄρτι εἰ δέον [ἐστὶν] λυπηθέντες ἐν ποικίλοις πειρασμοῖς). These 'various trials' will be discussed later in the epistle; the author's task now is to provide a framework to interpret them. This begins with the εἰ δέον, which implies an unavoidability and even necessity to their suffering. As Achtemeier says, this 'adds the note of inevitability to such trials,' but even more important, 'an inevitability in this context most likely of divine origin.'[75] Thus, at this point we begin to see how it is that their current trials are something not *outside* God's plan, but *within* it. This will become even more apparent as we proceed, but it is important to see here how this begins to explain the paradoxical situation that this verse proclaims: they rejoice (ἀγαλλιάω) even though they are suffering.[76] This is not to say that suffering becomes good; the author still wishes to console them that their

---

[75] ACHTEMEIER, *1 Peter*, 101. He also notes that, 'The conditional particle εἰ normally expresses a factual rather than a hypothetical condition, and it is probably to be understood in that sense here.' Contra ELLIOTT, *1 Peter*, 339, 'But suffering is *not a necessity*, as the qualifier "if it must be" (*ei deon* [*estin*]) makes clear.'

[76] Taking the participle λυπηθέντες in a concessive sense.

trials are only for a short time (ὀλίγος).[77] But ultimately they can rejoice in the midst of suffering because their trials are an instrument for their salvation. Their present reality of suffering fits within God's redemptive plan for them.

Verse 7 explains the purpose of these trials. *So that the genuineness of your faith* (ἵνα τὸ δοκίμιον ὑμῶν τῆς πίστεως), *more precious than gold which though perishable is tested by fire* (πολυτιμότερον χρυσίου τοῦ ἀπολλυμένου διὰ πυρὸς δὲ δοκιμαζομένου), *may redound to praise and glory and honor at the revelation of Jesus Christ* (εὑρεθῇ εἰς ἔπαινον καὶ δόξαν καὶ τιμὴν ἐν ἀποκαλύψει Ἰησοῦ Χριστοῦ). They suffer trials so that the character of their faith might be proved and strengthened, and that it might be praised and honored by God at the consummation. The focus here is on the molding of character. The subject of this verse, τὸ δοκίμιον, has the sense of 'proven character'[78] or 'genuineness as the result of a test.'[79] Faith (πίστις) in 1 Peter is an active commitment of devotion and allegiance to God and Jesus Christ.[80] This 'proven character' of their faith is a matured faith that has been strengthened in its allegiance through testing. (In Aristotelian terms: it is the 'habit' or 'learned disposition' [ἔθος] of faith.) It is this proven character of their faith that here is called much more valuable than gold (πολυτιμότερον χρυσίου).[81] Gold, which though perishable, and therefore not comparable to proven character, is tested (i.e. purified) by fire. The implication (from the lesser to the greater) is that the character of faith is also tested, proven, purified, and strengthened by 'fire' (i.e. trials).[82]

So, the purpose of their trials is to prove the character of their faith so that God might reward that character with praise, honor, and glory at the

---

[77] Cf. ACHTEMEIER, *1 Peter*, 101, 'The accusative ὀλίγον more likely refers to duration of time rather than to the relative unimportance of their suffering; the combination with ἄρτι implies the characteristic contrast in this letter between present suffering and future redemption.'

[78] ACHTEMEIER, *1 Peter*, 102. KELLY, *Peter & Jude*, 54, translates it as 'the sterling quality' of their faith.

[79] BDAG, 256.

[80] Cf. ELLIOTT, *1 Peter*, 340, 'In 1 Peter, "faith" (*pistis, pisteuo, pistos*) entails maintaining trust, loyalty, and commitment toward Jesus Christ (1:8, 9?; 2:6, 7) but primarily toward God (1:21 [2x]; also implied in 1:5, 9?; 5:9).'

[81] So ACHTEMEIER, *1 Peter*, 102, says, 'The emphasis here is not on faith itself so much as on the nature of faith that results from such trials. It is that tested and proved character (δοκίμιον) of faith which is more precious than gold (πολυτιμότερον) and which brings approval at the last judgment.' Cf. MICHAELS, *1 Peter*, 30. Both contra GOPPELT, *1 Peter*, 90–1.

[82] This analogy of character being tested by trials as metals are by fire can be found in both Hellenistic and Jewish writings. E.g., SENECA, *Prov.* 5.10; Ps. 66:10; Prov. 17:3; Zech. 13:9; Mal. 3:3; Wisd. 3:5–6; Sir. 2:1–9.

judgment. Once again, we see the intertwining of the two stories. The current circumstance of the churches in the midst of trials is related to God's plan of salvation in the present (working through trials to refine the character of their faith), and in the future (giving them praise, honor, and glory for their endurance and faith).[83] As before, present circumstance is directly related to future eschatological glory ἐν ἀποκαλύψει Ἰησοῦ Χριστοῦ.

Verse 8 brings us immediately back to the readers' story, and (again using a relative pronoun) picks up the Ἰησοῦς Χριστός above. In a seeming digression, the author speaks about their love for Christ: ὃν οὐκ ἰδόντες ἀγαπᾶτε. Here the readers are said to love him (Jesus) even though they have not seen (or met) him. Contextually, the purpose here is once again to highlight the eschatological reality as already underway. The temporal contrast is between their not having seen/met Jesus and their seeing/meeting him in the future ἀποκάλυψις just mentioned. But they already experience the love that they will have for him on that day now in the present. The next clause develops the same thought: *you do not see now, nevertheless believing you rejoice in him.*[84] Thus, while not yet experiencing the joy of the consummation, nevertheless these readers do, through their experience of faith and love,[85] already have a part in this eschatological reality. This is emphasized in a subordinate clause where they are said to rejoice with *unutterable and exalted joy* (χαρᾷ ἀνεκλαλήτῳ καὶ δεδοξασμένῃ), which points to eschatological rejoicing.[86]

Verse 9 finishes this subunit off with a participial phrase describing the reason for their rejoicing; they are obtaining (κομιζόμενοι) the goal of their faith: the salvation of their souls (ψυχῶν).[87] The focus here is on the

---

[83] Cf. ACHTEMEIER, *1 Peter*, 102, 'The thrust of these two verses is therefore that present trials may be greeted with joy, since they are necessary if faith is to have the kind of proved character that God finds acceptable at the final judgment.'

[84] It is also possible to take the εἰς ὃν with πιστεύοντες, and read *believing in him you rejoice*, but this loses the parallelism with the previous verse (i.e., you love him). Cf. ACHTEMEIER, *1 Peter*, 103. Also the parallelism between ἀγαπάω and ἀγαλλιάω, well demonstrated by MICHAELS, *1 Peter*, 33, shows that ἀγαλλιᾶσθε should be taken as a present tense, and not a futuristic present, as can also be clearly seen in the ἄρτι. Thus, the ἀγαλλιᾶσθε of v. 6 should be taken in the same way. Contra MARTIN, 'Present Indicative,' 311–2.

[85] Here πιστέω and ἀγαπάω are virtual synonyms. Cf. MICHAELS, *1 Peter*, 33, 'The tested "faith" of 1 Peter 1:6–7 and the love of Jesus mentioned in v 8 are simply two expressions for the same basic commitment.' Also cf. ELLIOTT, *1 Peter*, 343.

[86] Cf. ACHTEMEIER, *1 Peter*, 103–4. 'The joy…carries within itself a foretaste of the glorious future (cf. δόξα in v. 7) that awaits those who remain faithful to Christ. It is thus a present joy "lit up by the light of eternity."'

[87] ACHTEMEIER, *1 Peter*, 104, argues that the participle, 'must be understood here as describing a present activity and is probably best understood in a causal sense.'

appropriation of salvation in the present.[88] Selwyn describes κομίζεσθαι as, 'a good classical word meaning "carry off for oneself," with special reference to what is deserved or earned.'[89] Therefore, what is in view here is not simply a gift to be received, but something being appropriated through their faithful living in the midst of trials. Thus, they are said to be obtaining τὸ τέλος τῆς πίστεως [ὑμῶν],[90] and so they have cause to rejoice because they are, in the midst of their trials, obtaining the goal of their faith – σωτηρίαν ψυχῶν. Ψυχή here carries the sense of the 'inner person' or the 'heart', as it does elsewhere in 1 Peter (see 1:22; 2:11).[91] This is not to say that it should be thought of in sharp distinction from the body, as sometimes happens in Greek thought. Rather it is an *emphasis* on the inner person within a holistic understanding of the human person.[92] More specifically, the emphasis here (as in 1:22; 2:11) is on the inner *moral* nature. So when the author speaks here of the salvation of their souls he is emphasizing their moral transformation or sanctification, which is the product of their faith in the midst of trials. This moral transformation is not something divorced from eschatological salvation, but part of it, as we saw in verse 7 above. Therefore, these Christians rejoice because they are receiving their (eschatological) salvation now, in their sanctification through trials.

This subunit then returns to where it started: a joy in the midst of suffering because the character of their faith is being forged by trials. It is this same proven character (δοκίμιον) of faith that is more valuable than

---

[88] As a present participle dependent on a present finite verb, κομιζόμενοι is to be taken as referring to present 'receiving'.

[89] SELWYN, *1 Peter*, 132. SELWYN references PLATO, *Rep.* 615B and 621D as classical examples; the latter is especially pertinent. In the NT, see 2 Cor. 5:10; Eph. 4:8; Col. 3:25.

[90] Here τέλος has the sense of 'goal,' 'objective,' or 'purpose', and not 'end'. Cf. SELWYN, *1 Peter*, 132–3, 'τέλος in the N.T. is most commonly used of the temporal end or cessation. But the usage here conforms more closely to that which is normal in classical Greek, where τέλος = the logical end of a process or action, its issue, consummation, perfection and thus (in philosophical writings) its ideal or chief good.'

[91] Cf. SELWYN, *1 Peter* , who says that here ψυχή has a 'special reference to the spiritual side of men's lives.'

[92] As ELLIOTT, *1 Peter*, 344, notes, 'Here, and in the Bible generally, it [i.e., ψυχή] denotes not an entity within or distinguished from the human body but human beings in their entirety as *living beings*.' Unfortunately, ELLIOTT and ACHTEMEIER have both overcorrected against the 'Greek' dichotomy and emphasized the holistic aspect of ψυχή to the point where they cannot see variations of emphasis in usage (see ACHTEMEIER, *1 Peter*, 104). In 1 Peter ψυχή is used 6x: once to mean simply 'person' (3:20); twice to refer to the 'whole person' (2:25; 4:19 (this latter case is most likely a case of the Semitic use of ψυχή as simply a reflexive pronoun, see M. ZERWICK, *Biblical Greek: Illustrated by Examples*, SPIB 114 (Rome: Editrice Pontificio Istituto Biblico, 1963) §212)); and three times with emphasis on the inner moral nature (1:9, 22; 2:11).

gold, which they are obtaining now as the goal of their faith. This is why they rejoice with eschatological joy, because they are already receiving their eschatological salvation.[93] Thus, we see how the author, using this eschatological tension, intertwines the present story of the churches with the overarching reality of eschatological salvation – present and future. Also, we can see how the second subunit complements the first, and especially verse 5b. The second subunit is the present salvation complement to the future salvation promised in verse 5b; in addition, its focus on relating present salvation to the future compliments the first subunit's focus on relating future salvation to the present.

The third subunit (10–12) again intertwines the two stories, but this time the focus shifts to the *past*, and its connection to the present. The purpose is to show how the salvation of the readers fits within the grand narrative of God's plan of salvation prophesied in ages past. It also emphasizes the readers' privileged place in history, living in the messianic age, which the prophets tried to fathom and which angels stoop to see.[94]

The subunit begins with περὶ ἧς σωτηρίας, which takes up the σωτηρία from the end of the previous verse, but in terms of sense also points back the σωτηρία of verse 5b. As we mentioned above, it refers to the entirety of salvation. Verse 10 tells us how intensely the OT prophets pondered this salvation. *The prophets who prophesied of the grace that was to be yours searched and inquired about this salvation.*[95] In addition to this, they prophesied about the grace designated for these churches (περὶ τῆς εἰς ὑμᾶς χάριτος).[96] Thus, the salvation/grace the readers have experienced was prophesied by the OT prophets as they sought to understand and proclaim God's plan of salvation.[97]

Verse 11 sheds light on the work of the prophets, and the content of their prophecies. *They inquired what person or time was indicated by the Spirit of Christ within them when predicting the sufferings of Christ and*

---

[93] Cf. ACHTEMEIER, *1 Peter*, 104, 'σωτηρία is here an eschatological term. The sense [of v. 9] is that Christians now obtain by faith what they will only fully enter into at the end; the power of the new age is already at work and allows Christians in their present plight nevertheless to experience something of the eschatological joy awaiting them.'

[94] Cf. ACHTEMEIER, *1 Peter*, 105.

[95] The inclusion of NT era prophets is excluded by the fact that later it is said that they proclaimed the sufferings of Christ beforehand (προμαρτυρόμενον τὰ εἰς Χριστὸν παθήματα, v. 11b), which is in contrast to those who preached the gospel to these churches (ἃ νῦν ἀνηγγέλη ὑμῖν διὰ τῶν εὐαγγελισαμένων ὑμᾶς, v. 12b).

[96] ELLIOTT, *1 Peter*, 345, says, 'Here "salvation...is equated with "grace."'

[97] Cf. ELLIOTT, *1 Peter*, 345, where he says that salvation/grace, 'is stated to be intended specifically for the addressees (*eis hymas*), thereby continuing the focus on the readers that is so prominent in this unit.'

the subsequent glory (τὰ εἰς Χριστὸν παθήματα καὶ τὰς μετὰ ταῦτα δόξας).

The sufferings of Christ, the glories of his resurrection, and all of salvation that flows from them were predicted by the prophets, who struggled to comprehend what was revealed to them by τὸ ἐν αὐτοῖς πνεῦμα Χριστοῦ.[98] Salvation does not happen by accident, but according to God's plan.

According to verse 12, the prophets saw themselves as servants of future generations who would taste of the messianic age through the Spirit. *It was revealed to them that they were serving not themselves but you* (οἷς ἀπεκαλύφθη ὅτι οὐχ ἑαυτοῖς ὑμῖν δὲ διηκόνουν αὐτά), *in the things which have now been announced to you by those who preached the good news to you through the Holy Spirit sent from heaven, things into which angels long to look* (εἰς ἃ ἐπιθυμοῦσιν ἄγγελοι παρακύψαι). Once again, we are brought back to story of the readers and the privileged place that these Christians have in the story of God's salvation. This is further accentuated in the following clause, which says that this proclamation νῦν ἀνηγγέλη ὑμῖν διὰ τῶν εὐαγγελισαμένων ὑμᾶς. This again was no happenstance but part of the plan of God. The Gospel came *through* (διά) those who preached, not *from* them, for they preached [ἐν] πνεύματι ἁγίῳ ἀποσταλέντι ἀπ' οὐρανοῦ. These readers stand at the pinnacle in the history of God's revelation and salvation, the end times to which OT prophets looked forward. Theirs is a position of extreme privilege, even more privileged than the angels in heaven who long only to peek into this salvation.[99]

The benediction then functions to imprint on its readers a theological narrative worldview. Even more than painting a grand picture of reality with God's mighty salvific acts with angels as would-be onlookers, it tells a grand *story* of God's plan of salvation for his people. How it was predicted in the distant past, brought about in the recent past in Christ, and awaiting its consummation in a glorious future. Interwoven with this greater story is that of the readers, who have been given a new birth and promised a glorious future, and are realizing the benefits of that future glory now in the present in the midst of trials. Thus, the experiences of the readers, their past, present, and future, are placed within the context of a universe that is going somewhere, with their God at the helm. In this way, their current situation is charged with a significance immediately related to

---

[98] I.e., the 'preexistent' Christ; so ACHTEMEIER, *1 Peter*, 109–10.

[99] Cf. ELLIOTT, *1 Peter*, 350. 'Here in 1 Peter the thought heightens the exclusive privilege granted the addressees: not the ancient prophets, not even angels in heaven – despite their efforts and desires – have seen or heard the things proclaimed only to you!'

their future salvation, which is already being made manifest in the plan of God.

This story of salvation is further supplemented and expanded in the remainder of the first major section of the letter (1:13–2:10). Here we learn a great deal more about the story of Christ and his place within the meta-narrative of salvation. He was *destined before the foundation of the world but was made manifest at the end of the times* (1:20) to redeem a people through his precious blood, *like...a lamb without blemish or spot* (1:19). He was *rejected by men but chosen by God* (2:4), *who raised him from the dead and gave him glory* (1:21). Once again, this story is interlaced with that of the readers. It is the addressees who were redeemed by Christ's blood (1:18–19), and it was for them (δι' ὑμᾶς) that Christ was revealed in the last times.[100]

In addition to this, we learn more about the readers' story, and especially two particular areas: (1) their conversion and (2) their new identity as the chosen people of God. We are told not only that they were redeemed and born again (1:23; cf. 1:3), but also of their empty life (1:18) and *the evil desires they had in ignorance* (1:14) before their conversion. Likewise, the author praises their love for their fellow Christians that characterizes their life after conversion. Their conversion is a life-defining event for them as individuals and as a community, and the basis for their new communal identity. In 2:9 they are called γένος ἐκλεκτόν, βασίλειον ἱεράτευμα, ἔθνος ἅγιον, λαὸς εἰς περιποίησιν. These two important interrelated themes of conversion and communal identity will be dealt with in greater detail in the two chapters that follow. At this point, we need to think about how the salvation story laid out so far functions within the overall paraenetic aims of the epistle.

B. The Function of the Story

Wilson cautions that, 'In a paraenetic context...the astute interpreter will not construe its underlying narrative substructure as simply an addendum to the author's thought or the text's composition, but as *essential* to how the paraenesis functions morally to persuade, to convey values, to construct worldview, and to shape the self-identification of the audience over against hostile positions.'[101] The meta-narrative of salvation then functions at numerous levels as an integral tool in the paraenetic enterprise of moral transformation. In 1 Peter the story of salvation functions at three principal levels. First, it serves to contextualize ethics by picturing a

---

[100] Cf. ACHTEMEIER, *1 Peter*, 132, says that this passage 'has the effect of focusing the whole sweep of history on the readers and sets them, exiles and aliens that they are, at center stage in the drama of salvation.'

[101] WILSON, *Hope*, 192. Italics added.

universe in which the epistle's instructions are reasonable and significant. Secondly, it actively reshapes the value systems of these believers and calls for their commitment to the process of growth. Thirdly, it procures their allegiance to God by shaping their affective commitments toward him through reminders of his grace.

1. Contextualizing Ethics

One of the basic functions of a (narrative) worldview is to picture a world in which ethical norms become virtually self-evident. In 1 Peter the author constructs a theological narrative worldview that both grounds and reinforces his ethical teaching. The world he projects is one governed by the story of God's salvation. This worldview provides a normative framework within which these churches can interpret their own personal and corporate life stories. Within this context of God's gracious provision, the responses of adoration and obedience are only common sense. God's grace becomes their defining reality, and the appropriation of that grace becomes the defining aim of their existence. It is in this context that these young churches embrace the moral instructions given in the epistle as guidance for their transformations into mature Christian communities. Thus, the story of salvation provides the context for ethical instruction, seeing moral transformation as the locus of eschatological salvation in the present.

The deliberate intertwining of the two stories creates a web of connections between the over-arching reality of God's salvation and the life of the individual Christian. To experience the grace of God is to be invited to *participate* in that story. While the meta-narrative of salvation is fixed, for the individual Christian the story is still being written. At the same time, these individual biographies are informed and shaped by the contours of the story of God's eschatological salvation. The basic themes, structure, and especially conclusion of each individual story are fixed in the normative meta-narrative, but within this, each reader's story is still a contingent narrative under development.[102] The narratives of the readers are informed and directed by the meta-narrative, but are always in the

---

[102] Cf. MACINTYRE, *After Virtue*, 215–6, 'There is no present which is not informed by some image of some future and an image of the future which always presents itself in the form of a *telos*...towards which we are either moving or failing to move in the present. Unpredictability and teleology therefore coexist as part of our lives; like characters in a fictional narrative we do not know what will happen next, but nonetheless our lives have a certain form which projects itself towards our future. Thus the narratives which we live out have both an unpredictable and a partially teleological character.' Also see S. HAUERWAS and D. BURRELL, 'From System to Story: An Alternative Pattern for Rationality in Ethics,' in *Why Narrative?: Readings in Narrative Theology*, ed. S. HAUERWAS and L.G. JONES (Grand Rapids: Eerdmans, 1989), 178.

process of individualization, characterization, and growth. Thus, inherent in the way the overall story of salvation is constructed is an invitation for the Christian to participate in that story, developing his own story of salvation, within the larger narrative.[103] The meta-narrative provides a context for moral instruction and transformation.[104] The τέλος of the narrative worldview defines the τέλος for the individual.

As we saw above, Petrine eschatology is not a future reality only, but one that has already been inaugurated in the resurrection of Jesus Christ. This 'already/not yet' aspect of the letter's eschatological framework makes the teleological moral implications all the more potent. As we saw in the first subunit (3–5), the author speaks of the future hope, inheritance, and salvation as realities awaiting revelation in the coming of Christ, but also as present realities transforming the lives of these young Christians as they grow in maturity. Hence, they have cause to rejoice (with eschatological joy) because they are receiving the goal (τέλος) of their faith: the salvation of their souls (σωτηρία ψυχῶν), in the present. This picture of salvation provides the context for moral transformation and moral instruction.

This is especially the case in the second subunit (6–9), where the author develops the theme of salvation in the context of suffering. Here, according to Selwyn, 'the trials of the Christian life come to be regarded not as obstacles but as opportunities.'[105] Persecutions are not meant to be simply 'Stoically' endured, but joyfully embraced as a means of salvation. They are the 'refining fire' that produces a proven character (δοκίμιον) of faith, which is desirable above all other things and which will be praised and rewarded by God. It is this framework that undergirds and motivates the social ethics that will follow. Thus, in the midst of unjust suffering, they are called to 'do good', and in so doing mold their character of faith, and thereby obtain their salvation in their development as mature Christians. This picture of reality, with the salvific possibility of suffering,

---

[103] Cf. T. ENGBERG-PEDERSEN, 'Galatians in Romans 5–8 and Paul's Construction of Identity of Christ Believers,' in *Texts and Contexts: Biblical Texts in Their Textual and Situational Contexts*, ed. T. FORNBERG and D. HELLHOLM (Oslo: Scandinavian University Press, 1995), 495, '[Paul's] basic point [in Rom. 5–8]...is to make his addressees realize that through their own faith-response to the Christ event...*they have themselves become partners* in this world-encompassing story. In fact, once the see themselves in the light of that story and understand their own identity as being defined by it, they all together become centrally important participants in the decisive event in that story represented by Christ.' Italics original.

[104] Cf. WILSON, *Hope*, 195, 'In fact, a crucial feature of a text's narrative substructure emerges as the writer constructs for the recipients a "history," an historical context and perspective that impose a certain logic on the myriad experiences of life.'

[105] SELWYN, *1 Peter*, 81.

provides a hermeneutic of life for these suffering communities, as well as a hermeneutic for appropriating the author's moral instruction.[106] It provides a framework in which to understand and embrace the epistle's teachings on suffering summarized in 4:19: *Therefore let those who suffer according to God's will do right and entrust their souls to a faithful Creator.*

Thus, we can see that the story of salvation, in all its richness and complexity, provides a context for ethical instruction in 1 Peter.[107] The meta-narrative of God's salvation provides reasons, motives, context, and direction for moral action. As participants in a grand-narrative, these Christians are invited to shape their own salvation stories as an act of love and obedience. In practice, this appropriation of salvation comes chiefly through the instrument of faithful moral choices in the midst of unjust persecutions. In this way, the story of salvation supplies a coherent picture of reality that provides a context in which the epistle's ethical instructions can be understood and carried out.

2. Reshaping Values and Priorities

The benediction's narrative worldview not only gives a context for ethical instruction, it also imparts a system of values and priorities that encourages the process of moral transformation. As we saw in Seneca, a worldview serves as a map of value for all of reality, giving a proper estimation of all things that could claim one's admiration. For ethical instructions to be effective, it is necessary to comprehend the true value of, for example, moral integrity. For converts this can only take place through a radical shift in priorities and values, and the adoption of a new comprehensive system of values. Thus, in the context of paraenesis, worldview serves to reshape values and priorities. As we have seen before, this often involves bi-polar language that clarifies values for the convert by extolling new standards and deprecating old ones. Narrative worldviews, with their inherent union of beliefs and ethos, are particularly apt tools for this enterprise. As Wilson says:

The stories that are constituent of a worldview are in principle normative. Inasmuch as a narrative claims to make sense of the whole of reality, it necessitates a decision on the

---

[106] Cf. A.W. MUSSCHENGA, 'Narrative Theology and Narrative Ethics,' in *Does Religion Matter Morally?: The Critical Reappraisal of the Thesis of Morality's Independence from Religion*, ed. A.W. MUSSCHENGA, (Kampen: Kok Pharos, 1995), 187, 'Narrative ethics means to be a hermeneutic of moral experience.'

[107] Cf. SELWYN, *1 Peter*, 65, 'It is God's design and purpose for the universe and God's action which have called the Church into being through Christ's death and resurrection, and have given to the trials to which it was subject the character of a purifying judgment, and supply the strength and courage which it needs for its task. That is the background of the Church's life.'

part of the reader whether or not to embrace it as a controlling story over other stories. It is through this controlling set of stories that the reader interprets all secondary narratives, as well as all rival narratives. Narration, then, would appear to be a particularly effective implement for subverting or modifying competing stories and the worldviews united to them.[108]

Thus, a narrative worldview endorses a system of values and priorities and calls for the convert to align himself with those values. To give credence to a narrative is to adopt its system of values.

The world projected in 1 Peter is a moral universe, with God himself, the central character of the meta-narrative, defining the contours of that morality. The meta-narrative defines the parameters of a moral universe by showing the character of God as loving, faithful and righteous. The implications of this for the church are succinctly summed up later in 1:16: ἅγιοι ἔσεσθε, ὅτι ἐγὼ ἅγιος. Throughout the epistle, the moral universe defined by God's character serves as a backdrop for moral instruction. In 3:8–9, for example, the call to love and not return evil for evil is rooted in the character of God revealed in his actions toward his people – loving them, and graciously rescuing them in the face of their rebellion. Thus, the character of God, shown in his actions, directly informs the morality of his people.

Because God and his plan of salvation govern the epistle's narrative worldview, any other authority, whether earthly or spiritual, can only have a subordinate role to play. The epistle immediately places God's salvation at the center of the addressees' hermeneutic of life. All of reality is interpreted through this grid, and those narratives and sub-narratives directly related to salvation take precedence over all competing narratives. The meta-narrative of salvation becomes normative, and defines a new system of values and priorities.

This can be clearly seen for example in the attitude towards persecutions, which are transformed by reinterpretation through the story of salvation. While it would be natural to think that suffering was a sign of God's apathy or even malevolence, here it is reinterpreted as the central arena of salvation.[109] In verse 7, the focus is placed on the value of proven character. First, it is said to be *more precious even than gold*, which, while the most precious and honored substance in the ancient world, *will perish*. Secondly, this character will be the focus of God's joy, when it is showered with ἔπαινον καὶ δόξαν καὶ τιμὴν ἐν ἀποκαλύψει Ἰησοῦ Χριστοῦ. Thus, this proven character becomes a treasured possession to be valued above all else, even safety and relief from affliction.

---

[108] WILSON, *Hope*, 191.

[109] Cf. SELWYN, *1 Peter*, 79, 'It is this practical and spiritual adjustment to suffering which is the Apostle's main concern.'

From this it is clear that the author of 1 Peter constructs a narrative worldview with a system of values that reinforces his main objective of developing Christian maturity. This system of values, embodied in a comprehensive narrative worldview, endorses character development as the main instrument of appropriating eschatological salvation in the present. This provides not only a framework for ethical instruction, but also a rich soil for its reception. In this context, instructions are not only reasonable but also desirable as a tool for developing a refined character.

3. Procuring Allegiance to God

Philosophic paraenesis takes seriously the role of the emotions in the life of the convert, and seeks to educate and realign emotions to conform to virtue. As we saw with Seneca, misplaced devotion and fears are the true impediments to transformation. In the same way, 1 Peter, as an example of Christian paraenesis, aims to strengthen the affective commitments of its readers to Christianity. More precisely, it aims to strengthen their personal and corporate allegiance to God and Jesus Christ. The author of 1 Peter has deliberately shaped his theological reflections to win the allegiance of these churches to God. In the epistle, both 'faith' and 'love'[110] have the sense of a whole-hearted commitment or allegiance to God. So, we could say that 'procuring allegiance' toward God is, in the language of the epistle, strengthening their faith in and love for God.

The purpose of this is to bolster the readers' commitment to the process of moral renewal as an act of devotion and obedience. Shaping emotional commitments aids in the process of transformation by supplying not simply reasons but *motivations* for obedience. By strengthening their emotional ties to God, the author also strengthens their commitment to the process of growth, since procuring allegiance to God also procures allegiance to his design for salvation. This strategy also provides the addressees with new affective commitments that override others, checking illegitimate admirations and mistaken fears, and thus freeing them to embrace the process of growth.

For this reason, it is important not to forget that the benediction is a *benediction*. Right from the start, the epistle's theology is placed in the context of *worship*. As Michaels notes, 'To call God "blessed" is not to make a theological statement but to offer up to him one's praise.'[111] This worship is rooted in gratitude to God for his many gracious gifts, which the author catalogs. He has given them new birth (ἀναγεννάω), into a living hope (ἐλπίς ζῶσα), an inheritance (κληρονομία), and salvation (σωτηρία).

---

[110] I.e., love *for God*. 'Love' is also used to express the relationships among Christians in the church (e.g., 1:22).

[111] MICHAELS, *1 Peter*, 15.

All these wonderful gifts are given κατὰ τὸ πολὺ αὐτοῦ ἔλεος, with the rhetorical emphasis on the *greatness* and *extravagance* of his mercy.

The entire benediction (3–12) is carefully constructed with this aim of realigning affective commitments by eliciting gratitude and strengthening allegiance. The author emphasizes the living hope active now in their midst, which God has made possible by raising Christ from the dead. In addition, the author rhetorically stresses the impeccable character of their inheritance with the triad of α-privative adjectives: ἄφθαρτος καὶ ἀμίαντος καὶ ἀμάραντος. If that is not enough, this inheritance is secure because God himself is watching over it in heaven, while at the same time guarding them in his power through their faith. In all this, the focus is on what God has done, is doing, and will do for the readers. As Elliott notes, 'One of the most typical and remarkable features of 1 Peter as a letter of encouragement and exhortation is its constant stress on the "for-you-ness" of the gospel. This is not a writing of theological generalities "to whom it may concern" but a specific communication of "good news" for suffering believers in a "bad situation."'[112] The purpose of this stress on the 'for-you-ness' of God's salvation is to win their allegiance to him out of their gratitude for the great mercy he has shown them. Thus, the logic for the selection and arrangement of these theological truths is derived from the author's paraenetic aims; he is reshaping their devotions and procuring their allegiance.

These same paraenetic aims are well served by the author's eschatological framework. Not only have they been given a new birth (in the past) and are awaiting their salvation, which is ready to be revealed (in the future), but God is also giving them fruits of their salvation now (in the present). Through their trials, God is refining their faith, so that they might be more whole-hearted in their devotion and obedience to Him. As we have seen, trials then become the arena of salvation, not a sign of God's apathy. Therefore, they rejoice in their trials with the eschatological joy of salvation. In this, they affirm the work of God in their lives, as they hope for the future fulfillment of their salvation. Thus, they have reason to give their allegiance to him in faith and love, and embrace his plan of salvation.

The author reminds them of the love and devotion which they already possess for Christ, even though they have not seen him. And even though they are separated from him now and do not see him, they still believe and rejoice, because they are receiving the salvation of their souls. This affirmation that they already love him, serves as a tool to encourage the growth of this love. It shows them that this love is not misplaced, and that it is a taste of the love and communion they will have with Christ when he

---

[112] ELLIOTT, *1 Peter*, 353.

is revealed. So, love and devotion for Christ are a natural part of the salvation they are looking forward to and experiencing now.

Their salvation is placed within the over-arching story of God's plan of salvation, and thereby their present circumstances are placed within a larger story that is proceeding to its conclusion – once again emphasizing God's hand in their lives now. As Selwyn says, 'The author teaches very plainly that all Christians owe their position, and the Church its existence, not to any imminent logic of history, but to the mind and will of God.'[113] The author also wants to emphasize the privileged place they hold in God's plan. They are experiencing the salvation that the prophets only wished they could know and experience, and which angels long to only have a glimpse at. This long-awaited salvation is the Gospel that was preached to them. They are living in the messianic age, which is already revealing the consummation of God's salvation. Once again, the 'for-you-ness' of the gospel is emphasized to procure their allegiance to God and to His salvation, in hope for the future and obedience in the present.

The author then engineers his theology to suit his paraenetic motives. He creates a theological narrative worldview not only to contextualize the lives of his readers and reshape their values, but also to inform their devotions and win their allegiance to God. He does this by reminding them of the gracious gifts of God for them, and of His loving care for them. He is especially keen to persuade them of God's care for them in their present circumstance of suffering in trials. Thus, he points to the salvific purpose behind their trials, developing a 'habit' of faith (i.e., a deeper commitment to him), and to the great value of this refined faith. In all this, the author's aim is to mold and reinforce his reader's emotional commitment to God. The author shows them the extravagance of his favor, and elicits from them their gratitude and allegiance. In doing so, he is re-educating their devotions, and providing a fertile soil for his ethical instructions.

III. Conclusion

As we saw in Seneca and Philo moral precepts must be placed in the context of a worldview in order to be both comprehensible and effective. 1 Peter accomplishes this by using theology as a tool for shaping worldview. The author constructs a narrative worldview that contextualizes and reinforces his ethical instructions and thereby aids his paraenetic aim of moral transformation.[114] The benediction of 1:3–12 is designed to map a

---

[113] SELWYN, *1 Peter*, 76–7.

[114] Cf. W.A. MEEKS, *The Origins of Christian Morality: The First Two Centuries* (New Haven, CT: Yale University Press, 1993), 196, where, speaking of Pauline epistles,

narrative world that provides for the readers a meta-history by which they can interpret their own life stories, both individual and corporate.[115] The story of salvation provides them with a hermeneutic for their suffering, as well as for the epistle's ethical instructions.[116] Their persecutions and trials are reinterpreted, in the context of God's eschatological salvation, as the arena of salvation. In suffering, the character of their faith is strengthened through faithful obedience to God in the face of injustice.[117]

This picture of reality, with the appropriation of eschatological salvation in the present through the medium of active obedience, provides the context and motivating force for the ethical instructions that follow later on. It is in this context that the *Haustafel*, for example, is to be understood and embraced. Thus, theology and ethics here work together to further the author's paraenetic aims. The author has adeptly fashioned a theological narrative worldview that contextualizes his ethics. This narrative worldview not only provides the context for ethics, but is also itself a catalyst for ethical transformation. As we saw, in addition to providing a context for ethics, the narrative worldview also serves to reshape values and priorities, and to win the readers' allegiance to God and his plan of salvation. In this way, the author aims at a complete realignment of thought, values, and praxis for these Anatolian churches, so that they might grow up in their faith.

---

he states that, 'Paul's central concern was to use the narrative to form a moral community.'

[115] Cf. WILSON, *Hope*, 195, '[A] crucial feature of a text's narrative substructure emerges as the writer constructs for the recipients a "history," an historical context and perspective that impose a certain logic on the myriad experiences of life.'

[116] This actually provides an answer to one of the epistle's most perplexing and intractable problems: the relationship between 1:3–12 and the rest of the epistle. MARTIN, *Metaphor*, 39, claims that any justifiable interpretation of the epistle, 'must identify the relationship of 1:3–12 to the rest of the letter.' As with the Pauline thanksgivings, we ought to expect the benediction to provide some sort of hermeneutical key for the rest of the epistle. The attempts by MARTIN and D.W. KENDALL, 'The Literary and Theological Function of 1 Peter 1:3–12,' in *Perspectives on First Peter*, NABPRSSS (Macon, GA: Mercer University Press, 1986) to demonstrate how the benediction provides a thematic theological nexus that unifies the epistle are unconvincing. Seeing the benediction as a hermeneutical meta-narrative has the distinct advantage of answering this problem by showing how the benediction (and especially vv. 6–9) provides the key for understanding the remainder of the epistle. The benediction supplies a key for understanding how the moral transformation of these young Christian communities fits within the scheme of God's eschatological salvation.

[117] Cf. KELLY, *Peter & Jude*, 54.

Chapter Four

Conversion and Contrasts

Following on the previous chapter's examination of the story of the readers within the meta-narrative of God's salvation, in this chapter we focus on a particularly important element in the readers' story – their conversion. We will see how the author of 1 Peter, utilizing a Greco-Roman paraenetic literary strategy, uses reminders of conversion, together with antitheses that derive from conversion, as tools for achieving his paraenetic aims. Specifically, we will see how conversion becomes paradigmatic for all of life; and how conversion creates antitheses (e.g., life before and after conversion) that clarify moral distinctions and promote commitment to moral transformation.

I. Conversion in the Greco-Roman World

In his classic study of conversion in the ancient world, Nock documented how the level of commitment and allegiance required for membership in the pagan mystery religions was far less than that required by the philosophic schools. This was chiefly due to the strong demands for moral reformation central to the programs of the schools. Nock contrasted 'conversion' to philosophy with what he termed mere 'adhesion' in the cults. He said that we have 'little reason to expect that the adhesion of any individual to a cult would involve any marked spiritual reorientation, any recoil from his moral and religious past, any idea of starting a new life.'[1] Thus, *adhesion* is a casual association involving little or no call to allegiance or moral reform, but *conversion* involves radical commitment with a reorientation of one's life to conform to a radical shift in values and priorities. Meeks concurs that, 'In antiquity, conversion as moral transformation of the individual is the business of philosophy rather than of religion.'[2]

---

[1] A.D. NOCK, *Conversion: The Old and the New in Religion from Alexander the Great to Augustine of Hippo* (Oxford: Clarendon, 1933), 138.

[2] MEEKS, *Origins*, 23. Cf. NOCK, *Conversion*, 179–80, 'Plato spoke of the object of education as a "turning of the soul" (*Republic*, 518Dff.): the word *epistrophe*, later used by Christians of conversion, is applied to the effects of philosophy, meaning thereby an

But at this point we must be careful to ask whether conversion was *always* the 'business of philosophy'. Can we safely assume all members of the philosophic schools should be labeled 'converts'? Wilson defines conversion as, 'a comprehensive intellectual and spiritual reorientation... [which] initiates in some sense a new life progressing towards an established, personal goal, such as wisdom, virtue, or *eudaimonia*.'[3] While serious commitment to the philosophic life always involved 'in some sense a new life' directed toward *eudaimonia*, it is questionable that in all cases this required 'a comprehensive intellectual and spiritual reorientation', as is assumed by Malherbe, Wilson, Meeks and Stowers in their work of relating the environment of the philosophic schools to context for early Christian literature.[4] Nock's dichotomy works well in the contrast between the mysteries and philosophy, but is perhaps too blunt a tool to serve us in any detailed understanding of the environment of the philosophic schools.

The concept of conversion implies two things: (1) a strong sense of commitment and (2) a radical shift in life. Nock's dichotomy conflates these two elements by assuming that strong commitment always entails a radical reorientation, but this need not always be the case. This confusion could be clarified by the introduction of a third element called *adherence*, which describes a high level of commitment, but without a conscious *radical* shift in life. Adherence is not located between adhesion and conversion, neither is it a step along the way to conversion, but is rather another contrapole to adhesion. Adherence shares with conversion exclusive commitment, but does not share with conversion its strong sense of turning from one way of life to another. Like conversion, adherence does involve a life-defining choice, which sets the priorities and direction for one's existence. While this may involve *some* degree of change in life, it is not a *radical* shift, not what Wilson describes as 'a comprehensive intellectual and spiritual reorientation.'

This three-fold classification of adhesion, adherence, and conversion fits more naturally with the makeup of the philosophic schools of Greco-Roman antiquity. While there are dramatic examples of conversion to philosophy, just as often philosophy was pursued as the completion of a Roman gentleman's education.[5] In addition, the teachings of the schools attracted many attentive listeners, who nevertheless were not prepared to

---

orientation or focusing of the soul, the turning of men from carelessness to true piety, for which *conuersio* is used by Cicero (*On the Nature of the Gods*, i.77).'

[3] WILSON, *Hope*, 85.

[4] In his earlier work, *Moral World*, MEEKS showed more caution and used conversion in quotation marks (i.e., "conversion") with regard to the philosophic schools (e.g., 44).

[5] E.g., see VALERIUS MAXIMUS, *Sayings and Doings*.

make a strong commitment. Thus, even *within* the environment of the schools one can find examples of adhesion, adherence, and conversion.[6] Philosophers regularly deride the mere adhesion of hangers on, because they lack any real commitment to the philosophical life.[7] Philosophic literature is aimed at producing and educating adherents and converts. Paraenesis, for example, is addressed to adherents and converts, encouraging their fidelity to and growth in the philosophic life.

It is probably more accurate to think of 'adherents' and 'converts' not as two discrete realities, but rather as two endpoints on a continuum. The distinguishing factor being the intensity of an individual's conversion experience (i.e., the degree of a *conscious* change in life-direction). This 'degree of conversion' is dependent upon two things: first the convert's perception of the distance between his former life and new life; and second, the particular school's conception of its distance from the surrounding culture.

It is possible for a neophyte to see his commitment to a school as a natural extension of his previous life. More than likely, it will involve *some* level of change of lifestyle, but this shift need not be perceived as a radical one. Of course, this becomes much less likely for the more radical schools like the Cynics. Within this environment, where the school conceives of itself as 'outside' the culture, there is a strong sense of discontinuity, and typically a stronger sense of conversion.[8]

Meeks observes that, 'Conversion implies a change of reference groups and reference individuals – those groups and persons to whom we look, in fact or imagination, for standards, for approval or disapproval, for measures of how well we are doing.'[9] This shift of reference groups

---

[6] In applying adhesion to the environment of the philosophic schools, I am using it differently than NOCK, who reserves it for the popular religions. I am still using it in the same sense though – a casual association as opposed to serious commitment – but I have shifted it to describe something *within* the schools.

[7] E.g., PLUTARCH, *On Listening*, 46E, 'But young men of the opposite temperament, if they ever hear a single word directed against themselves, run away without looking back, and try to desert philosophy; and, although the sense of modesty which Nature has bestowed upon them is an admirable beginning for their salvation, they lose it through effeminacy and weakness, since they display no firmness under reproof, nor do they accept corrections with the proper spirit, but they turn away their ears toward agreeable and gentle converse of sundry flatterers or voluble talkers, who enchant them with useless and unprofitable but nevertheless pleasant utterances.'

[8] Cf. MEEKS, *Origins*, 22, 'It is among the Cynics, and among those Stoic philosophers influenced by the Cynics, that we most often hear of conversion as a rejection of or rescue from the perverted values of the dominant culture.'

[9] MEEKS, *Origins*, 48. Cf. EPICTETUS, *Discourses*, 3.16.11, 'It is for this reason that the philosophers advise us to leave even our own countries, because old habits distract us and do not allow a beginning to be made of another custom, and we cannot bear to have

explains why the school's conception of its relation to the wider culture is important for determining the degree of conversion. All the philosophic schools had some sense of distance from the popular culture,[10] but this varied in its extent. If joining a school meant the abandonment of most or all of one's previous reference groups or individuals, then there was a stronger sense of conversion. If, however, membership meant only minor shifts in reference groups or individuals, with a few deletions and additions, then there was less of a sense of conversion and thus we are closer to adherence than conversion. For schools that were more moderate, the degree of conversion was dependent upon the experience of the *individual* in his choice to join the school, and his perception of the extent of a shift in priorities, values, and allegiances.

This more nuanced view is more true to the social situation of the philosophic schools in the Greco-Roman world, and to the literature that they produced, which has come down to us. For example, it can explain why in his *Moral Epistles*, Seneca (a moderate Stoic and one-time advisor to Nero) never mentions conversion, or reminds Lucilius (the young aristocrat) to look to his conversion as a life-defining moment. There is not a strong sense of conversion, because there is not a strong sense of distance from the culture, and Lucilius' philosophic pursuits, while genuine, are an extension of his education as a Roman gentleman. By contrast, as we will see below, in the writings of the Cynic (Pseudo-) Diogenes there is a strong sense of cultural distance and thus, a strong sense of conversion. For the Platonist and former slave Epictetus, who combines a personal experience of conversion with a cultural distance somewhere between Seneca and the Cynics, conversion has a moderate role to play in his exhortations.

II. Remembrance and Antithesis in Paraenesis

Whether for converts or adherents, the choice of commitment to the philosophic life was 'only the beginning of a lengthy journey in which evidence of continuous progress was required.'[11] It is not surprising then that much philosophic literature, and especially paraenesis, concerns itself with what the Stoics termed προκοπή – progress in the moral life. But how does one attain progress? All the schools would have taken for granted

---

men meet us and say, "Look, So-and-so is philosophizing, although he is this sort of a person or that."'

[10] Cf. NOCK, *Conversion*, 185, '[T]here was a general antithesis of philosophic and common ethic and values.'

[11] WILSON, *Hope*, 88.

Aristotle's maxim that 'character is the result of habit.'[12] As Seneca says, 'you must learn first, and then strengthen your learning by action.'[13]

For converts especially, progress is neither simple nor guaranteed, since their transitions are so radical. Plutarch likens them to 'sailors who have left behind what is normal and familiar, but of having not yet become acquainted with and in possession of what is better: they are going round in circles in the intermediate area, and in the process often turn back towards where they have come from.' But he promises that habit and progress will give 'a light and brightness in philosophy, to replace the perplexity, uncertainty and vacillations which students of philosophy come across at first.'[14]

In the case of converts, character is the result of habit in the bad sense as well. If their turn to the philosophic way of life marked a turn from a life of self-indulgence, then their work of moral progress is all the more difficult. This same principle can apply to adherents as well, but again depends on the *degree* of their conversion.

In addressing converts, remembrance is a particularly potent paraenetic strategy.[15] By reminding the converts of their own life-defining choice of conversion, a paraenetic author can encourage his readers to remain true to that choice, and to renew their commitment to the program of personal transformation they embraced in their conversion. In this way, the convert's own biography becomes a tool in the paraenetic program of exhortation and encouragement.

For both adherents and converts the decision to embrace the philosophic life is a defining choice, but for converts there is the added element of a strong antithesis between life before and after this decision. This means that in the context of conversion remembrance includes a strong element of antithesis – contrasting the vacuity of life prior to conversion with the quality of life since. This involves a strong disparagement of the prior life, reinterpreting the pleasures of that life as depraved and enslaving (and therefore *now* undesirable). It also involves a remembrance of personal experiences of the enriched life within the school since conversion, and how the convert has been able to live out his beliefs.

Along these lines, Epictetus derides his students for not making a clean break with the past: 'You go back to the same things again; you have exactly the same desires as before, the same aversions, in the same way

---

[12] ARISTOTLE, *EN*, 1103a: ἡ ἠθικὴ ἐξ ἔθους περιγίνεται.

[13] SENECA, *EM*, 94.47.

[14] PLUTARCH, *Moral Progress*, 77D–E. WATERFIELD translation.

[15] Cf. WILSON, *Hope*, 93. The term 'remembrance' is taken from him. Much of paraenesis is set within the setting of remembering. Doctrinal and moral instructions, for example, are usually given as reminders of what the hearers already know.

you make you choices, your designs, and your purposes, you pray for the same things and are interested in the same things.'[16] He criticizes them for lives that show no evidence of change; they desire and pursue the same things they did before. Elsewhere, on a similar tack, he exhorts his students: 'flee from your former habits (φεύγετε ἔθη τὰ πρότερον)…if you would begin (εἰ θέλετε ἄρξασθαί) to be somebody some time (ποτέ τινες εἶναι).'[17] Rhetorically, Epictetus stresses the worthlessness of their former life, implying his students are 'nobodies' apart from reform. In both these examples, Epictetus relies on the antithesis of conversion – the contrast of the former life with the new. His intention is to underline this antithesis, and translate it into changed lives in practice. By emphasizing the antitheses conversion brings, he exposes the inconsistencies of his pupils, and calls them to live a life consistent with their initial choice to embrace the philosophic life. Only in this way will they be able to attain happiness.

This strong antithesis is also central to conversion *narratives*.[18] A fictive account of the conversion of Diogenes the Cynic (given in Diogenes' name)[19] provides a striking example of the antithesis inherent in conversion and how the act of conversion embodies the values of the entire philosophic journey.

I came to Athens, Father, and, when I heard that the companion of Socrates was teaching about happiness, I went to listen to him. Now he happened to be lecturing at the time about the two roads that lead to it. He said that they are two and not many (δύο καὶ οὐ πολλάς): the one a short cut, and the other the long way. …When we returned to him on the next day, I urged him to speak to us about the two roads. He quite readily rose from his seat and led us to town and straight through it to the Acropolis. And when we were near, he pointed out to us a certain pair of roads leading upward: the one short, rising up against the hill and difficult; the other long, smooth and easy. And as soon as he had brought us down, he said, "Such are the roads leading to the Acropolis, and the ones to happiness are like them. Each of you, choose the one you want and I will guide you."

---

[16] EPICTETUS, *Discourses*, 2.17.36–37.

[17] EPICTETUS, *Discourses*, 3.16.16. Cf. 3.22.13, 'First, in all that pertains to yourself directly you must change completely from your present practices, and must cease to blame God or man; you must utterly wipe out desire, and must turn your aversion toward the things which lie within the province of moral purpose, and these only; you must feel no anger, no rage, no envy, no pity; no wench must look fine to you, no petty reputation, no boy-favourite, no little sweet cake.'

[18] We possess few examples of 'conversion stories'. MEEKS, *Origins*, 23–4, cites the intriguing, *Tablet of Cebes* as an example. In addition to the letter cited below, (PSEUDO-) DIOGENES, *Epistle* 38, is also a conversion story.

[19] The collection of fifty-one epistles we possess today written in the name of DIOGENES of Sinope (4th-cent. BC Cynic) is a pseudepigraphic collection written at various times by at least four authors. For details of introduction, see A.J. MALHERBE, *The Cynic Epistles: A Study Edition*, SBLSBS 12 (Missoula, MT: Scholars Press, 1977), 14–21. Epistles 30 and 38, cited here, date from the first-century BC.

Then the others, fearstruck at the difficulty and steepness of the road, backed down and urged him to lead the along the long and smooth one. But since I was superior to the hardships (ἐγὼ δὲ κρείττων γενόμενος τῶν χαλεπῶν), I chose the steep and rough road, for the person hurrying on toward happiness must proceed even if it be through fire and sword (ἐπὶ γὰρ εὐδαιμονίαν ἐπειγομένῳ κἂν διὰ πυρὸς ἢ ξιφῶν βαδιστέον εἶναι). And after I chose this road, he took off my mantle and tunic, put a double coarse cloak around me, and hung a wallet from my shoulder, putting bread, drink, a cup, and a bowl into it. He attached an oil flask and a scraper on the outside of it, and gave me a staff too.[20]

The coarse cloak, wallet, and staff are the Cynic's identifying marks and only possessions in life. Thus, the conclusion of the scene is Diogenes becoming a Cynic. In the story, one cannot miss the strong antithesis of the two roads; especially with the emphasis that there are δύο καὶ οὐ πολλάς. Also significant is the demand for a choice between these two alternatives and the emphasis that this choice reveals moral character. Thus, the others chose the easy road because they were 'fearstruck at the difficulty', but Diogenes 'was superior to the hardships.'

In addition, the choice of conversion becomes paradigmatic for all of life; not because each moral choice is an act of conversion, but because the values embraced in the act of conversion are applicable to each moral 'crossroads'. Diogenes' rationale that, 'the person hurrying on toward happiness must proceed even if it be through fire and sword,' is applicable to all moral struggles, not only the act of conversion. While the act of conversion is a unique choice, it marks a change that sets a new course for his life, and is a choice that gives shape to that life.

In the last chapter we mentioned the teleological element of story in the Greco-Roman conception of the philosophic life, where life is seen as moving towards a personal goal of εὐδαιμονία. Within that story conversion becomes the defining moment in which this τέλος is first embraced. It also functions as a paradigmatic choice for the manner in which the story progresses towards that τέλος. Thus, the remembrance of conversion, as both a unique and paradigmatic act, is an essential part of the moral education of the convert in his pursuit of happiness.

The theme of conversion then serves as a powerful literary strategy operating on two fronts. First, it provides moral clarity by promoting those

---

[20] (PSEUDO-) DIOGENES, *Epistle* 30. This conversion account illustrates what was said above regarding the two factors that are relevant to the degree of conversion. The strength of DIOGENES' conversion lies in his being made a *Cynic*. His experience does not mark a strong point of departure from his previous life, but still possesses a strong degree of conversion because now he is a Cynic. The decision he made was consistent with his character, so it is not a radical shift in the sense of a new set of priorities. In some sense, this 'conversion' is really of revelation that he is a Cynic at heart. So, the strong sense of conversion comes from Cynicism and its cultural distinctiveness, not primarily from a radical shift of values and priorities.

values that were embraced in conversion, while at the same time denigrating the values that characterized the pre-conversion life, as we saw in Epictetus above. Secondly, it sustains commitment to the philosophic program of life transformation amidst the difficulties inherent in such a venture. As Porphyry says to his wife, the recent convert Marcella, 'the present situation is not so utterly unendurable for you if you disregard the irrational confusion caused by passion (τὴν ἐκ τοῦ πάθους ἀλόγιστον ταραχήν) and consider it no small thing to remember the divine doctrine (τῶν θείων λόγων) by which you were initiated into the right philosophy.'[21] Thus, conversion used as a paraenetic literary strategy clarifies fundamental values and strengthens fundamental commitments.

III. Remembrance and Antithesis in 1 Peter

Turning to 1 Peter, we find the same program at work with the author utilizing conversion as a tool for furthering his paraenetic aims. From conversion, the author draws out several lines of antithesis, all reinforcing moral distinctions and encouraging growth in moral maturity and Christian devotion.

In the past, this emphasis on the theme of conversion and its implications for the Christian life was given considerable attention by those interpreters who took this epistle as a baptismal homily.[22] While this was an improbable theory from the start, its greatest currency lay in the recognition of the importance of the theme of conversion in the epistle, and the implications drawn from conversion as a life-defining reality that informs the whole of Christian existence. So, while the theory has been justifiably discarded,[23] as van Unnik says, 'it will be wise to see that there is a kernel of truth in it.'[24]

In the previous chapter, we focused our attention on the first major section of the letter (1:3–12); here our focus is on the second major section of the epistle (1:13–2:3). Our author has concentrated his use of remembrance of conversion in this section. There are other allusions to this theme elsewhere in the epistle, which will be drawn upon where illustrative and important, but it is here, in the second major section, that

---

[21] PORPHYRY, *Marcella*, 139–40.

[22] E.g., BEARE, *1 Peter*, 51. The author 'is directly concerned not with thought but with conduct and character; and his ground of appeal lies not in doctrines as such, but in the living relationship which has been established between the Christian believer and God through the life, death, and resurrection of Christ and through entrance into the Christian community by baptism.'

[23] See ACHTEMEIER, 'Newborn Babes,' 208–9.

[24] VAN UNNIK, 'Christianity,' 80.

the author has chosen to focus on remembrance and antithesis. These dual themes of remembrance and the antitheses that arise from conversion serve to unify this section of the epistle, which has consistently been treated as disjointed and haphazard.[25] For reasons we will see below, this section can be further divided into two subsections (1:13–21, and 1:22–2:3).

Verse 13 functions as a transition from the first section to the second. *Therefore girding up your minds, being sober* (Διὸ ἀναζωσάμενοι τὰς ὀσφύας τῆς διανοίας ὑμῶν νήφοντες), *set your hope fully* (τελείως ἐλπίσατε) *upon the grace that is coming to you at the revelation of Jesus Christ* (ἐπὶ τὴν φερομένην ὑμῖν χάριν ἐν ἀποκαλύψει Ἰησοῦ Χριστοῦ). The benediction of 1:3–12 mapped out the framework for action, providing the story of salvation as the interpretive framework for life, and now the author begins his call to moral action molded by that framework.[26] The transition is marked by the particle διό, which begins the verse and which Selwyn classifies as 'the usual particle when an author passes from statement to inference.'[27] Rhetorically, the author accentuates this call to action with two circumstantial participles (ἀναζωσάμενοι, νήφοντες)[28] that precede the main imperatival verb: ἐλπίσατε. The author's strong call to action is rooted in the grounding realities expounded in the benediction.

---

[25] Most students of the epistle only dare to make the broadest generalizations about the overall theme of this section. ELLIOTT's description using the twin themes of hope and holiness (354–55) is typical. While applicable, this description is general enough to apply to the whole epistle, or most of its subsection. Likewise, PRASAD, *Foundations*, in his monograph on this passage, does not advance far beyond the general 'foundations of the Christian way of life.'

[26] It is customary to speak of this transition in terms of the dynamic of 'indicative and imperative' (e.g., BROX, *1. Petrusbrief*, 73–4). While ACHTEMEIER, *1 Peter*, 115, is right that, here 'as in early Christian proclamation in general, the imperative grows out of the indicative,' the terminology is not unproblematic. The idea that salvation precedes and gives shape to moral action is a central conviction of the NT authors, but, as was stated in the introduction, the shorthand of 'indicative and imperative' is an oversimplification that can produce confusion. To call the benediction 'theological' or 'didactic' and this section 'hortatory' is an oversimplification that fails to recognize the author's pragmatics. 1 Peter's theology is operating in a paraenetic mode; its function in the discourse goes far beyond constructing orthodox theology. For this reason, it is quite natural that our author freely alternates between indicative and imperative moods throughout the epistle. On the problem of 'indicative and imperative', see A. VERHEY, *The Great Reversal: Ethics and the New Testament* (Grand Rapids: Eerdmans, 1984), 104–5, and FURNISH, *Theology and Ethics*, 224–7.

[27] SELWYN, *1 Peter*, 139. Cf. ELLIOTT, *1 Peter*, 355.

[28] ACHTEMEIER, *1 Peter*, 118 n.11, says that these participles are 'most likely... adverbial participles of attendant circumstance, describing what accompanies the action of the main verb.' ACHTEMEIER is duly cautious of the so-called 'imperatival participle' (see his excursus on 117). For an overview of the issues, see the discussion in PRASAD, *Foundations*, 130–46.

The imperative harkens back to the eschatological ἐλπίς that was so central to the previous section; as does the χάρις, which refers back to verse 10, where it is synonymous with σωτηρία.

But what does the author mean by commanding his readers to 'hope'? In what sense is hoping an action to be commanded? The author is exhorting his audience to place their hope in the teleological eschatological reality of their salvation, which is coming at the Parousia. He has already proclaimed that this hope is the defining reality of their existence, and the lens through which they are to interpret their lives. Now he is calling them to action living sober lives, focusing their hearts and minds,[29] and placing all their hopes in God and in his salvation for them. To hope *fully* (τελείως, i.e., without reserve) in God means to cut all cords of security to false gods, and to hold exclusively to the grace of God as the only reliable security and source of life.[30] An implied antithesis, which becomes explicit below, already exists here between the trustworthiness of God and all other rivals for the hope of these churches. The remainder of this subsection (14–21) can be seen as an elucidation and expansion of this verse, particularizing what it means to hope fully.[31] These verses show that hope is not simply an attitude of the heart, but a commitment to see the appropriation of salvation in the present through personal and corporate transformation in the moral sphere.

In verse 14 the author strikes the chords of conversion and moral antithesis. *As obedient children* (ὡς τέκνα ὑπακοῆς), *do not be conformed to the passions of your former ignorance* (μὴ συσχηματιζόμενοι ταῖς πρότερον ἐν τῇ ἀγνοίᾳ ὑμῶν ἐπιθυμίαις). Their designation here as τέκνα ὑπακοῆς (lit. 'children of obedience'[32]) echoes the new birth of conversion mentioned in 1:3. That they are *obedient* children emphasized the essential

---

[29] SCHLATTER, *Petrus und Paulus*, 71, says that διάνοια here refers to 'the exertion of thought and will', and that this is equivalent to the 'Palestinian' use of καρδία. Cf. HORT, *1 Peter*, 65.

[30] Cf. W. BRANDT, 'Wandel als Zeugnis nach dem 1. Petrusbrief,' in *Verbum Dei Manet in Aeternum*, ed. W. FOERSTER (Witten: Luther Verlag, 1953), 15, 'Die Zukunft ist schon Gegenwart in der Hoffnung, die alle andern Ziele, auf die menschliches Hoffen sich sonst richtet, überspringt und beiseite schiebt.' HUTHER, *Peter & Jude*, 80, cites W.M.L. DE WETTE, *Kurze Erklärung der Briefe des Petrus, Judas und Jakobus*, vol. 3.1, *Kurzgefaßtes exegetisches Handbuch zum Neuen Testament* (Leipzig: Weidmann, 1847), 12, who describes this hoping as, 'ohne Zeifel, Kleinmuth, mit voller Hingebung der Seele.' This use of ἐλπίζω has affinities with LXX usage, where the verb most often means simply 'trust', with little or no eschatological connotation.

[31] Cf. ACHTEMEIER, *1 Peter*, 117, 'While v. 13 could stand alone because of its structure...its close ties to the content of the next three verses make it appropriate to see them as a unity of thought.'

[32] Probably a Semitism (See MICHAELS, *1 Peter*, 56); it emphasizes an essential characteristic (like 'children of light'), not source or origin (like 'children of God').

moral nature of their new life, which is to be characterized by obedience to God. Thus, the call to obedience comports with who they have become; they have been born anew as children of obedience. This new birth, however, creates an antithesis with their previous lives, since their pre-conversion lives were dominated by passions and characterized by ignorance.[33] As we saw above, this rhetorical device of denigrating pre-conversion existence is common in paraenetic literature.

Also common to paraenesis is the two-fold command to leave the old life and embrace the new. Verse 15 gives the positive command that follows the condemnation of their pre-conversion life. *But as he who called you is holy* (ἀλλὰ κατὰ τὸν καλέσαντα ὑμᾶς ἅγιον), *be holy yourselves in all your conduct* (καὶ αὐτοὶ ἅγιοι ἐν πάσῃ ἀναστροφῇ γενήθητε). Here we see what the author calls his readers *to*, not simply what he calls them *from*: to live a life that conforms to God's character of holiness.[34] What we have here is an antithesis between two ways of life (ἀναστροφαί). Ἀναστροφή is a keyword in 1 Peter (and especially in this subsection).[35] As van Unnik says, 'Christianity according to 1 Peter is not a certain set of ideas, but ἀναστροφή = *a way of life*.'[36] In 1 Peter, it carries the sense of a life that is defined and directed by some principle, either good or evil. To speak of what characterizes one's life as a whole, in the Aristotelian sense, is to speak of one's ἀναστροφή. Thus, when the author calls for holiness ἐν πάσῃ ἀναστροφῇ, he is calling for a transformation of what characterizes their lives as a whole, which is both molded by, and revealed in, their behavior.

Also present here is the idea that conversion is not only the act of an individual, but also refers to the action of God in conversion. It is God who calls and gives new birth. (This does not nullify the importance of the choice of the convert; *both* have their place and serve to complement one another.) Thus, in 1 Peter references to conversion can refer to either the actions of believers or the actions of God in election. The use of antithesis as a literary strategy is still valid even when God is in focus; in fact the antithesis is even *stronger*, because conversion involves the transforming agency of God, and not simply the will of an individual.

The metaphors used to describe this aspect of conversion often imply an absolute antithesis. 'New birth', for example, is a metaphor that implies an

---

[33] HORT, *1 Peter*, 69, comments that, 'Conduct ruled by desires is irregular and erratic, at the mercy of outward circumstances, not moulded by a consistent life principle.'

[34] SELWYN, *1 Peter*, 215, notes that, 'κατά expresses conformity to some standard, model, rule, or will.'

[35] 6 of 13 NT occurrences are in 1 Peter. The only other NT writing with more than one occurrence is 2 Peter with two.

[36] VAN UNNIK, 'Christianity,' 81.

absolutely new beginning with a note of irreversibility. In this way, conversion is something that happens to the convert as well as being a product of his own agency, which serves to strengthen the radical sense of conversion, and thereby aids our author realizing his paraenetic agendas.

So, we see in verse 15 that it is not merely the character of the *convert* in conversion that is life-defining (as we saw with Diogenes above), but the character of God is life-defining as well. Thus, κατὰ τὸν καλέσαντα ὑμᾶς ἅγιον καὶ αὐτοὶ ἅγιοι ἐν πάσῃ ἀναστροφῇ γενήθητε. In verse 16, this exhortation receives an OT endorsement in a quotation of a *Leitmotiv* from the book of Leviticus, Ἅγιοι ἔσεσθε, ὅτι ἐγὼ ἅγιός [εἰμι]. As in the OT context, the call to holiness is a call to distinctiveness and separateness from the surrounding culture in which they live and from which they came.[37] (We will see in the next chapter that this is a call to cultural separateness but not to cultural isolation.) Also, just as in the OT, the call to holiness comes as a result of the saving action of God (Exodus/conversion) and the new relationship that he has established with his people.

In verse 17, the author continues to explicate what it means to 'hope fully,' by reminding his readers that God is both their Father (who gave them 'new birth') and their judge. *And if you invoke as Father him who judges each one impartially according to his deeds* (καὶ εἰ πατέρα ἐπικαλεῖσθε τὸν ἀπροσωπολήμπτως κρίνοντα κατὰ τὸ ἑκάστου ἔργον), *conduct yourselves with fear throughout the time of your exile* (ἐν φόβῳ τὸν τῆς παροικίας ὑμῶν χρόνον ἀναστράφητε). Once again, it is the character of God, this time as an impartial judge who does not play favorites, which provides the basis for exhortation; but here God is to be feared not imitated. Calling on God as πατήρ refers to the church's activity in prayer (as in Mt. 6); but it is also another remembrance of conversion, of the initial paradigmatic calling on God that brought salvation.[38] 'The point,' as Achtemeier says so well, 'is that the Christian is not to presume on God's grace, a grace that includes in itself the call to transform one's

---

[37] Cf. N. HILLYER, *1 and 2 Peter, Jude*, NIBCNT 16 (Peabody, MA: Hendrickson, 1992), 45–6. While ACHTEMEIER, *1 Peter*, 122, is right that the form of the quotation better matches Lev. 19:2 than 11:44, the argument that this then refers to Israelites living in the promised land instead of referring to the situation of the Exodus, draws too fine a point. There is no reason to draw an either/or here. The temptations to unfaithfulness can be thought of either in terms of regression *or* assimilation. In his laudable rejection of *strong* Exodus motifs, ACHTEMEIER has over-corrected.

[38] As ELLIOTT, 365, notes, 'The metaphor of God as "father"…corresponds to the metaphor of the believers as "obedient children,"' which we have already seen relates to the new birth given by God.

life in obedience to God.'³⁹ Thus, they are to live in reverent fear, respecting God's character as their righteous judge and not presuming on his mercy.

The period of exile (τὸν τῆς παροικίας ὑμῶν χρόνον) is, once again, an expression of the antithesis of two periods of life that result from conversion. While Elliott is right to criticize interpretations that place the dichotomy between earthly and heavenly life, he fails to recognize fully that this antithesis finds its *origin* in the saving work of God. The point is that their status as aliens is something created by their conversion, not something possessed prior to conversion.⁴⁰ Again, the author's aim is to draw a strong line of distinction between life before and after conversion, in an effort to clarify moral thinking and strengthen commitment.

Since the ἀναστροφή before conversion is taken generally to be the same as the ἀναστροφή of the culture at large, this necessarily involves a social antithesis between the Christian community and their pagan neighbors. This is why they are considered to be aliens/strangers/exiles/sojourners. At the same time, their identity as God's people is rooted in the eschatological reality of God's salvation, which is coming in future judgment. Thus, there is also a sense in which they are strangers and sojourners because they are awaiting their salvation (see 4:2). But these two realities are not in tension with one another. Their cultural distinctiveness as the people of God is rooted in their hope of salvation.

This 'time of exile' finds its antithesis in the verse 18b, where the author speaks of his readers being ransomed ἐκ τῆς ματαίας ὑμῶν ἀναστροφῆς πατροπαραδότου. Again, the author underlines the 'worthlessness' and 'futility' (μάταιος) of their previous way of life. In the ancient world πατροπαράδοτος described those traditions that were faithfully adopted as ancient and venerable. For the author to denounce this

---

³⁹ ACHTEMEIER, *1 Peter*, 125. He continues, 'The consequence of being in intimate relationship ("Father") with the God who is the impartial judge of the world is to conduct one's life (ἀναστράφητε) in accordance with the will of God, here expressed as ἐν φόβῳ.' HUTHER, *Peter & Jude*, 87, notes that, in the context of impartial judgment, 'the plural [τὰ ἔργα] is generally found (Rom. ii. 6);' and that, 'by the singular the whole conduct of man (outwardly and inwardly) is conceived as a work of his life.' Thus, each person is judged according to their ἀναστροφή.

⁴⁰ While it is true that the metaphor of exile/sojourner would have had a deeper significance if some members of the churches were actually literal exiles/sojourners, Elliott's insistence this must be the case for the metaphor to hold any significance is unfounded. Tacit knowledge of the literal reality behind a metaphor is not necessary for a metaphor to be meaningful. Cf. F.W. DANKER, Review of *A Home for the Homeless*, *Int* 37.1 (1983): 84–88.

ἀναστροφή as ματαία is a very bold critique of Greco-Roman cultural practices.[41]

A. The Corruptible and the Incorruptible

Verses 18 and 19 introduce a new antithesis between the corruptible and the incorruptible and provide a warrant for the exhortation of verse 17 to live with due reverence. *You know* (εἰδότες) *that you were ransomed* (ἐλυτρώθητε) *from the futile ways inherited from your fathers, not with perishable things such as silver or gold* (οὐ φθαρτοῖς, ἀργυρίῳ ἢ χρυσίῳ), *but with the precious blood of Christ, like that of a lamb without blemish or spot* (ἀλλὰ τιμίῳ αἵματι ὡς ἀμνοῦ ἀμώμου καὶ ἀσπίλου Χριστοῦ). The image of redemption by silver or gold would not have been lost on the slaves in the congregation (2:18). But the value of corruptible silver and gold cannot be compared with the value of the precious blood of the pure and uncorrupted lamb: Jesus Christ.

Here the author is playing on an antithesis that has been building since verse 4, where he described the heavenly inheritance as ἄφθαρτον καὶ ἀμίαντον καὶ ἀμάραντον. In this antithesis, families of images cluster around two poles: the corruptible and the incorruptible. On one side are those 'earthly' things that will perish by rust or decay, things that are impermanent and of little value in comparison with those things that are 'heavenly' and incorruptible. But it is important to realize that the import of this antithesis is *moral*. Physically corruptible things signify moral corruptibility, not simply their susceptibility to the elements or the arrow of time. Likewise, those things eternal represent not simply the everlasting, but also goodness, faithfulness, and moral purity. Thus, the ontological distinction between things eternal and mortal, rhetorically, carries the moral antithesis of good and evil, incorruptible and corruptible.[42]

Thus, in verse 7 we saw how the author argued that faith was of greater worth that gold, which perishes, since genuine faith finds fruition in the eschatological realities of praise, glory, and honor. Later, he characterizes the pre-conversion life of the readers as a worthless tradition, controlled by wicked desires (ἐπιθυμίαι). In contrast to this are all those eternal and righteous things pertaining to God and his eschatological salvation. This is

---

[41] See W.C. VAN UNNIK, 'The Critique of Paganism in 1 Peter 1:18,' in *Neotestamentica et Semetica: Studies in Honour of Matthew Black*, ed. E.E. ELLIS and M. WILCOX (Edinburgh: T & T Clark, 1969) 129–42. Similar criticisms were not unknown in those philosophical circles that had little regard for popular values. E.g., (PSEUDO-) DIOGENES, *Epistle* 29.4, 'Poor soul, there is no harsher burden for you than the ways of your forefathers and of the tyrants. There is nothing else which more consistently destroys you.'

[42] In English 'corruptible' and 'incorruptible' have both senses of physical and moral, and so carry the meaning well.

why, in verses 18–19, corruptible silver and gold can be set against the incorruptibility and moral blamelessness of Christ. The antithesis is not, as is often assumed, between perishable silver and gold and the precious blood. The blood *is* more valuable/precious than gold and silver, but its superiority derives from its *pure incorruptible source.*[43] The fact that silver and gold are *physically* corruptible and Christ is *morally* incorruptible is insignificant.

This also explains how these verses can be a warrant for the injunctions in the previous verses to live a holy life in reverent fear. It is not because the readers are to be moved at the costliness/preciousness of Christ's sacrifice, but that they are to recognize that their salvation brings them into relationship with the incorruptible eschatological 'kingdom of God'. The inheritance they have received is incorruptible and kept for them. They are to hope fully in the grace to be given them by incorporating eschatological realities into their lives now. This translates into the practice and nurturing of incorruptible moral qualities that characterize God and his salvation. Thus, they are to be holy, just as he is holy. Their experience of God's incorruptible salvation calls for the elimination of corruptibility in their own hearts.

Again, the author's purpose in drawing these antitheses between the corruptible and the incorruptible is to foster his readers' allegiance to the incorruptible. His aim is to give them reason to hope fully in the coming salvation. Thus, he means to show that corruptible things are not worthy of their hope, and that the incorruptible are. In the next two verses (20–21) the author again emphasizes those things which set their salvation apart as worthy of their exclusive allegiance. As we mentioned in the previous chapter, the thrust of verse 20 is to underscore the privilege of the readers who are placed at the culmination of the story of God's salvation.[44] *He was destined* (προεγνωσμένου μὲν) *before the foundation of the world but was made manifest* (φανερωθέντος δὲ) *at the end of the times for your sake* (ἐπ' ἐσχάτου τῶν χρόνων δι' ὑμᾶς). At the same time, this verse also serves to extol both the antiquity and surety of their salvation. While the traditions inherited from their ancestors were venerable on the basis of their antiquity alone, here the ἀναστροφή πατροπαραδότου is surpassed by a salvation that can be traced back to a time before the creation of the world. The

---

[43] Cf. HUTHER, *Peter & Jude*, 89, 'τιμίῳ forms the antithesis to φθαρτοῖς, in so far as the perishable is destitute of true worth.'

[44] A privilege underlined by the emphatic δι' ὑμᾶς. Cf. SELWYN, *1 Peter*, 146, 'St. Peter thus focuses the whole divine counsel of redemption upon his readers, and sets them, strangers and pilgrims as they are, in the forefront of the drama of history. The fact would help them to realize the love of God and the privilege of their calling, and so would strengthen them in the midst of the world's indifference and cruelty.'

unassailability of their hope is also assured by God's power to bring it to conclusion. It was he that set Christ apart and revealed him, and it is he that will assuredly bring to fruition the object of their hope – their final salvation.[45]

Verse 21, continuing along similar lines, proclaims confidence in God through Christ. *Through him you have confidence in God* (τοὺς δι' αὐτοῦ πιστοὺς εἰς θεόν), *who raised him from the dead and gave him glory, so that your faith and hope are in God*. Achtemeier notes that the import of this confidence 'is that one can put one's trust in God because he has shown himself trustworthy in his redemptive action through Christ.'[46] The author continues to rehearse these redemptive acts, telling how he raised Christ from the dead and gave him glory (δόξα). These twin eschatological actions express the core of how God revealed himself in Christ to bring about salvation in the last times.[47] The body of the letter began in verse 3 with the proclamation that new birth and hope have come through the resurrection of Jesus Christ. Thus, the mention of resurrection points to both their status (new birth) and calling (hope) as Christians.[48] Here, the emphasis is on the latter. Again, the author's intent is to foster an exclusive hope in God, the bringer of salvation. The point he aims at here is that their hope finds its anchor not only in Christ, but ultimately in God himself. Thus, the final clause explains the purpose of God's actions, ὥστε τὴν πίστιν ὑμῶν καὶ ἐλπίδα εἶναι εἰς θεόν.[49] In his eschatological work through Christ God's intention was to open the door of salvation so that he

---

[45] Cf. ACHTEMEIER, *1 Peter*, 131, 'The passive voice of the two participles (προεγνωσμένου, φανερωθέντος), indicating that all of this is God's doing, adds further assurance to the claim that the redemption brought about by the death of Jesus is reliable precisely because it was due to the divine initiative.'

[46] ACHTEMEIER, *1 Peter*, 132.

[47] While the expression for glorification (δόξαν αὐτῷ δόντα) is unique among the NT writings, the resurrection and glorification of Christ are central tenets of early church kerygma, with numerous references scattered throughout the NT.

[48] Also, MICHAELS, *1 Peter*, 68, argues that the expression πιστοὺς εἰς θεόν connotes 'the break they have made with the past.' He notes that, 'The latter phrase [εἰς θεόν] is not superfluous, for it reminds the readers once more of their identity as Gentiles. They are believers in God, not (as Jews would have been) by virtue of their ancestral heritage (cf. v 18b) but through Jesus Christ (δι' αὐτοῦ). In the same way that "turning to God" (Acts 14:15; 15:19; 26:20; 1 Thess. 1:9) is used of Gentiles but not of Jews, and the "Gospel of God" (Mk. 1:14; Rom. 1:1; 15:16; 1 Thess. 2:2, 8–9) refers primarily to the Christian gospel as proclaimed to the Gentiles, so "believing in God" [πιστοὺς εἰς θεόν] is an appropriate expression for the experience of Gentile Christians.'

[49] The infinitive (εἶναι) with ὥστε here is taken as a purpose clause (i.e., *so that your faith and hope might be in God*) with SELWYN, *1 Peter*, 147–8, and MICHAELS, *1 Peter*, 70, but against ACHTEMEIER, *1 Peter*, 133; see BDF, 391§3.

might be the object of their faith and hope.[50] Therefore, because he has revealed his gracious will towards them and his unrivalled power to save, he is worthy of their hope. In the context of the antithesis with their previous life, he is worthy of their *exclusive* hope. The author's intention is to exalt the worthiness of God to the point that it outshines all possible alternatives. God is not only *a* sure hope, but their *only* sure hope, and therefore worthy of their full and unalloyed confidence.[51] This returns us to the beginning of this subsection and the call τελείως ἐλπίσατε in the coming grace/salvation.[52]

B. Pure Sincere Love

Verse 22 begins a new subsection that concludes in 2:3. *Having purified your souls by your obedience to the truth for a sincere love of the brethren* (Τὰς ψυχὰς ὑμῶν ἡγνικότες ἐν τῇ ὑπακοῇ τῆς ἀληθείας εἰς φιλαδελφίαν ἀνυπόκριτον), *love one another earnestly from the heart* (ἐκ [καθαρᾶς] καρδίας ἀλλήλους ἀγαπήσατε ἐκτενῶς). Once again, we see a strong emphasis on conversion and moral antitheses that arise out of conversion. In referring to the purification of their souls by obedience to the truth, the author is alluding to their conversion.[53] The perfective aspect of the participle ἡγνικότες emphasizes their new state of purification in contrast to their pre-conversion state of defilement. Here the sense of ἁγνίζω (especially in conjunction with τὰς ψυχάς) is of *moral* cleansing.[54] The mention of obedience recalls their new identity as *children of obedience* (1:14) as well as their *sanctification by the Spirit for obedience* (1:2).[55] ῾Η

---

[50] ACHTEMEIER, *1 Peter*, 133, notes that, 'The nature of faith, which includes trust, and the nature of hope, which includes confidence, are so related that we are probably correct in seeing here two aspects of the same reality.' This comports well with his conclusion that the τήν before πίστιν also applies to ἐλπίδα, since, 'the two nouns ought to be understood as coordinate, almost in the sense of a hendiadys.'

[51] Cf. SELWYN, *1 Peter* , 'The place of εἰς Θεόν, moreover, at the close of the sentence is emphatic, and there was good reason for it; for it served to distinguish Christianity from the contemporary pagan cults. They, too, professed to know divine beings – Dionysus, Attis, Horus – who had been raised from the dead and glorified, and who became themselves the object and term of worshippers' faith; Christianity, while it encouraged the worship of Christ and was therefore Christocentric, yet worshipped Him in the context of the Blessed Trinity, and His exaltation was that men's faith might rest there – in God.'

[52] Cf. MICHAELS, *1 Peter*, 70, 'By introducing hope at this point, he come full circle back to v 13.' This thematic return has the effect of setting this subsection off as a unit.

[53] So ELLIOTT, *1 Peter*, 382, 'This initial phrase recalls 1:14–16 and describes the active role that the addressees played in the process of conversion.'

[54] Cf. SELWYN, *1 Peter*, 149, and ACHTEMEIER, *1 Peter*, 136.

[55] As ELLIOTT, *1 Peter*, 384, notes, many later manuscripts (P, 𝔐) contain the addition of διὰ πνεύματος here.

ἀλήθεια (i.e., the gospel)[56] refers to what is sure and which corresponds to reality, in contrast to the ἄγνοια and ματαιότης of their previous way of life.[57] That the purification of their souls is accomplished by their *obedience* to the truth, and not simply 'believing the gospel', is another reminder that in conversion they have embraced a new ἀναστροφή, not simply a new set of ideas.

This moral purification has as its aim the transformation of human relationships, first within the church and then in relation to those outside. The former is the focus here, where sincere brotherly love is said to be the *goal* of their conversion.[58] Hence the command: ἀλλήλους ἀγαπήσατε. Such love must be 'sincere' (ἀνυπόκριτος), and so ἐκ καθαρᾶς καρδίας.

New birth entails membership in a new family (as Elliott has noted, ὁ οἶκος τοῦ θεοῦ), which is characterized by ἀγάπη. The fruit of conversion is love for one another as brothers and sisters in the new household of God. Love is at the center of who they are as a community, and the chief virtue they are meant to cultivate. Thus, the command here to love one another is reiterated in 2:17 and given as the first rule of community life in 4:8. Love then is the dynamic power for life in the Christian community. It is here, in their love for one another, that they appropriate their eschatological salvation. Growth in moral maturity and in the Christian life is acquired by and shown in an increasingly pure and fervent love for the brethren. Thus, it is correct to root the goal of sincere brotherly love in the purifying act of conversion.

The subordinate participial phrase of verse 23 provides a supporting warrant for the command to love one another. *You have been born anew, not of perishable seed but of imperishable* (οὐκ ἐκ σπορᾶς φθαρτῆς ἀλλὰ ἀφθάρτου), *through the living and abiding word of God* (διὰ λόγου ζῶντος θεοῦ καὶ μένοντος). Once more, the author employs the antithesis of the corruptible and the incorruptible. Here he uses it with reference to the seed by which they were born again – the word of God. Again, the antithesis derives from the nature of their conversion and supplies moral implications. Since the means by which God saved them[59] was the incorruptible seed of the word of God, then their community life is to reflect this same incorruptibility, exhibiting a sincere love from a pure

---

[56] See ACHTEMEIER, *1 Peter*, 136–7, and KELLY, *Peter & Jude*, 79.

[57] Cf. SELWYN, *1 Peter*, 149, notes that ἀλήθεια, 'is peculiarly appropriate here...as pointing the contrast between the truth of Christianity and the falsehood of heathenism (cf. ἀγνοίᾳ, verse 14, ματαίας, verse 18).'

[58] Cf. ACHTEMEIER, *1 Peter*, 137. 'Such sanctified lives have as their goal (telic εἰς) "brotherly love" (φιλαδελφία).'

[59] Whereas the circumstantial participial phrase that precedes the imperative deals with the convert's activity in conversion, here the focus shifts to *God's* activity in salvation, as is shown in the passive participle ἀναγεγεννημένοι.

heart.[60] Thus, we see that the author's portrayal of conversion as a purifying act of obedience, accomplished by means of the incorruptible word of God, provides a framework for his call for moral purity and sincere love. In this way, just as we saw in Greco-Roman paraenesis, the act of conversion becomes paradigmatic for all of life, and the antitheses that arise from conversion acquire a lasting moral validity.

The next two verses (24–25a), quoting Isa. 40:6, 8, elucidate the eternality of the word of God. *For 'All flesh is like grass and all its glory like the flower of grass. The grass withers, and the flower falls, but the word of the Lord abides for ever'* (τὸ δὲ ῥῆμα κυρίου μένει εἰς τὸν αἰῶνα). The poetic contrast here is between the eternality and incorruptibility of the word of the Lord and the fragile mortality and corruption of 'all flesh' (i.e., humanity). As we have seen before, an insurmountable chasm exists between the corruptible and the incorruptible, between those things bound to die and fade away and those eternal, immortal, and incorruptible. The author goes on to remind his readers that their new birth is rooted in the eternal and incorruptible ῥῆμα κυρίου, adding, τοῦτο δέ ἐστιν τὸ ῥῆμα τὸ εὐαγγελισθὲν εἰς ὑμᾶς (25b).

As before, this antithesis carries with it moral import. Thus, in the next verse (2:1), the author enjoins the readers to rid their lives of vices that are representative of human corruptibility and their pre-conversion lives. *So putting away all malice and all guile and insincerity and envy and all slander* ('Αποθέμενοι οὖν πᾶσαν κακίαν καὶ πάντα δόλον καὶ ὑποκρίσεις καὶ φθόνους καὶ πάσας καταλαλιάς). The connection with the thought of the previous verse is emphasized by the particle οὖν. They are to rid their lives of all those practices that do not comport with their new identity as those who have been born again through the incorruptible word of God. It is important to note that the vices of 2:1 all stand in opposition to the fostering of love in the community.[61] The author still has in mind the command of 1:22 to love one another; this is most obvious from the

---

[60] ELLIOTT, *1 Peter*, 387, states that the adverb ἐκτενῶς in the command ἀγαπήσατε ἐκτενῶς should be taken in the sense of 'continually'. He argues that, 'the following verses, which elaborate on the implications of this term, are concerned with the issue of imperishability, permanence, and endurance.' In doing so, he fails to see how 'imperishability, permanence, and endurance' are used as *moral* categories, and comport with love that is sincere and pure. Cf. Eph. 6:24, ἡ χάρις μετὰ πάντων τῶν ἀγαπώντων τὸν κύριον ἡμῶν Ἰησοῦν Χριστὸν ἐν ἀφθαρσίᾳ.

[61] Cf. ACHTEMEIER, *1 Peter*, 144–5, 'Taken together, they represent the kind of attitudes and actions in whose presence true community based on love is impossible.' Technically speaking, all vices are expressions of selfishness that destroy community life, so this is not so startling. The point here is that the author is setting up these vices as barriers to the love he has just commanded.

prohibition of ὑπόκρισις, in direct contrast with the command that love be ἀνυπόκριτος.

Ridding themselves of such vices is only the negative precursor to the author's positive command in 2:2. *Like newborn babes, long for the pure spiritual milk* (ὡς ἀρτιγέννητα βρέφη τὸ λογικὸν ἄδολον γάλα ἐπιποθήσατε), *that by it you may grow up to salvation* (ἵνα ἐν αὐτῷ αὐξηθῆτε εἰς σωτηρίαν). The metaphor of ἀρτιγέννητα βρέφη is an extension of the central metaphor of 'new birth' that pervades this entire section. The focus of the metaphor is on the craving of a newborn for its mother's milk as its only source of life and growth. The import of the metaphor is that the readers are to crave the nourishment of 'spiritual milk' for 'spiritual' growth in salvation. The meaning of τὸ λογικὸν ἄδολον γάλα, and especially τὸ γάλα, is notoriously difficult to unpack.[62]

C. Pure Spiritual Milk

The adjective ἄδολος is the most straightforward, here carrying the sense of 'pure', or more literally, 'guileless', in contrast to the 'guile/deceit' (δόλος) in the vice list in the previous verse. Thus, this 'milk' shares in the moral purity that characterizes all things incorruptible. Λογικός can have the sense of 'spiritual' as opposed to real physical milk, thus indicating the *metaphorical* nature of the milk, but this seems unlikely on two counts. First, the metaphor is already established with the previous phrase ὡς ἀρτιγέννητα βρέφη; in the context there is little chance of taking this milk as literal. Secondly, the author uses πνευματικός to denote both 'a spiritual house' and 'spiritual sacrifices' only three verses later; if his intended meaning is 'spiritual', he could have used πνευματικός here as well.[63]

The sense of λογικός is more likely here to be its more natural sense of 'reasonable', or 'that which is in accord with reason or truth.' This sense is widely attested in Greco-Roman literature and carries with it a strong moral connotation of reasonable in antithesis with the irrational passions (τὸ παθητικόν).[64] Hort notes that this sense fits well in the flow of the entire section, which began by calling its readers to *gird up the loins of your minds* while resisting conformity *to the desires of their former ignorance*, and which calls their conversion an *act of obedience to the truth*.[65] Thus λογικός describes something that is reasonable, in accord with

---

[62] HORT, *1 Peter*, 100, calls this '[a]n unquestionably difficult phrase.'

[63] Cf. MICHAELS, *1 Peter*, 87.

[64] See, e.g., PLUTARCH, *Flatterer*, 61D, '[O]ur soul has its two sides: on the one side are truthfulness, love for what is honourable and power to reason (τὸ μὲν ἀληθινὸν καί φιλόκαλον καὶ λογικὸν ἐχούσης), and on the other side irrationality, love of falsehood, and the emotional element (τὸ δ᾽ ἄλογον καὶ φιλοψευδὲς καὶ παθητικόν).'

[65] See HORT, *1 Peter*, 101.

the truth, and morally sound, not something spiritual in contrast to physical.

With respect to the meaning of τὸ γάλα, commentators find little agreement. Michaels offers the nebulous gloss of: 'the sustaining life of God given in mercy to his children.'[66] A more tangible proposal given by others is to take γάλα as 'the word of God' or 'the gospel', citing as evidence the ῥῆμα κυρίου just mentioned in the previous verse.[67] While this is plausible, the word of God is mentioned in this context for its *regenerative* power, not its power to nourish and cause growth. The word of God is, of course, instrumental in growth and spiritual nourishment, but the fact that this aspect is not in focus here raises doubts about its applicability. Further, where γάλα is used in a metaphorical sense elsewhere in the NT writings (1 Cor. 3:2; Heb. 5:12–14), it is neither used in the sense of 'the word of God' nor 'the gospel'.

In 1 Corinthians Paul uses γάλα to refer to 'elementary teaching', probably doctrinal and ethical, that he gave to the Corinthians, but the context tells us little more. Hebrews is more illustrative. As in 1 Cor. 3, γάλα is used here in a negative context, criticizing the readers for needing 'milk' when they ought to be eating 'solid food.' In Heb. 5:12 γάλα is equated with *the first principles of the word of God* (τὰ στοιχεῖα τῆς ἀρχῆς τῶν λογίων τοῦ θεοῦ). Here 'milk' is connected with the word of God, but the focus is on the 'first principles' of God's revelation; whatever they are. Verse 13 cryptically adds: *for every one who lives on milk is unskilled in the word of righteousness, for he is immature* (πᾶς γὰρ ὁ μετέχων γάλακτος ἄπειρος λόγου δικαιοσύνης, νήπιος γάρ ἐστιν). Verse 14 helps us by filling out the contrast between the immature and the mature.

But solid food is for the mature, for those who have their faculties trained by practice to distinguish good from evil (τελείων δέ ἐστιν ἡ στερεὰ τροφή, τῶν διὰ τὴν ἕξιν τὰ αἰσθητήρια γεγυμνασμένα ἐχόντων πρὸς διάκρισιν καλοῦ τε καὶ κακοῦ). The mature have learned wisdom (Aristotelian φρόνησις), but the immature have not yet acquired the skill of handling the word of righteousness, or of understanding the first principles of God's revelation. Thus, the immature need the milk of instruction that promotes moral growth, so that they can understand first principles and

---

[66] MICHAELS, *1 Peter*, 89. He qualifies his conclusions, however, saying, 'It is doubtful…that the significance of "pure spiritual milk" for Peter can be summed up in just one word or concept' (88).

[67] E.g., ACHTEMEIER, *1 Peter*, 147. 'It would…be appropriate for Christians who were rebegotten by the word of God to yearn for that word so they may experience further growth leading to salvation.' He also argues that 'some relationship between the divine word [λόγος] and the adjective λογικός seems most likely.'

grow in the art of discerning good from evil in each situation.[68] While, we need to be careful not to import too much of Heb. 5 back into 1 Peter 2:2,[69] it seems reasonable to see γάλα there as referring to Christian instruction (doctrinal and ethical) that promotes moral growth, as it does in Hebrews.

This sense of γάλα fits well with our conclusions regarding λογικός. The phrase τὸ λογικὸν ἄδολον γάλα, then, has the sense of 'sound and pure (doctrinal and ethical) instruction.' Γάλα would *include* the word of God as one source of instruction, but is not to be identified with it. This reading also fits well within the context of the letter as we have seen it so far. The appropriation of, or growth in, salvation is accomplished through growth in the moral sphere of life, which is shown in holiness, purity, and a love for fellow Christians. Thus, it is not surprising here that growth in salvation (i.e., in the conformity of one's life to the τέλος of eschatological salvation)[70] is nourished by instruction that encourages this moral growth. The moral nature of this γάλα also explains why the ridding of vices is a logical precondition to craving this instruction,[71] because only those who are engaged in purification are prepared to receive moral instruction.[72]

This subsection concludes in 2:3 with a final warrant for the command to crave the milk that will bring growth in salvation: *for you have tasted that the Lord is good* (εἰ ἐγεύσασθε ὅτι χρηστὸς ὁ κύριος). The phrase,

---

[68] C.R. KOESTER, *Hebrews: A New Translation with Introduction and Commentary*, AB 36 (New York: Doubleday, 2001), 302, takes λόγου δικαιοσύνης as 'reasoning about righteousness' and says that it refers to 'discernment or reasoning about good and evil.' This fits well with our explanation of the content and purpose of the γάλα. This metaphor of milk and solid food was not uncommon in Greco-Roman education. E.g., PHILO, *Husbandry*, 9, 'But seeing that for babes (νηπίοις) milk is food, but for grown men (τελείοις) wheaten bread, there must also be soul-nourishment (ψυχῆς γαλακτώδεις), such as is milk-like suited to the time of childhood, in the shape of the preliminary stages of school-learning, and such as is adapted to grown men, in the shape of instructions leading the way through wisdom and temperance (διὰ φρονήσεως καὶ σωφροσύνης) and all virtue (ἁπάσης ἀπρετῆς).' Milk, corresponded to a young boys education in mathematics/logic, and science, whereas solid food was philosophy/ethics. While using the metaphor, Hebrews does not follow this schema exactly. Milk is not 'doctrine' and solid food 'ethics'. What marks the mature is their moral maturity. If solid food is ethical instruction reserved for the mature, then how are the immature ever to become mature? Therefore, milk is basic Christian teaching including doctrinal and ethical teaching with the aim of growth in moral maturity.

[69] In 1 Peter there is no pejorative connotation to milk, as there is in Heb. (and 1 Cor.), so the need for milk is not a sign of immaturity but youth.

[70] In 2:2 the εἰς in εἰς σωτηρίαν is telic. So also ACHTEMEIER, *1 Peter*, 147.

[71] E. BEST, *1 Peter*, ed. M. BLACK, NCB (London: Oliphants, 1982), 97, notes that, 'Logically the putting away of sin precedes growth in goodness and so verse 1 precedes verse 2; in actual fact both are continuous processes.'

[72] Cf. BEST, *1 Peter*, 97, '[T]he ability to receive spiritual nourishment (the "milk") and the sharing of fellowship with other Christians are interdependent.'

adapted from LXX Ps. 33:9, seems relatively straightforward, but its meaning in the immediate context is far from clear. How does this verse provide a warrant to the command to crave the pure and reasonable milk of instruction? As Selwyn says, 'The meaning of the passage hardly lies on the surface.'[73] Some have seen the image of tasting the Lord as having eucharistic significance in a liturgical setting (especially those that already see baptism as the background).[74] Many others conclude from this clause that Christ himself is the γάλα of the previous verse, arguing that it is reasonable for the readers to crave what they have tasted is good.[75]

In the context, though, ἐγεύσασθε refers most naturally to conversion. Thus, the act of tasting is not a reference to the eucharist, but to the initial experience of the goodness of God in the act of conversion.[76] The confusion of Christ with the milk is another example of a failure to see how the author draws *moral implications* from *ontological categories* like goodness. The emphasis here is that they have tasted the *goodness* of the Lord, not that they have tasted *him*. Χρηστός here, just as in Ps. 33, refers to the moral perfection and trustworthiness of God shown in his redemptive acts.[77] Just as we have seen before, participation in the incorruptible purity (here 'goodness') of God in conversion is the motivation given for purity in life, and thus growth in salvation, or growth toward the teleological eschatological reality of salvation. In this way, this verse not only fits naturally into its context, but also forms a fitting conclusion to this section as a whole. It reminds the readers of the gracious goodness of God, which they experienced in their conversion, and also of their duty to incorporate this goodness into their daily lives as they grow in Christian maturity. It motivates their desire to 'hope fully'.

IV. The Function of the Conversion Strategy

As with Greco-Roman paraenetic, the main function of remembrance in 1 Peter is to clarify fundamental values and commitments. Within the overall paraenetic aim of the epistle, it seeks to promote clarity in the

---

[73] SELWYN, *1 Peter*, 156.

[74] E.g., KELLY, *Peter & Jude*, 87.

[75] So. ELLIOTT, *1 Peter*, 404; BEST, *1 Peter*, 97-99; and BEARE, *1 Peter*, 117.

[76] Cf. SELWYN, *1 Peter*, 156, 'The emphasis must, therefore, lie on the ἐγεύσασθε rather than on its object, the meaning being, "go on growing in grace, now that you have once begun."'

[77] Χρηστός is commonly used in reference to people to refer to their moral goodness. See LSJ, *s.v.* In this context, it does not carry the sense of 'kind', although the goodness of the Lord is shown in his kindness.

development of moral reasoning and to procure the readers' allegiance to God and his program of salvation.

A. Clarifying Values

The antithesis of pre-conversion life with post-conversion life provides a tool for clarifying fundamental values. In 1:14 the author characterizes the pre-conversion lives of his readers as marked by ἄγνοια and ruled by wicked ἐπιθυμίαι. Theirs was a futile way of life, inherited from their forefathers (1:18). With this life, he associates a catalog of vices: malice, deceit, hypocrisy, envy, and slander (2:1). In contradistinction to this are those values that characterize the new life after conversion: sincere love (1:22), holiness (1:15), self-control (1:13), and obedience (1:22).

The author admits no 'gray area' where these realities of virtues and vices commingle; the antithesis in absolute. This antithesis is reinforced by the author's rooting of moral values in the distinction of the corruptible and the incorruptible; a distinction that is both indisputable and absolute. Everyone recognizes that precious metals rust and decay and in this respect are in absolute antithesis with things eternal. Through this ontological antithesis the author underlines the absolute moral antithesis of good and evil.

These stark antitheses are important because all people live in the gray area where virtue and vice alike find a home in the human heart. This is why values need the clarifying light of antitheses, to distill what becomes confused in the soul. But antithesis not only clarifies moral reasoning; it also calls for commitment. While one quickly recognizes that ὑπόκρισις is antithetical to φιλαδελφία ἀνυπόκριτος, *practicing* love free from artifice comes less easily.

B. Clarifying Commitments

By introducing moral antithesis (an 'either/or'), our author is calling for a choice of allegiance to one side or the other; there are no middle positions. (As the philosopher in Diogenes' story said, 'there are only two roads, not many.') But our author is not simply *asking* his readers to choose; he is *shaping* their choice. This is why he disparages the wickedness of their pre-conversion existence, and extols their new life of holiness, self-control, and love.

Of course, he recognizes that their lives are not so easily compartmentalized. Their existence prior to conversion, no doubt had some good elements, and their life since has without question not been one of absolute moral purity, which is presupposed in his call to be rid of particular vices in 2:1. But the real issue is, what *principle* shaped their ἀναστροφή before conversion and what *principle* directs their ἀναστροφή since?

Rhetorically, the author's portrayal of the *nature* of conversion is essential to his agenda. He associates their pre-conversion life with their vices, and then he detaches them absolutely from that life. They have been 'born anew.' They are living a completely new existence as 'children of obedience.' There is no conceptual room for a mixture of their lives before and after conversion. They are thus completely disconnected from their previous existence. The reality of the situation, which the author recognizes, is that they do live an existence that is a mixture of the old and the new, but by drawing sharp antitheses, the author is helping to strengthen their commitments to their new life and cut their commitments to the old. It is also important in this regard that the nature of conversion is irreversibly in addition to being absolute. New birth is a completely new existence, but more important, it is irreversible; one cannot be unborn. Thus, the author utilizes the antithesis of conversion to shape the readers' commitment to their new life.

Antithesis is also used to strengthen their commitment to God and his program of salvation. As we saw above, conversion involves not only *their* decision, but also the saving will of God. It is he who has given them new birth through the gospel. In his saving actions toward them God has revealed his character, which stands in antithesis to all evil and all rival hopes. To be a member of God's family means to act as he does. Communion with a holy God, who is free from all vice, demands the same standard of conduct. So, in 1:15 the author commands them to be holy as God is holy.

In addition, as we saw most clearly in 1:19–20, the author sets up God as a rival to all counterfeit objects of their hope by extolling his graciousness toward them in Christ. His aim is to win the absolute allegiance of his hearers to God, to give them *reason* to hope fully in the salvation that is coming to them (1:13). God, who is eternal in nature and faithful to his promises, is the surest object of their trust.

By winning the readers' allegiance to God, the author also wins their commitment to the project of salvation. It is their experience of the goodness of the Lord in conversion (2:3) that is the basis for the author's command to seek out sound instruction in order to grow in salvation (2:2).

V. Conclusion

Antithesis is at the heart of the paraenetic enterprise. As Libanius said, 'Paraenesis is divided into two parts, encouragement and dissuasion (προτροπὴν καὶ ἀποτροπήν).'[78] Facilitating moral growth means advocating virtues and deprecating vices in order to clarify moral values and educate affective commitments.

In the context of conversion, we saw that Greco-Roman paraenetic authors use the literary strategy of remembrance to emphasize the centrality of the act of conversion as a life-defining moment, drawing an antithesis between life before and after conversion. Paraenetic authors engage in the practice of remembrance to exhort their readers to live a life consistent with the path of life they embraced in their conversion.

Likewise, in 1 Peter, our author utilizes the paraenetic literary strategy of remembrance to clarify values and commitments for his readers. He denigrates their pagan lifestyle before conversion as ἡ ματαία ἀναστροφή πατροπαράδοτος (1:18), characterized by both ἄγνοια and ἐπιθυμίαι (1:14). In contrast to this, he extols the purity, love, and holiness that characterize their new lives since conversion. This shift is not only a product of their own choice to call on God as Father (1:17) and obey the truth (1:22), but it is also a product of God's saving activity in giving them new birth (1:3, 23). It is he who has made them τέκνα ὑπακοῆς. The author's motive is to clarify for his readers the moral implications of these absolute antitheses by calling for a break with their pre-conversion ἀναστροφή.

Our author also utilizes the antithesis of corruptibility and incorruptibility to draw moral implications from ontological categories. He further associates pre-conversion existence with all that is earthly, mortal, and corruptible (e.g., silver, gold, perishable seed, grass), while at the same time associating conversion and post-conversion life with things heavenly, immortal and incorruptible (e.g., precious blood of Christ, word of God). The author's purpose is to remind his readers that their new life is one that is characterized by moral incorruptibility, because it comes from the immortal God through his incorruptible word.

In these various ways, the author of 1 Peter appropriates, with particular creativity and agility, the paraenetic literary strategy of remembrance to suit his paraenetic agenda of facilitating growth in Christian character within the communities he is addressing. His focus is on promoting moral integrity that is consistent with their new ἀναστροφή, which aids growth in both moral maturity and practical dependence on God.

---

[78] (PSEUDO-) LIBANIUS, *Epistolary Styles*, 5.

Chapter Five

Identity and 'Soft' Difference

In this third and final chapter on paraenetic theology in 1 Peter we will look at another aspect of the story of the salvation which God has brought about in the Anatolian churches. In the previous chapter, we saw how conversion demarcates an ethical dividing line between the immoral pagan lifestyle, which characterized life prior to conversion, and ἡ καλὴ ἀναστροφή, which accompanies faith. In addition, we saw how the author used this antithesis to further his paraenetic agenda by calling on his readers to abandon their pre-conversion lifestyle while embracing their new life.

In this chapter, we will examine how our author extends this dividing line to establish the social identity of the church as a distinct group vis-à-vis the surrounding pagan culture. Since the addressees have made a break with their pagan ways in conversion, the question of how they are to relate to their unbelieving neighbors and friends is a natural one for these communities. The author's answer is to reinforce their cultural distinctiveness as a unique people – a community called by God. Thus, their break with the past is extended from the individual level to the corporate as the new λαὸς θεοῦ. Our focus then for this chapter will be on the author's construction of a social identity for the church as a distinct chosen people, and the author's paraenetic agenda of reinforcing their commitment to moral reform by promoting a moral distinctiveness that avoids cultural isolationism.

The social agenda of 1 Peter has long been recognized as a distinctive feature of the letter,[1] but has been given increased attention in recent decades in the wake of Elliott's influential socio-scientific study *A Home for the Homeless*. Our procedure here will be to evaluate Elliott's description of the social aims of the author after an exegetical examination of our key passage: 2:4–10.

In the previous chapter, we saw how conversion was used as a literary strategy both in Greco-Roman paraenetic literature and in 1 Peter. Here however, the literary strategy of creating and reinforcing a social/group

---

[1] The first modern scholarly study on the subject was T. Spörri, *Der Gemeindegedanke im ersten Petrusbrief: Ein Beitrag zur Struktur des urchristlichen Kirchenbegriffs*, NTF 2.2 (Gütersloh: Bertelsmann, 1925).

identity finds no substantial correlate in Greco-Roman paraenetic epistles.[2] The main reason for this is that these epistolary traditions are, on the whole, confined to correspondence between *individuals*, and not to or from groups. In addition, an emphasis on group identity as a motivator for ethical living is almost completely absent in Hellenistic philosophy. The emphasis was much more focused on the individual as the locus of responsibility, action, and reform. It should be noted, however, that the Hellenistic schools did see close friendships within the circle of the school as an important characteristic of virtuous living. In addition, some schools formed separated communities (e.g., Pythagoreans and Epicureans) in which to practice their philosophy in relative isolation from the wider culture.[3] So, while social ties were important, and while the philosophic schools faced many of the same social issues of moral distinctiveness faced by the young Christian churches, the *strategies* used to address those problems were different.[4]

The chief difference in strategy comes in the use by Christian authors of corporate identity as a motivational tool. The absence of this approach in Greco-Roman paraenetic literature corresponds to the previously noted absence of 'meta-narrative' in Greco-Roman philosophy. In its construction of a social identity for the church, 1 Peter appropriates OT traditions of Israel as a distinct people called by God, for whom God's action in the world (i.e., the meta-narrative of salvation) is the basis for corporate identity. As Birch notes, 'For the Hebrew Bible the community receives its identity from divine initiative.'[5] Israelite, and later Christian, collective identity is rooted in the reality of the electing grace of God. Since this idea of the meta-narrative of God's redemptive actions is absent from Greco-Roman philosophy, so also is the social identity drawn from it in Jewish and Christian traditions.

As we have noted before, meta-narratives are intimately connected with moral action and character formation. Sociologists Somers and Gibson observe, 'Ontological narratives are used to define who we are; this in turn

---

[2] This is why in this chapter we are beginning with an exegetical study, whereas our normal pattern has been to study a particular paraenetic literary strategy and then see how that strategy was appropriated in 1 Peter. Here, since there is no correlate, we are beginning with exegesis and then moving on to evaluations of current theories and how they relate to the overall paraenetic agenda of the epistle.

[3] Cf. ASCOUGH, 'Associations,' 5–8.

[4] Acknowledging this difference, we will note below some basic similarities of approach between Seneca and 1 Peter.

[5] B.C. BIRCH, 'Moral Agency, Community, and the Character of God in the Hebrew Bible,' *Semeia* 66 (1995): 29.

is a precondition for knowing what to do.'[6] Because meta-narratives act as a context for moral actions, they are instrumental in the formation of character. As Bondi says, 'human beings are creatures formed in communities marked by allegiance to a normative story, and...this formation can best be discussed in the language of character.'[7] In applying this to ancient Israel, Birch argues that, 'For Israel, new identity is the necessary context for formation as moral community.'[8]

In turning to 1 Peter, then, it is not surprising that we find our author appropriating key phrases from the OT that articulate the identity of Israel as a unique people chosen and saved by God. Since our author's concern is with moral formation and character growth, the emphasis on social identity is a natural choice given the Jewish roots of his thinking. In promoting the social identity of these churches as distinct from the surrounding culture, he not only strengthens their cohesion as a group, but also provides them with interpretive images through which they can contemplate their moral agency at the corporate and personal level.[9]

I. Election, Identity, and Rejection

As a literary unit 1 Peter 2:4–10 is the conclusion/culmination of the first major section of the letter (1:3–2:10). The theme of the great ἔλεος of God, which opened this section in 1:3, is reiterated in the identification of the readers as those who have been shown mercy in 2:10.[10] The story of this mercy, having just focused on conversion, now devotes itself to God's creation of a new community of the redeemed. The movement here is from individual conversion to corporate identity.[11] As we will see below, this

---

[6] M.R. SOMERS and G.D. GIBSON, 'Reclaiming the Epistemological "Other": Narrative and the Social Construction of Identity,' in *Social Theory and the Politics of Identity*, ed. C. CALHOUN (Oxford: Blackwell, 1994), 61.

[7] R. BONDI, 'The Elements of Character,' *JRE* 12 (1984): 201, cited by B.C. BIRCH, 'Divine Character and the Formation of Moral Community in the Book of Exodus,' in *The Bible in Ethics: The Second Sheffield Colloquium*, JSOTSS 207 (Sheffield: Sheffield Academic Press, 1995), 122–3. SOMERS and GIBSON, 'Narrative and Identity,' 61, argue that, 'Ontological narratives make identity and the self something that one *becomes*.'

[8] BIRCH, 'Divine Character,' 133.

[9] Cf. W. MARXSEN, *New Testament Foundations for Christian Ethics*, trans. O.C. DEAN (Edinburgh: T & T Clark, 1993), 265, 'The author does not make statements that are crucial for his ethics by telling his readers what they must do, but by talking to them about *who they are*, how they became who they are, how that can be translated into concrete behavior and action, and what the resulting consequences are for them personally.'

[10] Cf. ELLIOTT, *1 Peter*, 407.

[11] So also MICHAELS, *1 Peter*, 93.

corporate identity forms the foundation for the epistle's social ethics with respect to both outsiders and those within the οἶκος of God.

Divine election, as Elliott notes, 'permeates this unit from start to finish,' and operates as the unit's 'integrating theme.'[12] For our author, God's activity in election is not focused primarily on salvation for the *individual*, but principally refers to his activity in forming a new *people*. The numerous titles used to encapsulate the corporate identity of the readers reflect an identity rooted in the saving activity of God. In addition, their identity is also linked to God's elect son Jesus Christ. As God's chosen Messiah he is the foundation stone for the house of God.

Tied to these two themes of identity and election is a third – the rejection of the elect. Just as Jesus was rejected, so also the church will be rejected. Identity breeds difference. Generally speaking, the same boundaries that define who is a member of a group also define who is outside. Every group has what sociologists refer to as an 'other' (i.e., outsiders). Here, those who reject Christ and the people of God are the 'other'. These three themes of election, identity, and rejection are the major threads knit together to form this unit. All three are introduced in verses 4–5, and given scriptural 'proofs' and expansion in verses 6–10.

The transition from the previous unit is jarring at first; 2:3 ends with *you have tasted that the Lord is good*, and 2:4 begins with *coming to him the living stone* (πρὸς ὃν προσερχόμενοι λίθον ζῶντα). In fact, both of these phrases are images of conversion drawn from LXX Ps. 33.[13] The *emphasis* of the latter image however is not on conversion *itself*, as in the former case, but on the 'stone', and with it the activity of God in building a community of those coming to Christ. The image of living stone is continued in verse 5 where it is applied to believers. *Like living stones you are being built into a spiritual house* (οἶκος πνευματικὸς), *to be a holy priesthood* (ἱεράτευμα ἅγιον), *to offer spiritual sacrifices* (πνευματικὰς θυσίας) *acceptable to God through Jesus Christ.* As converts are coming to Jesus, God is building them together (divine passive: οἰκοδομεῖσθε) into an οἶκος πνευματικὸς on the foundation stone of Christ.[14] That the Christians are called 'living stones' shows that their life and identity are drawn from connection with Christ.[15] His designation as a 'living stone' refers to his resurrection life and that he, as Selwyn puts it, 'communicates life to those who come to Him in faith.'[16]

---

[12] ELLIOTT, *1 Peter*, 411.

[13] 2:3 adopts the language of LXX Ps. 33:9 [MT 34:9], γεύσασθε καὶ ἴδετε ὅτι χρηστὸς ὁ κύριος, and 2:4a takes up 33:6, προσέλθατε πρὸς αὐτόν.

[14] See HORT, *1 Peter*, 105.

[15] So also ELLIOTT, *1 Peter*, 413.

[16] SELWYN, *1 Peter*, 159.

In verse 4 we learn that, although Christ was rejected (ἀποδοκιμάζω) by men, in God's sight he is ἐκλεκτός and ἔντιμος. Here our themes of election and rejection are applied to Christ. In an act of reversal, God honors his chosen who was rejected by men. The language of honor and shame, prevalent in the entire epistle, is especially concentrated in this unit.[17] This is not surprising given the important place of honor and shame in the social structures of the ancient world.[18] It is especially important to our author here because he is constructing a *competing* paradigm of honor and shame.[19] Here God honors what men have rejected.

This paradigm is intentionally transferable to the church, the living stones that make up the new community. As Achtemeier says, '[I]f the Christian community is elect and precious to God because it is based on Christ who is elect and precious to God, then it is also true that as that elect and precious Christ was rejected by human beings (2:4b) so will be the community constituted by him (2:7b–8).'[20] This explains why the rejection of Christ, which historically belongs to the history of Israel, is generalized as ὑπὸ ἀνθρώπων. It is meant to apply paradigmatically to the Christian community as well, to speak of their election by God and their rejection by men – in their case by their pagan neighbors. Thus, their new honor/shame, election/rejection paradigm is derived from their identification with Christ.

Election then is the line that distinguishes them from the 'other', and establishes their identity as the ones who are rejected by the larger culture. But election also establishes their corporate identity positively, by honoring the Christians as a people chosen by God for a special purpose. God is building them into an οἶκος πνευματικὸς εἰς ἱεράτευμα ἅγιον.

The meaning of οἶκος πνευματικός is not easily decrypted. We can begin by saying that the 'house' is obviously metaphorical. While οἶκος can mean simply 'dwelling', whether simple or palatial, in Jewish and Christian literature it is often used to refer to the Temple as 'God's house'. Most interpreters would take οἶκος πνευματικός as a reference to a 'spiritual temple' – a community of believers in which God dwells.[21] 1 Cor. 3:16–17 speaks of believers as the ναὸς θεοῦ in this sense.[22] This

---

[17] See B.L. CAMPBELL, *Honor, Shame, and the Rhetoric of 1 Peter*, SBLDS 160 (Atlanta: Scholars Press, 1998), 83–85.

[18] See B.J. MALINA, *The New Testament World: Insights from Cultural Anthropology*, 3rd ed. (Louisville, KY: Westminster John Knox, 2001), 27–57.

[19] See J.H. ELLIOTT, 'Disgraced Yet Graced: The Gospel According to 1 Peter in the Key of Honor and Shame,' *BTB* 25.4 (1995): 172–4.

[20] ACHTEMEIER, *1 Peter*, 152.

[21] E.g., SELWYN, *1 Peter*, 286–91, and ACHTEMEIER, *1 Peter*, 154–9.

[22] The Qumran community also understood themselves in terms of the Temple; see 1QS, 4Q174, and 4Q400.

interpretation is especially fitting in the context of 'priesthood' and (as we will see shortly) 'spiritual sacrifices'. Against this Elliott proposes that οἶκος be taken in the sense of 'household',[23] which is certainly a viable option.[24] At first it may seem as though Elliott is splitting hairs by distinguishing the complementary senses of 'temple' and 'community', but in the end he is correct.

The first difficulty with taking οἶκος πνευματικός to mean 'spiritual temple' is that the next phrase describes the readers as a 'holy priesthood'. First they *are* the temple, and then they are the priests *in* the temple. The mixing of metaphors is jarring; although insufficient in itself to disqualify this interpretation, it does raise doubts. The more substantial difficulty with this reading is that 'temple' is not a group descriptor. All of the other titles given here and in 2:9 have an adjective and a noun where the noun denotes a group: holy *priesthood*, chosen *race*, royal *priesthood*, holy *nation*, God's own *people*. In short, these are all *collective nouns*. Following this pattern, it is better to take οἶκος in the sense of 'household', or 'family'.[25] Thus, God is 'building them into a spiritual household to be a holy priesthood.' In addition, taking οἶκος in the sense of 'household' fits more easily with its use later in 4:17, where no cultic connotations cloud the issue. The designation of this household as 'spiritual' points both to its

---

[23] ELLIOTT, *1 Peter*, 414–8.

[24] See BDAG, *s.v.* §2.

[25] Commentators who take οἶκος in the sense of 'temple' would say that it *is* a group descriptor because, while the *sense* is that of metaphorical building, the *referent* is the community. (Linguists recognize a distinction between 'sense' (what a word *means*) and 'referent' (what a word *refers to*). See D. CRYSTAL, *A Dictionary of Linguistics and Phonetics*, ed. D. CRYSTAL, 4th ed., *The Language Library* (Oxford: Blackwell, 1997), 347, *s.v.* 'sense'.) As a community, the Christian church becomes a 'spiritual temple'. (E.g., see ACHTEMEIER, *1 Peter*, 155–6, where οἶκος is both a 'group' and a 'place'.) Again, the difficulty with this is that all of the other descriptors connote 'group' in terms of *both* sense and referent. Not only do they refer to the community but their senses also express an idea of community. Technically, they all share a semantic field that does not include 'temple'. That 'temple' is taken metaphorically makes no difference. At least three of the other titles ('race', 'nation', and 'priesthood') are used here metaphorically since none of these are to be taken in the 'literal' sense, which they possessed in their original contexts in the OT.

The reason why commentators are driven to take οἶκος as both a building and a people is that actually both are implied here. As we have seen, all of the other titles denote a people, but at the same time the metaphor of living stones being built up leads one towards the idea of a building. One has to resolve this tension somehow, but taking οἶκος to mean both temple and community is problematic for the reasons just mentioned. Rather, it should be taken as a play on the word οἶκος, where the author is using the word in the sense of 'household', while also playing on the *connotation* of 'house', as a building under construction. The same wordplay is operative, with a slightly different sense, in Eph. 2:19–22.

origins in the electing activity of God, and to the connection that binds all the members of this family together. Elliott argues that, '*Oikos pneumatikos* (*oikos tou theou* [4:17]) constitutes the root metaphor for Christian community in 1 Peter, the fundamental concept that identifies the collective identity of the Christians, their relation to God and to one another, and the basis of their behavior as a family or brotherhood.'[26]

Our author continues by pointing to the purpose for which God has created this spiritual family: *to be a holy priesthood, to offer spiritual sacrifices acceptable to God through Jesus Christ* (εἰς ἱεράτευμα ἅγιον ἀνενέγκαι πνευματικὰς θυσίας εὐπροσδέκτους [τῷ] θεῷ διὰ Ἰησοῦ Χριστοῦ). The title 'holy priesthood' is meant to add another layer to the community's identity as a household, and to encapsulate the identity of the church in relation to its vocation before God. The rare word ἱεράτευμα is taken from LXX Exod. 19:6,[27] where it is a title given by God to Israel at Sinai that identifies them as his chosen people. God calls Israel a βασίλειον ἱεράτευμα[28] καὶ ἔθνος ἅγιον. While both of these titles are used in 2:9, here in verse 5 they are conflated to form the single image of a ἱεράτευμα ἅγιον. The main thrust of this title is the same as it was for Israel, to set off this community as the elect and holy people of God, as Elliott has rightly emphasized.[29] This title also describes the community's vocation as a priesthood that offers spiritual sacrifices. It is not *only* an identity marker, it also denotes purpose.[30] But in what sense are they a 'priesthood', and what are πνευματικὰς θυσίας? Perhaps answering the second question will help us with the first.

Beginning with the most obvious point, spiritual sacrifices, like literal sacrifices, are acts of worship. Therefore, this community of priests is meant to offer praise to its God as spelled out in the complementary purpose clause given in verse 9. As recipients of his grace, they are to honor God by proclaiming his great deeds (ἀρεταί) of salvation. In

---

[26] ELLIOTT, *1 Peter*, 418. He also notes that, 'Familial imagery pervades this composition from beginning to end, and the model of household/family serves as the dominant ecclesial metaphor though which its consolation and exhortation are integrated' (418).

[27] As ELLIOTT, *1 Peter*, 419, notes, 'The word *hierateuma* here and in v 9 is unique in the NT. Its absence in secular Greek and its occurrence elsewhere only in LXX Exod. 19:6 (repeated in LXX Exod. 23:22 but not in the MT) decisively indicates its derivation from LXX Exod. 19:6.'

[28] There is a degree of disparity between the MT and LXX here. In the MT Israel is called מַמְלֶכֶת כֹּהֲנִים ('a kingdom of priests'), but in the LXX this becomes βασίλειον ἱεράτευμα ('a royal priesthood').

[29] See ELLIOTT, *1 Peter*, 419–23, and J.H. ELLIOTT, *The Elect and the Holy: An Exegetical Examination of 1 Peter 2:4–10 and the Phrase βασίλειον ἱεράτευμα*, NovTSup 12 (Leiden: E. J. Brill, 1966), 50–128.

[30] On the 'telic' force of this clause see ACHTEMEIER, *1 Peter*, 156.

addition, πνευματικὰς θυσίας also include conduct that reflects a call out of darkness and into light. As Elliott notes, 'Since the time of the prophets, thanksgiving and righteous conduct were considered equivalent, and in some instances superior, to animal sacrifices.'[31] He adds that, 'Among Israelites of the Diaspora for whom sacrifice at the Jerusalem Temple was not always possible, the equation of praise and moral conduct with such sacrifices was particularly welcomed.'[32] So, within Israel's history a precedent already exists for a moral connotation to 'spiritual sacrifices,' and it is this tradition that stands behind the usage here. As Michaels argues, 'In 1 Peter, as in Hebrews [13:15–16], the "spiritual sacrifices" are first of all something offered up to God as worship (ἀνενέγκαι) and, second, a pattern of social conduct.'[33] This emphasis on conduct is confirmed in the description of this priesthood as ἅγιον, which implies these 'priests' are morally upright as well as set apart by God.

It is important to note that our author has used two titles to describe the community's identity: οἶκος πνευματικὸς and ἱεράτευμα ἅγιον. The first relates to the community's identity as a family brought together by God, while the second relates to their identity as a worshipping community. The first image emphasizes the love and mutual belonging of the family. The second image emphasizes the glorification of God as the final motivation for all action. Thus, augmenting Elliott who focuses on the first of these aspects, these *twin* 'root metaphors' of οἶκος πνευματικός and ἱεράτευμα ἅγιον act as controlling images over the author's prescriptions for community life.

In the verses that follow 'scripture proofs' are adduced from three OT texts that build on the themes of election and rejection. Many keywords from these proofs have already been introduced in verses 4–5, but the primary keyword is λίθος, which links the proof texts to each other as well as to verses 4–5. Verse 6 begins the 'chain' (loosely quoting LXX Isa. 28:16): *For it stands in scripture: 'Behold, I am laying in Zion a stone* (ἰδοὺ τίθημι ἐν Σιὼν λίθον), *a cornerstone chosen and precious* (ἐκλεκτὸν ἔντιμον), *and he who believes in him will not be put to shame* (ὁ πιστεύων ἐπ' αὐτῷ οὐ μὴ καταισχυνθῇ).' This goes to substantiate the claim in verse 4 that Jesus is the living stone who is chosen and honored by God. The other focus of this text is that believers in Jesus will be rescued from shame. The next verse makes this connection explicit: *So to you honor as those who believe* (ὑμῖν οὖν ἡ τιμὴ τοῖς πιστεύουσιν). To those who believe God bestows honor. Again, the honor/shame motif is hard to miss.

---

[31] ELLIOTT, *1 Peter*, 421–2. He cites Hos. 6:6; Isa. 1:10–17; Ps. 49:13–23; 50:17–19; Amos 5:23; Mic. 6:6–8.

[32] ELLIOTT, *1 Peter*, 422. He cites Sir. 35:1; Jdt. 16:16; 2 En. 45:3; *Let. Aris.* 234.

[33] MICHAELS, *1 Peter*, 101.

Here honor is tied explicitly to belief in God's chosen one. Belief, as the correlate to election, is the demarcating feature between the Christian community, who are honored, and those outside who are shamed. As we are told in verse 7 (quoting LXX Ps. 117:22), those who do not believe become like the builders who rejected the stone, which later became the cornerstone, the stone of honor. Again, divine reversal turns the scales of honor and shame on their head. In verse 8a their rejection of the stone translates into their downfall and shame. The author briefly explains the metaphor, which is not difficult to decipher, that non-believers *stumble because they disobey the word* (προσκόπτουσιν τῷ λόγῳ ἀπειθοῦντες), where the word is the gospel message (cf. 4:17). He adds that unbelief, disobedience, and stumbling are what God destined (τίθημι) them for.[34]

The main *theme* of these verses is election/honor and rejection/shame, but the *focus* of these verses is on Christ the λίθος.[35] In addition, while Christ is the focus of attention, the main *actor* is God. It is he who places the stone in Zion, and it is he who exalts the stone after it has been rejected (thereby making it a stone of stumbling). It is he who will not allow those who believe in the stone to be shamed, and it is he who consigns the disobedient to ignominy. The result is two distinct groups: those who believe and those who do not. To those who trust in God's elect one, he gives honor, and to those who reject his elect, shame. In the divine paradigm of honor, attachment to his elect 'stone' is the only criterion that separates honor from shame; wealth, citizenship, occupation, familial ties, and possessions are all brushed aside as means of procuring honor.

Faith is the dividing line that separates the honored people of God from the remainder of humanity. Faith and its divine counterpart election determine identity and difference. This is especially clear in verse 9 where the communal titles pile on top of one another. *But you are a chosen race, a royal priesthood, a holy nation, God's own people* (ὑμεῖς δὲ γένος ἐκλεκτόν, βασίλειον ἱεράτευμα, ἔθνος ἅγιον, λαὸς εἰς περιποίησιν). The emphasis here is on a unique race/nation/people, whose identity is derived from their divine election; hence the priority of the first title γένος ἐκλεκτός. The author constructs an emphatic contrast (ὑμεῖς δέ) with those in the previous verse who were not elected to favor but destined to disobedience, thus underlining the polarity of identity and difference, and its origin in the mystery of the divine will. But the real focus of attention here is on the unique communal identity of the elect people of God. As has already been mentioned, each of these titles uses a collective noun denoting a 'community': γένος, ἱεράτευμα, ἔθνος, λαός. The plurality of

---

[34] Cf. ACHTEMEIER, *1 Peter*, 162–3.
[35] Cf. MICHAELS, *1 Peter*, 93, '[the author] comes to ecclesiology by way of Christology.'

titles is not meant to define multiple identities or roles, but to attest to the multifaceted reality of their single identity as the elect people of God. Rhetorically, the multiple titles also possess a cumulative weight that reinforces the reality of this identity.

Verse 10, the final verse in this section, reminds the readers that their new identity is rooted in a story – the meta-narrative of God's saving actions – *Once you were no people but now you are God's people* (οἵ ποτε οὐ λαὸς νῦν δὲ λαὸς θεοῦ); *once you had not received mercy but now you have received mercy* (οἱ οὐκ ἠλεημένοι νῦν δὲ ἐλεηθέντες). Just as we saw in the previous chapter, an absolute distinction is drawn between life before and after conversion, but here it is transposed into the key of social identity. Before, they possessed no identity (οὐ λαός), but now they are the honored people of God. Now they are collectively known simply as οἱ ἐλεηθέντες. And thus, we return to the theme of τὸ πολὺ ἔλεος, with which we began in 1:3. It is a fitting conclusion (as well as inclusion) that here identity is tied to being receivers of mercy. Their identity is rooted in the story of God's salvation story. But it is this derivative identity that gives a framework for their action, as a people who have been shown mercy.

This is also a fitting conclusion because it returns to the main point of this unit. While we have focused on issues of identity and difference, the 'other' is only a minor theme at present. Up to this point, nothing has been said *explicitly* about how the people of God are to relate to outsiders, although a great deal is already implied. As yet, rejection and difference are introduced in relation to Christ only, with *implications* for the community of the elect. The focus here is not yet on social ethics, but on communal identity rooted in the saving activity of God.[36] That said, this communal identity is purposefully constructed to provide a basis for social action, as will become clear in the following verses.

II. Aliens and Strangers

To answer our question about the relationship of the people of God to the surrounding pagan culture it is necessary to extend our exegetical study to include the two verses that follow: 2:11–12. These verses are the transition zone between the first major section of the epistle (1:3–2:10) and the second major section (2:13–4:19), where the social ethics of the epistle are made explicit. As Elliott notes, 'The linguistic and thematic links between these verses and what precedes and follows indicate their function as a *transitional statement* in which the moral and social implications of

---

[36] Cf. MICHAELS, *1 Peter*, 113. 'Peter's focus is on who they are before God, not on how they must behave in Roman society.'

the foregoing (1:3–2:10) are now introduced.'[37] These verses augment the preceding verses with additional identity images, which are focused on the relationship of the church to the outside world, and proclaim the centrality of righteous conduct in relationships with outsiders. Calling them πάροικοι and παρεπίδημοι, the author exhorts them to abstain from fleshly desires and to maintain their good ἀναστροφή among the 'Gentiles'.

To understand the thrust of this exhortation and the social ethics of the epistle we need first to understand these two additional identity markers πάροικοι and παρεπίδημοι. In recent years, Elliott has provided a great deal of both clarity and confusion on this issue, and has received some praise for the former, and ample criticism for the latter.[38] While rightly reacting against a 'spiritualized' interpretation of 'strangers on earth' awaiting their home in heaven, he has tended to overemphasize the 'literal' social status implied in these words. His basic argument[39] is that πάροικοι and παρεπίδημοι refer to the social status, *prior to conversion*, of Christians who have, since conversion, found a sense of belonging in the οἶκος τοῦ θεοῦ. After documenting that the literal sense of these words, as social status markers (πάροικος = 'resident alien', and παρεπίδημος = 'stranger'), dominates their utilization in the LXX as well as in secular Greek, he argues that this 'requires the assumption of a literal sense unless the context *requires* a metaphorical sense.'[40] So the readers are not 'strangers and aliens' in a spiritual sense, but in a literal socio-political sense.

That established, he goes on to argue that these words are not to be taken *only* literally, rather they are *both* literal and metaphorical. Recognizing the unlikelihood that all members of the churches addressed in this epistle were from a single social caste, he argues that *some* of the Christians were literal πάροικοι and παρεπίδημοι before conversion and that their pre-conversion social existence became paradigmatic for the *whole* community, as believers living lives of estrangement from the values that dominated life in the pagan world. Thus, the literal sense of social status,

---

[37] ELLIOTT, *1 Peter*, 456. Italics original. Also see his 'Detailed Comment' supporting this on pp. 474–6.

[38] His book *Home* received 30 reviews (see A. CASURELLA, *Bibliography of Literature on First Peter*, NTTS 23 (Leiden: Brill, 1996), 84) and a monograph in response: R. FELDMEIER, *Die Christen als Fremde: Die Metapher der Fremde in der antiken Welt, im Urchristentum und im 1. Petrusbrief*, WUNT 64 (Tübingen: Mohr (Siebeck), 1992).

[39] To be fair to ELLIOTT, where possible, I am using his statements from his commentary as his most recent expression of his views originally developed in *Home*.

[40] ELLIOTT, *1 Peter*, 461. Italics original. As to merits of this particular point, semantics is not a matter of statistics but of context. What a word mean elsewhere is not determinative for its meaning in a particular instance. Context determines the sense of a word from a range of possible senses.

which applied to *some* of the community, becomes transposed into a metaphorical sense for the *whole* community.[41] So, according to Elliott, the usage of πάροικοι and παρεπίδημοι in 1 Peter refers *metaphorically* to the social status of the *whole* community as a *result* of conversion.

Here Elliott's dichotomy between 'literal' and 'metaphorical' uses proves problematic. In reality, at issue here are one literal sense and *two* metaphorical senses. Elliott sets up a dichotomy of literal strangerhood versus metaphorical 'cosmic' strangerhood. But there is another metaphorical sense in play here, and that is the sense in which these Christians are strangers and aliens because they experience estrangement as a community with a decidedly different ethos than the wider culture in which they live. This strangerhood is something that they possess as a distinct people called by God. It is in this *second* metaphorical sense that Elliott argues these Christian communities are 'aliens and strangers'. When he rejects the metaphorical use of these terms, he is rejecting the first, and when he accepts the metaphorical usage he is accepting the second. So these Christians are metaphorical resident aliens, not because they are 'cosmically' estranged, as 'citizens of heaven', but because they live as a community distinct from their surroundings, and therefore experience a social estrangement *analogous* to literal πάροικοι and παρεπίδημοι.

What about Elliott's assertion that these terms are both literal and metaphorical? If it is true, we will find no evidence for it in the text. Once we admit that these terms are used metaphorically, there is no way to stuff a literal meaning back into them,[42] and no evidence that we ought to. As with all of the communal titles we have seen in 2:9 (γένος, ἱεράτευμα, ἔθνος, λαός), these two identity markers are both (1) metaphorical and (2) a result of election, which can be seen clearly in 1:1, where the churches are addressed as ἐκλεκτοὶ παρεπίδημοι. While Elliott is correct to find in 1 Peter the idea of a people without status finding status as God's people

---

[41] See ELLIOTT, *1 Peter*, 481. '[I]t is neither necessary nor advisable to require an absolute distinction between literal and figurative usage with respect to these Petrine terms. It is conceivable that their usage here reflects an historical process in which the condition of *some* addressees as actual strangers and resident aliens provided the experiential basis for eventually characterizing the condition of *all* Christians in a secular society.'

[42] If we say that πάροικοι and παρεπίδημοι describe metaphorically the post-conversion experience of the whole community, then we cannot, at the same time, say that they also describe literally the pre-conversion experience of some of the community. This would mean that these terms have not only dual senses but also dual referents. This does not exclude entirely the possibility that ELLIOTT's proposed history of these terms is true; it simply means that the text can give us no evidence to support the claim. This is one of the core problems of ELLIOTT's theory; on this point it is neither verifiable nor falsifiable.

(οἵ ποτε οὐ λαὸς νῦν δὲ λαὸς θεοῦ), nowhere do we see the author using *pre-conversion* status as an identity to *embrace*. All identity markers point to post-conversion existence. This comports with what we saw in the previous chapter where pre-conversion life is deprecated as worthless in contrast to post-conversion life. Pre-conversion identity is something to be left behind, not something to be embraced. In 2:11, when the author admonishes his readers to abstain as 'aliens and strangers' from fleshly desires, he is calling for a break with their previous life, which was characterized by ἐπιθυμίαι (1:14). Hence, πάροικοι and παρεπίδημοι cannot refer to pre-conversion existence, but rather to a cultural estrangement that is a *result* of conversion. It is precisely in breaking with their own cultural norms in the act of conversion that these Christians *became* social outsiders: πάροικοι and παρεπίδημοι. Elliott is likely correct that some of the Christians came from the socio-political class of οἱ πάροικοι; it would be surprising if none were. But this pre-conversion identity plays no necessary part in its usage in 1 Peter, where it is used metaphorically to speak of cultural estrangement resulting from election.[43] This means that the alleged prehistory of these terms,[44] as a descriptor of *pre-conversion* social status for *some* of the community, is unnecessary, cannot be supported from the text, and actually goes against the epistle's attitude toward pre-conversion identity.

Again, saying that these terms are used metaphorically does not mean they do not carry a chiefly *social* import. Elliott is correct to stress the social significance of these terms, but probably is too quick to draw a sharp dichotomy between the 'sociological' and 'cosmological' elements involved. He argues that, 'The constant perspective of this document is social not cosmological, and in this context *parepidēmos*, *paroikia*, and *paroikos* describe a condition of *social*, not cosmological, estrangement.'[45] Again, Elliott is right to deflate the 'strangers on earth' interpretation, but he goes too far it eliminating all 'cosmological' elements. For our author social estrangement has its origin in the electing grace of God. In this sense, it is both a social and a cosmological estrangement. Being πάροικοι

---

[43] ELLIOTT seems to assume that literal knowledge is *necessary* for a metaphor to have any real meaning, but linguistically this is not the case. While tacit knowledge supplies additional elements to one's apprehension of a metaphor, it is not a necessary precondition.

[44] One factor that speaks against ELLIOTT's historical reconstruction is that these terms arise as a self-designation of the addressees. This assumes that the term arose in one church community, and then spread to a significant number of other Anatolian churches. It further assumes that this self-designation was known to the author (or authorial community) in Rome, while the remainder of the epistle evidences little specific knowledge of the addressees, apart from their persecutions.

[45] ELLIOTT, *1 Peter*, 481.

and παρεπίδημοι involves another sense of cosmological estrangement in that the terms imply a temporal limit to strangerhood. This is picked up in 1:17, where the author refers to τὸν τῆς παροικίας ὑμῶν χρόνον. In the eschatology of the epistle, this refers to the time between conversion and the parousia of Christ. While a heaven/earth dichotomy is absent, a present/future age dichotomy is present in the use of the terms πάροικοι and παρεπίδημοι.[46]

In the logic of the epistle, this social estrangement has roots that go *beyond* the social. In the previous verses, we saw that the line that separates the church from the disobedient is faith. This creates a social divide with two humanities: the λαὸς θεοῦ and the unbelieving world, in verse 12a simply τὰ ἔθνη. But because the church does not detach itself from the world, the people of God become 'strangers' with respect to the culture at large. Holding differing allegiances from those around them, they become estranged. Abandoning their former practices, which characterize participation in the pagan world, they become outsiders to their friends and neighbors (cf. 4:3–4).

The temptation for these converts is to revert back to their former ἀναστροφαί in an effort to ease their estrangement by assimilation. This is exactly why our author emphasizes their identity as πάροικοι and παρεπίδημοι, because it reinforces their *difference* from the surrounding culture and thus weakens the lure of assimilation. Their estrangement then is not simply an unfortunate reality to be coped with, but something to be *fostered*.

There are two different senses in which they are 'strangers'. In the first sense, their neighbors reject them for being different. In the second sense, they are God's distinct holy people. Both are present in the epistle, but, especially in the context of the previous verses, the latter is in focus here.[47] This explains how strangerhood can be a virtue. Being rejected by one's neighbors is neither desirable nor laudable,[48] but maintaining a stance of moral distinctiveness is. Just as we saw with the communal titles in 2:9, πάροικοι and παρεπίδημοι emphasize the uniqueness and moral purity that is to characterize the elect people of God.[49] Thus, it becomes clear why the

---

[46] Cf. ACHTEMEIER, *1 Peter*, 175, esp. n.39.

[47] Contra ELLIOTT.

[48] In fact, as we will see below, it is precisely this sense of strangerhood that the author seeks to ameliorate.

[49] Because of the particular way in which ELLIOTT sees the use of πάροικοι and παρεπίδημοι developing out of their initial literal sociological use and then later being applied to the whole community because of its cultural estrangement, he sees them as fundamentally different from the titles given in 2:5, 9–10. The origin of those titles is the electing grace of God, but the origin of these titles is the sociological reality of the young churches, who saw the estrangement of πάροικοι and παρεπίδημοι as paradigmatic for

author emphasizes their identity as 'aliens and strangers' in exhorting his hearers to abstain from fleshly ἐπιθυμίαι (i.e., the social vices that characterize both their former lives and the culture at large); he is trying to reinforce their *difference* from the culture to release them from their past. By admonishing them to embrace their identity as 'aliens and strangers', the author constructs a social barrier between the covenant community and the outside world. But, this social barrier also marks a battle line in the heart of every convert. Hence, the call to abstain from the desires that 'wage war on your souls' reflects their calling to be πάροικοι and παρεπίδημοι. While reflected in differing external social practices, ultimately this barrier is *internal*.

Constructing this internal barrier, by embracing their identity as 'aliens and strangers', enables these Christians to maintain their good behavior while living in the midst of the 'Gentiles' (τὴν ἀναστροφὴν ἐν τοῖς ἔθνεσιν καλήν). This has two senses. First, it means that they maintain their moral distinctiveness while still living in close proximity with the pagan world. This is accomplished through the conscious strategy of seeing themselves as 'strangers' in their own culture (i.e., not identifying with the priorities that drive everyday pagan culture). Secondly, living in the midst of the 'Gentiles' means that their lives are on display before a 'watching world'. Here we move from the internal struggle with assimilation and sin to the outward witness of the redeemed community. The author's fundamental attitude toward relationships with outsiders is 'do good'. To a significant degree this agenda is directed towards improving the reputation of the church with outsiders and to winning converts, as can be seen in the purpose clause that finishes verse: *so that in case they speak against you as wrongdoers, they may see your good deeds and glorify God on the day of visitation* (ἵνα ἐν ᾧ καταλαλοῦσιν ὑμῶν ὡς κακοποιῶν ἐκ τῶν καλῶν ἔργων ἐποπτεύοντες δοξάσωσιν τὸν θεὸν ἐν ἡμέρᾳ ἐπισκοπῆς).

Here is the first explicit reference to the rejection of the church by outsiders, who slander (καταλαλέω) these Christians as 'evildoers'. This slander is probably not directed at a particular practice of the Christians that is perceived as 'evil', but an abusive slur directed at them because of the their general non-conformity, as in 4:3–4 where outsiders revile believers because they abstain from licentious behavior. As we said above, this is the other sense in which they are πάροικοι and παρεπίδημοι. But,

---

their own cultural estrangement. See, for example, ELLIOTT, *1 Peter*, 448, 'The formulation "elect strangers" (1:1) effectively expresses the paradox of the believers' estrangement in society, on the one hand, and their union with Jesus Christ and God, on the other.'

unlike their divinely given identity, this sense of estrangement is *not* desirable. Therefore, a central part of the author's social agenda for the community is to improve their relationship to the outside world through recognizably good conduct.[50] The hope is that their good lives will affect the opinions of outsiders (2:15), or at least make them ashamed of their fallacious slander (3:16), and on occasion win converts to the faith (3:1, 15). As we saw in 2:4–10, the ultimate motivation for action is the greater glory of God. Here the ultimate goal is that outsiders will give glory to God in the day of judgment[51] for the righteous lives of these Christians.[52] Thus, their stance toward outsiders is tied into their identity as God's ἱεράτευμα ἅγιον. In living holy lives, they both glorify God and win praise for him from the 'Gentiles'.

III. Identity and Difference

Every 'minority' group wrestles with the issues of identity and difference. How much do they identify with their surrounding culture and how much do they stress their difference? For some groups acceptance by the masses is a goal, or even a given from the start. Other groups seek to maximize difference by separating themselves in some way from the culture. One group might choose the path of assimilation while another the path of

---

[50] The adjective καλός, used here to modify ἔργα and ἀναστροφή, points to recognizable goods in Greco-Roman culture. Cf. ELLIOTT, *1 Peter*, 466, 'The term *kalos* has an aesthetic as well as moral connotation. It denotes conduct that is both morally just and aesthetically attractive, thus behavior that is in all senses worthy of honor. This double aspect of the term is obviously important to our author, who notes that honorable behavior and deeds will be "observed" (*epopteuontes*, v 12c) and thereby confirmed from experience as good and honorable.' As SELWYN, *1 Peter*, 170, notes, 'This point was of particular importance in a society which applied to the highest kind of human character the term καλὸς κἀγαθός, i.e. one whose intrinsic goodness is also beautiful in others' eyes.'

[51] Cf. ACHTEMEIER, *1 Peter*, 178, 'While it is possible that [ἐν ἡμέρᾳ ἐπισκοπῆς]... could refer to the time of the conversion of the nonbelievers, ...the use of this phrase in the Bible points to the time of the final judgment.'

[52] This verse is very likely dependent, in some way, on the Jesus tradition found in Mt. 5:16 for its basic idea and key terms. Whether these outsiders will glorify God from a position of belief or unbelief is uncertain. The teaching of the epistle as a whole includes a missionary agenda for living rightly before Gentiles, and it is difficult to see glorifying God as an activity of unbelievers (even on the day of judgment), so perhaps the ideal is for the Gentile recognition of the good lives of Christians to lead to conversion, and thus inclusion in the priesthood that glorifies God. But W.C. VAN UNNIK, 'The Teaching of Good Works in 1 Peter,' *NTS* 1 (1954–55): 105, cites 1 Enoch 62–63 as a Jewish precedent for Gentiles who glorify God in the final judgment even though they are condemned. So, this option remains a possibility.

isolation. These are the two options at the extremes. Most groups choose to place themselves somewhere in between, not wanting to sacrifice either their distinctiveness or their connection to the larger culture. But the reality is that this tension is very difficult to hold, and groups tend to move toward one pole or the other. As group members interact with their non-group neighbors, they experience the painful reality of difference and estrangement. There are two routes to alleviate this felt difference. The first is to reduce the difference (assimilation) and the second is to reduce the contact with non-group members (isolation). Thus, for groups who attempt to balance identity and difference, assimilation and isolation are two strong temptations pulling in opposite directions – to become either conformists or iconoclasts.

This conundrum is precisely the social reality addressed in 1 Peter.[53] What then is our author's advice – assimilate or isolate? In his study of the epistle's *Haustafel*, Balch argues that the author encourages assimilation. He argues that, 'The author of 1 Peter wrote to advise the Christians who were being persecuted about how they might become socially-politically acceptable to their society.' To accomplish this, 'Christians had to conform to the expectations of Hellenistic-Roman society so that society would cease criticizing the new cult.'[54] But this hardly fits the evidence of text, whether we are thinking of the whole epistle or only the *Haustafel*.[55] As we have seen, the author's strategy for relating to pagan neighbors *begins* with the identity of the Christians as 'aliens and strangers'. He begins by emphasizing and encouraging their *difference* with respect to their neighbors. Criticizing Balch, Elliott rightly maintains that, 'nothing in 1 Peter, including its discussion of household duties, indicates an interest in promoting social assimilation.'[56]

Elliott sees a different agenda at work. He argues that, 'the recommendations in 1 Peter were designed to urge an effective *balance*

---

[53] Cf. ELLIOTT, 'Situation and Strategy,' 69. 'As with any subsociety within the total social system, this tension between boundary maintenance (preserving the distinctive group values, beliefs, norms, identity, and limits set on intergroup contacts) and system linkage (contacts and interdependency among groups) aptly characterizes a dilemma reflected also in 1 Peter and the early Christian movement.'

[54] BALCH, *Wives*, 88.

[55] The suggestion by D.L. BALCH, 'Hellenization/Acculturation in 1 Peter,' in *Perspectives on First Peter*, ed. C.H. TALBERT, NABPRSSS (Macon, GA: Mercer University Press, 1986), 81, that 'Such acculturation meant that Petrine Christianity accepted hellenistic social values in tension with important values in Jewish tradition (in the Torah) and even in tension with the early Jesus movement,' represents a misguided reading of the historical traditions that lay behind the *Haustafel* as well as their utilization in this context.

[56] Cf. ELLIOTT, 'Situation and Strategy,' 72.

between intergroup communication and preserving lines of demarcation.'[57] While Elliott has, at times, been characterized as holding a position precisely the opposite of Balch (i.e., isolationist),[58] his position is more nuanced and balanced than that. In confronting the twin temptations of assimilation and isolation, Elliott argues, that '1 Peter in its entirety was designed to deal with *both* horns of this dilemma.'[59] It is true that Elliott has emphasized the importance of 'boundary maintenance' in the strategy of the author, but he sees this in consort with the aim of promoting internal community life. He also emphasizes strong 'familial' love within the community, perseverance in good works, and respect when dealing with outsiders.

Adopting the sect typologies of Wilson, Elliott interprets the social makeup of the addressees of 1 Peter as an example of a 'conversionist sect'. According to Elliott, the twin priorities of the conversionist sect are to maintain boundaries and to win converts. Thus, this model fits with the situation of the letter, where the author exhorts the readers to maintain their difference while still remaining enmeshed in society with the aim of winning converts. As Elliott points out, these twin priorities, while difficult to hold together, are actually complementary. It is precisely social distinctiveness that is the source of (possible) attraction to outsiders. If they were not different from the culture, then they would have nothing to offer.[60]

Following Wilson, Elliott uses the term 'sect' somewhat loosely, as simply a designation for a 'minority group'.[61] Thus, 'sect' does not necessarily imply an *isolationist* agenda. While there are serious shortcomings of this model, as we will see shortly, all too often critiques of Elliott have mistakenly assumed that by using the term 'sect' he was conceiving of these communities as something analogous to the Qumran community. While the identification of these Christian communities as 'sectarian' does imply a strong emphasis on 'boundary maintenance', it

---

[57] ELLIOTT, 'Situation and Strategy,' 74. Italics added.

[58] E.g., L. THURÉN, *The Rhetorical Strategy of 1 Peter: With Special Regard to Ambiguous Expressions* (Åbo, Finland: Åbo Akademis forlag, 1990), 36.

[59] ELLIOTT, 'Situation and Strategy,' 69. Italics original.

[60] Cf. ELLIOTT, *1 Peter*, 104. 'One important goal of this conversionist sect was the attraction and conversion of outsiders (2:12; 3:2), an aim that would be decisively thwarted if it espoused a strategy of social and moral accommodation.' Cf. M. VOLF, 'Soft Difference: Theological Reflections on the Relation Between Church and Culture in 1 Peter,' *ExAud* 10 (1994): 24, 'distance is a presupposition of mission.'

[61] Cf. B.R. WILSON, *Magic and the Millennium: A Sociological Study of Religious Movements of Protest Among Tribal and Third-World Peoples* (London: Heinemann, 1973), 34, where he explains that he uses 'sect', 'loosely and in general as pseudonymous with "minority religious movements."'

does not mean that these groups were necessarily isolationist.[62] What it does imply is a general negative attitude toward the culture,[63] where the basic model of interaction is one of conflict.[64]

The major shortcoming in Elliott's work is its lack of appreciation for the emphasis on πάροικοι and παρεπίδημοι as an identity to be *embraced*. Since he views these terms as referring to the unfortunate social status of the community resulting from rejection, he fails to see how these titles are the central identity markers which are prescribed for the community to embrace in its relation to pagan culture. This is unfortunate because in doing so he actually forfeits the key to understanding the author's agenda in addressing the 'two-horned' dilemma of isolation or assimilation.

As Volf argues, the key to overcoming this tension is not found in the '*degree* [to which] one stresses difference, but rather on what *basis* Christian identity is established.' As he explains, 'Identity can be forged through two related but clearly distinct processes: either through a *negative* process of rejecting the beliefs and practices of others, or through a *positive* process of giving allegiance to something distinctive.'[65] How identity is constructed (whether positively or negatively) affects how a group relates to the 'other'. Volf warns that:

When identity is forged primarily through the negative process of the rejection of the beliefs and practices of others, violence seems unavoidable, especially in situations of conflict. We have to push others away from ourselves and keep them at a distance, and we have to close ourselves off from others to keep ourselves pure of their taint. The violence of pushing and keeping away can express itself in subdued resentment, or it can break out in aggressive and destructive behavior.[66]

---

[62] Cf. ELLIOTT, *1 Peter*, 473, 'While aliens and strangers, the addressees are not urged to be isolationists who withdraw from society as did the community at Qumran. They are, rather, challenged to engage with society and present it a superior form of moral and religious life. This is the only practical strategy appropriate for such a sectarian movement that is intent on gaining new members through conversion while simultaneously preserving its distinctiveness.' Cf. J.H. ELLIOTT, *A Home for the Homeless: A Social-Scientific Criticism of 1 Peter, its Situation and Strategy* (Philadelphia: Fortress, 1981), 117.

[63] Cf. B. JOHNSON, 'On Church and Sect,' *ASR* 28 (1963): 542, where he distinguishes between the sociological models of 'church' and 'sect' based on their posture towards the culture. He argues that, 'A church is a religious group that *accepts* the social environment in which it exists. A sect is a religious group that *rejects* the social environment in which it exists.' Italics added. While the church/sect dichotomy is crude, this comment still touches on what distinguishes a group as a 'sect'.

[64] See ELLIOTT, *Home*, 112–8, for his description of the social 'conflict' faced by the sect.

[65] VOLF, 'Soft Difference,' 20. Italics added.

[66] VOLF, 'Soft Difference,' 21.

Since Elliott sees πάροικοι and παρεπίδημοι as a description of Christian social estrangement, instead of a prescription of divinely given identity, he is constructing identity vis-à-vis the pagan world *negatively*.[67] As Volf has rightly argued, this results in an essentially negative depiction of the pagan world and produces a climate of conflict. Not surprisingly, this fits Elliott's description of the situation addressed in 1 Peter:

> The readers...are reminded that they are in a state of war (2:11; 4:1) which implies a radical distinction between themselves the righteous and the impious sinners (4:17–18). They are the brotherhood faithful to God, whereas the Gentiles are in league with the devil (5:8–9). Hence Christians are encouraged to 'resist' these opposing forces (5:9) and to separate themselves thoroughly from all the ungodly ways of the Gentiles (1:14, 17; 2:11; 4:1–4).[68]

But here Elliott's model leads him astray. Constructing identity negatively forces him to posit a 'state of war' between the church and the pagan world, which finds little support in the text. As we saw in 2:11, the church's battle is not with the world outside, but with the fleshly desires that battle within the heart of every convert. Critiquing Elliott, Volf argues that:

> 1 Peter consistently establishes the difference positively, not negatively. There are no direct injunctions not to behave as non-Christians do. ...The statements that celebrate Christian calling 'out of darkness into his marvelous light' notwithstanding (2:9), 1 Peter does not operate with the stark black-and-white opposition between 'divine community' and 'satanic world.' Correspondingly, the author seems less interested in hurling threats against the unbelieving and aggressive non-Christian neighbors, than in celebrating Christians' special status before God (see 2:9f). ...When we encounter negative examples of how Christians should not behave, then our attention is drawn not so much to the life-style of non-Christians as to 'the *desires of the flesh* that wage war against the soul' (2:11). ...The force of the injunction is not 'Do not be as your neighbors are!' but 'Do not be as *you were!*'[69]

To construct identity negatively is to identify everything 'other' as evil, as when Elliott argues that, 'the letter reduces all the opposing forces to a common denominator: "Gentiles" (2:12; 4:3), "sinner(s)" (4:18), "your adversary, the devil" (5:8).'[70] But the emphasis in 1 Peter is with the church's *internal* struggle with evil, evidenced in the recurrent exhortations to good works. Because the author constructs identity

---

[67] ELLIOTT sees positive identity construction in 2:5, 9–10. But when talking about their identity as 'aliens and strangers' he constructs it negatively, as reflecting the social estrangement they suffer at the hands of their pagan neighbors.

[68] ELLIOTT, *Home*, 108.

[69] VOLF, 'Soft Difference,' 20–1.

[70] ELLIOTT, *Home*, 115.

positively, the 'other' is not an enemy; and since the conflict is internal, the need to fend off the outsider falls away. In the face of persecution, this means that the Christians can move *toward* their persecutors. As Volf notes:

Exhortation [in 1 Peter] is given not to repay evil for evil or abuse for abuse, but to *repay evil with blessing* (3:9)! ...When blessing replaces rage and revenge, the one who suffers violence refuses to retaliate in kind and chooses instead to encounter violence with an embrace. But how can people give up violence in the midst of a life-threatening conflict if their identity is wrapped up in rejecting the beliefs and practices of their enemies? Only those who refuse to be defined by their enemies can bless them.[71]

Volf's description of 1 Peter's attitude toward outsiders fits the evidence better than Elliott's sectarian model. Because their identity as 'aliens and strangers' is an essentially positive one, they are able to view their interaction with outsiders positively – to replace 'rage and revenge' with 'blessing'.

The 'violence' of pushing the other away is exactly the sort of response these Christians are tempted to embrace in retaliation for their mistreatment by their pagan neighbors. It is exactly this sort of fleshly desire that wage war κατὰ τῆς ψυχῆς, which the author seeks to extinguish. For them to embrace this sort of violence would mean a departure from the holy life they have been called to. In the midst of their sufferings, they must continue to choose to do good.[72] By embracing their identity as 'aliens and strangers' they choose to deny themselves the path to violence that their pagan neighbors have chosen as their response to *their* 'other': the church. In so doing, the Christians divorce themselves from a sinful response that would have been fully in keeping with their previous lives and the norms of pagan culture, and thus retain their difference from the culture by embracing their identity as aliens and strangers.

This difference is necessary for their mission; as Elliott noted above, the potential attraction of a minority group to outsiders is its positive difference from the culture. But what Elliott fails to see is that difference and mission come together in *identity*. It is precisely in their identity as 'aliens and strangers' that these Christians preserve their καλὴ ἀναστροφή, and it is this attractive lifestyle that has the potential to win approval and, in some cases, converts. Thus, as Volf notes, 'the boundaries that mark our

---

[71] VOLF, 'Soft Difference,' 21.

[72] We will see in another chapter how Christ is the ultimate example of one who continued to do good in the face of unjust suffering, and did not resort to 'violence' (2:21–5).

identities are both barriers *and* bridges.'[73] In maintaining their virtuous conduct 'as aliens and strangers', the Christians reveal their distinction from outsiders; but inherent in this distinction is an invitation. Because their identity is constructed positively, it does not exclude outsiders. Their identity as 'aliens and strangers' is both a barrier and a bridge; it both separates and invites. This is why Volf suggests that, 'It might be appropriate to call the missionary distance that 1 Peter stresses *soft difference.*' He argues that this does not mean, '*weak* difference, for in 1 Peter the difference is anything but weak.' It is 'strong, but not hard.'[74]

This difference is 'soft' primarily because it is *internal* (i.e., attitudinal). The barriers prescribed by the author are not external practices or rituals. True, these Christians are being persecuted because of their external distinctives, but the author prescribes good behavior not as a barrier to non-Christians but as a possible means of winning them over. The barriers these Christians construct are ones that guard their allegiance to God. They are barriers that block a return to their pre-conversion life. By adopting the identity of πάροικοι and παρεπίδημοι within their own culture, they denigrate their attachment to their pre-conversion values. The struggle is an internal one, thus the answer is also internal. Elliott is correct that these boundaries are given to maintain the integrity and cohesion of the group, but they are not constructed to exclude outsiders. Their purpose is to protect insiders from *themselves*, not from outsiders. From the outside these barriers are easily crossed, hence the difference is real but 'soft'.[75]

A. Seneca on Identity and Difference

It is interesting to note that Seneca's advice to Lucilius on how philosophers should relate to the wider culture is not very different. Observing that, 'The mere name of philosophy, however quietly pursued, is an object of sufficient scorn,' he asks, 'What would happen if we should begin to separate ourselves for the customs of our fellow-men?'[76] His advice is that, 'our life should observe a happy medium between the ways of a sage [i.e., iconoclasm] and the ways of the world at large [i.e.,

---

[73] M. VOLF, *Exclusion and Embrace: A Theological Exploration of Identity, Otherness, and Reconciliation* (Nashville: Abingdon Press, 1996), 66. Italics added.

[74] VOLF, 'Soft Difference,' 24. Italics original.

[75] Cf. S.J. GRENZ, 'Die begrenzte Gemeinschaft ("The Boundaried Community") and the Character of Evangelical Theology,' *JETS* 45.2 (2002): 304, 'This aspect of the biblical concept of election suggests that the ultimate goal of God's constituting a boundaried people is not to exclude but to include. In fact, rather than being established with the intent of keeping others out, boundaries are meant to be crossed. And this crossing of the boundaries is to run in both directions. The mandate of the boundaried community is to reach out beyond the border that delimits its identity.'

[76] SENECA, *EM*, 5.2.

assimilation]; all men should admire it, but they should understand it also (*suspiciant omnes vitam nostrum, sed agnoscant*).'[77] Seneca urges a path of balance between identity and difference. For Seneca the key to this balance is an *internal* difference from the norms of society. As he says, 'Inwardly, we ought to be different in all respects (*intus omnia dissimilia sint*), but our exterior should conform to society (*frons populo nostra conveniat*).'[78]

Also, as in 1 Peter, Seneca expects outsiders to notice, comprehend, and admire the virtuous life of the philosopher. As he said above, 'all men should admire it, but they should understand it also.' The point of this admiration is, as in 1 Peter, missionary. Seneca prescribes difference *for the sake of the other*. He urges Lucilius: 'Let us try to maintain a higher standard of life than that of the multitude, but not a contrary standard; otherwise we shall frighten away and repel the very persons whom we are trying to improve.'[79] As in 1 Peter, difference is meant to be attractive; if it repels others, then it fails to serve them.

Finally, it is interesting to note that Seneca shares with 1 Peter the paradoxical conviction that persecutors, who disparage philosopher and Christian alike for their distinctive behavior, can be won over by that same behavior. (This has proved an especially difficult puzzle in 1 Peter, so an example of a similar principle in Seneca may prove helpful.) Seneca urges that philosophers should live to 'a higher standard of life...but not a contrary one (*non ut contrariam*).' He admonishes Lucilius to live up to the *ideals* of society while living above its *norms*. For all societies, some distance exists between its images of ideals and its norms of practice. Seneca urges a rejection of those lascivious practices that are considered part of the norm in pagan society, while at the same time pursuing the recognizably ideals of the virtuous man. This is what he means by living by a higher standard of life, but not a contrary standard. So also 1 Peter urges that, though they are persecuted for their distinctive lifestyle and abstention from vice, Christians can expect to win the respect of (some of) their neighbors by living up to a recognizably high standard. Thus, through good behavior they may win over those who persecute them.[80]

---

[77] SENECA, *EM*, 5.5.

[78] SENECA, *EM*, 5.2. SENECA is not urging 'conformity' in everything. Internal differences will undoubtedly produce behavioral differences. His point is that one should not invent easily produced external differences, such as distinctive dress, which alienate outsiders.

[79] SENECA, *EM*, 5.3.

[80] While the social situations addressed by SENECA and 1 Peter are markedly different (i.e., differing degrees of social estrangement, and community v. individual address), and while SENECA does not adopt the strategy of corporate identity construction, it is still interesting to note how similar the two approaches are in dealing with the question of relations with outsiders.

IV. Paraenetic Aims

How then does our author's advice fit within the overall paraenetic aims of
the epistle? What is the relationship, if any, between character formation
and identity construction? To begin with, we can say that identity provides
a context for moral deliberation and action. Harned puts it well when he
argues that:

> Our conduct is shaped by the condition of our vision; we are free to choose or to struggle
> against only what we can see. Our vision, however, is determined by the most important
> images of the self from which we have fashioned our sense of identity. These furnish us
> with our perspective upon everything else; they finally legislate not only what we will
> and what we will not see, but the particular angle or point of view from which the whole
> of reality will be assessed. How we see ourselves, then, determines how we will conduct
> ourselves in relation to others, to the world, and even to God – and all this is ultimately a
> matter of images. If we cannot see ourselves as Christians, we shall scarcely be able to
> act except in the ways that the fashions of this world legitimate.[81]

As Harned maintains, images that inform identity, like 'holy priesthood' or
'aliens and strangers', are necessary for moral action because they are the
interpretive grids through which we see reality and through which we
contemplate responsibilities and actions. Thus, we should *expect* any
competent agenda of moral reform to also include a reform of identity that
provides new images of the self and/or the group.[82] This is especially true
in the context of social difference. As Harned argues, firm images of
identity are necessary if one hopes to live in a manner different from the
'ways that the fashions of this world legitimate.' Thus, it is not surprising
that, within his overall paraenetic agenda, our author spends so much
energy on the formation of corporate identity through a multiplication of
communal images.

By calling the readers to see themselves ὡς πάροικοι καὶ παρεπίδημοι,
our author has given them a means to accomplish their difficult task of
retaining moral purity while remaining open to the world. In this he is

---

[81] D.B. HARNED, *Creed and Personal Identity: The Meaning of the Apostles' Creed*
(Philadelphia: Fortress, 1981), 120, quoted in J.B. WEBSTER, 'Christology, Imitability
and Ethics,' *SJT* 39 (1986): 309.

[82] The distinction between group and individual identity is not as significant as it
might at first seem. Most sociologists define 'social identity theory' in terms of how the
individual member of a group is shaped by the group's identity. For example, the
standard definition by H. TAJFEL, 'Experiments in a Vacuum,' in *The Context of Social
Psychology: A Critical Assessment*, EMSP (London: Academic Press, 1972), 31, defines
social identity as, 'the individual's knowledge that he/she belongs to certain social
groups together with some emotional and value significance to him/her of the group
membership.'

doing far more than simply stating the ideal balance of identity and difference, or commanding the retention of such a balance. He is rendering, what Seneca calls 'effective paraenesis.' The author is providing psychological catalysts that support moral transformation. By providing images to embrace, he enables them to retain their καλὴ ἀναστροφή.

The cultural estrangement the churches experience produces a host of anxieties, temptations, and difficulties. While the author's agenda operates on many fronts, his focus is on the *moral* challenge produced by such estrangement. These Christians face a legion of temptations. Do they strike back, retaliating in kind for their abuse (verbal and physical)? Do they retreat from their neighbors, withdrawing from society? Do they simply try to blend in, abandoning the distinctive lifestyle that gives rise to their estrangement? For our author, all of these options represent not simply unhealthy dynamics for the life of the group, but a failure to live up to the life to which God has called them. To follow any of these paths would be a moral failure, because they all involve a failure to love God and one's neighbor. Thus, at heart this is an internal moral struggle, although it obviously has wide social ramifications in terms of the church's stance towards outsiders.

As we saw above, because the struggle is an internal one, the barriers to the world are also internal. Their war is with social vices not with society. Thus, the author's appeal to those being persecuted is to continue to do good. At the same time, the call to do good is the sum of the author's advice for relating to outsiders in the face of persecution. Doing good has the potential to win persecutors over to the faith. Thus, this agenda operates at both levels; it retains their moral purity as God's holy people, while at the same time it (potentially) improves their reputation with outsiders. Again, as we have seen, these two activities (difference and mission) are complementary, and should not be separated or set against one another, as though one of these is the *real* agenda of our author. That said, the author has stressed moral purity before God as the more 'basic' motivation for doing good. As we saw above, the church's identity as a holy priesthood means all its actions find their ultimate ground in the greater glory of God.

Thus, the author's agenda is to reinforce the commitment of these Christians to the work of salvation in their midst. Faced with the fiery trial of cultural estrangement and persecution, he admonishes them to remain committed to the sanctifying work of doing good, so that the genuineness of their faith might be revealed through these trials (1:6–7). Recognizing the painful temptation to cease from well-doing, he urges them to remain faithful to God and to their calling. This in large measure is the reason for the string of communal identity titles given in 2:5, 9–10. As we saw, these titles point to God's electing mercy as the source of these Christian communities, and in so doing serve to procure the allegiance of these communities for their gracious God. This is made explicit in the author's description of the vocation of this holy priesthood as ὅπως τὰς ἀρετὰς ἐξαγγείλητε τοῦ ἐκ σκότους ὑμᾶς καλέσαντος εἰς τὸ θαυμαστὸν αὐτοῦ φῶς in 2:9. Their existence is defined by a story; they are who they are because of the saving activity of God. Thus, their lives are directed in gratitude and love towards living out their calling as the elect and holy people of God.

We saw in 2:5 the two central corporate images that govern the epistle's social outlook. The first was the household of God, which points to God as the source of their community. The second was the holy priesthood, which points to the vocation of this household as living for the glory of God. Together, these two sum up the main thrust of the passage, which is to call these Christians to devotion to their God out of gratitude for his great mercy.[83] The author furthers his paraenetic agenda by procuring this affective allegiance to God.[84] As we have said before, our author is confronting two complementary challenges, which these suffering communities face. One is theological and the other is moral, but the two are inextricably linked together. Greater devotion to God translates into moral action, which in turn aids in the development of a more mature devotion. So we see that the author's emphasis on corporate identity being rooted in God's actions and calling for distinctive moral integrity fits within his overall paraenetic agenda of facilitating growth in Christian maturity.

---

[83] As an important side note, if we comprehend the agenda of the author in this way, then it is actually not the least surprising that he shows no care for the question of the relationship of the church to Israel. Obviously, the author has *some* concept of continuity between the two, since he feels comfortable simply applying OT titles to the church. But what that conception might be is immaterial to his purpose here. This freedom in applying titles used of Israel to these Anatolian churches, without explanation, has astounded some interpreters (e.g., ACHTEMEIER, *1 Peter*, 69). This is a perfect example that illustrates the paraenetic bent of the epistle. The author's theology is constructed to foster his pragmatic aims. There is no theology for theology's sake. The question of Israel and the church is an obvious one, which Paul and Luke both wrestled with, but as it does nothing to further this epistle's paraenetic aims, it is absent. The titles convey what they did in their OT contexts – this is the elect and holy people of God. For the author's purposes that is all that is needed.

[84] In a much more subtle way, the author also emphasizes the community's identity with Jesus, as the elect but rejected one. This not only underscores their devotion to him as well as God, but also prepares the way for the *imitatio Christi* motif that is to come, and which is the topic of another chapter below.

Chapter Six

Moral Instructions

In the previous chapters, we saw how theological discourse in 1 Peter functions in a paraenetic mode. In this chapter, our concern is with paraenesis-as-form: the form, content, and function of moral instructions. In previous chapters, a case had to be made for the paraenetic function of what is typically branded 'theology' in 1 Peter. Here, the paraenetic nature of moral instructions is not a matter of dispute, since paraenesis-as-form is one of the key elements of paraenesis-as-genre. It is, in fact, yet another strategy in the literary arsenal of the paraenetic author.

Because a large portion of 1 Peter is devoted to moral instructions, taking these together at once means that this chapter will cover roughly half of the epistle (2:13–5:11).[1] But because the paraenetic nature of the moral instructions in 1 Peter is uncontested, a summary treatment will be sufficient to establish the main features that describe the function of moral instructions in 1 Peter. In order to avoid a danger of overgeneralization, however, we will examine in detail the letter's *Haustafel* as a sizable and representative unit of moral instruction in 1 Peter.

The aim of this chapter is to describe how moral instructions (paraenesis-as-form) *function*, that is how they work to realize the paraenetic aims of the author. We will begin by constructing a basic taxonomy of moral instructions, classifying different types of instruction and the constituent parts that comprise them. We then move on to a discussion of the function of moral instruction within the context of Greco-Roman paraenetic epistles. As usual, this is followed by an application of these findings to the relevant materials in 1 Peter.

I. Form

We start by looking at some of the various forms in which instructions occur. Some are very simple and others more complex. In building a

---

[1] The christological passages within this range will be dealt with separately in the following chapter.

taxonomy of instructions[2] we will begin with the basic form of instruction, the simple exhortation, and add supporting elements as we go along. With each type of instruction, examples are given from the moral instructions of 1 Peter. Along with these, where possible, examples from the epistles of Isocrates are included for comparison. Our purpose here is twofold. First, building a taxonomy of moral instructions helps us to see the universals amidst the particulars, by revealing the building blocks that are utilized in constructing instructions. Secondly, this gives us a starting point for analyzing the function of instructions in general as well as the specialized functions of particular types of instruction.

A. Exhortation – The basic element of an instruction is the exhortation – that which prescribes a certain action or attitude as a duty to be embraced. Exhortations can appear alone or as a series of multiple commands.

> 2:17: Honor everyone. Love the brotherhood. Fear God. Honor the emperor.
> 5:5a: Likewise you that are younger be subject to the elders.
>
> ---
>
> *Dem.* 16: Fear the gods, honor your parents, respect your friends, obey the laws.
> *Nic.* 38: If there are men whose reputations you envy, imitate their deeds.

B. Exhortation with Motive – Motives strengthen exhortations by appealing to the benefits that result from practicing them.

> 5:6: Humble yourselves therefore under the mighty hand of God, *(Exhortation)*
>   that in due time he may exalt you. *(Motive)*
>
> ---
>
> *Dem.* 21: Train yourself in self-imposed toils, *(Exhortation)*
>   that you may be able to endure those which others impose upon you. *(Motive)*

C. Exhortation with Motive and Qualifications – Qualifications describe how the exhortation is to be carried out, or under what circumstances it is applicable.

> 5:2–4: Tend the flock of God that is your charge, *(Exhortation)*
>   not by constraint but willingly, *(Qualification)*
>   not for shameful gain but eagerly, *(Qualification)*

---

[2] This taxonomy is somewhat modeled on similar work done by R. BAUCKHAM in *James: Wisdom of James, Disciple of Jesus the Sage*, NTR (London: Routledge, 1999), see 35–69. The categories he used in delineating different types of instruction were particularly suited to the aphoristic nature of paraenesis in the epistle of James, and are not as applicable to 1 Peter. Therefore, instead of utilizing his categories I have coined my own.

not as domineering over those in your charge (*Qualification*)
    but being examples to the flock. (*Qualification*)
And when the chief Shepherd is manifested
you will obtain the unfading crown of glory. (*Motive*)

2:13–16: Be subject for the Lord's sake to every human institution, (*Exhortation*)
    whether it be to the emperor as supreme, or to governors
    as sent by him to punish those who do wrong
    and to praise those who do right. (*Qualification*)
      For it is God's will that by doing right
      you should put to silence the ignorance of foolish men, (*Motive*)
        living as free men, yet without using your freedom as a pretext
        for evil; but living as servants of God. (*Qualification*)

Dem. 13: Do honor to the divine power at all times, (*Exhortation*)
    but especially on occasions of public worship; (*Qualification*)
      for thus you will have the reputation both of sacrificing to the gods
      and of abiding by the laws. (*Motive*)

D. *Exhortation with Warrant*[3] – Warrants support exhortations by supplying a justifying general principle. It relates an exhortation to a fundamental principle, and thus provides it with a coherent rational justification.

4:7: The end of all things is at hand; (*Warrant*)
    therefore keep sane and sober for your prayers. (*Exhortation*)

5:5b: Clothe yourselves, all of you, with humility toward one another, (*Exhortation*)
    for 'God opposes the proud, but gives grace to the humble.' (*Warrant*)

Dem. 15: Consider that no adornment so becomes you as
    modesty, justice, and self-control; (*Exhortation*)
      for these are the virtues by which, as all men are agreed,
      the character of the young is held in restraint. (*Warrant*)

Dem. 22: Guard more faithfully the secret which is confided to you
    than the money which is entrusted to your care; (*Exhortation*)
      for good men ought to show that they hold their honor
      more trustworthy than an oath. (*Warrant*)

---

[3] The terms 'warrant' and 'backing' (below) are taken from the argumentation analysis of S.E. TOULMIN, *The Uses of Argument* (Cambridge: Cambridge University Press, 1958). I have not followed TOULMIN in any rigorous sense, as L. THURÉN does in *Argument and Theology*. My use of these terms, while inspired by TOULMIN, is only *analogous* to the ways in which he uses them. Warrants, for example, are never explicit in TOULMIN's system, only implied.

E. Exhortation with Warrant and/or Motive with Backing – Backing supports exhortations *indirectly* by providing support for warrants and motives. This can be done in various ways that include emotional appeals, additional warrants, or moral exemplars.

> 5:8–11: Be sober, be watchful (*Exhortation*)
> Your adversary the devil prowls around like a roaring lion,
> seeking some one to devour. (*Warrant*)
> Resist him, firm in your faith, (*Exhortation*)
> knowing that the same experience of suffering
> is required of your brotherhood throughout the world. (*Warrant*)
> And after you have suffered a little while, the God of all grace,
> who has called you to his eternal glory in Christ,
> will himself restore, establish, and strengthen you. (*Backing*)
> To him be the dominion for ever and ever. Amen. (*Backing*)

> *Dem.* 35: Whenever you purpose to consult with anyone about your affairs,
> first observe how he has managed his own; (*Exhortation*)
> for he who has shown poor judgment in conducting
> his own business will never give wise counsel
> about the business of others. (*Warrant*)
> The greatest incentive you can have to deliberation is to observe
> the misfortunes which spring from the lack of it; (*Motive*)
> for we pay the closest attention to our health
> when we recall the pains which spring from disease. (*Backing*)

F. Exhortation with Qualification, Warrant and/or Motive with Backing – Here all of the above are combined in various permutations.

> 3:15b–18:Always be prepared to make a defense to any one
> who calls you to account for the hope that is in you, (*Exhortation*)
> yet do it with gentleness and reverence,
> keeping your conscience clear, (*Qualification*)
> so that, when you are abused, those who revile your good
> behavior in Christ may be put to shame. (*Motive*)
> For it is better to suffer for doing right,
> if that should be God's will, than for doing wrong. (*Warrant*)
> For Christ also died for sins once for all, the righteous for the
> unrighteous, that he might bring us to God, being put to death
> in the flesh but made alive in the spirit; (*Backing*)

> 4:1–2: Since therefore Christ suffered in the flesh, (*Backing: Example*)
> arm yourselves with the same thought, (*Exhortation*)
> for whoever has suffered in the flesh has ceased from sin, (*Warrant*)
> so as to live for the rest of the time in the flesh no longer by
> human passions but by the will of God. (*Qualification*)

4:10–11: As each has received a gift, employ it for one another, *(Exhortation)*
         as good stewards of God's varied grace: *(Qualification)*
         whoever speaks, as one who utters oracles of God; *(Qualification)*
         whoever renders service, as one who renders it by the strength
         which God supplies; *(Qualification)*
            in order that in everything God may be glorified
            through Jesus Christ. *(Motive)*
         To him belong glory and dominion forever and ever. Amen. *(Backing)*

G. Antithetical Pairs – Here a positive exhortation is juxtaposed with an admonition (i.e., a negative exhortation) that specifies what actions are to be avoided while embracing the exhortation. Often the prohibition precedes the exhortation, placing the emphasis on the positive command.

4:12–14: Beloved, do not be surprised at the fiery ordeal
         which comes upon you to prove you, *(Admonition)*
            as though something strange were happening to you. *(Qualification)*
         But rejoice in so far as you share Christ's sufferings, *(Exhortation)*
         that you may also rejoice and be glad
         when his glory is revealed. *(Motive)*
            If you are reproached for the name of Christ, you are blessed,
            because the spirit of glory and of God rests upon you. *(Backing)*

3:14–15a: But even if you do suffer for righteousness' sake,
         you will be blessed. *(Warrant)*
            Have no fear of them, nor be troubled, *(Admonition)*
            but in your hearts reverence Christ as Lord. *(Exhortation)*

Dem. 39:   Never emulate those who seek to gain by injustice, *(Admonition)*
         but cleave rather to those who have suffered loss
         in the cause of justice; *(Exhortation)*
            for if the just have no other advantage over the unjust,
            at any rate they surpass them in their high hopes. *(Warrant)*

H. Combination – These various forms can, of course, be combined together to form an intricate coherent instruction.

4:15–19: Let none of you suffer as a murderer, or a thief,
         or a wrongdoer, or a mischief-maker; *(Admonition)*
            yet if one suffers as a Christian, let him not be ashamed,
            but under that name let him glorify God. *(Antithetical Pair)*
               For the time has come for judgment to begin
               with the household of God; *(Warrant)*
                  and if it begins with us, what will be the end of those who do not
                  obey the gospel of God? And 'If the righteous man is scarcely
                  saved, where will the impious and sinner appear?' *(Backing)*
            Therefore let those who suffer according to God's will *(Qualification)*
            do right and entrust their souls to a faithful Creator. *(Exhortation)*

As with so many things, form is suited to function. As we turn to look at the function of moral instructions in moral discourse we will see how these diverse forms of instructions are integral to the various ways in which they function.

II. Function

Prima facie, the function of moral instructions is quite obvious – they tell someone what to do. Instructions define ethical norms and practices and prescribe actions that flesh out philosophic principles. That is why they are exhortations that command. But there is more to them than simply this. In the context of Greco-Roman paraenesis, moral instructions also operate as a tool to foster growth in moral virtue. The value of instructions lies not simply in delineating duties, but also in aiding the acquisition of virtue by instigating virtuous deeds. As Seneca says, 'Virtue depends partly upon training and partly upon practice (*pars virtutis disciplina constat, pars exercitatione*); you must learn first, and then strengthen (*confirmes*) your learning by action.'[1] Because of this he concludes 'not only do the doctrines of wisdom help us, but the precepts also (*non tantum scita sapientiae prosunt, sed etiam praecepta*).'[2] Since virtue is a habit gained by practice, instructions (what Seneca calls 'precepts') are useful for growth in virtue because they initiate virtuous deeds.

Instructions also aid growth in virtue by fostering the skill of discernment (φρόνησις). Discernment is a necessary skill for virtuous living, and, like virtue, is only acquired by practice. As Seneca notes, our 'judgment as to Good and Evil [i.e., discernment] is itself strengthened by following up our duties (*praeterea ipsum de malis bonisque iudicium confirmatur officiorum exsecutione*).'[3] Virtuous deeds then promote both virtue and discernment. The reason for this is simply that instructions are examples of discernment (i.e., the skill of applying general principles to specific situations and determining what actions are required by virtue). The contemplation and practice of such instructions promotes the skill of φρόνησις. To aid this process some instructions include warrants, because they connect the principle with the exhortation.

Seneca uses the analogy of boys learning penmanship as a picture of how instructions promote discernment: 'Their fingers are held and guided by others so that they may follow the outlines of the letters; next, they are ordered to imitate a copy and base thereon a style of penmanship.' He

---

[1] SENECA, *EM*, 94.47.
[2] SENECA, *EM*, 94.47.
[3] SENECA, *EM*, 94.34.

concludes, 'Similarly, the mind is helped if it is taught according to direction (*sic animus noster dum eruditur ad praescriptum, iuvatur*).'[4] Therefore, imitating the wisdom encapsulated in instructions instills discernment. So, instructions are a benefit because they not only give one practice in performing virtuous deeds, thereby instigating growth in virtue, but also because they provide lessons in applying principles to real situations, thereby promoting the skill of φρόνησις.

Aristotle, and those who followed in his train, recognized the complexities of human life, and appreciated the unique circumstances that surround each moral deliberation. No two situations are exactly the same, and neither are any two people. It is precisely this complexity that gives φρόνησις a central role in the program of virtue. The skill of discernment is needed to see the right action in a particular circumstance, but it does not operate by brushing over the particularities of life and reducing the diversity of moral experience to a handful of manageable model scenarios. Rather it seeks to develop a sensitivity to particular circumstances that is informed by general principles.[5]

The makeup of instructions is also shaped by this appreciation of the complexities of life. The purpose of instructions is not to give responses to every conceivable situation; that would be impossible. Rather, in applying general principles to specific situations, instructions typically give commands of a *general* or *dispositional* nature. Characteristically, instructions prescribe a proper *attitude* that is meant to guide deliberation and action in a specific sphere of life. Thus, while instructions are situationally specific, they are dispositional in their prescriptions, often pointing to which particular virtue is most needed for that situation. Seneca confirms this, noting that, 'Of course there are slight distinctions, due to the time, of the place, or the person,' but he adds, 'even in these cases, precepts are given which have a general application.'[6] It is precisely this generality of application that makes instructions useful, because they are applicable to a general class of concrete life situations. Because instructions apply general principles to specific spheres of life, they are examples of discernment, but because they do not go so far as to prescribe concrete actions, discernment is still needed to determine the right action in a particular circumstance. In this way, the situationally specific yet

---

[4] SENECA, *EM*, 94.51. It is interesting to note that 1 Peter 2:21 uses the same analogy in describing Christ as a moral example (ὑπογραμμός) to be copied/followed.

[5] Cf. ANNAS, *Happiness*, 73, '[I]t is a shared assumption [among the schools] that such a disposition [i.e., discernment] is firm in relying on general principles, but must also always be sensitive to the complexities of particular situations.'

[6] SENECA, *EM*, 94.35.

dispositional nature of instructions serves to promote the acquisition of discernment.

Finally, instructions act to promote moral maturity simply because they encourage the pursuit of the virtuous life. Instructions are moral *exhortations*, reminding the listener of his duties and exhorting him to fulfill them. Oftentimes the real issue for the hearer is not one of discernment but of commitment, where one knows the path but does not take it. Here instructions are needed to encourage and to exhort. As Seneca argues:

> People say: "What good does it do to point out the obvious?" A great deal of good; for we sometimes know facts without paying attention to them. Advice is not teaching; it merely engages the attention and rouses us, and concentrates the memory, and keeps it from losing grip (*non docet admonitio, sed advertit, sed excitat, sed memoriam continet nec patitur elabi*). We miss much that is set before our very eyes. Advice is, in fact, a sort of exhortation. The mind often tries not to notice even that which lies before our eyes; we must therefore force upon it the knowledge of things that are perfectly well known (*ingerenda est itaque illi notitia rerum notissimarum*).[7]

Instructions then serve as an exhortation that stirs the hearer out of his complacency to virtuous action. Instructions are a catalyst to the proper function of the will. By 'engaging the attention and concentrating the memory,' instructions counteract a vast array of psychological impediments to virtue. As Seneca notes, one of the roles of instruction is to 'check and banish our emotions by a sort of official decree (*adfectus nostros velut edicto coercent et ablegant*).'[8] The emotions he has in mind here are those negative emotions that are enticements to vice. Instructions, according to Seneca, defeat these emotions by addressing our true natures. He argues that, 'The soul carries within itself the seed of everything that is honourable, and this seed is stirred to growth by advice, as a spark that is fanned by a gentle breeze develops its natural fire.'[9] Instructions, therefore, are a catalyst for virtue, providing encouragements and exhortations that 'fan the flames' of virtue in the face of laziness, self-indulgence and the allure of pleasure.

With respect to form, antithetical pairs and motive clauses operate at this level by promoting virtue in the face of affective resistance. Motive clauses provide the enticement of some long-term gain (e.g., εὐδαιμονία) that counters the attraction of the short-term gains promised by vice. Seneca applauds the utility of motive clauses, noting that, 'The counsel which assists suggestion by reason – which adds the motive for doing a

---

[7] SENECA, *EM*, 94.25.
[8] SENECA, *EM*, 94.47.
[9] SENECA, *EM*, 94.29.

given thing and the reward which awaits one who carries out and obeys such precepts – is more effective and settles deeper in the heart.'[1] Motive clauses redirect the desires of the listener away from the pleasures of vice, and towards the happiness that comes from a life rooted in virtue. Likewise, antithetical pairs rhetorically attack the path to vice while endorsing the road to virtue, reorienting emotional commitments and calling for action.

Summarizing, it is clear that instructions do a great deal more than simply specify moral norms; they also function in various ways to foster a life of virtue. First, instructions foster virtue by instigating virtuous deeds, the practice of which fosters virtue. Secondly, instructions nurture the development of the skill of φρόνησις through practice and imitation. Thirdly, instructions cultivate virtue by re-educating affective commitments: deprecating a life of vice while endorsing a desire for the fruits of virtue.

As we have seen before, fostering the life of virtue is typical of the paraenetic enterprise. Thus, we can easily see why moral instructions play such an important role in paraenesis as a genre. The central concern of paraenesis is with προκοπή (i.e., the progress from immaturity to maturity). Seneca recognizes that this road to maturity is a long one and argues that it is precisely for this reason that instructions are necessary. He says that since 'the approach to these qualities is slow, in the meantime, in practical matters, the path should be pointed out for the benefit of one who is still short of perfection, but is making progress (*interim etiam inperfecto sed proficienti demonstranda est in rebus agendis via*).'[2] Instructions, then, are a vital and indispensable[3] literary strategy at the disposal of a paraenetic author to further his agenda of promoting progress in the moral life.

A. *Function in 1 Peter*

What bearing then does this have on the moral instructions we find in 1 Peter? Are these instructions typical of Greco-Roman paraenesis-as-form and is their primary purpose the promotion of virtue? We have seen previously ample evidence that 1 Peter operates in a paraenetic mode. The

---

[1] SENECA, *EM*, 94.44.

[2] SENECA, *EM*, 94.50.

[3] As we have noted before, SENECA teaches that effective paraenesis is a marriage of doctrine and instructions. For instructions to be effective, they must be given a philosophic framework; but this framework does not make instructions superfluous. *Both* are needed in the work of character transformation. SENECA's basic argument in *EM* 95 is that precepts are ineffective apart from contextualizing dogmas. His *EM* 94 makes the complementary argument that dogmas without precepts are ineffective. Therefore, according to SENECA, instructions are a *necessary* element in the paraenetic venture of character formation.

letter clearly evidences a concern for growth, coupled with a focus on the centrality of the moral sphere as the arena of that growth (e.g., 2:1–3). It is reasonable to assume that the letter's concern to foster a καλὴ ἀναστροφή is furthered here in the instructions that give shape to the moral life of these Christian communities. If this is so, then we have little reason to suspect that the purpose of these instructions is any different than instructions in other examples of Greco-Roman paraenesis.

But here we must take care to appreciate the ways in which 1 Peter *differs* from the epistles of Isocrates, Seneca, or other comparable paraenetic epistles. The critical difference with respect to the question of epistolary purpose is the disparity in the situations being addressed. 1 Peter is written to address the problems of a particular collection of churches undergoing persecution. In general, Greco-Roman paraenetic epistles, while addressed to particular individuals, are not typically written to address a particular 'crisis situation', but could be written to almost anyone at almost any time.[4] Isocrates, for example, freely admits that some of his advice to Demonicus is not pertinent to his present station in life and will only be of use to him later on.[5]

So, we must take care not to *underestimate* the differences in situation and intention between 1 Peter and Greco-Roman paraenetic epistles. This is not a general letter that could be written to almost anyone at any time. It seeks to address a particular situation: a particular people in challenging circumstances at a particular time. Thus, we should be wary of taking the advice of the epistle too generally, as though it merely prescribed universal maxims about the good life.

Recognizing this however, the greater danger is that of *overestimating* the difference. We must also take care not to interpret these instructions as *so* particularized that they possess only short-term currency in response to the situation of suffering. This represents a greater danger because, in general, the historical model utilized in studying NT epistles is that of a 'crisis situation'. In trying to assess the import of an epistle in its historical setting, we typically attempt to discern the crisis (implied or explicit) being addressed. While this approach is often helpful, it can lead to distortions and oversimplifications. The difficulty here is that crises are specific short-term problems that require specific short-term solutions. In Galatians, for instance, the particular problem is the circumcision of

---

[4] Of course, there are some exceptions; PORPHYRY'S *Marcella* is an example.

[5] ISOCRATES, *Demonicus*, 44, 'Do not be surprised (καὶ μὴ θαυμάσῃς) that many things which I have said do not apply to you at your present age. For I also have not overlooked this fact, but I have deliberately chosen to employ this one treatise, not only to convey to you advice for your life now, but also to leave with you precepts for the years to come.'

Gentile converts to Christianity, and Paul's particular solution is abstention. The issue will continue to plague Paul's ministry, but for those who heed his advice in Galatia, the problem is solved.[6] If we apply this model to 1 Peter, then we are very likely to downplay the importance of the epistle's moral instructions for moral formation. Moral formation is a long-term goal; if we take the letter as solely seeking to address a short-term crisis of persecution, then moral formation will slip from view in our assessment of the author's strategy.

As we have noted before, this need not be the case if we see that the author's chief concern is not the potential for despondency in the face of trials, but the potential for moral failure, perhaps fueled by despondency, revealing itself in acts of vengeance. The author's focus is on the moral challenges of suffering.

While addressing the crisis of young churches facing persecution from their pagan neighbors, 1 Peter's response betrays both long-term and short-term goals. The author's exhortations to continue to do good in the face of unjust suffering advance *both* the short-term goal of winning a good reputation among hostile neighbors as well as the long-term goal of growth in moral maturity. The agenda here is not solely that of meeting a short-term crisis. This is most clearly seen in the general dispositional nature of the instructions given, which as we saw above characterize Greco-Roman paraenesis-as-form. Instead of specific commands like 1 Cor. 5:13, *Drive out the wicked person from among you,* we have in 2:17, *Honor all men. Love the brotherhood. Fear God. Honor the emperor.* In this verse, the advice given is situationally specific, delineating different duties in relation to specific groups, but general in what it prescribes (i.e., it prescribes *dispositions* instead of specific actions). In contrast, instructions that seek only to address a crisis give advice that is both situationally specific and specific in its prescriptions, as in 1 Cor. 5:13 above.

Even in those passages, like 3:14–15a, which directly address the issue of suffering, the advice given is dispositional; in response to suffering, the instructions there prescribe *attitudes* not specific actions. While our author does seek to console his readers in the midst of their persecution (e.g.,

---

[6] In reality this 'crisis situation' paradigm does not fit Galatians either, because there too, along with addressing the short-term crisis of circumcision, Paul includes general exhortations to moral fidelity consistent with Christian convictions (Gal. 5:13–6:10). Paul betrays a long-term goal of moral character formation. In fact, the issue of circumcision is raised, at least in part, because it is an impediment to that goal. Cf. J.M.G. BARCLAY, *Obeying the Truth: A Study of Paul's Ethics in Galatians.* SNTW (Edinburgh: T&T Clark, 1988).

4:13), his chief concern is with the moral challenge that arises from their situation. Thus, his response to suffering in 3:14–15a and elsewhere is to set down those attitudes that should govern the behavior of the Anatolian churches in the face of estrangement and violence. Again, this has long-term as well as short-term payoffs. In the short-term, it has the possibility of winning a good reputation and alleviating some of the tensions. Also, it addresses the immediate temptations of retaliation, isolation, and assimilation. But these temptations also pose a challenge to long-term growth, since moral character is formed over time through choices. Persecution then is a challenge to the project of long-term character formation. In answering the issue of persecution in the manner in which he does, our author is able to facilitate both his short-term as well as long-term agendas. We can see this all the more clearly in the example of the *Haustafel* in 2:18–3:7.

B. Haustafeln and Wisdom

The *Haustafel* in 1 Peter proves an illustrative example of the balance of short and long-term agendas pursued by our author. These instructions are directed to specific spheres of life and yet their advice is dispositional, prescribing attitudes that are to govern actions within the bounds of a particular relationship. The *Haustafel* seeks to ameliorate domestic tensions, but it also seeks to foster growth in character.

In the Greco-Roman world, interest in domestic life as a sphere of moral discourse has a rich and diverse heritage. While early NT form-critics located the origin of the *Haustafeln* among the Stoics, recent research[1] has shown that a concern for οἰκονομία had its roots in the thinking of Plato and Aristotle[2] and had a wide influence both in the Hellenistic schools[3] and in Hellenistic Judaism as well.[4] Thus, οἰκονομία was a relatively common topic for moral philosophy in the Greco-Roman world.

Elliott explains that, 'The societies of the Greco-Roman period were greatly concerned with the establishment and maintenance of "order" (*taxis*) in all areas of public and private life as a replication of an ordered universe (*kosmos*).'[5] This concern for order was the driving force behind dominant cultural practices that prized the recognition of one's proper

---

[1] See especially BALCH, *Wives*.

[2] See PLATO, *Laws*, 3:690 A–D; 6:771E–7; 824C, and ARISTOTLE, *Pol.*, 1253b; 1260a; *EN*, 1134b.

[3] See XENOPHON, *Oeconomicus*; PLUTARCH, *Moralia*, 138B–146A; ARIUS DIDYMUS, 2.148.16–19; SENECA, *Benefits*, 2.18.1–2; 3:18.1–4; PHILODEMUS, *Oeconomicus*; ALBINUS, *Introduction*, 27–33.

[4] See PHILO, *Joseph*, 38–39; *Decalogue*, 165–67; *Special Laws*, 2.225–27; 3.169–71; JOSEPHUS, *Apion*, 2.199; *Apology*, 2.206, 216; PS.-PHOCYLIDES, 175–227.

[5] ELLIOTT, *1 Peter*, 486.

place in the chain of superordination and subordination. It also found expression in a concern for domestic and civil order. As Elliott notes, 'After the Greek classical period, the household (*oikos*) and the city-state (*polis*) formed the fundamental and related building blocks of society.'[6] Thus, it is not surprising that we find such a keen interest in οἰκονομία among the philosophers. Seneca, for example, speaks of a particular 'department of philosophy which supplies precepts appropriate to the individual case, instead of framing them for mankind at large – which, for instance, advises how a husband should conduct himself towards his wife, or how a father should bring up his children, or how a master should rule his slaves.'[7] Here Seneca describes the *Haustafeln* as a species of moral instruction (*praeceptum*). Like other forms of moral instruction, its function is not simply to prescribe duties, but also to foster growth in moral maturity.[8] Later, Seneca identifies this 'department of philosophy' as wisdom (*iudicium*).[9] Thus, he sees the purpose of the *Haustafeln* as promoting the acquisition of wisdom as a necessary element in the virtuous life.

Examples of *Haustafeln* found in the NT writings[10] are manifestations of this concern for οἰκονομία in the ancient world. In 1 Peter this tradition is appropriated and adapted by the author to suit his paraenetic aims. The *Haustafel* proper (2:18–3:7) sits within the first large unit of moral instructions (2:13–3:12).[11] This *Haustafel* is preceded by a subunit (2:13–17) that begins with an exhortation of subordination to Roman authorities. Given the close ties drawn between civic and domestic morality in the ancient world, the close proximity of instructions concerning governing authorities and the *Haustafel* is not surprising.[12] The

---

[6] ELLIOTT, *1 Peter*, 505.

[7] SENECA, *EM*, 94.1. The tradition of addressing οἰκονομία in terms of the three essential relationships that comprised the οἰκός (i.e., husband and wife, father and son, master and slave) goes back to ARISTOTLE, in *Politics*, 1253b: 'The investigation of everything should begin with its smallest parts, and the primary and smallest parts of the household (μέρη οἰκίας) are master and slave (δεσπότης καὶ δοῦλος), husband and wife (πόσις καὶ ἄλοχος), father and children (πατὴρ καὶ τέκνα); we ought therefore to examine the proper constitution and character of each of these three relationships.'

[8] Cf. SENECA, *EM*, 95.45, where he says that instructions in οἰκονομία will be ineffective unless married to a system of doctrines, emphasizing that 'no one will do his duty as he ought, unless he has some principle to which he may refer his conduct (*nisi habuerit quo referat*).'

[9] SENECA, *EM*, 94.4.

[10] E.g., Eph. 5:22–6:9; Col. 3:18–4:1.

[11] Cf. ELLIOTT, *1 Peter*, 484.

[12] Cf. ELLIOTT, *1 Peter*, 505. '[I]n philosophic thought and moral exhortation, civil responsibilities (*politeia*) and domestic duties (*oikonomia*) were often discussed in tandem.'

concern for τάξις in both these arenas is shown in the use of the verb ὑποτάσσω both in 2:13 and in the *Haustafel* (2:18; 3:1, 5). This subunit ends with a string of commands in 2:17. The first imperative, πάντας τιμήσατε, echoes the command in 2:13, ὑποτάγητε πάσῃ ἀνθρωπίνῃ κτίσει, and is the governing imperative for the entire *Haustafel* that follows.[13] The circumstantial participles that begin each new subunit in the *Haustafel* (e.g., ὑποτασσόμενοι) particularize how to 'honor all' within a specific domestic sphere.[14]

1. Slaves

The *Haustafel* begins by addressing slaves/servants (οἰκέται) in 2:18–25. The materials in verses 21–25, where Christ is presented as a moral exemplar in his suffering, will be dealt with in detail in the following chapter on the *imitatio Christi* theme, so our interest here is focused on verses 18–20.

> 2:18–21: Servants, be submissive to your masters with all respect, (*Exhortation*)
> not only to the kind and gentle but also to the cruel. (*Qualification*)
> For one is approved if, mindful of God,
> he endures pain while suffering unjustly. (*Warrant*)
> For what credit is it, if when you do wrong and are beaten for it you take it patiently? But if when you do right and suffer for it you take it patiently, you have God's approval. (*Backing*)
> For to this you have been called, because Christ also suffered for you, leaving you an example, that you should follow... (*Backing: Example*)

The first thing that we observe here is that in its *form* this injunction to slaves utilizes the same building blocks we saw in the moral instructions

---

[13] The collocation of imperatives in 2:17 has been a cause for great speculation and consternation on the part of commentators (see E. BAMMEL, 'The Commands in 1 Peter II.17,' *NTS* 11 (1965): 279–81 for a brief survey). The first command (πάντας τιμήσατε) is the global command, as is obvious from the object πάντας. The aorist aspect reinforces this generality, since the aorist when used with imperatives typically envisions action as in some sense 'whole' or 'complete' (cf. McKAY, *Syntax*, 203–4). The remaining imperatives, all present aspect, are to be taken 'epexegetically', explaining how the church is to 'honor all'. It is not meant as a comprehensive explanation, since the activity of specification continues in the *Haustafel*. These three imperatives are *not* to be taken simply as examples of honoring all with the first command as a kind of heading (as e.g., MARTIN, *Metaphor*, 204–5, along with the NIV and NEB). While loving the brethren and honoring the emperor are examples of honoring all, fearing God is not (cf. ACHTEMEIER, *1 Peter*, 187), since πάντας refers only to *people* (as is clear from 2:13); instead this command extols reverence for God as the fundamental *motivation* for all action, as it is throughout the epistle, and more immediately in the *Haustafel* itself.

[14] The participles are not 'imperatival', cf. MARTIN, *Metaphor*, 204–5, and ACHTEMEIER, *1 Peter*, 194.

above. The *Haustafel* is another form of moral instruction, just as Seneca said above. As an instruction, it is built of the same elements that are common to all instructions: exhortation, specification, warrant, and backing. Its only distinguishing feature is the *topic*: οἰκονομία.

Secondly, it is important to note the situationally specific but attitudinal nature of the prescriptions given. The slaves are told to honor their masters by subordinating themselves (ὑποτάσσομαι) to them. As Elliott notes, the term ὑποτάσσω denotes, 'a recognition of and respect for order manifested in the acknowledgement of one's subordinate position in relation to those in authority, ...which involve[s] submission, deference to, subjection to, and obedience to superiors.'[15] The author's advice prescribes no concrete actions for the slaves, but rather the *mind-set* that is to control all their dealings with their masters. In all things they are to treat their masters with respect and deference. In addition, this is to be done ἐν παντὶ φόβῳ, which signals that reverence for God is the guiding motivation for treating their masters with respect.[16] This motivation is also attitudinal, describing the internal reality that is to shape concrete action.

Even as the circumstances become more specific, with slaves facing the challenge of suffering unjustly at the hands of wicked masters, the advice remains general. For those slaves who suffer unjustly for their faith[17] the author's advice is that they are to endure (ὑποφέρω/ὑπομένω) suffering and continue to honor their masters with respect and deference. As we have seen elsewhere, the author's chief concern is with the moral challenges that arise out of suffering. The purpose of his advice here is not to encourage passivity, but to discourage retaliation, either in extreme forms like flight or revolt[18] or in the myriad of subtler forms of disdain and disrespect.[19] What this will look like practically is left up to the individual slave to discern for himself, but the outlook that is to guide their response is a willingness to endure mistreatment for their faith because they are mindful

---

[15] ELLIOTT, *1 Peter*, 487.

[16] As in the previous verse, the object of fear/reverence is God. Apart from a scriptural allusion in 3:14, God is the sole legitimate object of φοβέομαι in 1 Peter. Cf. ACHTEMEIER, *1 Peter*, 188, 95.

[17] It is important to note here that the suffering that the slaves are commanded to endure is suffering for their faith, or as v. 20 expresses it suffering for 'doing good' (ἀγαθοποιΐα). Cf. ACHTEMEIER, *1 Peter*, 196.

[18] Not altogether uncommon responses for slaves in the ancient world. See K.R. BRADLEY, *Slavery and Society at Rome*, KTAH (Cambridge: Cambridge University Press, 1996), 107–31.

[19] This is confirmed in the use of Christ as an example of one who suffered injustice and did not retaliate, but instead chose to entrust himself to God and to continue in doing good.

of God (διὰ συνείδησιν θεοῦ), knowing that he looks upon such endurance with favor (χάρις).

The author's form of advice furthers both his short and long-term agendas. He gives advice that addresses the immediate concern of persecution, with a program designed at possibly alleviating this tension, but without a compromise of moral integrity. This immediate challenge, however, is also an opportunity for long-term growth in character. Choosing to continue in well-doing in the face of persecution will produce in the slaves a well-seated moral fortitude. Likewise, the form of advice (specific yet attitudinal) helps them to see how their faith shapes their moral lives in a particular sphere, but still necessitates the exercise of their own moral judgment in everyday decisions, thus aiding in the development of discernment.

2. Wives

We can see similar dynamics operating in the author's advice to wives. As before, while the situation is specific, the advice is general and pertains to attitudes that govern behavior.

> 3:1–6: Likewise you wives, be submissive to your husbands, *(Exhortation)*
> so that some, though they do not obey the word,
> may be won without a word by the behavior of their wives, *(Motive)*
> when they see your reverent and chaste behavior. *(Qualification)*
> Let not yours be the outward adorning with braiding of hair,
> decoration of gold, and wearing of fine clothing,
> but let it be the hidden person of the heart with the imperishable
> jewel of a gentle and quiet spirit, *(Antithetical Pair)*
> which in God's sight is very precious. *(Warrant)*
> So once the holy women who hoped in God used to adorn themselves
> and were submissive to their husbands, *(Backing: Example)*
> as Sarah obeyed Abraham, calling him lord.
> And you are now her children if you do right
> and let nothing terrify you. *(Backing: Example)*

Again the keyword ὑποτάσσομαι is adopted to inform wives of their proper disposition towards their husbands, honoring them by showing appropriate respect and deference. Specifically, the author has in mind the case of a Christian wife married to an unbelieving husband. The hope is that through her recognizable good life (ἀναστροφή) her husband might be won over (κερδαίνω) to the faith.[20] Again the focus here is on inner dispositions (ὁ

---

[20] The unbelief of the husband is shown not only by his disobedience to the gospel (ἀπείθεια τῷ λόγῳ), but especially in the hope that he may be won over (κερδαίνω) to it. Cf. D. DAUBE, 'Κερδαίνω as a Missionary Term,' *HTR* 40 (1947): 109–20, cited by ACHTEMEIER, *1 Peter*, 210.

κρυπτὸς τῆς καρδίας ἄνθρωπος). Wives are to 'win' their husbands not by means of external adornments, but by the manifestation of their incorruptible character in a gentle and peaceful spirit. This is how Sarah and other 'holy women' in the past 'adorned' (κοσμέω) themselves, subordinating themselves to their husbands. As with the slaves above, the motivation for subordination is rooted in a devotion to God and doing what is precious in his sight.

In his advice to wives, our author reveals not only his concern for the immediate difficulty of wives with unbelieving husbands, but also how this situation will affect the long-term growth in Christian character for these women. Throughout, his concern is with how inner convictions shape their ἀναστροφή, and that their lives would be characterized by ἀγαθοποιΐα, just as with Sarah and the other holy women in the past. Thus, our author's advice that these wives should subordinate themselves to their husbands serves both the short-term goal of winning husbands to the faith, as well as the long-term goal of growth in character.

3. Husbands

Likewise, our author's brief word to husbands also exhibits immediate as well as long-term concerns, focusing on the mind-set that is to direct how they live with their wives.

> 3:7: Likewise you husbands, live considerately with your wives, (*Exhortation*)
> bestowing honor on the woman as the weaker sex, (*Qualification*)
> since you are joint heirs of the grace of life, (*Warrant*)
> in order that your prayers may not be hindered. (*Motive*)

The author challenges husbands to live with their wives recognizing their comparative weakness (ἀσθενέστερον), but at the same time bestowing due honor (ἀπονέμω τιμήν) on them as fellow heirs of the grace of life (ὡς συγκληρονόμοις χάριτος ζωῆς). Thus, while wives receive special consideration as 'weaker vessels', this does not imply inferiority; there is an equality of person as fellow members in the church and fellow heirs of the same salvation. The author bluntly warns husbands that God will not hear the prayers of those who mistreat their wives.[21] In this way, the author reminds husbands that their spirituality is measured by how they honor their wives. His advice checks the husbands' proclivity toward domination

---

[21] Cf. ACHTEMEIER, *1 Peter*, 218, 'The point is clear: men who transfer cultural notions about the superiority of men over women in the Christian community lose their ability to communicate with God.' ELLIOTT, *1 Peter*, 582, explains that, '1 Peter reflects the common Christian conviction that prayer, as an expression of one's relationship to God and an act of praise, thanksgiving, confession, and petition, is directly affected by one's behavior toward other persons.'

in a patriarchal society, but leaves open precisely how they are to honor their wives as sisters in the Lord. Thus, once again the form of instruction prescribes moral consequences of Christian belief, but leaves the discernment of concrete everyday actions to the reader.

4. Wisdom

These verses that follow (8–12) do not technically belong to the *Haustafel* since they do not deal with οἰκονομία, but syntactically these verses constitute the conclusion to this subunit.[22] The adjectives in verse 8 (with the implied participle of being: ὄντες) are dependent upon the command πάντας τιμήσατε in 2:17, just as the participles in the *Haustafel* proper.[23] Syntactically there is no disjunction here; the discontinuity is only in the *topic*. While it is traditional to see a break here, the author does not signal a transition to a new unit until verse 13.[24] To understand the function of the *Haustafel* in its context we have to continue to the end of this unit of discourse in verse 12.

In verses 8–9 the author turns from addressing specific members of the household to addressing the whole household of God,[25] outlining those virtues that should characterize relationships within the church.

> 3:8–9: Finally, all of you, have unity of spirit, sympathy, love of the brethren,
> a tender heart and a humble mind. (*Exhortation*)
> Do not return evil for evil or reviling for reviling;
> but on the contrary bless (*Antithetical Pair*)
> for to this you have been called,
> that you may obtain a blessing. (*Warrant w/Motive*)

The first adjective ὁμόφρονες informs us that the author has in mind relations *within* the circle of believers, since this attitude (along with

---

[22] Cf. ACHTEMEIER, *1 Peter*, 220–1.

[23] So also ACHTEMEIER, *1 Peter*, 222, 'As in the case of the other passages that were addressed to various groups (2:18; 3:1; 3:7), this passage, addressed now to all readers (πάντες), may similarly be understood as dependent on the imperatives of 2:17, and as assuming the participle ὄντες to complete the meaning of the adjectives.' Cf. SELWYN, *1 Peter*, 188.

[24] Here a devotion to *Gattungen* has led commentators to see a break at the end of the *Haustafel*, where syntactically no break exists. To argue for a break in the discourse is to impose a contemporary form-critical category (*Haustafeln*) upon the text, against the witness of linguistic evidence.

[25] It is likely that the author's stress elsewhere on the church's identity as a household (οἶκός) is the reason for his augmentation of the οἰκονομία tradition in this way. (A point surprisingly lost on ELLIOTT.) The author makes a similar move in 5:1–5 where he addresses elders and young men in a mode analogous to the *Haustafeln* (ὁμοίως, νεώτεροι, ὑποτάγητε πρεσβυτέροις), advising both on how to respect and honor one another through recognition of their differences in station.

φιλαδελφία) does not characterize relationships with outsiders, but rather the unity and love of the family of God. The advice here prescribes *attitudes* that are to guide relationships within the church: unity, sympathy, brotherly love, compassion, and humility. The author then gives an example of how to practice such virtues. When conflicts do arise, he urges them not to return evil for evil, but to return a blessing instead. In doing so, the author gives a situationally specific application of the virtues cataloged in the previous verse.[26] Again, unsurprisingly, the author's advice is general and leaves room for the individual to discern how to bless his brother in response to slander. The form, again, realizes the short-term goal of unity and love in the church, but also the complementary long-term goal of growth in maturity. The command to meet a curse with a blessing reflects an *implicit* appropriation, in some manner, of the Jesus tradition regarding love for enemies (Mt. 5:39–42; Lk. 6:27–36), as does the promise that those who do so will receive a 'blessing' (Lk. 6:35). Our author seeks *explicit* legitimation for his advice in the wisdom language of Ps. 33.

Verses 10–12, loosely quoting LXX Ps. 33:13–17a, are the author's conclusion to this section and the context for the preceding *Haustafel*, placing these instructions within the context of wisdom for life. *For 'He that would love life and see good days, let him keep his tongue from evil and his lips from speaking guile; let him turn away from evil and do right; let him seek peace and pursue it. For the eyes of the Lord are upon the righteous, and his ears are open to their prayer. But the face of the Lord is against those that do evil.'* The command παυσάτω τὴν γλῶσσαν ἀπὸ κακοῦ is closely connected to the admonition to *not return evil for evil or slander for slander* in verse 9. But these verses serve more than just the immediately preceding verse; they are the context for the whole section.[27] The command to ἐκκλινάτω δὲ ἀπὸ κακοῦ καὶ ποιησάτω ἀγαθόν echoes one of the keywords of this section: ἀγαθοποιέω (2:14, 15, 20; 3:6), and embodies the fundamental response of the author to persecution at the hands of master and husbands. Likewise the command ζητησάτω εἰρήνην καὶ διωξάτω αὐτήν resonates with the overall outlook of the *Haustafel*. More specifically, the command μὴ λαλῆσαι δόλον echoes the declaration regarding Jesus' exemplary character found in 2:22: οὐδὲ εὑρέθη δόλος ἐν τῷ στόματι αὐτοῦ. Equally, the promise that the Lord hears the prayers of the righteous but rejects the evildoer in 3:12 echoes the sentiment in 3:7 that God will not hear the prayers of husbands who mistreat their wives.

---

[26] The reference here is still to relationships (and therefore conflict) within the church. Nothing in the context suggests that the topic has shifted to relationships with outsiders. Contra ACHTEMEIER, *1 Peter*, 225, and ELLIOTT, *1 Peter*, 606.

[27] Cf. ACHTEMEIER, *1 Peter*, 226.

So, we can see that this passage from Ps. 33 is intimately connected with this entire section and gives a conclusion to it, and thus also serves as a context in which to read the *Haustafel*.

Like Seneca, 1 Peter places the *Haustafel* in the context of wisdom. Instructions are an aid to those who desire ζωὴν ἀγαπᾶν καὶ ἰδεῖν ἡμέρας ἀγαθάς. The author utilizes the *Haustafel* as a tool to promote the acquisition of the long-term benefits of a virtuous life. Such benefits come through avoiding evil and deceit, and doing good and seeking peace with others, because these benefits are gifts from the Lord, and he looks with favor on the righteous, but looks down on the evildoer.

Thus, we can see clearly that the *Haustafel*, as a representative form of moral instruction in 1 Peter, functions to achieve both immediate and long-term ends. In the short-term, they regulate proper conduct with hostile outsiders in an effort to win respect and possibly converts. In the long-term, they work to foster growth in Christian maturity, through growth in moral integrity and discernment.

III. Conclusion

Thus, the author of 1 Peter, once again, utilizes a literary strategy typical of Greco-Roman paraenetic. By incorporating moral instructions into his epistle, our author signals his paraenetic aims. These instructions not only serve his short-term goals of restraining misconduct that might arise in response to suffering mistreatment, but, because they encourages a lifestyle characterized by virtuous living, they also serve to foster the long-term goal of growth in character.

By specifying how fundamental beliefs shape everyday behavior, moral instructions aid these converts in the process of conforming their lives to their convictions. As we saw, moral instructions serve not only to define ethical norms but also to aid growth in character and discernment, both in terms of intellectual development and affective reorientation. Moral instructions then are another effective tool in the hand of our author to achieve his paraenetic aim of advancing growth in Christian maturity.

Chapter Seven

Imitatio Christi

Like moral instructions, moral example (παράδειγμα) is a staple literary device in paraenesis. In pointing to the examples of virtuous men, a paraenetic author's precepts come to life in realized biographies, which serve to demonstrate the possibility and fruits of the virtuous life and to encourage imitation. The author of 1 Peter utilizes this standard paraenetic literary strategy by using Christ as an example to be both admired and followed.

It may seem odd that the *imitatio Christi* theme is examined here alongside moral instructions instead of with the previous chapters on paraenetic theology. The reason for this is that Greco-Roman moralists thought of moral exemplars as going hand in hand with moral instructions. As Fiore notes, 'Example and precept enjoyed a long and, as seems likely, natural relationship as complementary hortatory devices.'[1] Thus, given that background, it is more natural to treat them together, but this is another reminder of the degree to which theology and ethics are intricately linked in 1 Peter.

I. Example in Greco-Roman Paraenesis

In his epistolary handbook, which we looked at previously, Libanius gives as his prototypical paraenetic letter a call to imitate virtuous men: 'Always be an emulator (ζηλωτής), dear friend, of virtuous men (τῶν ἐναρέτων ἀνδρῶν). For it is better to be well spoken of when imitating good men than to be reproached by all men while following evil men.'[2] In this very concise example, Libanius combines a call to imitation with an antithetical precept. Thus, for him, precept, example, and moral antithesis comprise the basic elements of a paraenetic epistle. Libanius' prototype testifies to

---

[1] B. FIORE, *The Function of Personal Example in the Socratic and Pastoral Epistles*, AnBib 105 (Rome: Editrice Pontificio Istituto Biblico, 1986), 93–4. Cf. SENECA, *EM*, 84.10, 'I would have my mind of such a quality as this; it should be equipped with many arts, many precepts, and patterns of conduct taken from many epochs of history (*multarum aetatum exempla*); but all should blend harmoniously into one.'

[2] (PSEUDO-) LIBANIUS, *Epistolary Styles*, 52.

the common ancient opinion that παράδειγμα was an essential tool in paraenetic persuasion. This is demonstrated by the frequent use of moral example in Greco-Roman paraenetic literature; a literary strategy so ubiquitous only a minute sample can be given here.

Example can be described as the allusion to elements of an individual's biography for the purpose of extolling that individual's virtue (or disparaging their vice) as an example to be followed (or avoided). The exemplar can be a personage either fictional or historical, but the latter is preferable, since one of the purposes of example is to exhibit *realized* virtue. The individual may be living or dead, and he may be someone known personally or only by legend. The exemplar must be someone whose biography is, in some measure, known to the reader. As we will see, example does not aim to communicate biography as such, instead it highlights particular elements of an individual's biography to extol their virtuous character.

A. Examples and Instructions

Our first concern is to learn how examples *function* as a paraenetic literary strategy. Seneca observes that moral exemplars function in ways that are analogous to the functionality of instructions. In a passage extolling the use of examples he says, 'Nothing is more successful in bringing honourable influences to bear upon the mind, or in straightening out the wavering spirit that is prone to evil, than association with good men. For the frequent seeing, the frequent hearing of them little by little sinks into the heart and acquires the force of precepts.'[3] Seneca here is thinking of living examples, but the idea is applicable to all examples. His point is that association with virtuous men affects us, and so 'acquires the force of precepts.' But how do examples become like precepts?

To see how, we first must begin by recalling the nature of virtue and how precepts aid in the acquisition of virtue. As we saw in the previous chapter, because virtue is a disposition, it is acquired by practice, not only by contemplation. It is only through the practice of virtuous deeds that one begins to obtain virtue – the twin ability of discerning and carrying out the virtuous course of action in a particular circumstance. Therefore, precepts are helpful, not only because they *define* particular duties, but also because they *command* them. That is, precepts call for action as well as contemplation.

Given this explanation, it is easier to see the functional similarities between examples and instructions. Examples, like instructions, define duties and invite action. As Isocrates says, '[W]e exhort young men to the study of philosophy by praising others (προτρέπομεν ἐπὶ τὴν φιλοσοφίαν

---

[3] SENECA, *EM*, 94.40.

ἑτέρους ἐπαινοῦντες) in order that they, emulating (ζηλοῦντες) those who are eulogized, may desire (ἐπιθυμῶσιν) to adopt the same pursuits.'[4] Examples provide a pattern to follow and a person to emulate; in so doing, they define duties and invite action. In this way, their function is similar to that of instructions. Along similar lines, Philo portrays examples as the embodiment of instructions, or 'living laws':

These are such men as lived good and blameless lives, whose virtues stand permanently recorded in the most holy scriptures, not merely to sound their praises but for the instruction of the reader and as an inducement to him to aspire to the same (ἀλλὰ καὶ ὑπὲρ τοῦ τοὺς ἐντυγχάνοντας προτρέψασθαι καὶ ἐπὶ τὸν ὅμοιον ζῆλον ἀγαγεῖν); for in these men we have laws endowed with life and reason (οἱ γὰρ ἔμψυχοι καὶ λογικοὶ νόμοι ἄνδρες ἐκεῖνοι γεγόνασιν).[5]

So these virtuous men become embodied laws, realized instructions. As instructions are worthy of adherence, so examples are worthy of being followed. Exemplars are living instructions because they have lived lives in accord with Reason/Nature. Instructions are the application of reason to particular spheres of life, and exemplars display reasonable virtuous actions in specific situations. Thus, both instructions and examples involve the application of reason to particularities of life.[6]

At the same time examples also *differ* from instructions in many respects. Because examples are personal, they possess an element of concrete reality that is missing from instructions, which, despite their specificity, are still unrealized theory. Examples represent, by definition, things within the realm of human experience and possibility. Instructions depict only what is within the realm of human potentiality. Seneca uses this to his advantage to show his pupil Lucilius that the virtuous life is possible:

Change therefore to better associations: live with the Catos, with Laelius, with Tubero. Or, if you enjoy living with Greeks also, spend your time with Socrates and with Zeno: the former will show you how to die if it be necessary; the latter how to die before it is necessary. ...The only harbour safe from the seething storms of this life is scorn of the future, a firm stand, a readiness to receive Fortune's missiles full in the breast, neither skulking nor turning the back.

...Why, pray, my dear Lucilius, should a man fear toil, or a mortal death? Countless cases occur to my mind of men who think that what they themselves are unable to do is

---

[4] ISOCRATES, *Evagoras*, 77.

[5] PHILO, *Abraham*, 1.4–5.

[6] Cf. W.C. SPOHN, *Go and Do Likewise: Jesus and Ethics* (New York: Continuum, 1999), 33, '[S]ince virtues are skills, they need examples to show what they mean practically. They have to be displayed concretely to convey their tactical meaning. In order to grasp how courage and integrity operate, we need accounts of persons who have shown these virtues in the tangle of circumstances.'

impossible, who maintain that we utter words which are too big for man's nature to carry out. But how much more highly do I think of these men! They can do these things, but decline to do them. To whom that ever tried have these tasks proved false? To what man did they not seem easier in the doing? Our lack of confidence is not the result of difficulty; the difficulty comes from our lack of confidence.

If, however, you desire a pattern, take Socrates, a long-suffering old man, who was sea-tossed amid every hardship and yet was unconquered (*invictum*)... Amid all the disturbance of Fortune, he was undisturbed (*aequalis fuit in tanta inaequalitate fortunae*).

Do you desire another case? Take that of the younger Marcus Cato, with whom Fortune dealt in a more hostile and more persistent fashion. But he withstood her, on all occasions, and in his last moments, at the point of death, showed that a brave man can live in spite of Fortune, can die in spite of her (*ostendit tamen virum fortem posse invita fortuna vivere, invita mori*).

...You see that man can endure toil (*vides posse homines laborem pati*): Cato, on foot, led an army through African deserts. You see that thirst can be endured (*vides posse tolerari sitim*): he marched over sun-baked hills, dragging the remains of a beaten army and with no train of supplies, undergoing lack of water and wearing a heavy suit of armour; always the last to drink of the few springs which they chanced to find. You see that honour, and dishonour too, can be despised (*vides honorem et notam posse contemni*): for they report that on the very day when Cato was defeated at the elections, he played a game of ball. You see also that man can be free from fear of those above him in rank (*vides posse non timeri potentiam superiorum*): for Cato attacked Caesar and Pompey simultaneously, at a time when none dared fall foul of the one without endeavouring to oblige the other. You see that death can be scorned as well as exile (*vides tam mortem posse contemni quam exilium*): Cato inflicted exile upon himself and finally death, and war all the while.

And so, if only we are willing to withdraw our necks from the yoke, we can keep as stout a heart against such terrors as these. But first and foremost, we must reject pleasures; they render us weak and womanish; they make great demands upon us, and, moreover, cause us to make great demands upon Fortune. Second, we must spurn wealth: wealth is the diploma of slavery. Abandon gold and silver, and whatever else is a burden upon our richly furnished homes; liberty cannot be gained for nothing. If you set a high value on liberty, you must set a low value on everything else.[7]

Here Seneca uses the examples of Socrates and Cato to demonstrate that the philosophic life, while difficult, is not impossible. He emphasizes this rhetorically in the penultimate paragraph with the repeated phrase *vides posse*, 'you see it is possible'. The biographies of Socrates and Cato catalog how they *accomplished* what Seneca is promoting: liberty from the twists of Fortune. These men were unchanged by their tragic situations; thus, they are living examples of Seneca's Stoic ideal. They demonstrate the possibility of living that ideal, and thus move it from the realm of theory to human actuality and possibility.[8]

---

[7] SENECA, *EM*, 104.22–34.

[8] PHILO makes a similar point in *Abraham*, 1.5, saying that, 'Moses extolled them [i.e., virtuous men] for two reasons. First he wished to show that the enacted ordinances

B. An Emotional Connection

Examples also function at an emotional level by fostering admiration and love for the exemplar and then directing this affective commitment toward the virtues they embody. As Isocrates and Philo have already said, in example virtuous men are praised so that young men will admire them, and this admiration will lead them to follow their example. Examples establish a personal connection between exemplar and follower. Exemplars must be worthy of respect, because this emotional connection is primarily one of reverence directed toward the exemplar who is admirable for his virtuous life. In the beginning of his *Pericles*, Plutarch makes a similar point about the need for the exemplar to be worthy of admiration:

A color is suited to the eye if its freshness, and its pleasantness as well, stimulates and nourishes the vision; and so our intellectual vision must be applied (τὴν διάνοιαν ἐπάγειν δεῖ θεάμασιν) to such objects as, by their very charm, invite it onward to its own proper good (πρὸς τὸ οἰκεῖον αὐτὴν ἀγαθὸν ἐκκαλεῖ). Such objects are to be found in virtuous deeds (ἐν τοῖς ἀπ' ἀρετῆς ἔργοις); these implant in those who search them out (τοῖς ἱστορήσασιν) a great and zealous eagerness which leads to imitation (ἀγωγὸν εἰς μίμησιν). In other cases, admiration of the deed is not immediately accompanied by an impulse to do it.

...For it does not of necessity follow that, if the work delights you with its grace, the one who wrought it is worthy of your esteem. Wherefore the spectator is not advantaged by those things at sight of which no ardor for imitation arises in the breast (πρὸς ἃ μιμητικὸς οὐ γίνεται ζῆλος). ...But virtuous action straightway so disposes a man that he no sooner admires the works of virtue than he strives to emulate those who wrought them (ἀλλ' ἥ γε ἀρετὴ ταῖς πράξεσιν εὐθὺς οὕτω διατίθησιν ὥστε ἅμα θαυμάζεσθαι τὰ ἔργα καὶ ζηλοῦσθαι τοὺς εἰργασμένους). ...The Good creates a stir of activity towards itself, and implants at once in the spectator an active impulse; it does not form his character by ideal representation alone (ἠθοποιοῦν οὐ τῇ μιμήσει τὸν θεατήν), but through the investigation of its work it furnishes him with a dominant purpose (ἀλλὰ τῇ ἱστορίᾳ τοῦ ἔργου τὴν προαίρεσιν παρεχόμενον). For such reasons I have decided to persevere in my writing of Lives (βίους).[9]

So Plutarch says that a virtuous action alone is not enough, to be exemplary it must be the action of a virtuous man. Individuals, not actions, are exemplars. When a virtuous person performs virtuous deeds, then the beauty of his deeds fills us with admiration and drives us to imitation. So, for examples to be effective they must be worthy of our deepest respect and affection. Elsewhere, Plutarch stresses that this sort of affection for

---

are not inconsistent with nature; and secondly that those who wish to live in accordance with the laws as they stand have no difficult task, seeing that the first generations before any at all of the particular statutes was set in writing followed the unwritten law with perfect ease.'

[9] PLUTARCH, *Pericles*, 1.3–4; 2.2–4. We will deal shortly with the relationship between biography (βίος) and the use of example.

virtuous men is an absolutely essential element in progress in the moral life:

Furthermore, as has already been said, the translating of our judgments into deeds, and not allowing our words to remain mere words, but to make them into actions, is, above all else, a specific mark of progress (προκοπῆς). An indication of this is, in the first place, the desire to emulate what we commend, eagerness to do what we admire, and, on the other hand, unwillingness to do, or even to tolerate, what we censure. ...We must therefore believe we are making but little progress so long as the admiration which we feel for successful men remains inert within us and does not of its own self stir us to imitation (ἀκίνητον ἐξ ἑαυτοῦ πρὸς μίμησιν). ...Indeed a peculiar symptom of true progress is found in this feeling (καὶ γὰρ τοῦτο προκοπῆς ἀληθοῦς ἴδιόν ἐστι πάθος) of love and affection for the disposition (διάθεσιν) shown by those whose deeds we try to emulate, and in the fact that our efforts to make ourselves like them are always attended by a goodwill which accords to them respect and honour.

...Whenever, therefore, we begin so to love good men, that not only...do we regard as blessed the man himself who has self-control...but also, through our admiration and affection for his habit, gait, look, and smile, we are eager to join, as it were, and cement ourselves to him (συναρμόττειν καὶ συγκολλᾶν ἑαυτοὺς ὦμεν πρόθυμοι), then we must believe that we are truly making progress (τότε χρὴ νομίζειν ἀληθῶς προκόπτειν). Still more is this the case if we do not limit our admiration of the good to their days of unclouded fortune, but if, just as lovers fondly welcome even lisping or pallor in their fair ones, and as the tears and dejection of Pantheia in all her grief and wretchedness smote the heart of Araspes, so we do not shrink at the thought of the exile of Aristeides, the imprisonment of Anaxagoras, or the penury of Socrates, or the sentence pronounced on Phocion, but because we believe that virtue, even when attended by such afflictions, is worthy of our love (ἀλλὰ καὶ μετὰ τούτων ἀξιέραστον ἡγούμενοι τὴν ἀρετὴν), we try to approach close to it (ὁμόσε χωπῶμεν αὐτῇ), and at each experience of this sort give utterance to this sentiment of Euripides, "The noble honour find in everything."[10]

Here Plutarch encourages his readers to 'love good men' to the point of being, 'as it were, cemented' to them. He also admonishes them to not to shrink away from following them into their tragic circumstances. In this way virtuous men become guides and encouragers in difficulties and temptations. Thus, exemplars are not merely patterns to be followed, but persons to be revered and loved.

This emotional 'relationship' between exemplar and follower is essential to the proper function of examples. It is from this connection that the follower's commitment to the virtuous life draws its energy. The follower is not merely following doctrines or precepts, but is following in the footsteps of a real person. This means that to fail is to fail a person not an idea, and to succeed is to join in the honor of a virtuous man. Seneca speaks of exemplars as respected companions that guide us:

---

[10] PLUTARCH, *Progress*, 84B–85C.

Hear and take to heart this useful and wholesome motto: 'Cherish some man of high character, and keep him ever before your eyes, living as if he were watching you, and ordering all your actions as if he beheld them.' Such, my dear Lucilius, is the counsel of Epicurus; he has quite properly given us a guardian and an attendant (*custodem nobis et paedagogum dedit, nec inmerito*). We can get rid of most sins, if we have a witness who stands near us when we are likely to go wrong. The soul should have someone whom it can respect...Choose therefore a Cato; or, if Cato seems too severe a model, choose some Laelius, a gentler spirit. Choose a master whose life, conversation, and soul-expressing face have satisfied you; picture him always to yourself as your protector or your pattern (*illum tibi semper ostende vel custodem vel exemplum*). For we must indeed have someone according to whom we may regulate our characters; you can never straighten that which is crooked unless you use a ruler.[11]

Thus, exemplars become trusted companions, protectors as well as patterns, a witness of all our actions to shame us from dishonorable deeds. Exemplars become intimate friends who know our inner selves, and thus become moral guides.

The emotional connection of admiration and love is important because devotion to the virtuous exemplar vies with those emotional ties that would thwart the progress of virtue. Plutarch and Seneca take the emotional temptations of life seriously, and so they see example as a powerful and essential tool because it does battle at the emotional level as well as the cognitive, and it directs powerful emotional commitments in the direction of virtue. Hence, the emotional connection between exemplar and follower is an essential ingredient in effective moral examples.

C. What to Imitate?

But what *specifically* about exemplars is imitable? Are we, like Cato, to walk barefoot through the desert, or to drink the poison of Socrates? What about exemplars are we meant to emulate and imitate? Plutarch, at the beginning of his life of Alexander, explains his approach in writing his 'Lives' (βίοι):

I do not tell of all the famous actions of these men, nor even speak exhaustively at all in each particular case, but in epitome for the most part...For it is not Histories that I am writing, but Lives (οὔτε γὰρ ἱσορίας γράφομεν, ἀλλὰ βίους); and in the most illustrious deeds there is not always a manifestation of virtue or vice, nay, a slight thing (ἀλλὰ πρᾶγμα βραχὺ) like a phrase or a jest often makes a greater revelation of character (ἔμφασιν ἤθους ἐποίησε μᾶλλον) than battles where thousands fall, or the greatest armaments, or sieges of cities. Accordingly, just as painters get the likeness (ὁμοιότητας) in their portraits from the face and the expression of the eyes, wherein the character shows itself (οἷς ἐμφαίνεται τὸ ἤθος), but make very little account of the other parts of the body, so I must be permitted to devote myself rather to the signs of the soul in men

---

[11] SENECA, *EM*, 11.8–10.

(οὕτως ἡμῖν δοτέον εἰς τὰ τῆς ψυξῆς σημεῖα μᾶλλον), and by means of these to portray the life of each, leaving to others the description of the great contests.[12]

We of course must be careful not to confuse genres, mixing ancient biography and paraenetic epistles. But example in paraenetic literature does operate in a 'biographic mode',[13] and thus the function of example within paraenetic is closely related to the function of biography as a genre. For Plutarch (and others) the primary purpose of biography is moral education.[14] We saw above, in the excerpt from his *Pericles*, that his intention in writing βίοι is to encourage the imitation of virtuous men. Plutarch's point here regarding biography, that he focuses on details because they reveal the character of the individual, also applies to examples. Examples focus attention on particular details that reveal certain character traits of the exemplar, and it is those specific traits that are to be imitated. As Fiore says, 'When demonstration of virtues and vices is the aim, then the deeds or particular qualities given are witnesses not to the whole personality but to the aspect being considered.'[15] Thus, the author focuses our attention on those character traits of the exemplar he wishes to inculcate in his readers. He does this by citing specific deeds that reveal the inner dispositions of the exemplars; it is this virtuous character that is to be imitated, not (necessarily) the specific deed.

Therefore, one does not imitate Cato by marching an army through the desert on foot, but by practicing his virtue of enduring hard labor. Note again Plutarch's statement that, 'The Good creates a stir of activity towards itself, and implants at once in the spectator an active impulse; it does not form his character by ideal representation alone (ἠθοποιοῦν οὐ τῇ μιμήσει τὸν θεατήν), but through the *investigation of its work* it furnishes him with a *dominant purpose* (ἀλλὰ τῇ ἱστορίᾳ τοῦ ἔργου τὴν προαίρεσιν παρεχόμενον).'[16] Character formation (ἠθοποιία) is achieved through the contemplation of virtuous deeds and the appropriation of the virtuous

---

[12] PLUTARCH, *Alexander*, 1.1–3.

[13] R.A. BURRIDGE, *What are the Gospels?: A Comparison with Graeco-Roman Biography*, SNTSMS 70 (Cambridge: Cambridge University Press, 1992), 41, describes how genres have correlate 'modes' within other genres. He explains that, 'Whereas a genre can be described in terms of a noun, mode is better seen adjectivally. Thus, a tragedy is an example of that genre and we would have certain expectations arising from the appropriate conventions of tragedy; however, things may occur in a tragic mode in all sorts of different writings and genres without those conventions.' Here BURRIDGE is appropriating the work of FOWLER, *Kinds*, 106–11.

[14] Cf. LIVY, *City*, 1, Preface: 10–11. For a summary of the generic function of biography see BURRIDGE, *Gospels*, 55–81. He places βίος on a continuum between 'history' and 'encomium' (65).

[15] FIORE, *Personal Example*, 92.

[16] PLUTARCH, *Pericles*, 2.3. Italics added.

principle (προαίρεσις) enacted. Specific virtuous *deeds* are exemplary, because they reveal certain virtuous *dispositions*. Above Plutarch said that, 'a peculiar symptom of true progress is found in this feeling of love and affection for the disposition (διάθεσις) shown by those whose deeds we try to emulate.'[17] Thus, it is the *disposition* of the exemplar to which he attaches central importance as the locus of affective commitments, while deeds are admired because they *reveal* these inner dispositions.

One final passage from Isocrates' letter to Demonicus will illustrate many of the points we have tried to establish here regarding moral example. Isocrates enlists Demonicus' own father Hipponicus as an example to be followed. He extols Hipponicus for his virtuous principles illustrated in his virtuous life:

Nay, if you will but recall also your father's principles (προαιρέσεις), you will have from your own house a noble illustration (παράδειγμα) of what I am telling you. For he did not (οὐ) belittle virtue nor (οὐδέ) pass his life in indolence; on the contrary (ἀλλά), he trained his body by toil, and by his spirit he withstood dangers (τῇ δὲ ψυχῇ τοὺς κινδύνους ὑπέμενεν). Nor (οὐδέ) did he love wealth inordinately; but (ἀλλά), although (μέν) he enjoyed the good things at his hand as became a mortal, yet (δέ) he cared for his possessions as if he had been immortal. Neither did he order his existence sordidly (οὐδὲ ταπεινῶς διῴκει τὸν αὐτοῦ βίον), but was a lover of beauty (ἀλλὰ φιλόκαλος), munificent in his manner of life, and generous to his friends; and he prized more those who were devoted to him than those who were his kin by blood; for he considered that in the matter of companionship nature is a much better guide than convention (ἡγεῖτο γὰρ εἶναι πρὸς ἑταιρίαν πολλῷ κρείττω φύσιν νόμου), character than kinship (τρόπον γένους), and freedom of choice than compulsion (προαίρεσιν ἀνάγκης).

But all time would fail us if we should try to recount all his activities. On another occasion I shall set them forth in detail; for the present however, I have produced a sample of the nature of Hipponicus (δεῖγμα δὲ τῆς Ἱππονίκου φύσεως νῦν ἐξενηνόχαμεν), after whom you should pattern your life as after an ensample[18] (πρὸς ὃν δεῖ ζῆν σε ὥσπερ πρὸς παράδειγμα), regarding his conduct as your law (νόμον μὲν τὸν ἐκείνου τρόπον ἡγησάμενον), and striving to imitate and emulate your father's virtue (μιμητὴν δὲ καὶ ζηλωτὴν τῆς πατρῴας ἀρετῆς γιγνόμενον); for it were a shame, when painters represent the beautiful among animals, for children not to imitate the noble among their ancestors.[19]

Isocrates has 'produced a sample' (δεῖγμα) of Hipponicus' virtuous life, and thus given to Demonicus an outline of how his father is to be a model. The choice of his father ensures the deep connection between exemplar and follower. With artful rhetoric, Isocrates shows how Hipponicus attained the 'golden mean', not falling into this or that vice

---

[17] PLUTARCH, *Progress*, 84E.

[18] The translator (G. NORLIN) has used the old form of example (ensample) to pick up Isocrates' word play of παράδειγμα (ensample/example) with δεῖγμα (sample) in the previous clause.

[19] ISOCRATES, *Demonicus*, 9–11.

(οὐ/οὐδέ), but instead (ἀλλά) choosing virtue.[20] Thus, his life becomes a construct of realized precepts. Notice again that the aim of Isocrates in rehearsing Hipponicus' life is to reveal the principles (προαιρέσεις) that guided him, and it is these principles that Demonicus is to incorporate into his own life, motivated by his devotion to his father and to virtue.

With this basic description of the functionality of the use of moral examples as a foundation, we are now ready to look at the use of Christ as a moral exemplar in early Christian writings and in particular 1 Peter.

II. Christ as Example

When turning to the use of Christ as a παράδειγμα, it is especially important to remember that, as with Greco-Roman paraenetic, deeds are exemplary because they are enacted virtue. Imitation is not especially a matter of re-enacting *deeds*, but of re-enacting *virtue*. Thus, in Christian paraenesis, '[T]he story of Jesus is a *paradigm*, a normative pattern or exemplar that can be creatively applied in different circumstances. Disciples do not clone their master's life; they follow the master through discerning imaginations, graced emotions, and faithful community.'[21] Ignoring this simple principle has produced countless confusions on what it means to 'imitate Christ'.

It is also important to remember that Greco-Roman paraenetic authors always specify how an individual is an exemplar; they *explicitly* underline those aspects of an individual's biography that are to foster imitation. In so doing, authors place constraints within which the example can be applied. Within these boundaries, the example is flexible enough to be applied to the infinitely variable contingencies of a realized life, but the process of application is guided by the author's selective portrayal of the exemplar. This also means that exemplars can be used repeatedly for varying situations. Great men embody a whole host of virtues, and so are applicable as exemplars to a whole host of circumstances where particular virtues are required.

In Christian paraenesis, Christ serves as an example of those virtues the author judges are most needed to address a particular need in the church. The 'biography' of Christ is retold is such a way as to reveal a particular character trait that the author seeks to instill in his audience.[22] A prime

---

[20] I am indebted to FIORE, *Personal Example*, 65, for this rhetorical insight.

[21] SPOHN, *Likewise*, 10–11.

[22] Cf. S.E. FOWL, *The Story of Christ in the Ethics of Paul: An Analysis of the Function of the Hymnic Material in the Pauline Corpus*, JSNTSS 36 (Sheffield: JSOT Press, 1990), 202–3.

example of this is the 'Christ hymn' of Phil. 2:5–11, where Christ's humility and obedience are extolled by Paul as an example to follow.

The hymn of Phil. 2 is also a prime example of a unique aspect in the use of Christ as an example. Here, as elsewhere, Christ is not only an exemplar, but also a savior. He not only provides a model, but also the *means* for the moral life. Both of these are bound up together in the biography of Christ, because his biography is the story of salvation. The narrative of Christ's life, death, and resurrection *is* the Gospel message. As Webster notes, 'precisely because the Christ-hymn [in Phil. 2] is the recital of the saving history of Jesus Christ, then it is equally an exhortation to the Christian life as a life moulded by that same history.'[23] At the center of this 'saving history' of Christ in the Christ hymn is his death and resurrection; so, the story of Christ's work in salvation also becomes a story to be imitated. As Webster notes:

[I]ntrinsic to the Christological narrative is its function in forming Christian vision and identity, making him into a self with particular beliefs and dispositions which give direction to the moral life in choice and action. The Christological narrative is thus the story of both a gift and a call, at once indicative and imperative. To rehearse that story is to be recalled to both the source of salvation and the source of obligation. Moreover, because the story elicits "imitation", its relation to the moral life is not only that of a *source* of obligation; it also serves to specify the shape of human life in response to obligation. It thus provides not simply the initial impetus of Christian morality but also a perceptible form or contour for its growth.[24]

Thus, the story of Christ is an especially potent example because it is, in the words of Webster, 'both the source of salvation and the source of obligation.' For early Christian paraenesis, the cross of Christ became a central symbol of both salvation and obligation. Just as the Synoptics connect the cross of Christ with both ransom and discipleship,[25] so Paul[26] and 1 Peter see in Christ's work of salvation an example to be followed.[27]

---

[23] WEBSTER, 'Imitability and Ethics,' 320. Contra E. KÄSEMANN, 'Kritische Analyse von Phil. 2, 5–11,' *ZTK* 47 (1950): 313–60.

[24] WEBSTER, 'Imitability and Ethics,' 311. Later he notes that, 'That significance is not the significance of an abstract principle, but of a lived life, a determined piece of human history, a subjectivity in action' (325).

[25] Mk. 8:31–35 and par.

[26] E.g., Phil. 2. Cf. MEEKS, *Origins*, 197. 'Paul's use of the metaphor of the cross resists its translation into simple slogans. Instead he introduces into the moral language of the new movement a way of seeking after resonances in the basic story for all kinds of relationships of disciples with the world and with one another, so that the event-become-metaphor could become the generative center of almost endless new narratives, yet remain a check and control over those narratives.'

[27] Traditionally a distinction has been made between 'imitation' and 'discipleship/following'. Properly conceived, imitation is not a form of 'works

III. Imitatio Christi in 1 Peter

1 Peter is particularly famous for its *imitatio Christi* passages, which comprise the bulk of the letter's christological material. These three passages (2:21–25; 3:18; and 4:1) have often been seen as the key to understanding the thrust of the letter as a whole,[28] and have received ample treatment in the scholarly literature as texts of paramount importance. It is surprising then that one finds so little agreement among commentators on their interpretation. Although central to the theology of the epistle, these texts have generated a baffling diversity of interpretive schemes. As we will see, by applying the basic ideas about the use of imitation just outlined, it will be possible to clear away much of this confusion.

The first of these texts comes in 2:21–25. As the longest of the three texts, it is the richest in showing the nuances of how the author uses imitation for his paraenetic purposes, and so will be the focus of our attention. The two other texts (3:18; 4:1) will prove helpful at points in illuminating this primary text:

21 {a}   For to this you have been called,
  {b}   because Christ also suffered for you,
  {c}   leaving you an example,
  {d}   that you should follow in his steps.
22 {a}   He committed no sin;
  {b}   no guile was found on his lips.
23 {a}   When he was reviled, he did not revile in return;
  {b}   when he suffered, he did not threaten;
  {c}   but he trusted to him who judges justly.
24 {a} He himself bore our sins in his body on the tree,
  {b}   that we might die to sin and live to righteousness.
  {c}   By his wounds you have been healed.
25 {a}   For you were straying like sheep,
  {b}   but have now returned to the shepherd and guardian of your souls.

---

righteousness', because it is rooted in the work of Christ, as *both* vicarious and exemplary. It is only when theories of imitation are cut loose from the cross that they are in danger of promoting self-generated righteousness. Cf. R.B. HAYS, *The Moral Vision of the New Testament: Community, Cross, New Creation: A Contemporary Introduction to New Testament Ethics* (San Francisco: HarperSanFrancisco, 1996), 197, 'To be Jesus' disciple is to obey his call to bear the cross, thus to be like him...When "imitation of Christ" is understood in these terms, the often-proposed distinction between discipleship and imitation disappears.' Also see J.H. ELLIOTT, 'Backward and Forward "In His Steps": Following Jesus from Rome to Raymond and Beyond. The Tradition, Redaction, and Reception of 1 Peter 2:18–25,' in *Discipleship in the New Testament*, ed. F.F. SEGOVIA (Philadelphia: Fortress, 1985), 201–3.

[28] E.g., BROX, *1. Petrusbrief*, 128, 'Darüber hinaus liegt darin die Logik der Theologie des ganzen Briefes, nicht nur der Sklaven-Paränese.'

21 {a} εἰς τοῦτο γὰρ ἐκλήθητε,
   {b}   ὅτι καὶ Χριστὸς ἔπαθεν ὑπὲρ ὑμῶν
   {c}   ὑμῖν ὑπολιμπάνων ὑπογραμμὸν
   {d}   ἵνα ἐπακολουθήσητε τοῖς ἴχνεσιν αὐτοῦ,
22 {a} ὃς ἁμαρτίαν οὐκ ἐποίησεν
   {b}   οὐδὲ εὑρέθη δόλος ἐν τῷ στόματι αὐτοῦ,
23 {a} ὃς λοιδορούμενος οὐκ ἀντελοιδόρει
   {b}   πάσχων οὐκ ἠπείλει,
   {c}   παρεδίδου δὲ τῷ κρίνοντι δικαίως·
24 {a} ὃς τὰς ἁμαρτίας ἡμῶν αὐτὸς ἀνήνεγκεν
   {b}   ἐν τῷ σώματι αὐτοῦ ἐπὶ τὸ ξύλον,
   {c}   ἵνα ταῖς ἁμαρτίαις ἀπογενόμενοι τῇ δικαιοσύνῃ ζήσωμεν,
   {d} οὗ τῷ μώλωπι ἰάθητε.
25 {a} ἦτε γὰρ ὡς πρόβατα πλανώμενοι,
   {b}   ἀλλὰ ἐπεστράφητε νῦν ἐπὶ τὸν ποιμένα καὶ
              ἐπίσκοπον τῶν ψυχῶν ὑμῶν.

These verses come at the conclusion to the *Haustafel* directed towards servants/slaves (οἰκέται).[29] This is the first in a series of three subunits directed towards servants (2:18–25), wives (3:1–6), and husbands (3:7), which fits into a larger unit on the topic of public morality (2:13–3:12). The keyword for this unit is the verb ὑποτάσσω, used here in the sense of 'subordinate yourselves to X'. As we saw in the previous chapter, one of the purposes of this subordination was for the churches to gain a good reputation with their neighbors by living upright lives. Subordination is part of the letter's overall call for these Christians to do good in relation to all out of reverence for God, which is clear from the verses that precede the *Haustafel* to the servants in 2:15–17.

It is within this context that the author commands servants in verses 18–20 to be submissive (ὑποτάσσω) to their masters ἐν παντὶ φόβῳ, and *not only to the kind and gentle but also to the cruel* (σκολιοῖς). He explains, *For one is approved if, mindful of God, he endures pain while suffering unjustly. For what credit is it, if when you do wrong and are beaten for it you take it patiently? But if when you do right and suffer for it you take it patiently* (εἰ ἀγαθοποιοῦντες καὶ πάσχοντες ὑπομενεῖτε), *you have God's approval* (τοῦτο χάρις παρὰ θεῷ). It is at this point that our author ushers Christ in as an example to be followed, but before we can move on to that, we need to comment on this injunction to slaves in relation to their masters.

---

[29] As ACHTEMEIER, *1 Peter*, 194, notes, 'While there is little question that slaves are indeed addressed directly in these verses, it is also clear from the language that the address is to a broader Christian audience than simply slaves.' The slaves are the primary addressees here, but they function paradigmatically for all Christians suffering for their faith, and thus through the slaves the author also addresses (at a secondary level) all Christian readers suffering unjustly for their faith.

It has to be admitted that, today this passage strikes us as shockingly oppressive in its endorsement of an unjust power structure, especially since the author explicitly commands subordination to *cruel* (σκολιοί) masters. There can be little doubt that the institution of slavery in the ancient world was an unjust power structure, since by definition slaves were property and possessed little, if any, 'rights'. But this passage has all too often been read with the question of (the absence of) emancipation in mind. It has often been assumed that slaves are here commanded to simply submit in the face of whatever arbitrary suffering the master can inflict, as a shameless endorsement of the 'system'.

In reality, the situation addressed here is slaves who are being oppressed *for their faith*, in the parlance of 1 Peter, *for doing good*. The concern of the author is that, in the face of suffering for doing good, that they will shrink back from doing good. As Neugebauer says, 'The danger for those who suffer injustice is that they cease to do good, that they either do nothing at all, or do the wrong thing.'[30] Thus, the author sees no merit in the endurance of suffering and submission as such, as the author makes clear in verse 20a.[31] What is approved by God (χάρις παρὰ θεῷ[32]) is to endure unjust suffering (i.e., suffering for doing good; ἀγαθοποιοῦντες καὶ πάσχοντες[33]) out of respect for God (ἐν παντὶ φόβῳ,[34] διὰ συνείδησιν θεοῦ). God does not, however, look with favor on taking a beating for wicked behavior.

---

[30] F. NEUGEBAUER, 'Zur Deutung und Bedeutung des 1. Petrusbriefes,' *NTS* 26 (1980): 80, 'In der Tat ist es die Gefahr derer, die Unrecht leiden, daß sie aufhören, das Gute weiter zu tun, daß sie entweder gar nichts machen oder das Falsche.' English translation from BORING, *1 Peter*, 119.

[31] Cf. M. JONES-HALDEMAN, 'The Function of Christ's Suffering in 1 Peter 2:21' (Th.D., Andrews University, 1988), 192. 'The Christian slave, therefore, is not called to suffering; rather he is called, as a member of God's people, to doing good.' Also see NEUGEBAUER, 'Deutung und Bedeutung,' 80, 'Der Unrecht Leidende soll sich nicht auf sein Leiden zurückziehen, gerade nicht in Passivität versinken, soll schon gar nicht mit gleicher Münze zurückzahlen (2.23, 3.9), sondern unbeirrt das Tun des Guten und Rechten fortsetzen. Leiden versetzt den Christen weder in die Regungslosigkeit noch ins bloße Reagieren, sondern gegenüber dem Unrecht und unter dem Leiden behält das Gute die Aktivität und die Initiative.'

[32] ACHTEMEIER, *1 Peter*, 196, says that, 'χάρις here does not have its usual meaning of divine grace; rather it is used in the sense of something pleasing to God.' Cf. SELWYN, *1 Peter*, 176. As ELLIOTT, *1 Peter*, 518, notes, the structure of the antithetical parallelism in v. 20 shows that χάρις is synonymous with κλέος, 'credit' or 'praise'.

[33] MICHAELS, *1 Peter*, 142, explains that, 'The words, "when you do good and suffer" explain Peter's reference to "suffering unjustly" in the preceding verse.'

[34] The φόβος prescribed here is reverence for God, not for masters. Cf. ACHTEMEIER, *1 Peter*, 194–5.

Our postmodern era is, for good reason, especially sensitive to the inequality of power structure and the rights of the oppressed. But this can be overemphasized to the point that power *itself* becomes evil, and therefore only those who hold power are capable of wickedness. While victims do have a 'moral high-ground' in relation to their victimization, this does not make them sinless moral agents.[35] Here our author addresses the oppressed, and his concern is to blunt their potential sin of either ceasing to do good, in an effort to obviate their suffering, or worse, retaliating in kind.[36]

It is in this context that Christ becomes a model for enduring unjust suffering and continuing to do good out of reverence for God. Commentators who have misunderstood the advice to the slaves have also misunderstood how Christ is to be a model. Kelly, for example, argues that, 'Submissive acceptance of treatment that is patently unfair is a fine and Christian thing precisely because the Lord Himself behaved in that way.'[37] As we will see below, Christ is an example because, in the face of unjust suffering, he neither retaliated with vengeance nor slacked from his obedience to God's will.

Before we can pursue this, however, we are forced to deal with a much deeper problem. The central difficulty of this text is that (it appears) Christ's work as 'savior' is given as an example to be followed.[38] But we know that it is precisely in his work as savior that his life is least imitable. Clearly, some elements of Christ's story are not applicable to the life of the servants, but determining which elements are exemplary and which are not has proven difficult in practice. Even a great commentator like Selwyn missteps here, concluding that the example of Christ 'was intended to include the "sin bearing" as well as the meekness of the Master.'[39]

The most obvious solution is simply to divide up the text on theological grounds, so that all elements pertaining to Christ's vicarious sacrifice are eliminated from the realm of imitation. This is a sound principle, but it

---

[35] See VOLF, *Exclusion and Embrace*, 79–85.

[36] Cf. F.V. FILSON, 'Partakers with Christ: Suffering in First Peter,' *Int* 9 (1955): 409, '[T]he repeated exhortation to do the right hints that under persecution, to avoid suffering, the Christian may shirk his duty, shrink from steady expression of his faith in life, and so take the easy way.' Elsewhere he adds that, '[T]he Christian must not respond to opposition or ill-treatment with hate or retaliation. The example of Christ should teach them that' (406).

[37] KELLY, *Peter & Jude*, 118.

[38] While our author does not use the word σωτήρ, I am using the term savior as a shorthand word to describe the work of substitutionary atonement achieved by Christ on the cross. For the sake of continuity, the term is picked up from WEBSTER's description of the function of the *imitatio Christi* theme in the previous section.

[39] SELWYN, *1 Peter*, 180.

quickly proves an unworkable solution, because the different elements are too closely connected to permit neat division.

Right from the start, in 2:21, we are confronted with this difficulty of the complex interweaving of these elements of savior and example. The τοῦτο, to which these slaves are 'called', refers back to the τοῦτο γὰρ χάρις of verse 19 and the τοῦτο χάρις παρὰ θεῷ of verse 20 (i.e., that which is commendable before God – bearing of suffering for doing good). 2:21b, ὅτι καὶ Χριστὸς ἔπαθεν ὑπὲρ ὑμῶν, which introduces Christ as an exemplar, leads us into the intractable difficulty of trying to separate the exemplary from the vicarious. On the one hand, this clause seems to be talking about Christ's vicarious atonement (ἔπαθεν ὑπὲρ ὑμῶν), but on the other hand this 'suffering' is identified with the suffering of the servants, since Christ *also* (καί) suffered. Christ's suffering is somehow *for* the slaves, but also at the same time an *example* to be followed. Christ is at once savior and exemplar. There are various solutions to this paradox. Some commentators see this statement as only exemplary with little if any reference to the atoning value of his death,[40] while others see only a hint of example in a statement primarily about the vicarious atonement of Jesus.[41] Most commentators split the difference between these two extremes, but no two agree on how to balance these conflicting elements of savior and exemplar.

One of the core difficulties is the phraseology employed here: Χριστὸς ἔπαθεν, instead of a more traditional (i.e., Pauline) Χριστὸς ἀπέθανεν. What does it mean to say that 'Christ suffered'? Is there a difference between this and 'Christ died'? Solving this riddle may help us to answer the deeper question about how specifically Christ is an example. So, we must first begin by looking at this phrase: Χριστὸς ἔπαθεν ὑπὲρ ὑμῶν.

A. The Suffering Christ

1 Peter is not the only NT writing to speak of Christ 'sufferings' in this way; Luke-Acts and Hebrews also refer to the death of Christ by saying that he 'suffered'.[42] What is unique in 1 Peter 2:21 is the use of the phrase

---

[40] E.g., ACHTEMEIER, *1 Peter*, 199.

[41] E.g., GOPPELT, *1 Peter*, 202.

[42] W. MICHAELIS, 'πάσχω,' *TDNT*, 5:913, notes that, 'In Lk. 22:15; 24:26, 46; Ac. 1:3; 3:18; 17:3 there is a special and uniform sense to the degree that πάσχω is here abs[olute]…and manifestly means "to die," as in Hb. and 1Pt.' Later he observes that, 'Though the author of Hb. could use ἀποθανεῖν for death, including violent death (7:8; 9:27; 10:28; 11:4, 13, 21, 37) he never uses this for the death of Jesus…but speaks of the παθεῖν of Jesus' (917).

ἔπαθεν ὑπὲρ ὑμῶν;[43] and it is this phrase that is so striking for its similarity to the Pauline *Sterbensformel* ἀπέθανεν ὑπὲρ ἡμῶν, which Paul uses in reference to the vicarious death of Christ.[44] Does this mean that ἔπαθεν ὑπὲρ ὑμῶν simply means 'he died for you'? A strong case can be made that it does. 2:24 certainly takes it this way when it tells how Christ τὰς ἁμαρτίας ἡμῶν...ἀνήνεγκεν ἐν τῷ σώματι αὐτοῦ ἐπὶ τὸ ξύλον. This possibility is strengthened by the parallel phrase in 3:18, Χριστὸς ἅπαξ περὶ ἁμαρτιῶν ἔπαθεν.[45] Thus, Kelly concludes that, 'suffered...is equivalent to "died" when used of Christ.'[46] But why, if the author meant to say 'Christ died for you,' did he not say simply ἀπέθανεν ὑπὲρ ὑμῶν?[47] Why use the confusing expression ἔπαθεν ὑπὲρ ὑμῶν? An answer frequently given is that he used ἔπαθεν, with the sense of 'he died', so that he could make a link between the death of Christ and the suffering of the slaves. As Blazen puts it:

[N]ot only was it *possible* for Peter to use πάσχειν ("to suffer") for death, it was also *valuable* that he should do so. It enabled him to speak on two important fronts and yet connect the two together. By the use of this one term he could speak about the death of Christ and also of the sufferings of Christians... Thus, what Christ did and what Christians are called upon to be a part of and to do are brought into fundamental relationship through the one motif of πάσχειν.[48]

But this explanation is problematic, since it sees no *real* connection between Christ and the slaves, and is therefore a weak explanation of how he is to be an exemplar to them in their suffering. In the end, this theory sees the use of πάσχω as a linguistic trick, a catchword to link two disparate realities. A theory that established a *real* connection between Christ and the slaves would be preferable.

To address this problem, others have proposed that πάσχω here refers to the sufferings of Christ *in his passion*. As Michaels says, 'The emphasis from here [verse 21] to the end of v 23 is on Jesus' behavior (in the events

---

[43] But note with MICHAELIS, 'πάσχω,' 5:918, that, 'Though in Hb. παθεῖν is never combined with ὑπὲρ ἡμῶν etc. (cf. 1 Pt. 2:21; 3:18), this thought is implied (cf. simply 10:12; 13:12).'

[44] E.g., Rom. 5:8, ἔτι ἁμαρτωλῶν ὄντων ἡμῶν Χριστὸς ὑπὲρ ἡμῶν ἀπέθανεν.

[45] Cf. 1 Cor. 15:3b, Χριστὸς ἀπέθανεν ὑπὲρ τῶν ἁμαρτιῶν ἡμῶν.

[46] KELLY, *Peter & Jude*, 168. Cf. E. LOHSE, *Märtyrer und Gottesknecht: Untersuchungen zur urchristlichen Verkündigung vom Sühntod Jesu Christi*, FRLANT 46 (Göttingen: Vandenhoeck & Ruprecht, 1955), 52 n.82. '1 Peter frequently speaks of Christ's having suffered, and thereby Christ's death is meant.'

[47] There is ample textual evidence that many scribes thought he should have. 𝔓[81] ℵ and some later texts read ἀπέθανεν instead of ἔπαθεν in 2:21. This variant reading is even more strongly attested at 3:18, as we will see below.

[48] I.T. BLAZEN, 'Suffering and Cessation from Sin According to 1 Peter 4:1,' *AUSS* 21.1 (1983): 29–30. Italics added.

leading up to his death) as a example to Peter's readers of "doing good" in the face of both verbal and physical abuse.'[49] This explanation sees the reference to Jesus' suffering as an allusion to his suffering in his passion *prior to death*, not a reference to his death.[50] The advantages of this approach are substantial, primarily because it has the power to explain how Jesus can be an *example* to the slaves as one who suffered unjustly and yet continued to do good. The materials of verses 22–23, largely taken from Isa. 53, are used to interpret the passion of Christ in a way that is applicable to the slaves. These verses show how Christ, though suffering unjustly, did not retaliate in kind.

This interpretation does not take the expression ἔπαθεν ὑπὲρ ὑμῶν as synonymous with the Pauline formula ἀπέθανεν ὑπὲρ ἡμῶν. (We cannot simply assume that the Pauline sense should be imported here.) The ὑπὲρ ὑμῶν is not taken as a sign of vicarious sacrifice, but defining the recipients of the example left by Christ.[51] This becomes clearer if we include verse 21cd, καὶ Χριστὸς ἔπαθεν ὑπὲρ ὑμῶν ὑμῖν ὑπολιμπάνων ὑπογραμμὸν ἵνα ἐπακολουθήσητε τοῖς ἴχνεσιν αὐτοῦ. In this scheme, therefore, the theme of Christ's vicarious atonement is not introduced until verse 24, *after* the materials talking about his passion prior to his death. This interpretation is able to explain how Christ's suffering was *for* the slaves but also how it was *analogous* to their suffering (i.e., that he *also* suffered *for them*), and so it answers one of our chief difficulties in interpreting this text.

Unfortunately, it is wrong. This reading completely fails to make sense of the use of ἔπαθεν in 3:18, where there is little doubt that ἔπαθεν refers to the vicarious sacrificial *death* of Christ for sins. The ἅπαξ and δίκαιος ὑπὲρ ἀδίκων, are typical expressions in the context of vicarious atonement. And of course, the mention of being put to death (θανατωθείς) is an indisputable sign that ἔπαθεν here refers to death.[52] Thus, the explanation that it refers

---

[49] MICHAELS, *1 Peter*, 143.

[50] Cf. JONES-HALDEMAN, 'Christ's Suffering,' 220.

[51] Cf. MICHAELS, *1 Peter*, 143.

[52] This is reflected in the textual tradition which heavily favors ἀπέθανεν over ἔπαθεν. 𝔓[72] ℵ A and C read Χριστὸς ἅπαξ περὶ ἁμαρτιῶν ὑπὲρ ἡμῶν/ὑμῶν ἀπέθανεν. Despite this strong manuscript evidence, today few doubt that the correct reading is Χριστὸς ἅπαξ περὶ ἁμαρτιῶν ἔπαθεν, even though it is only attested in B, 𝔐 and (with the addition of ὑπὲρ ἡμῶν) L. (See B. ALAND et al., eds., *Catholic Letters*, vol. 4, *Novum Testamentum Graecum Editio Critica Maior* (Stuttgart: Deutsche Bibelgesellschaft, 2000), 1.2.164.) The report of B.M. METZGER, ed., *A Textual Commentary on the Greek New Testament*, 2nd ed. (Stuttgart: Deutsche Bibelgesellschaft/United Bible Societies, 1994), 623, expresses the consensus well, '[A] majority of the Committee preferred the reading περὶ ἁμαρτιῶν ἔπαθεν because (*a*) this verb, which is a favorite of the author (it occurs elsewhere in 1 Peter eleven times), carries on the thought of ver. 17, whereas ἀποθήσκειν (which occurs nowhere else in the epistle) abruptly introduces a new idea; (*b*) in view of

to the passion of Jesus *prior* to his death does not fit here, and must be rejected. Michaels admits that, 'ἔπαθεν, which in 2:21 referred to the events leading up to Christ's death, here encompasses the death itself.'[53]

But even here, things are not as simple as they might seem. As in 2:21, here in 3:18, 'Christ *also* suffered' (καὶ Χριστὸς...ἔπαθεν). So here, as before, Christ is somehow exemplary.[54] Once again, as in 2:21, the context speaks to the question of suffering for doing good: *But even if you do suffer for righteousness' sake, you are blessed* (εἰ καὶ πάσχοιτε διὰ δικαιοσύνην, μακάριοι). *...For it is better to suffer for doing right* (ἀγαθοποιοῦντας), *if that should be God's will, than for doing wrong.* (3:14a, 17). Therefore, here Christ must again be an example of suffering for doing good, since he *also* suffered. So, Christ's 'suffering' seems to refer to his sufferings *and* to his death.

At this point we are forced to acknowledge Χριστὸς ἔπαθεν as a reference to the whole of Christ's passion, that is to his sufferings *and* his death, seen as a unit. As Cervantes-Gabarrón argues, 1 Peter, like Luke-Acts and Hebrews, uses πάσχω to speak of 'the passion and death of Christ, considered as a whole, as a single event.'[55] Therefore, when our author says that 'Christ suffered' he is speaking of the whole passion story, his suffering and his death. It is not an issue of choosing between the two. While the author may *emphasize* one at a particular time, the two are inseparable. This begins to explain how our author can speak of Christ as both an example and at the same time as a vicarious savior, since it does not separate his exemplary sufferings from his vicarious death.

To understand this fully, though, we must turn to our text in 4:1. This text is closely connected with, and in fact a resumption of, the thought of

---

the presence of the expression περὶ ἁμαρτιῶν scribes would be more likely to substitute ἀπέθανεν for ἔπαθεν than vice versa.'

[53] MICHAELS, *1 Peter*, 202.

[54] It is interesting to note that 𝔓[72] and ℵ, which read ἀπέθανεν for ἔπαθεν, both omit the καί here, since there can be no logical connection between Christ's death and the suffering of the readers.

[55] J. CERVANTES-GABARRÓN, 'La Pasión de Jesuchristo en la Primera Carta de Pedro: Centro Literario y Teológico de la Carta' (Ph.D., Pontificiae Universitatis Gregorianae, 1991), 167. 'El uso de este verbo en relación con Cristo en el NT se encuentra también en los Sinópticos, Hechos, Hebreos y 1Pedro, y se refiere a la Pasión y Muerte de Cristo, considerados como un todo, como un único acontecimiento, pero al mismo tiempo pone de relieve los sufrimientos que precedieron a la muerte de Jesús.' Cf. T.P. OSBORNE, 'Guide Lines for Christian Suffering: A Source-Critical and Theological Study of 1 Peter 2,21–25,' *Bib* 64 (1983): 391. Curiously, both OSBORNE and CERVANTES GABARRÓN claim this use for the 'Synoptics', when it only belongs to Luke. Mark and Matthew speak of suffering and death as separate events, not as a single event (e.g., Mt. 16:21; Mk. 8:31).

3:18, after the digression of the *Descensus Christi*.[56] This is most clearly
seen in the reference to Christ suffering in the flesh (σαρκί) just as he was
put to death in the flesh (θανατωθεὶς...σαρκί) in 3:18. From this it is also
clear that 4:1 is concerned with Christ suffering in the flesh, prior to his
resurrection and preaching which were done 'in the spirit'. Of all our
imitatio passages this is the most obscure, and it has produced the greatest
diversity of interpretations. The two most significant options take this as
either (1) an expression of Jewish martyr theology, where the righteous
suffering of a martyr secures atonement for the people,[57] or (2) drawing on
Paul's baptismal union with Christ in Rom. 6:1–11, where believers are to
die to sin in their union with Christ's death.[58] Neither of these alternatives
is convincing since (1) neither martyrdom nor atonement is in view here
and (2) while baptism is mentioned in this context (3:21), 1 Peter, here and
elsewhere, is completely lacking in a Pauline participationist union with
Christ. As Elliott concludes, 'The statement is neither a piece of baptismal
theology nor an echo of Israel's martyr theology.'[59]

So, what *is* this text about? First of all, we can say that Christ again is
an exemplar of something. The readers are commanded also (καί) to arm
themselves (ὑμεῖς...ὁπλίσασθε) with the same thought (τὴν αὐτὴν ἔννοιαν).
Just as they were to prepare themselves for action by ἀναζωσάμενοι τὰς
ὀσφύας τῆς διανοίας ὑμῶν in 1:13, here they are told to arm themselves
with a certain mental attitude. As Achtemeier notes, ἔννοιαν refers to
'mental activity...in the form of intention or disposition in the sphere of
moral actions.'[60] The καί means that they are to adopt the ἔννοιαν of
Christ. But what is this attitude or conviction of Christ that they are to
adopt? The answer given by the logic of this verse is (curiously) that he

---

[56] Cf. MICHAELS, *1 Peter*, 224, 'Peter lingers instead at the point where the
magnificent digression began – i.e., 3:18a and the theme of Christ's suffering.'

[57] E.g., LOHSE, 'Parenesis and Kerygma,' 51, 'First Peter 4:1, in a parenthesis of the
paraenesis that challenges the readers to arm themselves (ὁπλίσασθε), makes use of the
idea, which can be documented only in Palestinian Judaism, that the dying person,
especially the martyr, through his suffering and death secures atonement for his sins or
even for those of another.' He documented this idea in his influential work *Märtyrer und
Gottesknecht*.

[58] E.g., W.J. DALTON, *Christ's Proclamation to the Spirits: A Study of 1 Peter
3:18–4:6*, 2d ed., AnBib 23 (Rome: Editrice Pontificio Istituto Biblico, 1989), 221–5.

[59] ELLIOTT, *1 Peter*, 717.

[60] ACHTEMEIER, *1 Peter*, 277. Cf. BLAZEN, 'Cessation,' 32, 'ἔννοιαν in 1 Pet 4:1
contains two basic ingredients: insight and intention.' Elsewhere he also notes that, 'In
the LXX the word occurs almost exclusively in the Wisdom Literature (Sus 2:8 is the
only exception), and most of its uses are to be found in Proverbs...It is concerned with
the intellectual side of man, but as enlisted in and directed to practical and moral
ends...Here ἔννοια denotes what a person with his reason and will intends to do in the
moral sphere' (31).

'suffered in the flesh' (παθόντος σαρκί).⁶¹ Since this denotes action and not intention, it must be inferred that the author has in mind some conviction of Christ exhibited in his suffering.⁶² We have already seen before how Christ is an example of one who endures suffering for doing good and continues to do good. All of that applies here, but what is especially in focus is his fundamental commitment to do the will of God. It is this conviction that motivates his choices to endure suffering and continue to do good. The import of the statement that 'Christ suffered in the flesh' is not that he suffered as such, but that he actively chose to continue to do good in obedience to God's will for him out of reverence for God.

This becomes clear in the implications drawn out for the readers in 4:1c–2: *for whoever has suffered in the flesh has ceased from sin* (ὅτι ὁ παθὼν σαρκὶ πέπαυται ἁμαρτίας), *so as to live for the rest of the time in the flesh no longer by human passions but by the will of God* (εἰς τὸ μηκέτι ἀνθρώπων ἐπιθυμίαις ἀλλὰ θελήματι θεοῦ τὸν ἐπίλοιπον ἐν σαρκὶ βιῶσαι χρόνον). The idea here is not that suffering has morally cleansing powers *per se*, but that choosing to continue to do good in the midst of suffering involves a denial of the 'flesh', which is willing to compromise in order to alleviate suffering, or to retaliate in order to satisfy the desire for vengeance. With respect to Christ, 'suffering in the flesh' carries with it the idea of obedience to God's will, of choosing to do what is right in the midst of suffering. The point here is that obedience to God is a learned disposition (a virtue), which is gained through repeated choices. If one is able to make those choices under difficult circumstances, which exacerbate the temptation to abandon what is good, then their disposition forming value is even stronger. This basic principle is stated here in an absolute form, as maxims often are, ὁ παθὼν σαρκὶ πέπαυται ἁμαρτίας.⁶³ This maxim is directed at the readers and does not speak directly of Christ's experience, since he did not cease from sin (i.e., having never sinned, he could not cease from it). It does, however, speak analogically of Christ's passion, in that through his choices in suffering he overcame sin. As Heb. 5:8 puts it, although he was a Son, he learned obedience through what

---

⁶¹ As we will see shortly, the ὅτι clause, *for whoever has suffered in the flesh has ceased from sin*, is not to be taken epexegetically as an explanation of Christ's ἔννοιαν, as does DAVIDS, *First Peter*, 148, but as a warrant for the command given.

⁶² Cf. MICHAELS, *1 Peter*, 225, 'It is likely therefore that "the same resolve" has to do not with the sheer fact that Christ "suffered in the flesh" but with the attitude of mind that he brought to that moment of crisis (cf. 2:22–23; also perhaps Phil 2:5).'

⁶³ The use of the perfect πέπαυμαι here emphasizes the (idealized) *state*, reached after one has suffered (i.e., a freedom from sin that arises out of habitual good works in the midst of suffering). As ZERWICK, *Biblical Greek*, says, 'The use of the perfect in the NT thus shows that the author has in mind the notion of a state of affairs resultant upon the action' (§288). Also see, BDF §344, and the examples given: 1 John 2:5, and Jas. 2:10.

he suffered (καίπερ ὢν υἱός, ἔμαθεν ἀφ' ὧν ἔπαθεν τὴν ὑπακοήν). To say that he learned obedience does not mean that his righteousness was incomplete, but that, since obedience is a disposition, he had to learn it through practice.[64] Hebrews, like 1 Peter, connects this obedience with Christ's sufferings in his passion. Michaelis notes that in Heb. 5:8, 'ἔμαθεν, like ἔπαθεν, relates to the individual stages of the passion beginning with Gethsemane and ending with the death.'[65] Thus, through his obedient suffering in his passion Jesus learned obedience, or as Hebrews says elsewhere, he was 'made perfect through suffering' (2:10; cf. 5:9). This is the sense in which Christ's suffering in the flesh is analogous to the principle stated in 4:1c, and also explains how he is an example of one who suffered and conquered sin.[66]

Also *assumed* here is the idea (developed explicitly in Hebrews) that Christ's righteousness, perfected in suffering, was a pre-requisite for his vicarious death. The importance of this has already been stressed in 1:19 where the author reminds his readers that their redemption came through the τιμίῳ αἵματι ὡς ἀμνοῦ ἀμώμου καὶ ἀσπίλου Χριστοῦ. Christ's righteousness is a pre-condition of his sacrifice. The same is the case in 3:18, where the righteousness of Christ is directly connected with his vicarious sacrifice (δίκαιος ὑπὲρ ἀδίκων).[67] Thus, the obedience of Christ is an essential element in the passion narrative; it is not simply a prelude to his redemptive work, but an element of it. While a minor theme in the NT writings, the redemptive effect of the 'active obedience' of Christ is attested to most strongly in Phil. 2:6–11; Rom. 5:19; and Heb. 2:9–10, 17–18; 5:8–10.[68] Here in 1 Peter, it finds its expression in the use of the

---

[64] Cf. KOESTER, *Hebrews*, 290, 'Thus to say that Jesus "learned obedience" means that he practiced it.'

[65] MICHAELIS, 'πάσχω,' 917–8.

[66] FIORE, *Personal Example*, 93, notes that, 'In the case of an educational model toward which the pupil is expected to strive, the prototype includes moral qualities as well as exemplary deeds and incarnates a degree of perfection which the student earnestly desires to attain.'

[67] Cf. E. SCHWEIZER, *Lordship and Discipleship*, SBT 28 (London: SCM, 1960), 33, 'Here the idea of vicarious suffering has already been adopted. But here too his righteousness is shown by his suffering, and, what is more, by his innocent suffering.'

[68] R.N. LONGENECKER, 'The Foundational Conviction of New Testament Christology: The Obedience/Faithfulness/Sonship of Christ,' in *Jesus of Nazareth: Essay on the Historical Jesus and New Testament Christology*, ed. J.B. GREEN and M. TURNER (Grand Rapids: Eerdmans, 1994), 475, goes so far as to call this 'the foundational conviction of New Testament christology.' He argues that, 'the various terms and expression used in the NT with respect to Christ are to be understood as pictorial representations, graphic metaphors, and/or similes that stem from a basic conviction that has to do with the obedience, faithfulness, and sonship of Christ – with its corollary being the trustful obedience of the believer in response. In the case of Christ, I suggest that all the titles

succinct phrase 'he suffered'. As we have seen, this expression has in mind the *entirety* of the passion, including his sufferings and death, but also includes the active obedience of Christ.

Now we can see why the traditional scheme of sufferings being exemplary and death being salvific breaks down. In 1 Peter the whole of the passion is redemptive. His sufferings prior to death play a part in the salvation that Christ brought. So, they are more than exemplary. Conversely, as we will see below, the sacrificial vicarious death of Christ is (in a certain sense) exemplary. So, the whole of the passion story is both redemptive and exemplary; throughout Christ is both savior and example. This is hardly surprising, however, if we keep in mind Webster's statement: 'The Christological narrative is...the story of both a gift and a call, at once indicative and imperative.'[69]

B. Following in His Steps

In returning to our primary text (2:21–25), we are now in a position to see the implication of καὶ Χριστὸς ἔπαθεν ὑπὲρ ὑμῶν. Verses 22–23 have long been recognized as an explication of how Christ's attitude in his suffering are an example for the suffering slaves. Verse 22 shows that he was innocent of wrongdoing and therefore suffered unjustly, just as the slaves should.[70] The next verse shows that when he suffered he did not return evil for evil, but entrusted himself to God. So, likewise, the slaves are also to endure unjust suffering and not retaliate in kind to their masters who persecute them, but instead entrust themselves to God, looking to him to vindicate them. These verses highlight Jesus' actions with a particular aim of giving a model of enduring suffering to the slaves. But Jesus' actions also serve to reveal his righteousness; he endures suffering and continues to do good. His decision to refrain from retaliation and to trust God has not only exemplary but redemptive value as well. He suffered as an exemplar *and* as a savior. His righteous suffering made his vicarious sacrifice possible.

Thus, the statement that Χριστὸς ἔπαθεν ὑπὲρ ὑμῶν applies to these verses and the vicarious bearing of sin in verse 24. As in Paul, ὑπὲρ ὑμῶν

---

ascribed to him in the NT and all the metaphors used in description of the nature and effects of his work are founded ultimately on the early Christians' conviction regarding the full obedience and entire faithfulness of Jesus of Nazareth, God's Son *par excellence*, with this complete filial obedience seen as having been exercised throughout his life and coming to ultimate expression in his death on the cross.'

[69] WEBSTER, 'Imitability and Ethics,' 311.

[70] Cf. ELLIOTT, *1 Peter*, 529, 'The Isaian portrait of the innocent suffering servant (*pais*, 52:13; *paidion* 53:2) of God provides our author with a model for describing Jesus Christ as a similar innocent suffering servant of God whom in turn, serves as an apposite model for innocently suffering servants/slaves.'

can mean 'for your advantage' as well as 'in your stead'.[71] The *vicarious* aspect of Christ's suffering probably does not come into play until verse 24, but as his sufferings were a necessary precondition of his sin bearing, they can properly be spoken of as sufferings that have redemptive value for the servants. He suffered 'for them' in his righteous obedience. Commentators who see only the exemplary aspect in view in these two verses are forced to see either (1) exemplary value only in 'Christ suffered for you', and thus he suffered for you to give you an example,[72] or to see (2) this statement as only applying to the vicarious suffering of verse 24. The former is unacceptable because, as we have seen Christ's πάθημα must include his atoning death (as in 2:24 and 3:18), while the latter forces us to make verses 21c–23 as an intrusion to the thought and flow of the passage. Only by adopting the interpretation outlined here can the statement that Χριστὸς ἔπαθεν ὑπὲρ ὑμῶν make sense of verses 21–24 as a whole.

While this interpretative scheme may sound novel, it is not without historical precedent. Polycarp, in his letter to the Philippians (ca. 115),[73] gives a paraphrase[74] of this passage in which he speaks of the redemptive aspects of Christ's passion *as a whole*:

---

[71] Cf. E. KÄSEMANN, *Perspectives on Paul*, trans. M. KOHL, NTL (London: SCM, 1971), 39. 'The central theme is always the "for us". It covers the two meanings: "for our advantage" and "in our stead".'

[72] So MICHAELS, *1 Peter*, 143, and ACHTEMEIER, *1 Peter*, 198–9.

[73] So P. HARTOG, *Polycarp and the New Testament: The Occasion, Rhetoric, Theme, and Unity of the Epistle to the Philippians and its allusions to New Testament Literature*, WUNT II 134 (Tübingen: Mohr (Siebeck), 2002), 169. M.W. HOLMES, ed., *The Apostolic Fathers: Greek Texts and English Translations*, Updated ed. (Grand Rapids: Baker, 1999), 204, notes that, '[T]he letter is customarily dated within weeks (or at most months) of the time of Ignatius's death.' Elsewhere, he notes that 'There has long been a virtually unanimous consensus that Ignatius was martyred during the reign of Trajan (A.D. 98–117)' (131). J.B. LIGHTFOOT, *The Apostolic Fathers: Clement, Ignatius and Polycarp: Revised Texts with Introductions, Notes, Dissertations and Translations*, 2nd ed., 5 vols. (London: Macmillan, 1889), 2.1.30, places Ignatius' martyrdom, 'within a few years of A.D. 110, before or after.' H. KOESTER, *Introduction to the New Testament*, Hermeneia: Foundations and Facets (Philadelphia: Fortress Press, 1982), 281, argues for a later date, 'in Trajan's last years, i.e., 110–117 CE.'

[74] HARTOG, *Polycarp*, 189, states that, 'No one doubts that Polycarp clearly uses 1 Peter.' POLYCARP's familiarity with and use of 1 Peter has been recognized from an early date. As LIGHTFOOT, *Apostolic Fathers*, 2.1.596, notes, 'the large and repeated use made by Polycarp of the First Epistle of S. Peter…was sufficiently prominent to attract the notice of Eusebius.' LIGHTFOOT is referring to *HE*, 4.14.9, where Eusebius says that, 'Polycarp, in his…letter to the Philippians…has made some quotations from the first epistle of Peter.' In addition, P.V.M. BENECKE, 'Polycarp,' in *The New Testament in the Apostolic Fathers* (Oxford: Clarendon, 1905), 87, notes that this particular passage is, 'very strongly Petrine,' and that, 'there is a striking identity of thought, even where the form is different.'

Let us, therefore, hold steadfastly and unceasingly to our hope and the guarantee of our righteousness, who is Christ Jesus, "who bore our sins in his body upon the tree," "who committed no sin, and no deceit was found in his mouth"; instead for our sakes (ἀλλὰ δι' ἡμᾶς) he endured all things (πάντα ὑπέμεινεν), in order that we might live in him (ἵνα ζήσωμεν ἐν αὐτῷ).[75]

Polycarp does not limit Christ's redemptive suffering to the cross, but says that he endured *all things* (πάντα ὑπέμεινεν). In our 1 Peter text ὑπομένω is a synonym of πάσχω, and carries with it the sense not simply of passive suffering or passive endurance, but the *active choice* to remain faithful to God in the face of suffering for doing good.[76] Just as Polycarp saw *all* of Christ's sufferings as 'for us', so 1 Peter has the whole passion in mind when it says that καὶ Χριστὸς ἔπαθεν ὑπὲρ ὑμῶν.

Of course this includes his sin-bearing, as verse 24a says, *He himself bore our sins in his body on the tree* (ὃς τὰς ἁμαρτίας ἡμῶν αὐτὸς ἀνήνεγκεν ἐν τῷ σώματι αὐτοῦ ἐπὶ τὸ ξύλον). Christ's sufferings on the cross vicariously atone for sins; here we clearly have ὑπὲρ ὑμῶν in the sense of 'in your stead'. Here, most commentators are agreed that Christ role as example has disappeared from view, having concluded in the previous verse, since his vicarious atoning death is not an action to be imitated. But, is it possible that there is an exemplary element in mind here? Is not Christ's bearing of sins an active obedience to the will of God? Is not his death an example of continuing to do good in the face of unjust suffering?[77] It certainly is. Thus, the author speaks of Christ's work on the 'tree' as *both* vicarious and exemplary; again, Christ is at the same moment savior and exemplar.

This becomes more clear in the purpose clause of 24b: *that we might die to sin and live to righteousness* (ἵνα ταῖς ἁμαρτίαις ἀπογενόμενοι τῇ δικαιοσύνῃ ζήσωμεν). Christ acts as *savior* in providing atonement for sins are meant to bring practical freedom from sin in a life characterized by

---

[75] *Phil.* 8:1. Text and translation are from HOLMES, ed., *Apostolic Fathers*, 214–15.

[76] LOHSE, *Märtyrer und Gottesknecht*, 58 n.110, notes, '[I]n keeping with the high estimate of Christ's sufferings as an example, in the second century there is increasingly frequent mention of Christ's ὑπομένειν in suffering. This ὑπομένειν functions as an example for the Christians' patient suffering. Cf. *Barn.* 5:1, 6, 12; Ign. *Pol.* 3:2; Pol. *Phil.* 1:2; 8:1–2; Justin *Apol.* I.50.1; 63.10, 16; *Dial.* 68.1; 121.2.' The association of ὑπομένω with martyrdom is not present in POLYCARP, the way it is in the letters of IGNATIUS and the *Martyrdom of Polycarp*. Cf. ELLIOTT, *1 Peter*, 528, and HARTOG, *Polycarp*, 142–4. Also see J.W. VAN HENTEN, 'Zum Einfluß jüdischer Martyrien auf die Literatur des frühen Christentums: II. Die Apostolischen Väter,' *ANRW*, II.27.1:700–23.

[77] The same point is made in the Christ hymn in Phil. 2. HAYS, *Moral Vision*, 29, notes that, 'Christ's obedience to the point of death (2:8) is offered to the Philippians as a pattern for their obedience (2:12). Just as he obediently suffered, so the Philippians should stand firm in the gospel, even when it requires them to suffer (1:27–30).'

righteousness. The implications drawn from Christ's vicarious work as savior are *moral*. This opens up the path for Christ as example. The focus here is not on freedom from the *penalty* of sin (although that is assumed; see 1:18–19), but freedom from the ongoing *power* of sin. Since the emphasis here is on the moral implications of the atonement, Christ's applicability as a moral example fits the context quite naturally. If, on the other hand, the focus were on *legal* satisfaction in the atonement, then the context would not be set to speak of Christ as an example. As we have already seen in 4:1, Christ is a model of one who conquered sin and learned obedience through choosing to do God's will. Likewise, here he serves as an example for those who seek to make a break with sin and live in righteousness (cf. Rom 6:10–12).[78]

Because the vicarious actions of Christ are here given as exemplary, we see again how the old paradigm of simply separating the redemptive and the exemplary elements breaks down. How then *are* we to know what is exemplary? How do we know which elements to include and which to exclude from the 'model' of Christ? We have seen that Christ's entire passion is portrayed as both redemptive and exemplary. Are the slaves, then, to follow Christ in martyrdom, or to somehow suffer for others, or for Christ himself?[79] How do we know which elements are truly exemplary and which are not?

The simple answer is that the author has told us. It is not a question to be solved theologically, but by a close reading of the text. Just as in Greco-Roman paraenesis, our author here has specified how Christ is to be an example. The instruction to the slaves in verses 18–20 tells us what is χάρις παρὰ θεῷ, namely the endurance of suffering in doing good and entrusting oneself to God. In doing this, Christ is an exemplar. Those aspects of his passion that do not illustrate this principle are not exemplary (i.e., his atoning sacrifice *for others*). Verses 19–20 nowhere speak of suffering for others; they are concerned with doing good in the face of suffering for doing good. Thus, when verse 21 says that *Christ also suffered for you* the 'also' applies to the 'suffered' and not to the 'for you'.[80] The traditional instinct to separate the vicarious from the

---

[78] MICHAELS, *1 Peter*, 148, agrees that, 'The thought here is close to Paul's in Rom 6:11.'

[79] E.g., BLAZEN, 'Cessation,' 45, argues that, 'The fundamental ingredient in Christ's suffering for the right was his suffering for others. ...Since there is a fundamental parallel and relationship between Christ's suffering and ours, could it be that 4:1c, by way of implication carries the thought that as Christ has suffered *for us* to bring us to God (3:18), we are armed with the same thought when we suffer *for him*.'

[80] Cf. OSBORNE, 'Guide Lines,' 390, 'thus καί is related to ἔπαθεν ("he suffered") and not to ὑπὲρ ὑμῶν ("for you").' Contra ACHTEMEIER, *1 Peter*, 198–9, 'the implication is that Christ did good and suffered, so also slaves do good and suffer, and that as Christ

exemplary is correct, because that is what the *context* calls for. But the vicarious death of Christ is still exemplary as an act of obedience in the midst of suffering. So Christ's action in bearing sin is exemplary for its obedience, but not in its vicariousness. Likewise the other sufferings of Christ are exemplary in their display of righteous behavior in the face of suffering unjustly, but not exemplary in their value for others. As Achtemeier rightly says, 'Our conduct follows his in the *manner* of suffering but not in the *effects* of that suffering.'[81]

Having clarified what is exemplary about Christ's sufferings, what *specifically* do these verses commend as actions to be followed? Christ's refusal to threaten in retaliation for suffering maps easily onto the experience of the slaves, but what about his sin-bearing? Having excluded the vicarious element, where is the correlate? Once again, as in Greco-Roman paraenetic, it is not the *specific activity* that is given as an example, but the *disposition* that is revealed in that action. As Osborne notes, '[T]he term [ὑπογραμμός] as used in 1 Peter does not indicate the exact action which the slaves are to perform; rather it points to important characteristics of Christ's sufferings which are to serve as "guide lines" for the slaves' suffering.'[82] So when our author extols Christ because *when he suffered, he did not threaten*, it reveals Christ's commitment not to meet evil with evil, but to continue to do good in the face of gross injustice. It is this *disposition* of Christ that is exemplary. Practically speaking this may involve a choice to refrain from threats in the face of suffering, but it is not confined to this.[83] The application of the principle is left up to the slave in his particular circumstance. Likewise, Christ's sin bearing exemplifies this same commitment to do good in the face of injustice. His absolute devotion and obedience to God are exemplary for the slaves, who are called to abandon sin and live lives devoted to doing righteousness in obedient devotion to God. As Michaels explains, 'Living for δικαιοσύνη, or "what is right," is to Peter the equivalent of living for God or for Christ.'[84] Thus, Christ is an example in his commitment to follow God's will and do good in the face of radical injustice.

---

suffered for them, so they also are called to suffer "for him," that is because of their devotion to him.'

[81] P.J. ACHTEMEIER, 'Suffering Servant and Suffering Christ in 1 Peter,' in *The Future of Christology: Essays in Honor of Leander E. Keck*, ed. A.J. MALHERBE and W.A. MEEKS (Minneapolis: Fortress, 1993), 177 n.2. Italics added.

[82] OSBORNE, 'Guide Lines,' 392.

[83] Cf. MICHAELS, *1 Peter*, 145. 'Peter's emphasis in quoting Isa 53:9b is not so much on the fact that Christ's speech was free of deceit and treachery in particular as that it was free of every kind of evil speaking.'

[84] MICHAELS, *1 Peter*, 149.

C. Following the Shepherd

Our core christological text concludes with an emotive appeal in verses 24c–25. We saw that Greco-Roman paraenetic authors choose exemplars that the hearer respects and admires. Here in 1 Peter, Christ is an especially potent exemplar to the slaves as he is their Lord, whom they worship and love (1:8). The remainder of this passage underscores this connection by reminding them of his love and care for them, and thereby reinforces the affective power of Christ as an example.

First, he reminds them that Christ's work on the tree was really *for them*. Verse 24c, recalling Isa. 53:5 says, οὗ τῷ μώλωπι ἰάθητε. The author shifts from first to second person to focus the attention on the slaves as the beneficiaries of Christ's saving work. His aim is to elicit their gratitude to Christ, which strengthens their emotional connection to him. Secondly, he reminds them of their need for 'healing' and of Christ's gracious care for them in verse 25. *For you were straying like sheep* (ἦτε γὰρ ὡς πρόβατα πλανώμενοι)*, but have now returned to the Shepherd and Guardian of your souls* (ἀλλὰ ἐπεστράφητε νῦν ἐπὶ τὸν ποιμένα καὶ ἐπίσκοπον τῶν ψυχῶν ὑμῶν).

The first phrase reminds them of their pre-conversion life, using the language of Isa. 53:6, in which they wandered like aimless sheep in a life characterized by immorality. But they have been saved from that rebellious wandering; they have been returned to the fold. The passive ἐπεστράφην denotes God's action in their conversion.[85] The ἀλλα...νῦν construction emphasizes the contrast with their previous life and gives the aorist verb a perfective sense.[86] Not only have they been rescued from their wandering, but also they have been placed under the care of Christ, their shepherd and guardian.[87] Once again, the author elicits their gratitude by reminding his readers of their life before conversion and of God's saving gracious action towards them. In addition, he paints a picture of Christ as their shepherd

---

[85] ACHTEMEIER, *1 Peter*, 204, describes ἐπιστρέφω as 'virtually a technical term [in the NT] for the conversion of Gentiles.' It is not meant to imply anything about their residing with the Shepherd prior to their wandering; the focus of the metaphor is on their return (i.e., conversion). See ACHTEMEIER, *1 Peter*, 204. ELLIOTT, *1 Peter*, 538, also notes that, 'The contrast in v 25 a/b of former alienation and present reconciliation with God recalls the similar double contrast in 2:10.'

[86] So ACHTEMEIER, *1 Peter*, 204 n.207.

[87] ACHTEMEIER, *1 Peter*, 204, argues that, 'While the word "shepherd" is regularly used in the OT to refer to God, the absence of any reference to God as shepherd in the NT combined with its use as a descriptor of Jesus in the NT, the specific reference to Jesus as "chief shepherd" (ἀρχιποίμνη) in 1 Pet 5:10, and the connection of v. 24c with 25 by means of the explanatory conjunction γάρ, make it more likely that it here refers to Jesus.'

and guardian, who has not only provided for their salvation on the cross, but also continues to care for them, to lead them, and to protect them. In all this, the author seeks to procure their devotion to Christ out of appreciation of his love for them, shown in his actions past and present. By doing so, the author strengthens their emotional connection to Christ, and thus strengthens his effectiveness as a model to follow. They will follow Christ not only because he is a good moral example, but also because he is their savior and shepherd.

As in Greco-Roman paraenetic, this emotional connection and commitment is important because it counteracts the emotional appeal of what is familiar or comfortable. Here, it counteracts the strong emotional appeal of vengeance and assimilation. The author is able to use the slaves' devotion to Christ as a tool in helping them overcome these temptations.

IV. Conclusion

By using Christ as an example, our author has reinforced his injunction to the servants/slaves to refrain from evil in the face of suffering unjustly for their faith. In adopting this literary strategy, he is appropriating the use of παράδειγμα common in Greco-Roman paraenesis. Christ's actions and his commitments in his passion (sufferings and death) provide a model of faithful obedience to God in the midst of suffering gross injustice. In his death he also provides atonement for sin as a lamb without defect, and so becomes both a savior and an example to the slaves.[88] As we saw, these two elements are distinguishable but inseparable. The use of Christ as an example here reinforces and furthers the author's paraenetic agenda of promoting growth in Christian character, by calling on the servants (and paradigmatically the whole church) to endure suffering faithfully by sustaining their moral distinctiveness and integrity in the face of persecutions.

---

[88] Cf. WEBSTER, 'Imitability and Ethics,' 321–2, 'Jesus' history...furnishes at one and the same time the objective possibility of the new life of the Christian believer and its structure as a form of human conduct.'

Chapter Eight

Reflections and Prospects

Nearly half a century ago, Willem van Unnik insisted that, in approaching 1 Peter, it is 'not over-emphasizing a particular idea, but following the clue which leads to the heart of the writer's intention, if one tries to understand what he meant by καλὰ ἔργα and ἀγαθοποιΐα.'[1] The purpose of this thesis has been to follow this 'clue which leads to the heart of the writer's intention.' We have attempted to show that character formation is the central concern of the author of 1 Peter, and that this explains his strong emphasis on both καλὰ ἔργα and ἀγαθοποιΐα. To facilitate his character forming goals, our author has adapted several literary/rhetorical strategies that were common in Greco-Roman paraenetic epistles. As we saw, these strategies go far beyond simply providing moral precepts, but involve a complex integration of theological and ethical discourse designed to foster maturity in Christian convictions and praxis.

I. Reflections

We began our study by examining the nature of Greco-Roman paraenetic epistles. We saw that this epistolary tradition was well suited to both the environment and aims of the Hellenistic schools. Paraenesis developed as a tool for encouraging neophytes in their struggle to reform their lives to exhibit virtue. Because virtue is only gained through practice, one of the distinguishing features of paraenesis is a preponderance of practical advice, often in the form of moral precepts and maxims. But paraenetic authors recognized that advice by itself was not enough to bring about substantial progress (προκοπή) in moral maturity; to be effective, paraenesis must also address the obstacles to progress – misplaced devotions and mistaken ideas. To do this paraenetic authors developed a variety of literary devices, which included summary doctrinal statements, virtue and vice lists, moral exemplars, and remembrance and antithesis.

---

[1] W.C. VAN UNNIK, 'The Teaching of Good Works in 1 Peter.' *NTS* 1 (1954–55): 93. SELWYN, 89, notes that ' ἀγαθοποιεῖν is, indeed, one of the keywords of the Epistle, occurring more frequently, in one form or another, than in the whole of the rest of the New Testament put together.'

Thus, philosophic paraenesis is a multifaceted approach to character formation (ἠθοποιία), which takes into account the complexities of intellectual, emotional, and social ties that can impede progress in the venture of conforming one's life to one's convictions.

Our next step was to make the initial case for taking 1 Peter as an epistle of this type, by demonstrating that it not only utilizes paraenetic literary strategies, but that it also shares with paraenesis an overarching concern for furthering character development. We saw that the author's response to persecutions went beyond mere consolation to address the moral and theological challenges of suffering. This is why the fundamental 'answer' the author gives to suffering is the command to do good. He is addressing the dangers presented by temptations to cultural isolation and assimilation, but also to retaliation and despondency. Thus, the author's response facilitates several concurrent agendas, but central to these is his concern for growth in Christian character; the above temptations are confronted as impediments to that growth. In 1:6–7, the author shows that his response to persecutions is directly related to his concern for character formation. There he highlights the value of a practical faith that is refined by fire. It is this proven character (δοκίμιον) of faith, which is a result of righteous living in the face of unjust suffering, which the author extols as more precious than gold and the ultimate purpose for their suffering. Thus, we saw that 1 Peter is engaged in the typically paraenetic enterprise of facilitating character formation by promoting moral integrity.

In the chapters that followed, we detailed five specific paraenetic literary strategies and examined how they function within the overall paraenetic strategy of 1 Peter. The first strategy we examined was narrative worldview. In the benediction of 1:3–12, the author outlines a narrative worldview centered on God's salvific acts and the place of the readers within that overarching 'meta-narrative' of God's eschatological salvation. As we saw in Seneca and Philo, worldview constructs are a vital ingredient in paraenesis because they supply an ideational context for moral deliberation and education. The benediction constructs a theological narrative worldview that provides both intellectual grounding and affective motivation for the moral instructions that come later in the epistle. In addition, the meta-narrative of salvation has a normative role in shaping the individual biographies of the readers as they appropriate salvation through moral transformation. It also serves to realign commitments by fostering allegiance to God and to his program of salvation. In these ways, the benediction serves to foster the author's paraenetic agenda of character formation.

The second strategy we examined was remembrance, where a paraenetic author clarifies values and commitments by reminding his readers that their conversion was a paradigmatic life-defining event that involves a fundamental shift in values and priorities. In this rhetorical device pre-conversion existence is identified with vice while post-conversion life is identified with virtue. In 1 Peter, the author denigrates the readers' pre-conversion lifestyle as ἡ ματαία ἀναστροφή πατροπαράδοτος (1:18), which was characterized by ignorance and wicked desires (1:14). In contrast to this, he extols the sincere love (1:22), holiness (1:15), self-control (1:13), and obedience (1:22) that characterize their lives since conversion. The purpose of this remembrance is to facilitate a break with well-rehearsed vices, while at the same time instilling a desire for virtue. The paraenetic author recognizes that reforming one's character does not happen in an instant, but he characterizes conversion in the language of antithesis to clarify values and commitments for the neophyte struggling to put into practice the life first embraced in conversion. In 1 Peter, the author emphasizes the absolute antithesis brought about in conversion through images of new birth like ἀρτιγέννητα βρέφη in 2:2 and τέκνα ὑπακοῆς in 1:14.[2] Conversion is not only a matter of the covert's choice, but also God's work in giving them new birth. Remembrances of conversion and the absolute antitheses that derive from conversion further our author's paraenetic goal of promoting growth in moral integrity and aid the readers in translating their beliefs in practice.

The third strategy we looked at was the author's construction of a distinctive corporate identity for the church vis-à-vis the pagan world. Appropriating corporate imagery from the OT, the author constructs a corporate identity that is rooted in the saving activity of God and meets the twin temptations of cultural assimilation and isolation. The author begins by using two titles that encapsulate the community's new identity: οἶκος πνευματικὸς and ἱεράτευμα ἅγιον. The first relates to the community's identity as a family brought together by God, while the second relates to their identity as a worshipping community. The first image emphasizes the love and mutual belonging of the family. The second image emphasizes the glorification of God as the final motivation for all action. These two corporate images act as controlling images over the author's prescriptions for community life and social ethics throughout the remainder of the epistle.

In addition, the author calls his readers to embrace their God-given identity as πάροικοι and παρεπίδημοι, in order to urge them to retain their moral distinctiveness. As we saw, because the church's identity is defined by the electing activity of God and not their difference from others, it does not promote animosity towards outsiders. The church's battle is not with outsiders but with sin. The struggles the author addresses are moral

---

[2] Both of these images harken back to the new birth first mentioned in 1:3.

temptations towards assimilation and isolation, which are intensified by social ostracism. Thus, by calling the readers to see themselves ὡς πάροικοι καὶ παρεπίδημοι, our author has given them a means to accomplish their difficult task of retaining moral purity while still remaining open to the world. The author's strategy functions at many levels; in addition to creating an environment that facilitates evangelism while retaining community boundaries, he also furthers his paraenetic concern of promoting moral integrity. By providing various complementary corporate images, the author enables his readers to retain their καλὴ ἀναστροφή, and helps them realize growth in Christian character.

The fourth paraenetic strategy that came under our examination was our author's extensive use of moral instructions (i.e., paraenesis-as-form). These instructions not only serve the author's short-term goals of restraining misconduct that might arise in response to suffering mistreatment, but, because they encourages a lifestyle characterized by virtuous living, they also serve to foster the long-term goal of growth in character. By specifying how fundamental beliefs shape everyday behavior, moral instructions aid these converts in the process of conforming their lives to their convictions. As we saw, moral instructions serve not only to define ethical norms but also to aid growth in character and discernment, both in terms of intellectual development and affective reorientation. Moral instructions then are another effective tool in the hand of our author to achieve his paraenetic aim of advancing growth in maturity.

Our fifth and final look at the use of paraenetic strategies in 1 Peter focused on the use of Jesus as a moral exemplar. After cataloging several of the functional features of παράδειγμα in Greco-Roman paraenesis, we turned to applying these insights to the major christological passages in 1 Peter, which are dominated by an *imitatio Christi* theme. We found that the faithful obedience of Christ in his passion (which includes his death) has both salvific and exemplary value. Through his obedience, he won salvation for his church, but he also left an example of reverent obedience to God's will in the face of suffering radical injustice. In this way, his actions in his passion become a model for slaves who suffer unjustly for their faith, and by extension, for all Christians who suffer unjustly. The example of Christ precludes a myriad of possible responses that would entail retaliation, disrespect, and hatred. Instead, the servants are called to continue to do good out of reverence for God. Again, this comports with the author's overall concern to confront the moral challenges of persecution and to encourage the practice of sustained moral integrity and through this growth in Christian character.

These christological texts are a prime example of the inseparability of theology and ethics in 1 Peter. As we saw, exegetical approaches that sought to separate theology and ethics (i.e., Jesus as savior from Jesus as exemplar) are incapable of understanding these texts on their own terms. Only an integrated approach is able to see how Christ is simultaneously both savior and exemplar. The two elements are distinguishable but inseparable.

These *imitatio Christi* texts also present, in microcosm, a window into the nature of the whole epistle. Here we see a succinct clear illustration of theology operating in a paraenetic mode. As theology, it is fascinating in itself, with one of the few clear instances in the NT writings of the atoning death of Jesus being expressed in the language of the servant song of Isaiah 53. Yet, as we saw, the implications drawn by the author are *ethical* not 'doctrinal'. This is another example of paraenetic theology, where theology is brought to bear to further the paraenetic aims of the author.

As we have seen, this kind of pragmatically shaped theology is not limited to these christological texts, but describes the author's use of theology at all points in the epistle. Theological discourse operates at multiple levels to further the author's paraenetic agenda. It provides an ideational context for ethical deliberation, but it also provides motivational structures that encourage character formation; it not only instructs but also calls for a realignment of affective commitments. Therefore, it is clear that the old paradigm of 'indicative and imperative', which neatly separates theology and ethics, is inherently limited as a tool for studying 1 Peter. As we have seen, theology and ethics function together to serve the author's aim of encouraging growth in Christian character. This does not mean that theology becomes subsumed under ethics, but rather that theology and ethics operate *together* to realize the paraenetic aim of character formation. As we saw, the author of 1 Peter uses theology (in various forms) and ethical instruction (in various forms) as complementary modes of discourse to render what Seneca called 'effective paraenesis'.

II. Prospects

The foundation for the interpretation of any example of human communication is genre. This is especially the case when interpreting communication cross-culturally, where the genre cues are not automatic, as they are in most everyday communication. In examining literature from another culture and another time, genre determination is critical to hermeneutical fidelity. The first thing that this thesis establishes for future Petrine research is a firm foundation for understanding the generic form of

1 Peter as a paraenetic epistle. This thesis places 1 Peter within its historical context as a communicative act from the ancient world, with certain agendas and tools of realizing those agendas encoded in its genre. It also provides a set of tools for understanding the function of certain paraenetic strategies in 1 Peter, which in turn provide guidelines for exegesis.

This work has also laid the groundwork for further research into the complementary function of theology and ethics in 1 Peter, with theology and ethics operating in the same sphere, not separated. By understanding 1 Peter as paraenesis, we can more deeply explore the intertwining of theology and ethics in this epistle, which has perpetually fascinated interpreters, but has been hidden in a methodological cul-de-sac. More work remains to be done on how different passages function together paraenetically to render effective paraenesis and shape Christian character.

What is true for 1 Peter is also true for much of the epistolary literature of early Christianity. Looking at the Pauline epistles through the generic lens of paraenesis is a mine of interpretation that has only begun to be explored by Malherbe and Wilson. All of the paraenetic strategies outlined in this thesis would be directly applicable to material in Paul's letters; narrative worldview, remembrance and antithesis, social identity, moral instructions, and *imitatio Christi* all find deep resonances in the writings of Paul. Knowing how these different strategies function can provide new ways for reading specific texts, just as here in 1 Peter.

The paraenetic interpretive lens also has potential for seeing theology and ethics functioning as complements in the Pauline epistles. Ethics then would cease to be an add-on, or something that operates in a sphere independent from theology. The question of the relationship between theology and ethics is central in our understanding of Paul, as exhibited in the vast amount of literature in the last three decades on 'Paul and the Law'. Yet virtually all of this research takes 'Law' as either an idea (i.e., law as a theological construct) or interprets the function of law in Kantian deontological categories. The possibility of other ways of relating Paul's theology and ethics, or that Paul's 'inconsistencies' with respect to the law are his deliberations on different understandings of that relationship, has yet to be explored in any depth. This thesis has shown that there are alternative constructions for relating theology and ethics.

Finally, it is hoped that this thesis will add to and foster biblical research that is shaped by the reality that early Christian literature was written to shape human life, not simply to communicate ideas. This is, of course, a conviction that most NT specialists would adhere to, but one all too often neutered by our methodologies. This work has attempted to be an example of a methodology *shaped* by this conviction. May others follow.

Bibliography

Ancient Sources

ARISTOTLE, *EN*
Greek text: Aristotelis. *Ethica Nicomachea*. Edited by I. Bywater. Oxford Classical Texts. Oxford: Oxford University Press, 1894.
English text: *Nicomachean Ethics*, 2nd ed. Translated by Terence Irwin. Indianapolis: Hackett, 1999.

CICERO, *Gods*
Latin text: M. Tulli Ciceronis. *De Natura Deorum*, 2nd ed. Edited by W. Ax. Bibliotheca Scriptorum Graecorum et Romanorum Teubneriana. Stuttgart: Tübner Verlagsgesellschaft, 1933.
English text: Cicero. *On the Nature of the Gods*. Translated by Patrick Gerard Walsh. Oxford World's Classics. Oxford: Oxford University Press, 1998.

(PSEUDO-) CRATES, *Epistles*
Greek and English texts: *The Cynic Epistles: A Study Edition*. Edited by Abraham J. Malherbe. Society of Biblical Literature Sources for Biblical Study, edited by Wayne A. Meeks, Vol. 12. Missoula, MT: Scholars Press, 1977.

(PSEUDO-) DEMETRIUS, *Epistolary Types*
Greek and English texts: *Ancient Epistolary Theorists*. Edited by Abraham J. Malherbe. Atlanta, GA: Scholars Press, 1988.

(PSEUDO-) DIOGENES, *Epistles*
Greek and English texts: *The Cynic Epistles: A Study Edition*. Edited by Abraham J. Malherbe. Society of Biblical Literature Sources for Biblical Study, edited by Wayne A. Meeks, Vol. 12. Missoula, MT: Scholars Press, 1977.

DIO CHRYSOSTOM, *Orations*
Greek text: Dionis Chrysostomi. *Orationes*. Edited by Guy de Budé. 2 Vols. Bibliotheca Scriptorum Graecorum et Romanorum Teubneriana. Stuttgart: Tübner Verlagsgesellschaft, 1915–19.
English text: Dio Chrysostom. Translated by H. Lamar Crosby. 5 Vols. Loeb Classical Library. London: Heinemann, 1951.

EPICTETUS, *Discourses*
Greek text: Épictète. *Entretiens*. Edited by Joseph Souilhé and Amand Jagu. 4 Vols. Collection des Universités de France. Paris: Les Belles Lettres, 1943–65.
English text: Epictetus. *The Discourses*. Translated by W. A. Oldfather. 2 Vols. Loeb Classical Library. London: Heinemann, 1925.

EUSEBIUS, *HE*
Greek text: Eusebius. *Die Kirchengeschichte*. Edited by Eduard Schwartz. 3 Vol. Leipzig: J. C. Hinrich, 1903–09.
English text: Eusebius. *The Ecclesiastical History*. Translated by Kirsopp Lake, J. E. L. Oulton. 2 Vols. Loeb Classical Library. London: Heinemann, 1926–32.

ISOCRATES, *Demonicus*, *Nicocles*, and *Evagoras*
Greek text: Isocrate. *Discours*. Edited by Georges Mathieu and Émile

4 Vols. Collection des Universités de France. Paris: Les Belles Lettres, 1938.
English text: *Isocrates*. Translated by George Norlin. 3 Vols. Loeb Classical Library. London: Heinemann, 1928.

JUSTIN, *Apology* and *Dialogue*
Greek text: *Iustini Martyris Apologiae pro Christianis*. Edited by Miroslav Marcovich. Patristische Texte und Studien. Berlin: de Guyter, 1994. AND *Iustini Martyris Dialogus cum Tryphone*. Edited by Miroslav Marcovich. Patristische Texte und Studien. Berlin: de Guyter, 1997.
English text: Justin Martyr. *The First and Second Apologies*. Translated by Leslie William Barnard. Ancient Christian Writers, Vol. 56. New York: Paulist Press, 1997. AND Justin Martyr. *Dialogue with Trypho*. Translated by Thomas B. Falls. Fathers of the Church, edited by Michael Slusser, vol. 3. Washington, D.C.: Catholic University of America Press, 2003.

(PSEUDO-) LIBANIUS, *Epistolary Styles*
Greek and English texts: *Ancient Epistolary Theorists*. Edited by Abraham J. Malherbe. Atlanta, GA: Scholars Press, 1988.

LIVY, *City*
Latin text: Titi Livi. *Ab Urbe Condita: Libri 1–5*. Edited by Robert Maxwell Ogilvie. Oxford Classical Texts. Oxford: Oxford University Press, 1974.
English text: *Livy Vol. I*. Translated by B. O. Foster. Loeb Classical Library. Cambridge, MA: Harvard University Press, 1962.

PHILO, *Heir*, *On Creation*, *Husbandry*, *Moses*, and *Abraham*
Greek and English texts: *Philo*. Translated by Francis H. Colson, George H. Whitaker, and Ralph Marcus. 12 vols. Loeb Classical Library. London: Heinemann, 1929–62.

PLATO, *Republic*
Greek text: Platon. *La République*. Edited by Émile Chambry. 3 Vols. Collection des Universités de France. Paris: Les Belles Lettres, 1932–4.
English text: Plato. *The Republic*. Translated by Georges Maximilien Antoine. Indianapolis: Hacket, 1974.

PLUTARCH, *On Listening*, *Moral Progress*, and *Flatterer*
Greek text: Plutarchus. *Moralia*. 7 Vols. Bibliotheca Scriptorum Graecorum et Romanorum Teubneriana. Leipzig: Tübner Verlagsgesellschaft, 1953–78.
English text: *Plutarch's Moralia*. 16 Vols. Loeb Classical Library. London: Heinemann, 1927–76. OR (where noted) Plutarch. *Essays*. Translated by Robin Waterfield. Penguin Classics. London: Penguin Books, 1992.

PLUTARCH, *Pericles and Alexander*
Greek text: Plutarchus. *Vitae Parallelae*. Edited by Konrat Ziegler. 2 Vols. Bibliotheca Scriptorum Graecorum et Romanorum Teubneriana. Leipzig: Tübner Verlagsgesellschaft, 1964–70.
English text: *Plutarch's Lives*. Translated by Bernadotte Perrin. 11 Vols. Loeb Classical Library. London: Heinemann, 1914.

PORPHYRY, *Marcella*
Greek text: Porphyre. *Lettre à Marcella*. Edited by Édouard des Places. Collection des Universités de France. Paris: Les Belles Lettres, 1982.
English text: *Porphyry the Philosopher: To Marcella*. Translated by Kathleen O'Brien Wicker. Society of Biblical Literature Texts and Translations Vol. 28, Graeco-Roman Religion Series Vol. 10. Atlanta: Scholars Press, 1987.

, *EM*
text: L. Annaei Senecae. *Ad Lucilium Epistulae Morales*. Edited by L. D.

Reynolds. 2 Vols. Oxford Classical Texts. Oxford: Oxford University Press, 1965. English text: Seneca. *Ad Lucium Episulae Morales*. Translated by Richard M. Gummere. 3 Vols. Loeb Classical Library. London: Heinemann, 1917–25.

TERENCE, *Self-Tormentor*
Latin and English texts: *Terence I*. Translated by John Barsby. Loeb Classical Library. Cambridge, MA: Harvard University Press, 2001.

VALERIUS MAXIMUS, *Sayings and Doings*
Latin text: Valère Maxime. *Faits et Dits Mémorable*. Edited by Robert Combès. 2 Vols. Collection des Universités de France. Paris: Les Belles Lettres, 1995. English text: Valerius Maximus. *Memorable Sayings and Doings*. Translated by D. R. Schackleton Bailey. Loeb Classical Library. Cambridge, MA: Harvard University Press, 2000.

XENOPHON, *Oeconomicus*
Greek text: Xénophon. *Économique*. Edited by Pierre Chantraine. Collection des Universités de France. Paris: Les Belles Lettres, 1949. English text: Xenophon. *Momorabilia and Oeconomicus*. Translated by E. C. Marchant. Loeb Classical Library. London: Heinemann, 1923.

1 Peter Commentaries

ACHTEMEIER, PAUL J. *1 Peter: A Commentary on First Peter*. Hermeneia, edited by Eldon Jay Epp. Minneapolis: Fortress, 1996.

BEARE, FRANCIS WRIGHT. *The First Epistle of Peter: The Greek Text with Introduction and Notes*, 3rd ed. Oxford: Blackwell, 1970.

BECK, JOHANN TOBIAS. *Erklärung der Briefe Petri*. Edited by Julius Lindenmeyer. Gütersloh: Bertelsmann, 1896.

BEST, ERNEST. *1 Peter*. New Century Bible, edited by Matthew Black. London: Oliphants, 1982.

BIGG, CHARLES. *A Critical and Exegetical Commentary on the Epistles of St. Peter and St. Jude*, 2nd ed. International Critical Commentary, edited by S. R. Driver, A. Plummer and C. A. Briggs. Edinburgh: T&T Clark, 1902.

BORING, M. EUGENE. *1 Peter*. Abingdon New Testament Commentaries. Nashville: Abingdon Press, 1999.

BROX, NORBERT. *Der erste Petrusbrief*, 4th edition. Evangelisch-katholischer Kommentar zum Neuen Testament, edited by Norbert Brox, Joachim Gnilka, Jürgen Roloff, et al., Vol. 21. Zürich: Benziger Verlag, 1993.

CALVIN, JEAN. *The Epistle of Paul the Apostle to the Hebrews and the First and Second Epistles of St. Peter*. Translated by William B. Johnston. Calvin's New Testament Commentaries, edited by David W. Torrance and Thomas F. Torrance, Vol. 12. Grand Rapids: Eerdmans, 1994.

CRANFIELD, C. E. B. *The First Epistle of Peter*. London: SCM, 1950.

DAVIDS, PETER H. *The First Epistle of Peter*. New International Commentary on the New Testament, edited by F. F. Bruce and Gordon Fee. Grand Rapids: Eerdmans, 1990.

DE WETTE, WILHELM MARTIN LEBERECHT. *Kurze Erklärung der Briefe des Petrus, Judas und Jakobus*. Kurzgefaßtes exegetisches Handbuch zum Neuen Testament, Vol. 3.1. Leipzig: Weidmann, 1847.

ELLIOTT, JOHN H. *1 Peter: A New Translation with Introduction and Commentary.* Anchor Bible, edited by William Fox Albright and David Noel Freedman, Vol. 37B. New York: Doubleday, 2000.

FRONMÜLLER, G. F. C. *The Epistles General of Peter.* Translated by Jacob Isidor Mombert. Lange's Commentary on the Holy Scripture: New Testament, edited by Philip Schaff, Vol. 9.2. Edinburgh: T&T Clark, 1870. Original publication: *Die Briefe Petri und der Brief Judä,* 2nd edition. Theologisch-homiletisches Bibelwerk des Neuen Testamentes, edited by J. P. Lange, Vol. 14. Bielefeld: Velhagen & Klasing, 1862.

GOPPELT, LEONARD. *A Commentary on 1 Peter.* Translated by John E. Alsup, edited by Ferndinand Hahn. Grand Rapids: Eerdmans, 1993. Original publication: *Der Erste Petrusbrief.* Meyers Kritisch-exegetischer Kommentar über das Neue Testament, edited by Ferndinand Hahn, Vol. 12/1. Göttingen: Vandenhoeck & Ruprecht, 1978.

HILLYER, NORMAN. *1 and 2 Peter, Jude.* New International Biblical Commentary, New Testament Series, edited by W. Ward Gasque, Vol. 16. Peabody, MA: Hendrickson, 1992.

HORRELL, DAVID G. *The Epistles of Peter and Jude.* Epworth Commentaries, edited by Ivor H. Jones. Peterborough: Epworth Press, 1998.

HORT, F. J. A. *The First Epistle of St. Peter I.1–II.17: The Greek Text with Introductory Lecture, Commentary, and Additional Notes.* London: Macmillan, 1898.

HUTHER, JOHANN EDUARD. *Critical and Exegetical Handbook to the General Epistles of Peter and Jude.* Translated by D. B. Croom and Paton J. Gloag. Edinburgh: T&T Clark, 1881. Original publication: *Kritisch exegetisches Handbuch über den 1. Brief des Petrus, den Brief des Judas und den 2. Brief des Petrus,* 4th edition. Kritisch-exegetischer Kommentar über das Neue Testament, edited by Heinrich A. W. Meyer, Vol. 12. Göttingen: Vandenhoeck & Ruprecht, 1877.

KELLY, JOHN NORMAN DAVIDSON. *A Commentary on the Epistles of Peter and Jude.* Black's New Testament Commentaries, edited by Henry Chadwick. London: Black, 1969.

KISTEMAKER, SIMON. *Exposition of the Epistles of Peter and of the Epistle of Jude.* New Testament Commentary. Grand Rapids: Baker, 1987.

MICHAELS, J. RAMSEY. *1 Peter.* Word Bible Commentary, edited by David A. Hubbard and Glenn W. Barker, Vol. 49. Waco: Word, 1988.

REICKE, BO IVAR. *The Epistles of James, Peter, and Jude: Introduction, Translation, and Notes.* Anchor Bible, edited by William Fox Albright and David Noel Freedman, Vol. 37. Garden City, NY: Doubleday, 1964.

SCHELKLE, KARL HERMANN. *Die Petrusbriefe, der Judasbrief.* Herders theologischer Kommentar zum Neuen Testament, edited by Alfred Wikenhauser and Anton Vögtle, Vol. 13.2. Freiburg: Herder, 1961.

SCHLATTER, ADOLF. *Petrus und Paulus nach dem Ersten Petrusbrief.* Stuttgart: Calwer, 1937.

SCHRAGE, WOLFGANG, and HORST ROBERT BALZ. *Die katholischen Briefe: die Briefe des Jakobus, Petrus, Johannes und Judas.* Das Neue Testament Deutsch, edited by Gerhard Friedrich, Vol. 10. Göttingen: Vandenhoeck & Ruprecht, 1973.

SELWYN, EDWARD GORDON. *The First Epistle of St. Peter: The Greek Text with Introduction, Notes and Essays,* 2nd ed. London: MacMillan, 1947.

WINDISCH, HANS. *Die katholischen Briefe,* edited by Herbert Preisker, 3rd edition. Handbuch zum Neuen Testament, edited by Andreas Lindemann, Vol. 15. Tübingen: Mohr (Siebeck), 1951

1 Peter Studies

ACHTEMEIER, PAUL J. 'Newborn Babes and Living Stones: Literal and Figurative in 1 Peter.' In *To Touch the Text: Biblical and Related Studies in Honor of Joseph A. Fitzmyer, S.J.*, edited by Maurya P. Horgan and Paul J. Kobelski, 207–36. New York: Crossroad, 1989.

ACHTEMEIER, PAUL J. 'Suffering Servant and Suffering Christ in 1 Peter.' In *The Future of Christology: Essays in Honor of Leander E. Keck*, edited by Abraham J. Malherbe and Wayne A. Meeks, 176–88. Minneapolis: Fortress, 1993.

BALCH, DAVID L. 'Hellenization/Acculturation in 1 Peter.' In *Perspectives on First Peter*, edited by Charles H. Talbert, 79–101. National Association of Baptist Professors of Religion Special Studies Series, Vol. 9. Macon, GA: Mercer University Press, 1986.

BALCH, DAVID L. *Let Wives be Submissive: The Domestic Code in 1 Peter.* Society of Biblical Literature Monograph Series, edited by James Crenshaw and Robert Tannehill, Vol. 26. Chico, CA: Scholars Press, 1981.

BAMMEL, E. 'The Commands in 1 Peter II.17.' *New Testament Studies* 11 (1965): 279–81.

BECHTLER, STEVEN RICHARD. *Following in His Steps: Suffering, Community, and Christology in 1 Peter.* Society of Biblical Literature Dissertation Series, edited by E. Elizabeth Johnson, Vol. 162. Atlanta, GA: Scholars Press, 1998.

BOISMARD, M. E. *Quatre hymnes Baptismales dans la première Épître de Pierre.* Lectio Divina, Vol. 30. Paris: Éditions du Cerf, 1961.

BLAZEN, IVAN T. 'Suffering and Cessation from Sin According to 1 Peter 4:1.' *Andrews University Seminary Studies* 21.1 (1983): 27–50.

BRANDT, WILHELM. 'Wandel als Zeugnis nach dem 1. Petrusbrief.' In *Verbum Dei Manet in Aeternum*, edited by Werner Foerster, 10–25. Witten: Luther Verlag, 1953.

BULTMANN, RUDOLF. 'Bekenntnis- und Liedfragmente im ersten Petrusbrief.' *Coniectanea Neotestamentica* 11 (1947): 1–14.

CAMPBELL, BARTH L. *Honor, Shame, and the Rhetoric of 1 Peter.* Society of Biblical Literature Dissertation Series, edited by E. Elizabeth Johnson, Vol. 160. Atlanta: Scholars Press, 1998.

CASURELLA, ANTHONY. *Bibliography of Literature on First Peter.* New Testament Tools and Studies, edited by Bruce M. Metzger and Bart D. Ehrman, Vol. 23. Leiden: Brill, 1996.

CERVANTES-GABARRÓN, JOSÉ. 'La Pasión de Jesuchristo en la Primera Carta de Pedro.' Centro Literario y Teológico de la Carta.' Unpublished Doctoral thesis, Pontificiae Universitatis Gregorianae, 1991.

COMBRINK, H. J. B. 'The Structure of 1 Peter.' *Neotestamentica* 9 (1975): 34–63.

CROSS, F. L. *1. Peter: A Paschal Liturgy.* Oxford: A. R. Mowbray, 1954.

DALTON, WILLIAM JOSEPH. *Christ's Proclamation to the Spirits: A Study of 1 Peter 3:18–4:6*, 2nd edition. Analecta Biblica, Vol. 23. Rome: Editrice Pontificio Istituto Biblico, 1989.

DANKER, FREDERICK W. Review of *A Home for the Homeless: A Sociological Exegesis of 1 Peter, its Situation and Strategy* by John H. Elliott. Interpretation 37.1 (1983): 84–88.

DAVIES, PAUL E. 'Primitive Christology in 1 Peter.' In *Festschrift to Honor F. Wilbur Gingrich: Lexicographer, Scholar, Teacher, and Committed Christian Layman*, edited by Eugene Howard Barth and Ronald Edwin Cocroft, 115–22. Leiden: Brill, 1972.

DE VILLIERS, J. L. 'Joy in Suffering in 1 Peter.' *Neotestamentica* 9 (1975): 64–86.

DU TOIT, A. B. 'The Significance of Discourse Analysis for New Testament Interpretation and Translation: Introductory Remarks with Special Reference to 1 Peter 1:3–13.' *Neotestamentica* 8 (1974): 54–79.

ELLIOTT, JOHN H. '1 Peter, Its Situation and Strategy: A Discussion with David Balch.' In *Perspectives on First Peter*, edited by Charles H. Talbert, 61–78. National Association of Baptist Professors of Religion Special Studies Series, Vol. 9. Macon, GA: Mercer University Press, 1986.

ELLIOTT, JOHN H. 'Backward and Forward "In His Steps": Following Jesus from Rome to Raymond and Beyond. The Tradition, Redaction, and Reception of 1 Peter 2:18–25.' In *Discipleship in the New Testament*, edited by Fernando F. Segovia, 184–209. Philadelphia: Fortress, 1985.

ELLIOTT, JOHN H. 'Disgraced Yet Graced: The Gospel According to 1 Peter in the Key of Honor and Shame.' *Biblical Theology Bulletin* 25.4 (1995): 166–78.

ELLIOTT, JOHN H. *The Elect and the Holy: An Exegetical Examination of I Peter 2:4–10 and the Phrase βασίλειον ἱεράτευμα.* Supplements to Novum Testamentum, Vol. 12. Leiden: Brill, 1966.

ELLIOTT, JOHN H. *A Home for the Homeless: A Sociological Exegesis of 1 Peter, its Situation and Strategy*. Philadelphia: Fortress, 1981.

ELLIOTT, JOHN H. 'The Rehabilitation of an Exegetical Step-Child: 1 Peter in Recent Research.' *Journal of Biblical Literature* 95.2 (1976): 243–54.

ELLIOTT, JOHN H. 'Salutation and Exhortation to Christian Behavior on the Basis of God's Blessings (1:1–2:10).' *Review and Expositor* 79 (1982): 415–25.

FELDMEIER, REIHARD. *Die Christen als Fremde: Die Metapher der Fremde in der antiken Welt, im Urchristentum und im 1. Petrusbrief.* Wissenschaftliche Untersuchungen zum Neuen Testament, edited by Martin Hengel and Otfried Hofius, Vol. 64. Tübingen: Mohr (Siebeck), 1992.

FILSON, FLOYD V. 'Partakers with Christ: Suffering in First Peter.' *Interpretation* 9 (1955): 400–12.

GOLDSTEIN, HORST. 'Die Kirche als Schar derer, die ihrem leidenden Herrn mit dem Ziel der Gottesgemeinschaft nachfolgen: Zum Gemeindeverständnis von 1 Petr 2,21–25 und 3,18–22.' *Bibel und Leben* 15 (1974): 38–54.

HALL, RANDY. 'For to This You Have Been Called: The Cross and Suffering in 1 Peter.' *Restoration Quarterly* 19 (1976): 137–47.

HEMER, COLIN J. 'The Address of 1 Peter.' *Expository Times* 89 (1977–78): 239–43.

HERZER, JENS. *Petrus oder Paulus? Studien über das Verhältnis des Ersten Petrusbriefes zur paulinischen Tradition.* Wissenschaftliche Untersuchungen zum Neuen Testament, edited by Martin Hengel and Otfried Hofius, Vol. 103. Tübingen: Mohr (Siebeck), 1998.

HIEBERT, D. EDMOND. 'Following Christ's Example: An Exposition of 1 Peter 2:21–25.' *Bibliotheca Sacra* 139 (1982): 32–45.

HIEBERT, D. EDMOND. 'The Suffering and Triumphant Christ: An Exposition of 1 Peter 3:18–22.' *Bibliotheca Sacra* 139 (1982): 146–58.

HORRELL, DAVID G. 'The Product of a Petrine Circle? A Reassessment of the Origin and Character of 1 Peter.' *Journal for the Study of the New Testament* 86 (2002): 29–60.

JOBES, KAREN H. 'Got Milk? Septuagint Psalm 33 and the Interpretation of 1 Peter 2:1–3.' *Westminster Theological Journal* 63 (2002): 1–14.

JONES-HALDEMAN, MADELYN. 'The Function of Christ's Suffering in 1 Peter 2:21.' Unpublished Th.D. thesis, Andrews University, 1988.

KENDALL, DAVID WALTER. 'The Introductory Character of 1 Peter 1:3–12.' Unpublished Ph.D. thesis, Union Theological Seminary, 1984.

KENDALL, DAVID WALTER. 'The Literary and Theological Function of 1 Peter 1:3–12.' In *Perspectives on First Peter*, edited by Charles H. Talbert, 103–20. National Association of Baptist Professors of Religion Special Studies Series, Vol. 9. Macon, GA: Mercer University Press, 1986.

KIRK, GORDON E. 'Endurance in Suffering in 1 Peter.' *Bibliotheca Sacra* 138 (1981): 46–56.

LANGKAMMER, HUGOLINUS. 'Jes 53 und 1 Petr 2,21–25: Zur christologischen Interpretation der Leidenstheologie von Jes 53.' *Bibel und Liturgie* 60 (1987): 90–98.

LASH, C. J. A. 'Fashionable Sports: Hymn-Hunting in 1 Peter.' In *Studia Evangelica Vol. VII*, edited by Elizabeth A. Livingstone, 293–97. Texte und Untersuchungen: Zur Geschichte der altchristlichen Literatur, Vol. 126. Berlin: Akademie Verlag, 1982.

LOHSE, EDUARD. 'Parenesis and Kerygma in 1 Peter.' Translated by John Steely. In *Perspectives on First Peter*, edited by Charles H. Talbert, 37–59. National Association of Baptist Professors of Religion Special Studies Series, Vol. 9. Macon, GA: Mercer University Press, 1986. Original publication: 'Paränese und Kerygma im 1. Petrusbrief.' *Zeitschrift für die neutestamentliche Wissenschaft* 45 (1954): 68–89.

LOVE, JULIAN PRINCE. 'The First Epistle of Peter.' *Interpretation* 8 (1954): 63–87.

MARTIN, TROY W. 'The Present Indicative in the Eschatological Statements of 1 Peter 1:6, 8.' *Journal of Biblical Literature* 111.2 (1992): 307–14.

MARTIN, TROY W. *Metaphor and Composition in 1 Peter*. Society of Biblical Literature Dissertation Series, edited by Pheme Perkins, Vol. 131. Atlanta, GA: Scholars Press, 1992.

METZNER, RAINER. *Die Rezeption des Matthäusevangeliums im 1. Petrusbrief: Studien zum traditionsgeschichtlichen und theologischen Einfluss des 1. Evangeliums auf den 1. Petrusbrief.* Wissenschaftliche Untersuchungen zum Neuen Testament, 2nd series, edited by Martin Hengel and Otfried Hofius, Vol. 74. Tübingen: Mohr (Siebeck), 1995.

MILLAUER, HELMUT. *Leiden als Gnade: eine traditionsgeschichtliche Untersuchung zur Leidenstheologie des ersten Petrusbriefes.* Europäische Hochschulschriften, series 23: Theologie, Vol. 56. Bern: Herbert Lang, 1976.

MOULE, C. F. D. 'The Nature and Purpose of 1 Peter.' *New Testament Studies* 3 (1956–57): 1–11.

NAUCK, WOLFGANG. 'Freude im Leiden: Zum Problem einer urchristlichen Verfolgungstradition.' *Zeitschrift für die neutestamentliche Wissenschaft* 45 (1955): 68–80.

NEUGEBAUER, F. 'Zur Deutung und Bedeutung des 1. Petrusbriefes.' *New Testament Studies* 26 (1980): 61–86.

OMANSON, ROGER. 'Suffering for Righteousness' Sake (3:13–4:11).' *Review and Expositor* 79 (1982): 439–50.

OSBORNE, THOMAS P. 'Christian Suffering in the First Epistle of Peter.' Unpublished S.T.D. thesis, Université Catholique de Louvain, 1981.

OSBORNE, THOMAS P. 'Guide Lines for Christian Suffering: A Source-Critical and Theological Study of 1 Peter 2,21–25.' *Biblica* 64 (1983): 381–408.

PATSCH, HERMANN. 'Zum alttestamentlichen Hintergrund von Römer 4.25 und 1. Petrus 2.24.' *Zeitschrift für die neutestamentliche Wissenschaft* 60 (1969): 273–79.

PERDELWITZ, EMIL RICHARD. *Die Mysterienreligion und das Problem des 1. Petrusbriefes: ein literarischer und religionsgeschichtlicher Versuch.*

Religionsgeschichtliche Versuche und Vorarbeiten, Vol. 11.3. Giessen: Töpelmann, 1911.

PIPER, JOHN. 'Hope as the Motivation of Love: 1 Peter 3:9 12.' *New Testament Studies* 26 (1979–80): 212–31.

POH, CHU LUAN EILEEN. 'The Social World of 1 Peter: Socio-Historical and Exegetical Studies.' Unpublished Ph.D. thesis, King's College London, 1998.

PRASAD, JACOB. *Foundations of the Christian Way of Life According to 1 Peter 1,13–25: An Exegetico-theological Study.* Analecta Biblica, Vol. 146. Rome: Pontificio Istituto Biblico, 2000.

PROSTMEIER, FERDINAND-RUPERT. *Handlungsmodelle im ersten Petrusbrief.* Forschung zur Bibel, edited by Rudolf Schnackenburg and Josef Schreiner, Vol. 63. Würzburg: Echter, 1990.

RICHARD, EARL. 'The Functional Christology of First Peter.' In *Perspectives on First Peter*, edited by Charles H. Talbert, 121–39. National Association of Baptist Professors of Religion Special Studies Series, Vol. 9. Macon, GA: Mercer University Press, 1986.

SCHELKLE, KARL HERMANN. 'Das Leiden des Gottesknechtes als Form christlichen Lebens (nach dem ersten Petrusbrief).' *Bibel und Kirche* 16 (1961): 14–16.

SCHWEIZER, EDUARD. 'Zur Christologie des ersten Petrusbriefs.' In *Anfänge der Christologie: Festschrift für Ferdinand Hahn zum 65. Geburtstag*, edited by Cilliers Breytenbach and Henning Paulsen, 369–82. Göttingen: Vandenhoeck & Ruprecht, 1991.

SELWYN, EDWARD GORDON. 'Eschatology in 1 Peter.' In *The Background of the New Testament and its Eschatology: Studies in Honour of C. H. Dodd*, edited by W. D. Davies and D. Daube, 394–401. Cambridge: Cambridge University Press, 1956.

SELWYN, EDWARD GORDON. 'The Persecutions in 1 Peter.' *Bulletin of the Studiorum Novi Testamenti Societas* 1 (1950): 39–50.

SIEFFERT, E. A. 'Die Heilsbedeutung des Leidens und Sterbens Christi nach dem ersten Briefe des Petrus.' *Jahrbücher für deutsche Theologie* 20 (1875): 371–440.

SNYDER, SCOT. 'Participles and Imperatives in 1 Peter: A Re-examination in the Light of Recent Scholarly Trends.' *Filología Neotestamentaria* 8 (1995): 187–98.

SOUČEK, JOSEF BOHUMIL. 'Das Gegenüber von Gemeinde und Welt nach dem ersten Petrusbrief.' In *Bibelauslegung als Theologie*, edited by Petr Pokorný, 199–209. Wissenschaftliche Untersuchungen zum Neuen Testament, edited by Martin Hengel and Otfried Hofius, Vol. 100. Tübingen: Mohr (Siebeck), 1997.

SPÖRRI, THEOPHIL. *Der Gemeindegedanke im ersten Petrusbrief: ein Beitrag zur Struktur des urchristlichen Kirchenbegriffs.* Neutestamentliche Forschungen, edited by Otto Schmitz, Vol. 2.2. Gütersloh: Bertelsmann, 1925.

STROBEL, AUGUST. 'Macht Leiden von Sünde frei? Zur Problematik von 1. Petr. 4,1f.' *Theologische Zeitschrift* 19 (1963): 412–25.

THOMPSON, JAMES W. '"Be Submissive to Your Masters": A Study of 1 Peter 2:18–25.' *Restoration Quarterly* 9 (1966): 66–78.

THURÉN, LAURI. *Argument and Theology in 1 Peter: The Origins of Christian Paraenesis.* Journal for the Study of the New Testament Supplement Series, edited by Stanley E. Porter, Vol. 114. Sheffield: Sheffield Academic Press, 1995.

THURÉN, LAURI. The Rhetorical Strategy of 1 Peter: With Special Regard to Ambiguous Expressions. Åbo, Finland: Åbo Akademis Forlag, 1990.

VAN UNNIK, WILLEM C. 'Christianity According to 1 Peter.' *Expository Times* 68 (1956): 79–83.

VAN UNNIK, WILLEM C. 'The Critique of Paganism in 1 Peter 1:18.' In *Neotestamentica et Semetica: Studies in Honour of Matthew Black*, edited by E. Earle Ellis and Max Wilcox, 129–42. Edinburgh: T&T Clark, 1969.

VAN UNNIK, WILLEM C. 'First Letter of Peter.' In *The Interpreter's Dictionary of the Bible*, edited by George Arthur Buttrick, 3:758–66. New York: Abingdon, 1962.

VAN UNNIK, WILLEM C. 'The Teaching of Good Works in 1 Peter.' *New Testament Studies* 1 (1954–55): 92–110.

VOLF, MIROSLAV. 'Soft Difference: Theological Reflections on the Relation Between Church and Culture in 1 Peter.' *Ex Auditu* 10 (1994): 15–30.

WEIß, BERNHARD. *Der petrinische Lehrbegriff: Beiträge zur biblischen Theologie, sowie zur Kritik und Exegese des ersten Briefes Petri und der petrinischen Reden.* Berlin: Wilhelm Schulze, 1855.

WENDLAND, ERNST R. '"Stand Firm in the Grace of God!" A Study of 1 Peter.' *Journal of Translation and Textlinguistics* 13 (2000): 25–102.

Other Works

ADAMS, EDWARD. *Constructing the World: A Study in Paul's Cosmological Language.* Studies of the New Testament and its World, edited by John Barclay, Joel Marcus and John Riches. Edinburgh: T&T Clark, 2000.

ALAND, BARBARA, KURT ALAND, GERD MINK, and KLAUS WACHTEL. *Catholic Letters.* Novum Testamentum Graecum Editio Critica Maior, edited by The Institute for New Testament Textual Research, Vol. 4. Stuttgart: Deutsche Bibelgesellschaft, 2000.

ALEXANDER, LOVEDAY. 'Paul and the Hellenistic Schools: The Evidence of Galen.' In *Paul in His Hellenistic Context*, edited by Troels Engberg-Pedersen, 60–83. Studies in the New Testament and Its World, edited by John Riches. Minneapolis: Fortress, 1995.

ANNAS, JULIA. *The Morality of Happiness.* Oxford: Oxford University Press, 1993.

ASCOUGH, RICHARD S. 'Greco-Roman Philosophic, Religious, and Voluntary Associations.' In *Community Formation: In the Early Church and in the Church Today*, edited by Richard N. Longenecker, 3–19. Peabody, MA: Hendrickson, 2002.

AUNE, DAVID EDWARD. *The New Testament in its Literary Environment.* Library of Early Christianity, edited by Wayne A. Meeks, Vol. 8. Philadelphia: Westminster Press, 1987.

AUSTIN, J. L., *How to Do Things with Words.* Cambridge, MA.: Harvard University Press, 1962.

BARCLAY, JOHN M. G., *Obeying the Truth: A Study of Paul's Ethics in Galatians.* Studies in the New Testament and its World, edited by John Barclay and John Riches. Edinburgh: T&T Clark, 1988.

BENECKE, P. V. M. 'Polycarp.' In *The New Testament in the Apostolic Fathers*, edited by Committee of the Oxford Society of Historical Theology, 84–104. Oxford: Oxford University Press, 1905.

BERGER, KLAUS. 'Hellenistische Gattungen im Neuen Testament.' In *Aufstieg und Niedergang der römischen Welt: Geschichte und Kultur Roms im Spiegel der neueren Forschung*, edited by Hildegard Temporini and Wolgang Haase, II.25.2:1031–432. Berlin: de Gruyter, 1984.

BERGER, PETER L., and Thomas LUCKMANN. *The Social Construction of Reality: A Treatise in the Sociology of Knowledge.* Garden City, NY: Anchor Books, 1967.

BETZ, HANS DIETER. *Nachfolge und Nachahmung Jesu Christi im Neuen Testament.* Beiträge zur historischen Theologie, edited by Gerhard Ebeling, Vol. 37. Tübingen: Mohr (Siebeck), 1967.

BETZ, HANS DIETER. 'Introduction.' In *Plutarch's Ethical Writings and Early Christian Literature*, edited by Hans Dieter Betz, 1–10. Studia ad Corpus Hellenisticum Novi Testamenti, edited by H. D. Betz, G. Delling and W. C. van Unnik, Vol. 4. Leiden: Brill, 1978.

BIRCH, BRUCE C. 'Divine Character and the Formation of Moral Community in the Book of Exodus.' In *The Bible in Ethics: The Second Sheffield Colloquium*, edited by John W. Rogerson, Margaret Davies and M. Daniel Carroll Rodas, 119–35. Journal for the Study of the Old Testament Supplement Series, edited by David J. A. Clines and Philip R. Davies, Vol. 207. Sheffield: Sheffield Academic Press, 1995.

BIRCH, BRUCE C. 'Moral Agency, Community, and the Character of God in the Hebrew Bible.' *Semeia* 66 (1995): 23–39.

BONDI, RICHARD. 'The Elements of Character.' *Journal of Religious Ethics* 12 (1984): 201–218.

BRADLEY, KEITH R. *Slavery and Society at Rome.* Key Themes in Ancient History, edited by P. A. Cartledge and P. D. A. Garnsey. Cambridge: Cambridge University Press, 1996.

BROWN, GILLIAN, and GEORGE YULE. *Discourse Analysis.* Cambridge Textbooks in Linguistics. Cambridge: Cambridge University Press, 1983.

BROWN, WILLIAM P., editor. *Character and Scripture: Moral Formation, Community, and Biblical Interpretation.* Grand Rapids: Eerdmans, 2002.

BULTMANN, RUDOLF. 'Das Problem der Ethik bei Paulus.' *Zeitschrift für die neutestamentliche Wissenschaft* 23 (1924): 123–40.

BURGESS, THEODORE CHALON. *Epideictic Literature.* Studies in Classical Philology. Chicago: University of Chicago Press, 1902.

BURRIDGE, RICHARD A. *What are the Gospels?: A Comparison with Graeco-Roman Biography.* Society for New Testament Studies Monograph Series, edited by Graham N. Stanton, Vol. 70. Cambridge: Cambridge University Press, 1992.

COLEMAN, ROBERT, 'The Artful Moralist: A Study of Seneca's Epistolary Style.' *Classical Quarterly* NS 24 (1974): 276–89.

CRAFFERT, PIETER F. 'An Exercise in the Critical Use of Models: The "Goodness of Fit" of Wilson's Sect Model.' In *Social Scientific Models for Interpreting the Bible: Essays by the Context Group in Honor of Bruce J. Malina*, edited by John J. Pilch, 21–46. Biblical Interpretation Series, edited by R. Alan Culpepper and Rolf Rendtorff, Vol. 53. Leiden: Brill, 2001.

CRISP, ROGER, and MICHAEL A. SLOTE. *Virtue Ethics.* Oxford Readings in Philosophy. Oxford: Oxford University Press, 1997.

CRITES, STEPHEN. 'The Narrative Quality of Experience.' In *Why Narrative?: Readings in Narrative Theology*, edited by Stanley Hauerwas and L. Gregory Jones, 65–88. Grand Rapids: Eerdmans, 1989.

CRYSTAL, DAVID. *A Dictionary of Linguistics and Phonetics*, 4th edition. The Language Library, edited by David Crystal. Oxford: Blackwell, 1997.

DAUBE, DAVID. 'Κερδαίνω as a Missionary Term.' *Harvard Theological Review* 40 (1947): 109–20.

DEICHGRÄBER, REINHARD. *Gotteshymnus und Christushymnus in der frühen Christenheit: Untersuchungen zur Form, Sprache und Stil der frühchristlichen Hymnen.* Studien zur Umwelt des Neuen Testaments, Vol. 5. Göttingen: Vandenhoeck & Ruprecht, 1967.

DEISSMANN, GUSTAV ADOLF. *Light From the Ancient East: The New Testament Illustrated by Recently Discovered Texts of the Graeco-Roman World.* Translated by Lionel R. M. Strachan, revised edition. London: Hodder and Stoughton, 1927. Original Publication: *Licht vom Osten: Das Neue Testament und die neuentdeckten Texte der hellenistisch-römischen Welt*, 4th edition. Tübingen: Mohr, 1923.

DIBELIUS, MARTIN. *From Tradition to Gospel.* Translated by Bertram Lee Woolf. London: Ivor, Nicholson and Watson, 1934. Original publication: *Die Formgeschichte des Evangeliums*, 2nd edition. Tübingen: Mohr (Siebeck), 1933.

DIBELIUS, MARTIN. 'Zur Formgeschichte des Neuen Testaments (außerhalb der Evangelien).' *Theologische Rundschau* NS 3 (1931): 207–41.

DIBELIUS, MARTIN. *James: A Commentary on the Epistle of James.* Revised by Heinrich Greeven. Translated by Michael A. Williams. Hermeneia, edited by Helmut Koester. Philadelphia: Fortress, 1976. Original publication: *Der Brief des Jakobus.* Edited by Heinrich Greeven. Kritisch-exegetischer Kommentar über das Neue Testament, Vol. 15. Gottingen: Vandenhoeck & Ruprecht, 1964.

DODD, C. H. *Gospel and Law: The Relation of Faith and Ethics in Early Christianity.* Bampton Lectures in America, Vol. 3. Cambridge: Cambridge University Press, 1951.

ENGBERG-PEDERSEN, TROELS. 'Galatians in Romans 5–8 and Paul's Construction of Identity of Christ Believers.' In *Texts and Contexts: Biblical Texts in Their Textual and Situational Contexts*, edited by Tord Fornberg and David Hellholm, 477–505. Oslo: Scandinavian University Press, 1995.

ENGBERG-PEDERSEN, TROELS. *Paul and the Stoics.* Edinburgh: T&T Clark, 2000.

FANNING, BUIST M. *Verbal Aspect in New Testament Greek.* Oxford: Clarendon Press, 1990.

FIORE, BENJAMIN. 'Parenesis and Protreptic.' In *Anchor Bible Dictionary*, edited by David Noel Freedman, 5:162-65. New York: Doubleday, 1992.

FIORE, BENJAMIN. *The Function of Personal Example in the Socratic and Pastoral Epistles.* Analecta Biblica, Vol. 105. Rome: Editrice Pontificio Istituto Biblico, 1986.

FOWL, STEPHEN E. *The Story of Christ in the Ethics of Paul: An Analysis of the Function of the Hymnic Material in the Pauline Corpus.* Journal for the Study of the New Testament Supplement Series, edited by David Hill, Vol. 36. Sheffield: Journal for the Study of the Old Testament Press, 1990.

FOWLER, ALASTAIR. *Kinds of Literature: An Introduction to the Theory of Genres and Modes.* Cambridge, MA: Harvard University Press, 1982.

FURNISH, VICTOR PAUL. *Theology and Ethics in Paul.* Nashville, TN: Abingdon, 1968.

GAMMIE, John G. 'Paraenetic Literature: Toward the Morphology of a Secondary Genre.' *Semeia* 50 (1990): 41–77.

GAVENTA, BEVERLY ROBERTS. *From Darkness to Light: Aspects of Conversion in the New Testament.* Overtures to Biblical Theology, edited by John R. Donahue, Vol. 20. Philadelphia: Fortress Press, 1986.

GEERTZ, CLIFFORD. 'Ethos, World View, and the Analysis of Sacred Symbols.' In *The Interpretation of Cultures*, 126–41. New York: Basic Books, 1973.

GRENZ, STANLEY J. 'Die begrenzte Gemeinschaft ("The Boundaried Community") and the Character of Evangelical Theology.' *Journal of the Evangelical Theological Society* 45.2 (2002): 301–16.

GUTHRIE, DONALD. *New Testament Introduction*, 4th ed. Downers Grove, IL: Inter-Varsity Press, 1990.

HARNACK, ADOLF. *Die Chronologie der altchristlichen Literatur bis Eusebius.* Geschichte der altchristlichen Literatur bis Eusebius. Leipzig: J. C. Hinrich, 1897.

210 Bibliography

HARNED, DAVID BAILY. *Creed and Personal Identity: The Meaning of the Apostles' Creed*. Philadelphia: Fortress, 1981.

HARTOG, PAUL. *Polycarp and the New Testament: The Occasion, Rhetoric, Theme, and Unity of the Epistle to the Philippians and its allusions to New Testament Literature*. Wissenschaftliche Untersuchungen zum Neuen Testament, 2nd series, edited by Jörg Frey, Martin Hengel and Otfried Hofius, Vol. 134. Tübingen: Mohr (Siebeck), 2002.

HAUERWAS, STANLEY, and DAVID BURRELL. 'From System to Story: An Alternative Pattern for Rationality in Ethics.' In *Why Narrative?: Readings in Narrative Theology*, edited by Stanley Hauerwas and L. Gregory Jones, 158–90. Grand Rapids: Eerdmans, 1989.

HAUERWAS, STANLEY, and L. GREGORY JONES, editors. *Why Narrative?: Readings in Narrative Theology*. Grand Rapids: Eerdmans, 1989.

HAYS, RICHARD B. *The Faith of Jesus Christ: An Investigation of the Narrative Substructure of Galatians 3:1–4:11*. Society of Biblical Literature Dissertation Series, edited by William Baird, Vol. 56. Chico, CA: Scholars Press, 1983.

HAYS, RICHARD B. *The Moral Vision of the New Testament: Community, Cross, New Creation: A Contemporary Introduction to New Testament Ethics*. San Francisco: HarperSanFrancisco, 1996.

HOLMES, MICHAEL WILLIAM, editor. *The Apostolic Fathers: Greek Texts and English Translations*, updated ed. Grand Rapids: Baker, 1999.

HORSLEY, G. H. R., editor. *New Documents Illustrating Early Christianity Vol. 4: A Review of the Greek Inscriptions and Papyri Published in 1979*. North Ryde, NSW: The Ancient History Documentary Research Centre Macquarie University, 1987.

HURSTHOUSE, ROSALIND. *On Virtue Ethics*. Oxford: Oxford University Press, 1999.

JANOWSKI, BERND, and PETER STUHLMACHER, editors. *Der leidende Gottesknecht: Jesaja 53 und seine Wirkungsgeschichte*. Forschungen zum Alten Testament, edited by Bernd Janowski and Hermann Spieckermann, Vol. 14. Tübingen: Mohr (Siebeck), 1996.

JOHNSON, B. 'On Church and Sect.' *American Sociological Review* 28 (1963): 539–49.

JUDGE, E. A. 'The Early Christians as a Scholastic Community.' *Journal of Religious History* 1 (1960-61): 4–15; 125–37.

KÄSEMANN, ERNST. 'Kritische Analyse von Phil. 2, 5–11,' *Zeitschrift für Theologie und Kirche* 47 (1950): 313–60.

KÄSEMANN, ERNST. *Perspectives on Paul*. Translated by Margaret Kohl. New Testament Library, edited by Alan Richardson, C. F. D. Moule, C. F. Evans, et al. London: SCM, 1971.

KECK, LEANDER E. 'Rethinking "New Testament Ethics."' *Journal of Biblical Literature* 115.1 (1996): 3–16.

KOESTER, CRAIG R. *Hebrews: A New Translation with Introduction and Commentary*. Anchor Bible, edited by William Fox Albright and David Noel Freedman, Vol. 36. New York: Doubleday, 2001.

KOESTER, HELMUT. *Introduction to the New Testament*. 2 Vols. Hermeneia: Foundations and Facets, edited by Robert W. Funk. Philadelphia: Fortress Press, 1982. Original publication: Helmut Köster. *Einführung in das Neue Testament im Rahmen der Religionsgeschichte und Kulturgeschichte der hellenistischen und römischen Zeit*. Berlin: de Gruyter, 1980.

KWON, SOON-GU. *Christ as Example: The Imitatio Christi Motive in Biblical and Christian Ethics*. Acta Universitatis Upsaliensis. Uppsala Studies in Social Ethics, Vol. 21. Uppsala, Sweden: Uppsala University Library, 1998.

LIGHTFOOT, JOSEPH BARBER. *The Apostolic Fathers: Clement, Ignatius and Polycarp: Revised Texts with Introductions, Notes, Dissertations and Translations*, 2nd ed. London: Macmillan, 1889.

LOHSE, EDUARD. *Märtyrer und Gottesknecht: Untersuchungen zur urchristlichen Verkündigung vom Sühntod Jesu Christi*. Forschungen zur Religion und Literatur des alten und neuen Testaments, edited by Rudolf Bultmann, Vol. 46. Göttingen: Vandenhoeck & Ruprecht, 1955.

LONGENECKER, BRUCE W. 'Narrative Interest in the Study of Paul.' In *Narrative Dynamics in Paul: A Critical Assessment*, edited by Bruce W. Longenecker, 3–16. Louisville: Westminster John Knox, 2002.

LONGENECKER, RICHARD N. 'The Foundational Conviction of New Testament Christology: The Obedience/Faithfulness/Sonship of Christ.' In *Jesus of Nazareth: Essay on the Historical Jesus and New Testament Christology*, edited by Joel B. Green and Max Turner, 473–88. Grand Rapids: Eerdmans, 1994.

LOUGHLIN, GERARD. *Telling God's Story: Bible, Church and Narrative Theology*. Cambridge: Cambridge University Press, 1996.

MACINTYRE, ALASDAIR C. *After Virtue: A Study in Moral Theory*, 2nd ed. London: Duckworth, 1985.

MALHERBE, ABRAHAM J. 'Hellenistic Moralists and the New Testament.' In *Aufstieg und Niedergang der römischen Welt: Geschichte und Kultur Roms im Spiegel der neueren Forschung*, edited by Hildegard Temporini and Wolfgang Haase, II.26.1:267–333. Berlin: de Gruyter, 1992.

MALHERBE, ABRAHAM J. *Moral Exhortation: A Greco-Roman Sourcebook*. Library of Early Christianity, edited by Wayne A. Meeks, Vol. 4. Philadelphia: Westminster Press, 1986.

MALHERBE, ABRAHAM J. *Paul and the Thessalonians: The Philosophic Tradition of Pastoral Care*. Philadelphia: Fortress Press, 1987.

MALHERBE, ABRAHAM J. *The Letters to the Thessalonians: A New Translation with Introduction and Commentary*. The Anchor Bible, edited by William Fox Albright and David Noel Freedman, Vol. 32B. New York: Doubleday, 2000.

MALINA, BRUCE J. *The New Testament World: Insights from Cultural Anthropology*, 3rd ed. Louisville: Westminster John Knox, 2001.

MARXSEN, WILLI, *New Testament Foundations for Christian Ethics*. Translated by O. C. Dean. Edinburgh: T&T Clark, 1993. Original publication: *"Christliche" und christliche Ethik im Neuen Testament*. Gütersloh: Gütersloher Verlagshaus, 1989.

MCDONALD, J. IAN H. *The Crucible of Christian Morality*. Religion in the First Christian Centuries, edited by Deborah Sawyer. London: Routledge, 1998.

MCGRATH, ALISTER E. 'In What Way Can Jesus be a Moral Example for Christians.' *Journal of the Evangelical Theological Society* 34.3 (1991): 289–98.

MCKAY, K. L. *A New Syntax of the Verb in New Testament Greek*. Studies in Biblical Greek, edited by D. A. Carson. New York: Peter Lang, 1994.

MEEKS, WAYNE A. *The Moral World of the First Christians*. Library of Early Christianity, edited by Wayne A. Meeks, Vol. 6. Philadelphia: Westminster Press, 1986.

MEEKS, WAYNE A. *The Origins of Christian Morality: The First Two Centuries*. New Haven, CT: Yale University Press, 1993.

METZGER, BRUCE MANNING, editor. *A Textual Commentary on the Greek New Testament*, 2nd ed. Stuttgart: Deutsche Bibelgesellschaft/United Bible Societies, 1994.

MICHAELIS, WILHELM. 'πάσχω.' In *Theological Dictionary of the New Testament*, edited by Gerhard Friedrich, 5:904–39. Grand Rapids: Eerdmans, 1967.

MUSSCHENGA, ALBERT W. 'Narrative Theology and Narrative Ethics.' Translated by Birgit Kooijman. In *Does Religion Matter Morally? The Critical Reappraisal of the Thesis of Morality's Independence from Religion*, edited by Albert W. Musschenga, 173–204. Morality and the Meaning of Life, edited by Albert W. Musschenga and Paul J. M. van Tongeren, Vol. 2. Kampen: Kok Pharos, 1995.

NOCK, A. D. *Conversion: The Old and the New in Religion from Alexander the Great to Augustine of Hippo*. Oxford: Clarendon Press, 1933.

NUSSBAUM, MARTHA CRAVEN. *The Fragility of Goodness: Luck and Ethics in Greek Tragedy and Philosophy*. Cambridge: Cambridge University Press, 1986.

NUSSBAUM, MARTHA CRAVEN. *The Therapy of Desire: Theory and Practice in Hellenistic Ethics*. Martin Classical Lectures. Princeton: Princeton University Press, 1994.

PETERSEN, NORMAN R. *Rediscovering Paul: Philemon and the Sociology of Paul's Narrative World*. Philadelphia: Fortress Press, 1985.

REED, JEFFREY T. *A Discourse Analysis of Philippians: Method and Rhetoric in the Debate Over Literary Integrity*. Journal for the Study of the New Testament Supplement Series, edited by Stanley E. Porter, Vol. 136. Sheffield: Sheffield Academic Press, 1997.

REED, JEFFREY T. 'The Epistle.' In *Handbook of Classical Rhetoric in the Hellenistic Period (330 B.C.–A.D. 400)*, edited by Stanley E. Porter, 171–93. Leiden: Brill, 1997.

SCHRAGE, WOLFGANG. 'The Formal Ethical Interpretation of Pauline Paraenesis.' Translated by George S. Rosner and Brian S. Rosner. In *Understanding Paul's Ethics: Twentieth-Century Approaches*, edited by Brian S. Rosner, 301–35. Grand Rapids: Eerdmans, 1995. Original Publication: 'Zur formalethischen Deutung der paulinischen Paränese.' *Zeitschrift für evangelische Ethik* 4 (1960): 207–33.

SCHWEIZER, EDUARD. *Lordship and Discipleship*. Studies in Biblical Theology, edited by C. F. D. Moule and F. V. Filson, Vol. 28. London: SCM, 1960. Original publication: *Erniedrigung und Erhöhung bei Jesus und seinen Nachfolgern*. Zurich: Zwingli Verlag, 1955.

SEARLE, JOHN R. *Speech Acts: An Essay in the Philosophy of Language*. Cambridge: Cambridge University Press, 1969.

SMYTH, HERBERT WEIR. *Greek Grammar*. Cambridge, Mass.: Harvard University Press, 1980.

SOMERS, MARGARET R., and GLORIA D. GIBSON. 'Reclaiming the Epistemological "Other": Narrative and the Social Construction of Identity.' In *Social Theory and the Politics of Identity*, edited by Craig Calhoun, 37–99. Oxford: Blackwell, 1994.

SPOHN, WILLIAM C. *Go and Do Likewise: Jesus and Ethics*. New York: Continuum, 1999.

STATMAN, DANIEL, editor. *Virtue Ethics: A Critical Reader*. Edinburgh: Edinburgh University Press, 1997.

STOWERS, STANLEY KENT. *Letter Writing in Greco-Roman Antiquity*. Library of Early Christianity, edited by Wayne A. Meeks, Vol. 5. Philadelphia: Westminster Press, 1986.

TAJFEL, HENRI. 'Experiments in a Vacuum.' In *The Context of Social Psychology: A Critical Assessment*, edited by Joachim Israel and Henri Tajfel, 69–119. European Monographs in Social Psychology, edited by Henri Tajfel, Vol. 2. London: Academic Press, 1972.

TAYLOR, CHARLES. *Sources of the Self: The Making of the Modern Identity*. Cambridge: Cambridge University Press, 1989.

THURÉN, LAURI. *Derhetorizing Paul: A Dynamic Perspective on Pauline Theology and the Law*. Wissenschaftliche Untersuchungen zum Neuen Testament, edited by Martin Hengel and Otfried Hofius, Vol. 124. Tübingen: Mohr (Siebeck), 2000.

TOULMIN, STEPHEN EDELSTON. *The Uses of Argument*. Cambridge: Cambridge University Press, 1958.

VAN HENTEN, JAN WILLEM. 'Zum Einfluß jüdischer Martyrien auf die Literatur des frühen Christentums: II. Die Apostolischen Väter.' In *Aufstieg und Niedergang der römischen Welt: Geschichte und Kultur Roms im Spiegel der neueren Forschung*, edited by Hildegard Temporini and Wolgang Haase, II.27.1:700–23. Berlin: de Gruyter, 1993.

VERHEY, ALLEN. *The Great Reversal: Ethics and the New Testament*. Grand Rapids: Eerdmans, 1984.

VOLF, MIROSLAV. *Exclusion and Embrace: A Theological Exploration of Identity, Otherness, and Reconciliation*. Nashville: Abingdon Press, 1996.

WEBSTER, JOHN B. 'Christology, Imitability and Ethics.' *Scottish Journal of Theology* 39 (1986): 309–26.

WEIß, BERNHARD. *A Manual of Introduction to the New Testament*. Translated by A. J. K. Davidson. Foreign Biblical Library, edited by W. Robertson Nicoll. London: Hodder & Stoughton, 1887. Original publication: *Lehrbuch der Einleitung in das Neue Testament*. Berlin: W. Hertz, 1886.

WILKEN, ROBERT LOUIS. *The Christians as the Romans Saw Them*. New Haven: Yale University Press, 1984.

WILSON, BRYAN R. 'An Analysis of Sect Development.' *American Sociological Review* 24 (1959): 3–15.

WILSON, BRYAN R. *Magic and the Millennium: A Sociological Study of Religious Movements of Protest Among Tribal and Third-World Peoples*. London: Heinemann, 1973.

WILSON, WALTER T. *The Hope of Glory: Education and Exhortation in the Epistle to the Colossians*. Supplements to Novum Testamentum, Vol. 88. Leiden: Brill, 1997.

WOLTERS, ALBERT M. 'On the Idea of Worldview and its Relation to Philosophy.' In *Stained Glass: Worldviews and Social Science*, edited by Paul A. Marshall, S. Griffioen and Richard J. Mouw, 14–25. Christian Studies Today. Lanham, MD: University Press of America, 1989.

WRIGHT, N.T. *The New Testament and the People of God*. Christian Origins and the Question of God, Vol. 1. London: SPCK, 1992.

ZERWICK, MAXIMILLIAN. *Biblical Greek: Illustrated by Examples*. Edited by Joseph Smith. Scripta Pontificii Instituti Biblici, Vol. 114. Rome: Editrice Pontificio Istituto Biblico, 1963.

Index of Ancient Sources

Old Testament

Genesis
14:20   69
12:7   71

Exodus
24:3–8   67
19:6   123
23:22   123

Leviticus
19:2   102
11:4   102

1 Kings
5:21   69

Psalms
17:47   69
34:9 (lxx 33:9)   113, 120
34:13–17   161
49:13–23   124
50:17–19   124
65:20   69
66:10   76
67:36   69
118:22   125

Proverbs
17:3   76

Isaiah
1:10–17   124
28:16   124
40: 6–8   109
52:13   185
53   180, 197
53: 2   185
53:5–6   190
53:9   189

Daniel
12:13   72

Hosea
6:6   124

Amos
5:23   124

Micah
6:6–8   124

Zechariah
13:9   76

Malachi
3:3   76

New Testament

Matthew
5:16   132
5:39–42   161
6   102
16:21   181

Mark
1:14   106
8:31   181
8:31–35   173

Luke
6:27–36   161
22:15   178
24:26, 46 178

Acts
1:3   178
3:18   178
14:15   106
15:19   106
17:3   178
26:20   106

Romans
1:1   106
2:6   103
5–8   83
5:19   184
6:1–11   182
6:10–12   188
8:18   40
15:16   106

1 Corinthians
3:2   111
3:16–17   121
5:13   153
15:3   179

2 Corinthians
1:3   70
5:10   78
11:32   72

Galatians
3:23   72
5:13–6:10 153
5:25   1

Ephesians
2:19–22   122
1:3   70
4:8   78
5:22–6:9   155
6:24   109

Philippians
1:27–30   187
2:5   183
2:5–11   173, 187

2:6–10   184
2:12   187
4:772

Colossians
3:18–4:1   155
3:25   78

1 Thessalonians
1:9   106
2:2   106
2:8–9   106

Hebrews
2:9–10   184
2:17–18   184
5:8   184
5:8–10   184
5:12–14   111
7:8   178
9:27   178
10:12   179
10:28   178
11:4   178
11:13   178
11:21   178
11:37   178
13:12   179
13:15–16   124

James
2:10   183

1 Peter
1:1   68, 129, 131
1:1–2   66–8
1:2   48, 68–9, 108
1:3   39, 44, 69, 81, 100,
           116, 119, 126, 195
1:3–5   40, 69, 70, 73, 75, 83
1:3–12   39, 42, 46, 69, 87–8,
           98–9, 194
1:3–2:10   69, 81, 119, 126–7
1:3–2:12   2, 9
1:3–4:11   38
1:4   71, 104
1:5   64, 72, 74–6, 79
1:6   40, 73–5
1:6–7   46, 65, 77, 141, 194
1:6–8   40

1:6–9	69, 73–5, 83, 89	2:7–9	121
1:7	76, 78, 85, 104	2:9	81, 122–5, 128, 130, 142
1:8	76–7, 190		
1:9	74–7, 79	2:9–10	39, 130, 136, 141
1:9–10	72	2:10	69, 119, 126, 129
1:10	72, 74, 79	2:11	69, 78, 129, 136
1:10–12	69, 74, 79	2:11–12	126
1:10–17	65	2:12	41, 73, 130, 132, 134, 136
1:11	79		
1:12	79–80	2:13	155–6
1:13	48, 99, 111, 114–5, 182, 195	2:13–16	145
		2:13–17	155
1:13–21	99	2:13–3:12	155, 175
1:13–2:3	43, 69, 98	2:13–4:19	126
1:14	81, 100, 108, 114, 116, 129, 136, 195	2:13–5:11	143
		2:13–5:12	9, 38
1:14–16	107	2:14	161
1:14–21	100	2:15	41, 132, 161
1:15	101–2, 114–5, 195	2:15–17	175
1:16	85, 102	2:17	108. 144, 153, 156, 160
1:17	102, 116, 130, 136		
1:18	39, 81, 103–4, 106, 114, 116, 195	2:17–19	47
		2:18	104, 155, 160
1:18–19	64, 81, 105, 188	2:18–20	175–7
1:19	104, 184	2:18–24	65
1:19–20	115, 188	2:18–25	156, 175, 196–7
1:20	64, 67, 70, 81	2:18–3:7	38, 154–5
1:20–21	105	2:19	178
1:21	76, 81, 106, 188	2:19–20	48
1:22	39, 78, 86, 107, 109, 114, 116, 195	2:20	157, 161, 176, 178
		2:21	149, 178–9, 181
1:22–2:3	99	2:21–25	38, 137, 156, 174–5, 185–6, 189
1:23	39, 108, 116		
1:23–25	48	2:22	161, 180
1:24–25	109, 190	2:23	176, 179–80
2:1	38, 41, 114	2:24	4, 179, 180, 186–7
2:1–3	152	3:1	132, 155, 160
2:2	44, 45, 72, 110–1, 115, 195	3:1–6	158, 175
		3:2	47, 134
2:2–3	39	3:5	155
2:3	107, 112, 115, 120	3:5–6	38
2:4	81, 120–21	3:6	161
2:4–5	120, 124	3:7	159, 160–1, 175
2:4–10	69, 117, 119, 132	3:8	38
2:4–12	3, 42	3:8–9	85, 160
2:5	120, 123, 130, 136, 141–2	3:8–12	160
		3:9	137, 176
2:6	76, 124	3:10–12	161
2:6–10	120	3:12	160–1
2:7	76, 124–5	3:13	160

3:14	157, 181	4:13	40, 153
3:14–15	147, 153	4:15–18	65
3:15	132	4:15–19	147
3:15–18	146	4:17	122–3, 125
3:16	40, 73, 132	4:17–18	136
3:17	181	4:18	136
3:17–18	65	4:19	47, 64, 84
3:18	39, 174, 179–82, 184, 186, 188	5:1	40, 68
		5:1–4	65
3:19	73	5:1–5	45, 160
3:21	182	5:2–4	144
4:1	48, 136, 174, 181–2, 184, 188	5:5	48, 144–5
		5:6	144
4:1–2	146, 183	5:8	137
4:1–4	41, 136	5:8–9	136
4:2	103	5:8–11	146
4:3	38, 136	5:9	76, 136
4:3–4	130–1	5:9–10	65
4:4	40	5:10	40, 190
4:4–5	65	5:12	7, 47–9
4:7	41, 145	5:12–14	68
4:8	108		
4:10	48	*1 John*	
4:10–11	147	2:5	183
4:12–13	65		
4:12–14	147		

Greco-Roman

Aristotle *EN*		Dio Chrysostom *Orations*	
1094a	16	44.10	29
1098a	17		
1103a	95	Epictetus *Discourses*	
1134b	154	1.4.26	20
		3.16.11	93
Aristotle *Politics*		2.17.36–37	96
1253b	154	3.16.16	96
1260a	154	3.22.13	96
Albinus *Introduction*		Isocrates *Demonicus*	
27–33	154	5	24
		9	30
Arius Didymus		9–11	171
2.148.16–19	154	13	145
3:18.1–4	154	15	28, 145
		16	144
Cicero *Gods*		20	27
i.77	92	21	29, 144

22   145
23   28
30   27
39   28, 147
44   152
46   34
51   27

Isocrates *Nicocles*
38   144

Isocrates *Evagoras*
77   165

Livy *City* 1   170

M. Rufus *Fragmenta*
1.5.15–1.6.3   23

Oxyrhynchus
Papyri 3069   51

Philodemus
Oeconomicus   154

Plato *Laws*
3:690 A–D   154
6:771E–777   154
824C   154

Plato *Republic*
518D   91
615B   78
621D   78

Plutarch *Alexander*
1.1–3   170

Plutarch *Flatterer*
61D   110

Plutarch *Moralia*
138B–146A   154

Plutarch *On Listening*
46E   93

Plutarch *Pericles*
1.3–4   20, 167
2.2–4   20, 167

2.3   170–1

Plutarch *Progress*
77D–E   95
84B–85C   168
84E   171

Porphyry *Marcella*
139–40   98

(Pseudo-) Crates *Epistles*
15   29

(Pseudo-) Demetrius *Epistolary Types*
1   22

(Pseudo-) Diogenes *Epistles*
38   96
29.4   104

(Pseudo-) Libanius *Epistolary Styles*
45   23
5   24, 115–6
52   163
30   97

(Pseudo-) Phocylides,
175–227   154

Seneca *Benefits*
2.18.1–2   154

Seneca *EM*
5.2   138–9
5.3   139
5.5   138–9
11.8–10   169
84.10   163
94.1   38, 155
94.4   155
94.25   29, 150
94.28   27
94.29   150
94.32   29, 32
94.34   148
94.35   149
94.36   28
94.40   164
94.44   34, 151
94.47   95, 148, 150

94.50	151		95.59	30, 58
94.51	149		95.65–7	29
95.10	58–9		104.22 34	166
95.12	30, 58, 60			
95.34	59		Seneca *Providence*	
95.35	33		5:10	76
95.37	32, 59			
95.38	33, 59		Terence *Self-Tormentor*	
95.44	30, 59		77	61
95.45	30, 155			
95.48	61		Xenophon	
95.51–3	61		*Oeconomicus*	154
95.54	59–60			
95.58–9	60			

Jewish

Qumran			Philo *Special Laws*	
1QS	121		2.225–27	154
1QS 11:7	72		3.169–71	154
4Q174	121			
4Q400	121		*1 Enoch*	
			62–63	132
Josephus *Apion*				
2.199	154		*2 Enoch*	
			45:3	124
Josephus *Apology*				
2.206	154		*1 Esdras*	
2:216	154		4:40	69
Philo *Abraham*			*1 – 4 Maccabees* 50	
1.4–5	165, 167			
			Judith	
Philo *Creation*			16:16	124
1.1–3	62–63			
			Letter of Aristeas	
Philo *Decalogue*			234	124
165–67	154			
			Psalms of Solomon	
Philo *Husbandry*			14:10	72
9	112		15:5	72
Philo *Joseph*			*Sirach/Ecclesiasticus*	
38–39	154		2:1–9	76
			35:1	124
Philo *Moses*				
2.48	63		*Susanna*	
2.51	64		2:8	182

Tobit			*Wisdom of Solomon*	
11:17	69		3:5–6	76
13:2	69			
13:8	69			

Early Church

Barnabas			1.63.10	187
5:1, 6, 12	187		1.63.16	187
Eusebius *HE*			Justin *Trypho*	
4.14.9	186		68.1	187
			121.2	187
Ignatius *Polycarp*				
3:2	187		Polycarp *Philippians*	
			1:2	187
Justin *Apology*			8:1–2	187
1.50.1	187			

Index of Modern Authors

Achtemeier, P. J. 38, 40–2, 48, 65, 67,
    69, 71–81, 98–100, 102, 103, 106–7,
    111–2, 121–3, 125, 130, 132, 142,
    156–60, 161, 175–6, 178, 182, 186,
    188–90
Adams, E. 66
Aland, B. 180
Alexander, L. 49
Annas, J. 17, 149
Ascough, R. S. 45, 118
Aune, D. E. 21, 23
Austin, J. L. 11

Balch, D. L. 41, 42, 133, 154
Balz, H. R. 48, 68
Bammel, E. 156
Barclay, J. M. G. 153
Bauckham, R. 144
Beare, F. W. 38, 40, 44, 48, 70–1, 113
Benecke, P. V. M. 186
Berger, K. 13
Berger, P. 64
Best, E. 112
Betz, H. D. 25
Bigg, C. 47–8, 67
Birch, B. C. 118–9
Blazen, I. T. 179, 182, 188
Bondi, R. 119
Boring, M. E. 65–67
Brandt, W. 100
Brown, G. 10
Brown, W. P. 9
Brox, N. 40, 48, 68, 73, 99, 174
Bultmann, R. 1
Burgess, T. C. 21
Burrell, D. 82
Burridge, R. A. 170

Calvin, J. 46
Campbell, B. L. 121
Casurrella, A. 127
Cervantes-Gabarrón, J. 181

Cranfield, C. E. B. 2
Crisp, R. 16
Crites, S. 56
Cross, F. L. 37
Crystal, D. 122

Dalton, W. J. 182
Danker, F.W. 103
Daube, D. 158
Davids, P. H. 39, 73, 183
de Wette, W. M. L. 100
Deichgräber, R. 4, 69, 70
Deissmann, G. A. 13
Dibelius, M. 3, 5, 25, 26, 38
Doty, W. 13

Elliott, J. H. 2, 3, 5, 42–3, 67, 70, 72–3,
    75–8, 79–80, 87, 99, 102, 107, 109,
    113, 117, 119–24, 126–38, 154–5,
    157, 159–61, 174, 176, 182, 185,
    187, 190
Engberg-Pedersen, T. 7, 8, 49, 62, 83

Fanning, B. M. 74
Feldmeier, R. 127
Filson, F. V. 177
Fiore, B. 163, 170, 172, 184
Fowl, S. E. 172
Fowler, A. 52, 170
Fronmüller, G. F. C. 1
Furnish, B. 3, 99

Gammie, J. G. 15, 21, 24, 27
Geertz, C. 31
Gibson, G. D. 119
Goppelt, L. 47, 67, 73, 76, 178
Grenz, S. J. 138
Guthrie, D. 40

Harnack, A. 37
Harned, D. B. 140
Hartog, P. 186

Hauerwas, S. 16, 82
Hays, R., B. 66, 174, 187
Herzer, J. 3
Hillyer, N. 102
Holmes, M. W. 186, 187
Hort, F. J. 72, 100–1, 110, 120
Hursthouse, R. 16
Huther, J. E. 71, 100, 103, 105

Johnson, B. 135
Jones, L. G. 16
Jones-Haldeman, M. 176, 180
Judge, E. A. 50

Käsemann, E. 173, 186
Kelly, J. N. D. 40, 48, 72, 76, 89, 108, 113, 177, 179
Kendall, D. W. 2, 89
Kern, P. H. 10
Koester, C. R. 112, 184
Koester, H. 186

Lightfoot, J. B. 186
Lohse, E. 5, 40, 179, 182, 187
Longenecker, B. W. 66
Longenecker, R. N. 184
Loughlin, G. 56
Luckman, T. 64

MacIntyre, A. C. 16,18, 57, 82
Malherbe, A. J. 6, 25–6, 32, 51
Malina, B. J. 121
Martin, T. W. 2, 6, 43, 73, 77, 89, 156
Marxsen, W. 119
McKay, K. L. 73, 156
Meeks, W. A. 88, 91–3, 173
Metzger, B. M. 180, 183
Michaelis, W. 178–9, 184
Michaels, J. R. 71–73, 76–7, 86, 100, 106–7, 110–1, 119, 124–6, 176, 180–3, 186, 188–9
Musschenga, A. W. 84

Neugebauer, F. 176
Nock, A. D. 91, 93, 94
Norlin, G. 171
Nussbaum, M. C. 19

Osborne, T. P. 181, 188–9

Perdelwitz, E. R. 37
Petersen, N. R. 66
Piper, J. 41
Prasad, J. 6, 99

Reed, J. T. 10, 22
Reike, B. I. 38
Richard, E. 2

Schlatter, A. 39–40, 68, 73, 100
Schrage, W. 48, 68
Schweizer, E. 184
Searle, J. R. 11
Selwyn, E. G. 1, 3, 65, 70, 71, 73, 78, 83–85, 88, 99, 101, 105, 106–108, 113, 120–1, 132, 160, 176, 177
Slote, M. A., 16
Smyth, H. W. 73
Somers, M. R. 119
Spohn, W. C. 165, 172
Spörri, T. 117
Statman, D. 16
Stowers, S. K. 20–22, 51

Tajfel, H. 140
Taylor, C. 56
Thurén, L. 4, 5, 134, 145
Toulmin, S. E. 145

van Henten, J. W. 187
van Unnik, W. C. 2, 98, 101, 104, 132, 193
Vanhoozer, K. J. 11
Verhey, A. 99
Volf, M. 134–138, 177

Webster, J. B. 140, 173, 177, 185, 191
Weiß, B. 1, 3, 5
Wilson, B. R. 134
Wilson, W. T. 6, 7, 23, 25, 31–2, 55, 57–8, 62, 68, 81, 83–5, 89, 92, 94–5
Windisch, H. 37
Wolters, A. M. 55
Wright, N. T. 55

Yule, G. 10

Zerwick, M. 78

Subject Index

adhesion 91–3
adherence 92–5
admonition 28, 30, 147
affective commitments 17, 26, 33, 35, 82, 86, 116, 162, 171, 194, 196–7
  see also role of emotions
allegiance to God 76, 82, 86, 88, 89, 105, 115, 138, 142, 194
analogy and genealogy 12, 50–2
antithesis 24, 29, 32–34, 42–3, 58, 84, 91, 95–101, 104–5, 107–8, 114–6, 193, 195, 198
– antithetical pair 28, 147, 150–1, 163
argumentation analyis 4, 145
Asia Minor 10, 67, 154
atonement 67, 68, 81, 104, 116, 173, 177–86, 197
authorship 51
authorial intentionality 6, 7, 10, 11, 193
baptismal homily 37–8, 98, 113
biography 20, 167, 169–70
boundary maintenance 42, 133–4
  see also social barriers
character 159, 170
– Christian 7, 12, 47, 113, 116, 142, 159, 191, 194, 196, 198
– formation (ἠθοποιία) 8, 9, 15, 16, 17, 20, 24, 26, 45, 49, 52, 82, 119, 140, 154, 158, 162, 170, 193, 194, 197–8
– mature 46, 76, 86
– moral 17, 20, 97
character ethics interpretation 9
Christ hymn 173
classical rhetorical handbooks 10, 22
consolation 40, 41, 194
consummation 71, 74, 77, 80, 82, 88, 100, 106, 112, 130
contextualizing ethics 31–2, 44, 58, 60, 63, 81–2, 84, 88, 197
conversion 7, 9, 21, 24–5, 33, 39, 43, 45, 48, 52, 57, 69, 70, 81, 91–8, 101–2, 106–10, 113–7, 129, 190
– degree of 93–5
– irreversibility of 34, 102, 115
– narratives 96–7
– paradigmatic 97, 109, 195
corporate identity 9, 42, 81, 103, 109, 117–120, 124–9, 131, 132, 138, 142, 195, 198
– construction 135–8, 140
– titles 3, 67, 121–6, 128, 140–2, 195
corruptible and incorruptible 104–9, 113, 114, 116
creation 47, 63–7, 81, 105
cultural alienization 10, 41, 67, 94, 103, 127–41, 154, 195–6
cultural assimilation 41–2, 45, 52, 130, 132–3, 135, 139, 154, 194–6
cultural distinctiveness 40, 41, 103, 117, 119, 130, 131, 135, 137, 139, 141–2, 191
  see also holiness
cultural isolation 45, 52, 102, 117–8, 133–5, 138, 154, 194–6
dependence on God 7–8, 46, 116
discipleship 173–4
discourse analysis 10–1
doing good 47, 52, 83, 131, 137, 141, 159, 176–7, 180–1, 187–9, 193, 196
  see also good works
epistolary handbooks 22, 163
election 39, 46, 49, 67, 68, 101, 116–121, 123, 125, 126, 128–9, 130, 142
epistolary occasion 39, 44–45, 152
eschatology 40, 65, 71–5, 83, 87, 100, 103–4, 112–3, 130
ethics 16
– deontological 16, 198
– consequentialist 16
ethos 55–7
exile 66–7, 102–3
Exodus theme 102
faith 76, 78, 83, 85, 87–9

form-criticism 3–5
– form/*Gattung* 5, 23, 38, 50, 160
genre 5–8, 22–3, 37, 49, 51–2, 66, 170, 197–8
glory of God 132, 141–2, 195
good works 47, 134, 136, 193
   see also doing good
Greco-Roman ethics 5, 16, 18, 20
– ethical principles 19, 148–149, 170–2,
Greco-Roman philosophy 15–20, 23, 32, 49–50, 62, 118
– doctrines 58–61, 78, 151
Greco-Roman philosophic schools 15–6, 19–21, 25–27, 29, 31, 35, 45, 49, 91–4, 118, 149, 154, 193
– Cynics 93–4, 96–7
– Epicureans 118
– Platonists 94
– Pythagoreans 118
– Stoics 26, 62, 83, 93–4, 154, 166
Greek tragedy 20, 46, 170
group cohesion 119, 138
habit 17, 18, 20, 29, 47, 76, 84, 88, 95, 148, 164, 183
happiness (εὐδαιμονία) 16–7, 21, 25, 30, 34, 62, 92, 97, 150
Haustafeln 5, 25, 38, 41, 50, 89, 133, 154–62
– slaves 156–8, 175
– wives 158–9, 175
– husbands 159–60, 175
heart 78, 100, 114, 131
Hellenization 20–1, 49, 133
holiness 85, 101–2, 105, 112, 114–6, 123–4, 132, 137, 140, 142, 195
   see also cultural distinctiveness
hope 40–1, 71, 83, 87, 100, 103, 105, 107, 113, 115
honor and shame 121, 124–5
household of God 108, 117, 120–3, 160, 195
identity 10, 140
– marker 123, 127, 129
identity and difference 10, 120–1, 125–6, 132, 139, 140–1
identification with Christ 121
imitation of Christ 69, 142, 156–7, 161, 163, 172–91, 196–7
imperatival participles 156, 160

indicative and imperative 1, 2, 11, 12, 99, 173, 185, 197
inheritance 71–2, 83, 87
Judaism 49, 51, 62–5, 69, 72, 106, 118, 123, 133, 182
judgment 102–3, 132
letter v. epistle 12–3
life as a unity 17–20, 31, 101
life transformation 8, 23, 31, 98
   see also moral transformation
lifestyle (ἀναστροφή) 44, 49, 101, 103–5, 115–7, 127, 130–1, 137, 141, 152, 158–9, 196
liminality 24–5, 28, 34, 45, 48–9
literal v. metaphorical 127–9
living stone 120, 124–5
love 109–10, 112, 114, 116, 141–2, 190, 195
– brotherly 108, 160–1
– familial 124, 134, 195
– friendship 34
Messiah 70, 120
– messianic age 70, 74, 80, 88
monotheism 49
moral disposition 17–9, 28, 153–4, 170–1, 183, 189
moral education 22, 29, 97, 112, 170
moral exemplar (παράδειγμα) 7, 27, 30, 34, 38, 163–72, 190–1, 193, 196
moral instruction 7, 24, 26–7, 29, 35, 38, 41–4, 58–60, 63–4, 82–84, 88–9, 143–56, 162–4, 193, 196, 198
moral maturity 9, 35, 45, 62, 82, 108, 111, 150, 153, 161
moral maxim 24, 27–8, 30, 193
moral progress (προκοπή) 7, 15, 23, 25, 58, 61, 94–5, 112, 116, 151, 168, 171, 193
moral purity 107–8, 130, 140–1, 196
moral reform 91
moral transformation 78, 81, 83, 89, 91, 141, 153
motive clause 28, 144–6, 150–1
missional agenda 131–2, 137–9, 141, 153, 158, 162, 196
mystery religions 91–2
narrative 7, 20, 56
– life as narrative 56, 61–2, 82, 97
narrative substructure 66

Nature/Reason 19, 27, 59, 61, 63, 150,
    165
obedience 47, 82, 89, 100, 107, 195
  – of Jesus 173, 177, 183–89, 196
paraenesis 4, 5, 24, 26, 38, 93
  – as a form 5, 8, 143
  – as a genre 5, 6, 8, 12, 16, 35, 143, 151
paraenetic epistle 1, 21, 101
  – 1 Peter 5, 6, 8, 15, 47, 52
  – aims 8, 26, 43–4, 52–3, 87–8, 98, 102,
    116–7, 140, 142, 151, 162, 195
  – Greco-Roman 2, 6, 7, 13, 20–1, 39,
    51, 58, 109, 113, 117–8, 143, 148,
    152, 164, 172, 188–91, 193
paraenetic literary strategies 7–11, 25,
    32, 35, 38, 91, 95, 97, 116, 143, 162,
    164, 191, 193–4, 198
paraenetic theology 12, 117, 163, 197
persecution 39, 40, 45, 85, 131, 153
  see also suffering
pre-existent Christ 80
priesthood 123, 140, 142, 195
protrepsis 21–3, 31, 64
Qumran community 121, 134–5
reference groups 93–4
relationship to Pauline epistles 3, 198
remembrance 32, 91, 95, 97–9, 102, 113,
    116, 193–5, 198
resurrection 69, 71, 80, 83–4, 106–7,
    173
reverence for God 47, 103, 105, 157,
    176–7, 196
rhetoric 22, 33–4, 115, 171
rhetorical criticism 10
role of emotions 17, 19, 24–5, 32, 59,
    86, 150, 167–9, 190–1, 193–4
  see also affective commitments
savior 173, 177–8, 185, 190–1, 197
sect 134–5
self-control 18, 28, 114
shepherd 190–1
short-term v. long-term goals 152–4,
    158–9, 162, 196
slavery 104, 157, 174, 176, 179–80,
    188–91, 196

social barriers 131, 138, 196
  see also boundary maintenance
social ethics 3, 120, 126–7, 195
social-scientific criticism 10, 43, 117
socialization 57
socio-rhetorical criticism 9
speech-act theory 11
spiritual milk 110–3
spiritual sacrifices 123–4
symbolic universe 57, 65
suffering 40, 69, 75, 78, 84, 137, 152,
    161, 176–7, 190–1, 196
  see also persecution
  – as a means of growth 45–6, 49, 52, 76,
    83, 87
  – moral challenge of 44, 46, 153, 157,
    194
  – of Jesus 80, 177–91
  – theological challenge of 46, 194
τέλος 20, 25, 31, 57, 83, 97, 112
teleology 56, 60
temple 121–2
theology and ethics 1–4, 7, 11, 15, 61,
    65, 69, 89, 197–8
verbal aspect 73–4, 156
virtue 15–9, 21, 23, 24, 26, 28, 29–32,
    34, 59, 148, 162, 165, 171, 193
  – virtue and vice 18, 20, 24, 33–4,
    109–10, 114–6, 139, 150–1, 164, 170,
    195
  – virtue and vice lists 24–5, 27, 29, 38,
    193
virtue ethics 16
wisdom (φρόνησις) 15, 17, 19–20, 28–9,
    43, 58, 111–2, 148–51, 155, 158,
    160–2, 165, 196
worldview 25–6, 30–2, 35, 43–4, 55, 58,
    60–1
  – meta-narrative of salvation 62, 68, 72,
    75, 79, 81, 84–5, 91, 99, 117–8, 126,
    142, 194
  – narrative worldview 9, 31, 39, 44, 56,
    57, 63–6, 69, 80, 82, 85, 88–9, 194,
    198

Wissenschaftliche Untersuchungen zum Neuen Testament

Alphabetical Index of the First and Second Series

Ådna, Jostein: Jesu Stellung zum Tempel. 2000. *Volume II/119.*
– (Ed.): The Formation of the Early Church. 2005. *Volume 183.*
– and *Kvalbein, Hans* (Ed.): The Mission of the Early Church to Jews and Gentiles. 2000. *Volume 127.*
Alkier, Stefan: Wunder und Wirklichkeit in den Briefen des Apostels Paulus. 2001. *Volume 134.*
Anderson, Paul N.: The Christology of the Fourth Gospel. 1996. *Volume II/78.*
Appold, Mark L.: The Oneness Motif in the Fourth Gospel. 1976. *Volume II/1.*
Arnold, Clinton E.: The Colossian Syncretism. 1995. *Volume II/77.*
Ascough, Richard S.: Paul's Macedonian Associations. 2003. *Volume II/161.*
Asiedu-Peprah, Martin: Johannine Sabbath Conflicts As Juridical Controversy. 2001. *Volume II/132.*
Avemarie, Friedrich: Die Tauferzählungen der Apostelgeschichte. 2002. *Volume 139.*
Avemarie, Friedrich and *Hermann Lichtenberger* (Ed.): Auferstehung – Ressurection. 2001. *Volume 135.*
Avemarie, Friedrich and *Hermann Lichtenberger* (Ed.): Bund und Tora. 1996. *Volume 92.*
Baarlink, Heinrich: Verkündigtes Heil. 2004. *Volume 168.*
Bachmann, Michael: Sünder oder Übertreter. 1992. *Volume 59.*
Bachmann, Michael (Ed.): Lutherische und Neue Paulusperspektive. 2005. *Volume 182.*
Back, Frances: Verwandlung durch Offenbarung bei Paulus. 2002. *Volume II/153.*
Baker, William R.: Personal Speech-Ethics in the Epistle of James. 1995. *Volume II/68.*
Bakke, Odd Magne: 'Concord and Peace'. 2001. *Volume II/143.*
Baldwin, Matthew C.: Whose *Acts of Peter*? 2005. *Volume II/196.*
Balla, Peter: Challenges to New Testament Theology. 1997. *Volume II/95.*
– *The Child-Parent Relationship in the New Testament and its Environment. 2003. Volume 155.*

Bammel, Ernst: Judaica. Volume I 1986. *Volume 37.*
– Volume II 1997. *Volume 91.*
Bash, Anthony: Ambassadors for Christ. 1997. *Volume II/92.*
Bauernfeind, Otto: Kommentar und Studien zur Apostelgeschichte. 1980. *Volume 22.*
Baum, Armin Daniel: Pseudepigraphie und literarische Fälschung im frühen Christentum. 2001. *Volume II/138.*
Bayer, Hans Friedrich: Jesus' Predictions of Vindication and Resurrection. 1986. *Volume II/20.*
Becker, Eve-Marie and *Peter Pilhofer* (Ed.): Biographie und Persönlichkeit des Paulus. 2005. *Volume 187.*
Becker, Michael: Wunder und Wundertäter im früh-rabbinischen Judentum. 2002. *Volume II/144.*
Bell, Richard H.: The Irrevocable Call of God. 2005. *Volume 184.*
– No One Seeks for God. 1998. *Volume 106.*
– Provoked to Jealousy. 1994. *Volume II/63.*
Bennema, Cornelis: The Power of Saving Wisdom. 2002. *Volume II/148.*
Bergman, Jan: see *Kieffer, René*
Bergmeier, Roland: Das Gesetz im Römerbrief und andere Studien zum Neuen Testament. 2000. *Volume 121.*
Betz, Otto: Jesus, der Messias Israels. 1987. *Volume 42.*
– Jesus, der Herr der Kirche. 1990. *Volume 52.*
Beyschlag, Karlmann: Simon Magus und die christliche Gnosis. 1974. *Volume 16.*
Bittner, Wolfgang J.: Jesu Zeichen im Johannesevangelium. 1987. *Volume II/26.*
Bjerkelund, Carl J.: Tauta Egeneto. 1987. *Volume 40.*
Blackburn, Barry Lee: Theios Anēr and the Markan Miracle Traditions. 1991. *Volume II/40.*
Bock, Darrell L.: Blasphemy and Exaltation in Judaism and the Final Examination of Jesus. 1998. *Volume II/106.*
Bockmuehl, Markus N.A.: Revelation and Mystery in Ancient Judaism and Pauline Christianity. 1990. *Volume II/36.*
Bøe, Sverre: Gog and Magog. 2001. *Volume II/135.*

Böhlig, Alexander: Gnosis und Synkretismus. Teil 1 1989. *Volume 47* – Teil 2 1989. *Volume 48.*

Böhm, Martina: Samarien und die Samaritai bei Lukas. 1999. *Volume II/111.*

Böttrich, Christfried: Weltweisheit – Mensch-heitsethik – Urkult. 1992. *Volume II/50.*

Bolyki, János: Jesu Tischgemeinschaften. 1997. *Volume II/96.*

Bosman, Philip: Conscience in Philo and Paul. 2003. *Volume II/166.*

Bovon, François: Studies in Early Christianity. 2003. *Volume 161.*

Brocke, Christoph vom: Thessaloniki – Stadt des Kassander und Gemeinde des Paulus. 2001. *Volume II/125.*

Brunson, Andrew: Psalm 118 in the Gospel of John. 2003. *Volume II/158.*

Büchli, Jörg: Der Poimandres – ein paganisier-tes Evangelium. 1987. *Volume II/27.*

Bühner, Jan A.: Der Gesandte und sein Weg im 4. Evangelium. 1977. *Volume II/2.*

Burchard, Christoph: Untersuchungen zu Joseph und Asenath. 1965. *Volume 8.*

– Studien zur Theologie, Sprache und Umwelt des Neuen Testaments. Ed. von D. Sänger. 1998. *Volume 107.*

Burnett, Richard: Karl Barth's Theological Exegesis. 2001. *Volume II/145.*

Byron, John: Slavery Metaphors in Early Judaism and Pauline Christianity. 2003. *Volume II/162.*

Byrskog, Samuel: Story as History – History as Story. 2000. *Volume 123.*

Cancik, Hubert (Ed.): Markus-Philologie. 1984. *Volume 33.*

Capes, David B.: Old Testament Yaweh Texts in Paul's Christology. 1992. *Volume II/47.*

Caragounis, Chrys C.: The Development of Greek and the New Testament. 2004. *Volume 167.*

– The Son of Man. 1986. *Volume 38.*

– see *Fridrichsen, Anton.*

Carleton Paget, James: The Epistle of Barnabas. 1994. *Volume II/64.*

Carson, D.A., O'Brien, Peter T. and *Mark Seifrid* (Ed.): Justification and Variegated Nomism.
Volume 1: The Complexities of Second Temple Judaism. 2001. *Volume II/140.*
Volume 2: The Paradoxes of Paul. 2004. *Volume II/181.*

Ciampa, Roy E.: The Presence and Function of Scripture in Galatians 1 and 2. 1998. *Volume II/102.*

Classen, Carl Joachim: Rhetorical Criticsm of the New Testament. 2000. *Volume 128.*

Colpe, Carsten: Iranier – Aramäer – Hebräer – Hellenen. 2003. *Volume 154.*

Crump, David: Jesus the Intercessor. 1992. *Volume II/19.*

Dahl, Nils Alstrup: Studies in Ephesians. 2000. *Volume 131.*

Deines, Roland: Die Gerechtigkeit der Tora im Reich des Messias. 2004. *Volume 177.*

– Jüdische Steingefäße und pharisäische Frömmigkeit. 1993. *Volume II/52.*

– Die Pharisäer. 1997. *Volume 101.*

– and *Karl-Wilhelm Niebuhr* (Ed.): Philo und das Neue Testament. 2004. *Volume 172.*

Dettwiler, Andreas and *Jean Zumstein* (Ed.): Kreuzestheologie im Neuen Testament. 2002. *Volume 151.*

Dickson, John P.: Mission-Commitment in Ancient Judaism and in the Pauline Communities. 2003. *Volume II/159.*

Dietzfelbinger, Christian: Der Abschied des Kommenden. 1997. *Volume 95.*

Dimitrov, Ivan Z., James D.G. Dunn, Ulrich Luz and *Karl-Wilhelm Niebuhr* (Ed.): Das Alte Testament als christliche Bibel in orthodoxer und westlicher Sicht. 2004. *Volume 174.*

Dobbeler, Axel von: Glaube als Teilhabe. 1987. *Volume II/22.*

Dryden, J. de Waal: Theology and Ethics in 1 Peter. 2006. *Volume II/209.*

Du Toit, David S.: Theios Anthropos. 1997. *Volume II/91.*

Dübbers, Michael: Christologie und Existenz im Kolosserbrief. 2005. *Volume II/191.*

Dunn, James D.G.: The New Perspective on Paul. 2005. *Volume 185.*

Dunn , James D.G. (Ed.): Jews and Christians. 1992. *Volume 66.*

– Paul and the Mosaic Law. 1996. *Volume 89.*

– see *Dimitrov, Ivan Z.*

Dunn, James D.G., Hans Klein, Ulrich Luz and *Vasile Mihoc* (Ed.): Auslegung der Bibel in orthodoxer und westlicher Perspektive. 2000. *Volume 130.*

Ebel, Eva: Die Attraktivität früher christlicher Gemeinden. 2004. *Volume II/178.*

Ebertz, Michael N.: Das Charisma des Gekreu-zigten. 1987. *Volume 45.*

Eckstein, Hans-Joachim: Der Begriff Syneidesis bei Paulus. 1983. *Volume II/10.*

– Verheißung und Gesetz. 1996. *Volume 86.*

Ego, Beate: Im Himmel wie auf Erden. 1989. *Volume II/34*

Ego, Beate, Armin Lange and *Peter Pilhofer* *(Ed.):* Gemeinde ohne Tempel – Community without Temple. 1999. *Volume 118.*

– und *Helmut Merkel* (Ed.): Religiöses Lernen in der biblischen, frühjüdischen und früh-christlichen Überlieferung. 2005. *Volume 180.*

Eisen, Ute E.: see *Paulsen, Henning.*

Elledge, C.D.: Life after Death in Early Judaism. 2006. *Volume II/208.*

Ellis, E. Earle: Prophecy and Hermeneutic in Early Christianity. 1978. *Volume 18.*

– The Old Testament in Early Christianity. 1991. *Volume 54.*

Endo, Masanobu: Creation and Christology. 2002. *Volume 149.*

Ennulat, Andreas: Die 'Minor Agreements'. 1994. *Volume II/62.*

Ensor, Peter W.: Jesus and His 'Works'. 1996. *Volume II/85.*

Eskola, Timo: Messiah and the Throne. 2001. *Volume II/142.*

– Theodicy and Predestination in Pauline Soteriology. 1998. *Volume II/100.*

Fatehi, Mehrdad: The Spirit's Relation to the Risen Lord in Paul. 2000. *Volume II/128.*

Feldmeier, Reinhard: Die Krisis des Gottessohnes. 1987. *Volume II/21.*

– Die Christen als Fremde. 1992. *Volume 64.*

Feldmeier, Reinhard and *Ulrich Heckel* (Ed.): Die Heiden. 1994. *Volume 70.*

Fletcher-Louis, Crispin H.T.: Luke-Acts: Angels, Christology and Soteriology. 1997. *Volume II/94.*

Förster, Niclas: Marcus Magus. 1999. *Volume 114.*

Forbes, Christopher Brian: Prophecy and Inspired Speech in Early Christianity and its Hellenistic Environment. 1995. *Volume II/75.*

Fornberg, Tord: see *Fridrichsen, Anton.*

Fossum, Jarl E.: The Name of God and the Angel of the Lord. 1985. *Volume 36.*

Foster, Paul: Community, Law and Mission in Matthew's Gospel. *Volume II/177.*

Fotopoulos, John: Food Offered to Idols in Roman Corinth. 2003. *Volume II/151.*

Frenschkowski, Marco: Offenbarung und Epiphanie. Volume 1 1995. *Volume II/79 –* Volume 2 1997. *Volume II/80.*

Frey, Jörg: Eugen Drewermann und die biblische Exegese. 1995. *Volume II/71.*

– Die johanneische Eschatologie. Volume I. 1997. *Volume 96.* – Volume II. 1998. *Volume 110.*

– Volume III. 2000. *Volume 117.*

Frey, Jörg and *Udo Schnelle (Ed.):* Kontexte des Johannesevangeliums. 2004. *Volume 175.*

– and *Jens Schröter* (Ed.): Deutungen des Todes Jesu im Neuen Testament. 2005. *Volume 181.*

Freyne, Sean: Galilee and Gospel. 2000. *Volume 125.*

Fridrichsen, Anton: Exegetical Writings. Edited by C.C. Caragounis and T. Fornberg. 1994. *Volume 76.*

Gäckle, Volker: Die Starken und die Schwachen in Korinth und in Rom. 2005. *Volume 200.*

Garlington, Don B.: 'The Obedience of Faith'. 1991. *Volume II/38.*

– Faith, Obedience, and Perseverance. 1994. *Volume 79.*

Garnet, Paul: Salvation and Atonement in the Qumran Scrolls. 1977. *Volume II/3.*

Gemünden, Petra von (Ed.): see *Weissenrieder, Annette.*

Gese, Michael: Das Vermächtnis des Apostels. 1997. *Volume II/99.*

Gheorghita, Radu: The Role of the Septuagint in Hebrews. 2003. *Volume II/160.*

Gräbe, Petrus J.: The Power of God in Paul's Letters. 2000. *Volume II/123.*

Gräßer, Erich: Der Alte Bund im Neuen. 1985. *Volume 35.*

– Forschungen zur Apostelgeschichte. 2001. *Volume 137.*

Green, Joel B.: The Death of Jesus. 1988. *Volume II/33.*

Gregg, Brian Han: The Historical Jesus and the Final Judgment Sayings in Q. 2005. *Volume II/207.*

Gregory, Andrew: The Reception of Luke and Acts in the Period before Irenaeus. 2003. *Volume II/169.*

Grindheim, Sigurd: The Crux of Election. 2005. *Volume II/202.*

Gundry, Robert H.: The Old is Better. 2005. *Volume 178.*

Gundry Volf, Judith M.: Paul and Perseverance. 1990. *Volume II/37.*

Hafemann, Scott J.: Suffering and the Spirit. 1986. *Volume II/19.*

– Paul, Moses, and the History of Israel. 1995. *Volume 81.*

Hahn, Ferdinand: Studien zum Neuen Testament.
Vol. I: Grundsatzfragen, Jesusforschung, Evangelien. 2006. *Volume 191.*
Vol. II: Bekenntnisbildung und Theologie in urchristlicher Zeit. 2006. *Volume 192.*

Hahn, Johannes (Ed.): Zerstörungen des Jerusalemer Tempels. 2002. *Volume 147.*

Hannah, Darrel D.: Michael and Christ. 1999. *Volume II/109.*

Hamid-Khani, Saeed: Relevation and Concealment of Christ. 2000. *Volume II/120.*

Harrison; James R.: Paul's Language of Grace in Its Graeco-Roman Context. 2003. *Volume II/172.*

Hartman, Lars: Text Centered New Testament Studies. Ed. von D. Hellholm. 1997. *Volume 102.*

Hartog, Paul: Polycarp and the New Testament. 2001. *Volume II/134.*

Heckel, Theo K.: Der Innere Mensch. 1993. *Volume II/53.*

– Vom Evangelium des Markus zum viergestaltigen Evangelium. 1999. *Volume 120.*

Heckel, Ulrich: Kraft in Schwachheit. 1993. *Volume II/56.*

– Der Segen im Neuen Testament. 2002. *Volume 150.*

– see *Feldmeier, Reinhard.*

– see *Hengel, Martin.*

Heiligenthal, Roman: Werke als Zeichen. 1983. *Volume II/9.*

Hellholm, D.: see *Hartman, Lars.*

Hemer, Colin J.: The Book of Acts in the Setting of Hellenistic History. 1989. *Volume 49.*

Hengel, Martin: Judentum und Hellenismus. 1969, ³1988. *Volume 10.*

– Die johanneische Frage. 1993. *Volume 67.*

– Judaica et Hellenistica. Kleine Schriften I. 1996. *Volume 90.*

– Judaica, Hellenistica et Christiana. Kleine Schriften II. 1999. *Volume 109.*

– Paulus und Jakobus. Kleine Schriften III. 2002. *Volume 141.*

Hengel, Martin and *Ulrich Heckel* (Ed.): Paulus und das antike Judentum. 1991. *Volume 58.*

Hengel, Martin and *Hermut Löhr* (Ed.): Schriftauslegung im antiken Judentum und im Urchristentum. 1994. *Volume 73.*

Hengel, Martin and *Anna Maria Schwemer:* Paulus zwischen Damaskus und Antiochien. 1998. *Volume 108.*

– Der messianische Anspruch Jesu und die Anfänge der Christologie. 2001. *Volume 138.*

Hengel, Martin and *Anna Maria Schwemer* (Ed.): Königsherrschaft Gottes und himmlischer Kult. 1991. *Volume 55.*

– Die Septuaginta. 1994. *Volume 72.*

Hengel, Martin; Siegfried Mittmann and *Anna Maria Schwemer* (Ed.): La Cité de Dieu / Die Stadt Gottes. 2000. *Volume 129.*

Herrenbrück, Fritz: Jesus und die Zöllner. 1990. *Volume II/41.*

Herzer, Jens: Paulus oder Petrus? 1998. *Volume 103.*

Hill, Charles E.: From the Lost Teaching of Polycarp. 2005. *Volume 186.*

Hoegen-Rohls, Christina: Der nachösterliche Johannes. 1996. *Volume II/84.*

Hoffmann, Matthias Reinhard: The Destroyer and the Lamb. 2005. *Volume II/203.*

Hofius, Otfried: Katapausis. 1970. *Volume 11.*

– Der Vorhang vor dem Thron Gottes. 1972. *Volume 14.*

– Der Christushymnus Philipper 2,6-11. 1976, ²1991. *Volume 17.*

– Paulusstudien. 1989, ²1994. *Volume 51.*

– Neutestamentliche Studien. 2000. *Volume 132.*

– Paulusstudien II. 2002. *Volume 143.*

Hofius, Otfried and *Hans-Christian Kammler:* Johannesstudien. 1996. *Volume 88.*

Holtz, Traugott: Geschichte und Theologie des Urchristentums. 1991. *Volume 57.*

Hommel, Hildebrecht: Sebasmata. Volume 1 1983. *Volume 31* – Volume 2 1984. *Volume 32.*

Horbury, William: Herodian Judaism and New Testament Study. 2006. *Volume 193.*

Hvalvik, Reidar: The Struggle for Scripture and Covenant. 1996. *Volume II/82.*

Jauhiainen, Marko: The Use of Zechariah in Revelation. 2005. *Volume II/199.*

Johns, Loren L.: The Lamb Christology of the Apocalypse of John. 2003. *Volume II/167.*

Joubert, Stephan: Paul as Benefactor. 2000. *Volume II/124.*

Jungbauer, Harry: „Ehre Vater und Mutter". 2002. *Volume II/146.*

Kähler, Christoph: Jesu Gleichnisse als Poesie und Therapie. 1995. *Volume 78.*

Kamlah, Ehrhard: Die Form der katalogischen Paränese im Neuen Testament. 1964. *Volume 7.*

Kammler, Hans-Christian: Christologie und Eschatologie. 2000. *Volume 126.*

– Kreuz und Weisheit. 2003. *Volume 159.*

– see *Hofius, Otfried.*

Kelhoffer, James A.: The Diet of John the Baptist. 2005. *Volume 176.*

– Miracle and Mission. 1999. *Volume II/112.*

Kieffer, René and *Jan Bergman* (Ed.): La Main de Dieu / Die Hand Gottes. 1997. *Volume 94.*

Kim, Seyoon: The Origin of Paul's Gospel. 1981, ²1984. *Volume II/4.*

– Paul and the New Perspective. 2002. *Volume 140.*

– "The 'Son of Man'" as the Son of God. 1983. *Volume 30.*

Klauck, Hans-Josef: Religion und Gesellschaft im frühen Christentum. 2003. *Volume 152.*

Klein, Hans: see *Dunn, James D.G..*

Kleinknecht, Karl Th.: Der leidende Gerechtfertigte. 1984, ²1988. *Volume II/13.*

Klinghardt, Matthias: Gesetz und Volk Gottes. 1988. *Volume II/32.*

Koch, Michael: Drachenkampf und Sonnenfrau. 2004. *Volume II/184.*

Koch, Stefan: Rechtliche Regelung von Konflikten im frühen Christentum. 2004. *Volume II/174.*

Köhler, Wolf-Dietrich: Rezeption des Matthäusevangeliums in der Zeit vor Irenäus. 1987. *Volume II/24.*

Köhn, Andreas: Der Neutestamentler Ernst Lohmeyer. 2004. *Volume II/180.*

Kooten, George H. van: Cosmic Christology in Paul and the Pauline School. 2003. *Volume II/171.*

Korn, Manfred: Die Geschichte Jesu in veränderter Zeit. 1993. *Volume II/51.*

Koskenniemi, Erkki: Apollonios von Tyana in der neutestamentlichen Exegese. 1994. *Volume II/61.*

–: The Old Testament Miracle-Workers in Early Judaism. 2005. *Volume II/206.*

Kraus, Thomas J.: Sprache, Stil und historischer Ort des zweiten Petrusbriefes. 2001. *Volume II/136.*

Kraus, Wolfgang: Das Volk Gottes. 1996. *Volume 85.*

– and *Karl-Wilhelm Niebuhr* (Ed.): Frühjudentum und Neues Testament im Horizont Biblischer Theologie. 2003. *Volume 162.*

– see *Walter, Nikolaus.*

Kreplin, Matthias: Das Selbstverständnis Jesu. 2001. *Volume II/141.*

Kuhn, Karl G.: Achtzehngebet und Vaterunser und der Reim. 1950. *Volume 1.*

Kvalbein, Hans: see *Ådna, Jostein.*

Kwon, Yon-Gyong: Eschatology in Galatians. 2004. *Volume II/183.*

Laansma, Jon: I Will Give You Rest. 1997. *Volume II/98.*

Labahn, Michael: Offenbarung in Zeichen und Wort. 2000. *Volume II/117.*

Lambers-Petry, Doris: see *Tomson, Peter J.*

Lange, Armin: see *Ego, Beate.*

Lampe, Peter: Die stadtrömischen Christen in den ersten beiden Jahrhunderten. 1987, [2]1989. *Volume II/18.*

Landmesser, Christof: Wahrheit als Grundbegriff neutestamentlicher Wissenschaft. 1999. *Volume 113.*

– Jüngerberufung und Zuwendung zu Gott. 2000. *Volume 133.*

Lau, Andrew: Manifest in Flesh. 1996. *Volume II/86.*

Lawrence, Louise: An Ethnography of the Gospel of Matthew. 2003. *Volume II/165.*

Lee, Aquila H.I.: From Messiah to Preexistent Son. 2005. *Volume II/192.*

Lee, Pilchan: The New Jerusalem in the Book of Relevation. 2000. *Volume II/129.*

Lichtenberger, Hermann: see *Avemarie, Friedrich.*

Lichtenberger, Hermann: Das Ich Adams und das Ich der Menschheit. 2004. *Volume 164.*

Lierman, John: The New Testament Moses. 2004. *Volume II/173.*

Lieu, Samuel N.C.: Manichaeism in the Later Roman Empire and Medieval China. [2]1992. *Volume 63.*

Lindgård, Fredrik: Paul's Line of Thought in 2 Corinthians 4:16-5:10. 2004. *Volume II/189.*

Loader, William R.G.: Jesus' Attitude Towards the Law. 1997. *Volume II/97.*

Löhr, Gebhard: Verherrlichung Gottes durch Philosophie. 1997. *Volume 97.*

Löhr, Hermut: Studien zum frühchristlichen und frühjüdischen Gebet. 2003. *Volume 160.*

– see *Hengel, Martin.*

Löhr, Winrich Alfried: Basilides und seine Schule. 1995. *Volume 83.*

Luomanen, Petri: Entering the Kingdom of Heaven. 1998. *Volume II/101.*

Luz, Ulrich: see *Dunn, James D.G.*

Mackay, Ian D.: John's Raltionship with Mark. 2004. *Volume II/182.*

Maier, Gerhard: Mensch und freier Wille. 1971. *Volume 12.*

– Die Johannesoffenbarung und die Kirche. 1981. *Volume 25.*

Markschies, Christoph: Valentinus Gnosticus? 1992. *Volume 65.*

Marshall, Peter: Enmity in Corinth: Social Conventions in Paul's Relations with the Corinthians. 1987. *Volume II/23.*

Mayer, Annemarie: Sprache der Einheit im Epheserbrief und in der Ökumene. 2002. *Volume II/150.*

Mayordomo, Moisés: Argumentiert Paulus logisch? 2005. *Volume 188.*

McDonough, Sean M.: YHWH at Patmos: Rev. 1:4 in its Hellenistic and Early Jewish Setting. 1999. *Volume II/107.*

McGlynn, Moyna: Divine Judgement and Divine Benevolence in the Book of Wisdom. 2001. *Volume II/139.*

Meade, David G.: Pseudonymity and Canon. 1986. *Volume 39.*

Meadors, Edward P.: Jesus the Messianic Herald of Salvation. 1995. *Volume II/72.*

Meißner, Stefan: Die Heimholung des Ketzers. 1996. *Volume II/87.*

Mell, Ulrich: Die „anderen" Winzer. 1994. *Volume 77.*

Mengel, Berthold: Studien zum Philipperbrief. 1982. *Volume II/8.*

Merkel, Helmut: Die Widersprüche zwischen den Evangelien. 1971. *Volume 13.*
– see *Ego, Beate.*
Merklein, Helmut: Studien zu Jesus und Paulus. Volume 1 1987. *Volume 43.* – Volume 2 1998. *Volume 105.*
Metzdorf, Christina: Die Tempelaktion Jesu. 2003. *Volume II/168.*
Metzler, Karin: Der griechische Begriff des Verzeihens. 1991. *Volume II/44.*
Metzner, Rainer: Die Rezeption des Matthäusevangeliums im 1. Petrusbrief. 1995. *Volume II/74.*
– Das Verständnis der Sünde im Johannesevangelium. 2000. *Volume 122.*
Mihoc, Vasile: see *Dunn, James D.G.*
Mineshige, Kiyoshi: Besitzverzicht und Almosen bei Lukas. 2003. *Volume II/163.*
Mittmann, Siegfried: see *Hengel, Martin.*
Mittmann-Richert, Ulrike: Magnifikat und Benediktus. *1996. Volume II/90.*
Mournet, Terence C.: Oral Tradition and Literary Dependency. 2005. *Volume II/195.*
Mußner, Franz: Jesus von Nazareth im Umfeld Israels und der Urkirche. Ed. von M. Theobald. 1998. *Volume 111.*
Mutschler, Bernhard: Das Corpus Johanneum bei Irenäus von Lyon. 2005. *Volume 189.*
Niebuhr, Karl-Wilhelm: Gesetz und Paränese. 1987. *Volume II/28.*
– Heidenapostel aus Israel. 1992. *Volume 62.*
– see *Deines, Roland*
– see *Dimitrov, Ivan Z.*
– see *Kraus, Wolfgang*
Nielsen, Anders E.: "Until it is Fullfilled". 2000. *Volume II/126.*
Nissen, Andreas: Gott und der Nächste im antiken Judentum. 1974. *Volume 15.*
Noack, Christian: Gottesbewußtsein. 2000. *Volume II/116.*
Noormann, Rolf: Irenäus als Paulusinterpret. 1994. *Volume II/66.*
Novakovic, Lidija: Messiah, the Healer of the Sick. 2003. *Volume II/170.*
Obermann, Andreas: Die christologische Erfüllung der Schrift im Johannesevangelium. 1996. *Volume II/83.*
Öhler, Markus: Barnabas. 2003. *Volume 156.*
Okure, Teresa: The Johannine Approach to Mission. 1988. *Volume II/31.*
Onuki, Takashi: Heil und Erlösung. 2004. *Volume 165.*
Oropeza, B. J.: Paul and Apostasy. 2000. *Volume II/115.*
Ostmeyer, Karl-Heinrich: Taufe und Typos. 2000. *Volume II/118.*

Paulsen, Henning: Studien zur Literatur und Geschichte des frühen Christentums. Ed. von Ute E. Eisen. 1997. *Volume 99.*
Pao, David W.: Acts and the Isaianic New Exodus. 2000. *Volume II/130.*
Park, Eung Chun: The Mission Discourse in Matthew's Interpretation. 1995. *Volume II/81.*
Park, Joseph S.: Conceptions of Afterlife in Jewish Insriptions. 2000. *Volume II/121.*
Pate, C. Marvin: The Reverse of the Curse. 2000. *Volume II/114.*
Peres, Imre: Griechische Grabinschriften und neutestamentliche Eschatologie. 2003. *Volume 157.*
Philip, Finny: The Origins of Pauline Pneumatology. 2005. *Volume II/194.*
Philonenko, Marc (Ed.): Le Trône de Dieu. 1993. *Volume 69.*
Pilhofer, Peter: Presbyteron Kreitton. 1990. *Volume II/39.*
– Philippi. Volume 1 1995. *Volume 87.* – Volume 2 2000. *Volume 119.*
– Die frühen Christen und ihre Welt. 2002. *Volume 145.*
– see *Becker, Eve-Marie.*
– see *Ego, Beate.*
Pitre, Brant: Jesus, the Tribulation, and the End of the Exile. 2005. *Volume II/204.*
Plümacher, Eckhard: Geschichte und Geschichten. Aufsätze zur Apostelgeschichte und zu den Johannesakten. Herausgegeben von Jens Schröter und Ralph Brucker. 2004. *Volume 170.*
Pöhlmann, Wolfgang: Der Verlorene Sohn und das Haus. 1993. *Volume 68.*
Pokorný, Petr and *Josef B. Souček:* Bibelauslegung als Theologie. 1997. *Volume 100.*
Pokorný, Petr and *Jan Roskovec* (Ed.): Philosophical Hermeneutics and Biblical Exegesis. 2002. *Volume 153.*
Popkes, Enno Edzard: Die Theologie der Liebe Gottes in den johanneischen Schriften. 2005. *Volume II/197.*
Porter, Stanley E.: The Paul of Acts. 1999. *Volume 115.*
Prieur, Alexander: Die Verkündigung der Gottesherrschaft. 1996. *Volume II/89.*
Probst, Hermann: Paulus und der Brief. 1991. *Volume II/45.*
Räisänen, Heikki: Paul and the Law. 1983, ²1987. *Volume 29.*
Rehkopf, Friedrich: Die lukanische Sonderquelle. 1959. *Volume 5.*
Rein, Matthias: Die Heilung des Blindgeborenen (Joh 9). 1995. *Volume II/73.*
Reinmuth, Eckart: Pseudo-Philo und Lukas. 1994. *Volume 74.*

Reiser, Marius: Syntax und Stil des Markusevangeliums. 1984. *Volume II/11.*

Rhodes, James N.: The Epistle of Barnabas
and the Deuteronomic Tradition. 2004.
Volume II/188.

Richards, E. Randolph: The Secretary in the
Letters of Paul. 1991. *Volume II/42.*

Riesner, Rainer: Jesus als Lehrer. 1981, ³1988.
Volume II/7.

– Die Frühzeit des Apostels Paulus. 1994.
Volume 71.

Rissi, Mathias: Die Theologie des Hebräer-
briefs. 1987. *Volume 41.*

Roskovec, Jan: see *Pokorný, Petr.*

Röhser, Günter: Metaphorik und Personifikation
der Sünde. 1987. *Volume II/25.*

Rose, Christian: Die Wolke der Zeugen. 1994.
Volume II/60.

Rothschild, Clare K.: Baptist Traditions and
Q. 2005. *Volume 190.*

–: Luke Acts and the Rhetoric of History.
2004. *Volume II/175.*

Rüegger, Hans-Ulrich: Verstehen, was Markus
erzählt. 2002. *Volume II/155.*

Rüger, Hans Peter: Die Weisheitsschrift aus der
Kairoer Geniza. 1991. *Volume 53.*

Sänger, Dieter: Antikes Judentum und die
Mysterien. 1980. *Volume II/5.*

– Die Verkündigung des Gekreuzigten und
Israel. 1994. *Volume 75.*

– see *Burchard, Christoph*

Salier, Willis Hedley: The Rhetorical Impact of
the Sēmeia in the Gospel of John. 2004.
Volume II/186.

Salzmann, Jorg Christian: Lehren und
Ermahnen. 1994. *Volume II/59.*

Sandnes, Karl Olav: Paul – One of the
Prophets? 1991. *Volume II/43.*

Sato, Migaku: Q und Prophetie. 1988.
Volume II/29.

Schäfer, Ruth: Paulus bis zum Apostelkonzil.
2004. *Volume II/179.*

Schaper, Joachim: Eschatology in the Greek
Psalter. 1995. *Volume II/76.*

Schimanowski, Gottfried: Die himmlische
Liturgie in der Apokalypse des Johannes.
2002. *Volume II/154.*

– Weisheit und Messias. 1985. *Volume II/17.*

Schlichting, Günter: Ein jüdisches Leben Jesu.
1982. *Volume 24.*

Schnabel, Eckhard J.: Law and Wisdom from
Ben Sira to Paul. 1985. *Volume II/16.*

Schnelle, Udo: see *Frey, Jörg.*

Schröter, Jens: see *Frey, Jörg.*

Schutter, William L.: Hermeneutic and
Composition in I Peter. 1989. *Volume II/30.*

Schwartz, Daniel R.: Studies in the Jewish
Background of Christianity. 1992.
Volume 60.

Schwemer, Anna Maria: see *Hengel, Martin*

Scott, Ian W.: Implicit Epistemology in the
Letters of Paul. 2005. *Volume II/205.*

Scott, James M.: Adoption as Sons of God.
1992. *Volume II/48.*

– Paul and the Nations. 1995. *Volume 84.*

Shum, Shiu-Lun: Paul's Use of Isaiah in
Romans. 2002. *Volume II/156.*

Siegert, Folker: Drei hellenistisch-jüdische
Predigten. Teil I 1980. *Volume 20* – Teil
II 1992. *Volume 61.*

– Nag-Hammadi-Register. 1982. *Volume 26.*

– Argumentation bei Paulus. 1985. *Volume 34.*

– Philon von Alexandrien. 1988. *Volume 46.*

Simon, Marcel: Le christianisme antique et son
contexte religieux I/II. 1981. *Volume 23.*

Snodgrass, Klyne: The Parable of the
Wicked Tenants. 1983. *Volume 27.*

Söding, Thomas: Das Wort vom Kreuz.
1997. *Volume 93.*

– see *Thüsing, Wilhelm.*

Sommer, Urs: Die Passionsgeschichte des
Markusevangeliums. 1993. *Volume II/58.*

Souček, Josef B.: see *Pokorný, Petr.*

Spangenberg, Volker: Herrlichkeit des Neuen
Bundes. 1993. *Volume II/55.*

Spanje, T.E. van: Inconsistency in Paul? 1999.
Volume II/110.

Speyer, Wolfgang: Frühes Christentum im
antiken Strahlungsfeld. Volume I: 1989.
Volume 50.

– Volume II: 1999. *Volume 116.*

Stadelmann, Helge: Ben Sira als Schriftgelehr-
ter. 1980. *Volume II/6.*

Stenschke, Christoph W.: Luke's Portrait of
Gentiles Prior to Their Coming to Faith.
Volume II/108.

Sterck-Degueldre, Jean-Pierre: Eine Frau
namens Lydia. 2004. *Volume II/176.*

Stettler, Christian: Der Kolosserhymnus. 2000.
Volume II/131.

Stettler, Hanna: Die Christologie der Pastoral-
briefe. 1998. *Volume II/105.*

Stökl Ben Ezra, Daniel: The Impact of
Yom Kippur on Early Christianity. 2003.
Volume 163.

Strobel, August: Die Stunde der Wahrheit. 1980.
Volume 21.

Stroumsa, Guy G.: Barbarian Philosophy. 1999.
Volume 112.

Stuckenbruck, Loren T.: Angel Veneration and
Christology. 1995. *Volume II/70.*

Stuhlmacher, Peter (Ed.): Das Evangelium und
die Evangelien. 1983. *Volume 28.*

– Biblische Theologie und Evangelium. 2002. *Volume 146.*

Sung, Chong-Hyon: Vergebung der Sünden. 1993. *Volume II/57.*

Tajra, Harry W.: The Trial of St. Paul. 1989. *Volume II/35.*

– The Martyrdom of St.Paul. 1994. *Volume II/67.*

Theißen, Gerd: Studien zur Soziologie des Urchristentums. 1979, ³1989. *Volume 19.*

Theobald, Michael: Studien zum Römerbrief. 2001. *Volume 136.*

Theobald, Michael: see *Mußner, Franz.*

Thornton, Claus-Jürgen: Der Zeuge des Zeugen. 1991. *Volume 56.*

Thüsing, Wilhelm: Studien zur neutestamentlichen Theologie. Ed. von Thomas Söding. 1995. *Volume 82.*

Thurén, Lauri: Derhethorizing Paul. 2000. *Volume 124.*

Tolmie, D. Francois: Persuading the Galatians. 2005. *Volume II/190.*

Tomson, Peter J. and *Doris Lambers-Petry* (Ed.): The Image of the Judaeo-Christians in Ancient Jewish and Christian Literature. 2003. *Volume 158.*

Trebilco, Paul: The Early Christians in Ephesus from Paul to Ignatius. 2004. *Volume 166.*

Treloar, Geoffrey R.: Lightfoot the Historian. 1998. *Volume II/103.*

Tsuji, Manabu: Glaube zwischen Vollkommenheit und Verweltlichung. 1997. *Volume II/93*

Twelftree, Graham H.: Jesus the Exorcist. 1993. *Volume II/54.*

Urban, Christina: Das Menschenbild nach dem Johannesevangelium. 2001. *Volume II/137.*

Visotzky, Burton L.: Fathers of the World. 1995. *Volume 80.*

Vollenweider, Samuel: Horizonte neutestamentlicher Christologie. 2002. *Volume 144.*

Vos, Johan S.: Die Kunst der Argumentation bei Paulus. 2002. *Volume 149.*

Wagener, Ulrike: Die Ordnung des „Hauses Gottes". 1994. *Volume II/65.*

Wahlen, Clinton: Jesus and the Impurity of Spirits in the Synoptic Gospels. 2004. *Volume II/185.*

Walker, Donald D.: Paul's Offer of Leniency (2 Cor 10:1). 2002. *Volume II/152.*

Walter, Nikolaus: Praeparatio Evangelica. Ed. von Wolfgang Kraus und Florian Wilk. 1997. *Volume 98.*

Wander, Bernd: Gottesfürchtige und Sympathisanten. 1998. *Volume 104.*

Watts, Rikki: Isaiah's New Exodus and Mark. 1997. *Volume II/88*

Wedderburn, A.J.M.: Baptism and Resurrection. 1987. *Volume 44.*

Wegner, Uwe: Der Hauptmann von Kafarnaum. 1985. *Volume II/14.*

Weissenrieder, Annette: Images of Illness in the Gospel of Luke. 2003. Volume II/164.

–, *Friederike Wendt* and *Petra von Gemünden* (Ed.): Picturing the New Testament. 2005. *Volume II/193.*

Welck, Christian: Erzählte ‚Zeichen'. 1994. *Volume II/69.*

Wendt, Friederike (Ed.): see *Weissenrieder, Annette.*

Wiarda, Timothy: Peter in the Gospels. 2000. *Volume II/127.*

Wifstrand, Albert: Epochs and Styles. 2005. *Volume 179.*

Wilk, Florian: see *Walter, Nikolaus.*

Williams, Catrin H.: I am He. 2000. *Volume II/113.*

Wilson, Walter T.: Love without Pretense. 1991. *Volume II/46.*

Wischmeyer, Oda: Von Ben Sira zu Paulus. 2004. *Volume 173.*

Wisdom, Jeffrey: Blessing for the Nations and the Curse of the Law. 2001. *Volume II/133.*

Wold, Benjamin G.: Women, Men, and Angels. 2005. *Volume II/2001.*

Wright, Archie T.: The Origin of Evil Spirits. 2005. *Volume II/198.*

Wucherpfennig, Ansgar: Heracleon Philologus. 2002. *Volume 142.*

Yeung, Maureen: Faith in Jesus and Paul. 2002. *Volume II/147.*

Zimmermann, Alfred E.: Die urchristlichen Lehrer. 1984, ²1988. *Volume II/12.*

Zimmermann, Johannes: Messianische Texte aus Qumran. 1998. *Volume II/104.*

Zimmermann, Ruben: Christologie der Bilder im Johannesevangelium. 2004. *Volume 171.*

– Geschlechtermetaphorik und Gottesverhältnis. 2001. *Volume II/122.*

Zumstein, Jean: see *Dettwiler, Andreas*

Zwiep, Arie W.: Judas and the Choice of Matthias. 2004. *Volume II/187.*

For a complete catalogue please write to the publisher
Mohr Siebeck • P.O. Box 2030 • D–72010 Tübingen/Germany
Up-to-date information on the internet at www.mohr.de